# The Psychological Foundations of Culture

# The Psychological Foundations of Culture

*Edited by*

**Mark Schaller**
*University of British Columbia*

**Christian S. Crandall**
*University of Kansas*

2004

LAWRENCE ERLBAUM ASSOCIATES, PUBLISHERS
Mahwah, New Jersey London

Lawrence Erlbaum Associates, Inc., Publishers
10 Industrial Avenue
Mahwah, New Jersey 07430

Cover design by Kathryn Houghtaling Lacey

**Library of Congress Cataloging-in-Publication Data**

The psychological foundations of culture / edited by Mark Schaller, Christian S. Crandall.
p. cm.
Includes bibliographical references and index.
ISBN 0-8058-3839-2 (cloth : alk. paper) – ISBN 0-8058-3840-6 (pbk. : alk. paper)
1. Social change—Psychological aspects. 2. Culture—Origin—Psychological aspects. 3. Ethnopsychology. I. Schaller, Mark, 1962- II. Crandall, Christian S., 1959-

GN514.P78 2004
306—dc21

2003040839

Books published by Lawrence Erlbaum Associates are printed on acid-free paper, and their bindings are chosen for strength and durability.

Printed in the United States of America
10 9 8 7 6 5 4 3 2 1

# Contributors

Glen Adams, University of Kansas
Jamie Arndt, University of Missouri
Holly Arrow, University of Oregon
Scott Atran, University of Michigan
Martin J. Bourgeois, University of Wyoming
K. L. Burns, University of Oregon
Erica Carranza, Princeton University
Chi-yue Chiu, University of Illinois
Anna Clark, University of Melbourne
Dov Cohen, University of Illinois
Lucian Gideon Conway III, Indiana State University
Christian S. Crandall, University of Kansas
Jeff Greenberg, University of Arizona
Helen C. Harton, University of Northern Iowa
Steven J. Heine, University of British Columbia
Maria Janicki, Simon Fraser University
Yoshihisa Kashima, University of Melbourne
Dennis Krebs, Simon Fraser University
Arie W. Kruglanski, University of Maryland
Ivy Y. –M. Lau, University of Hong Kong
Sau-lai Lee, University of Hong Kong
Darrin R. Lehman, University of British Columbia
Anthony Lyons, University of Melbourne
Hazel Rose Markus, Stanford University
Allison McIntyre, University of Melbourne
Ara Norenzayan, University of British Columbia
Deborah Prentice, Princeton University
Tom Pyszczynski, University of Colorado–Colorado Springs
Linda Richter, Columbia University
Mark Schaller, University of British Columbia
Jeff Schimel, University of Alberta
Sheldon Solomon, Skidmore College
Joseph A. Vandello, University of South Florida

# Contents

# INTRODUCTION

CHAPTER

# 1

# The Psychological Foundations of Culture: An Introduction

Mark Schaller
University of British Columbia

Lucian Gideon Conway III
Indiana State University

Christian S. Crandall
University of Kansas

In his influential book *Folkways*, William Graham Sumner (1906, p. 3) wrote that culture results from "the frequent repetition of petty acts." He noted too that these cultural folkways "are not creations of human purpose and wit" but are instead "products of natural forces which men unconsciously set in operation" (Sumner, 1906, p. 4).

Sumner's work was social psychological in the broadest sense of the term. He addressed a topic, culture, that is fundamental to intellectual disciplines that seek to describe and understand the nature of human groups and societies. And he did so by referring to the basic psychological processes that govern the thoughts and actions of individuals. Here, for example, is his brief overview of the origins of cultural customs:

> Ways of doing things were selected, which were expedient. They answered the purpose better than other ways, or with less toil and pain. . . . [T]he struggle to maintain existence was carried on, not individually, but in groups. Each profited by the other's experience; hence there was concurrence towards that which proved to be most expedient. All at last adopted the same way for the same purpose; hence the ways turned into customs and became mass phenomena. (Sumner, 1906, p. 2)

There is no missing the role of psychological phenomena in this summary. Hedonic relevance and reinforcement, observation and imitation, social influence and persuasion: These processes are fundamental to our descriptions of human psychology. And there is no mistaking the eventual cultural consequences of these processes. The details of Sumner's analysis may be oversimplified, but the implication is profound: If we are to fully understand culture, we must know the essentially psychological "natural forces" through which individuals unintentionally create, sustain, and change the cultures that they comprise.

A century has passed since Sumner wrote his book on folkways—plenty of time for cognitive and social scientists to explore and articulate the psychological foundations of culture. Indeed, the discipline of psychology is largely defined by the research on the details of those basic processes of cognition, motivation and interpersonal influence that Sumner alluded to. But although Sumner's work is seminal within disciplines that treat cultures—rather than individuals—as a primary unit of analysis, it has had little impact within psychology (see Brewer, 2003, for discussion of one exception). Consequently, there is very little published work that follows Sumner's lead and shows explicitly how culture is created and sustained by the thoughts and actions of individuals. The purpose of this book is to help fill that void.

## THE GOALS AND THEMES OF THIS BOOK

The book is intended to address questions that apply to specific cultures, and to culture in general. The primary questions are these: How is it that cultures come into existence at all? How do cultures come to have particular customs and characteristics rather than others? How do cultures persist and change over time?

In the spirit of Sumner's *Folkways*, we believe that any attempt to substantially address these questions requires sustained inquiry into the specific things—customs, traditions, beliefs, and other social norms—that comprise cultures. To do this, we must focus on the individuals who traffic in these things and so conspire (usually unintentionally) to create, maintain, and change cultures. It is here that we find the central role of psychological processes: Individuals' thoughts, motives, and other cognitions govern how they interact with and influence one another; these interpersonal consequences in turn govern the emergence, persistence, and change of culture.

Psychological analyses of this sort allow us to gain special and unique insights into culture. We can learn how it is that specific beliefs, behaviors, and traditions come to be widespread while others do not. We can discover how these particular features of populations come to form a coherent thing that is perceived as culture. We can explore in detail the many subtle processes the lead some aspects of culture to persist and others to change. We can ask and answer questions about a variety of cognitive and contextual variables—some obvious, some surprising and subtle—that alter the emergence and evolution of cultures over time.

This thematic goal of this book is, in a sense, the complementary opposite of that underlying work in cross-cultural psychology (e.g., Adamopoulos & Kashima, 1999; Berry et al., 1997). Cross-cultural psychology explores the influence of culture on individual-level psychological processes, and so brings an anthropological frame of inquiry to psychological questions. This book is designed to place a psychological frame of inquiry around questions usually addressed by sociologists and anthropologists. In doing so, the book is intended to reveal that psychological inquiry in the foundations of culture is a useful—perhaps even necessary—complement to other forms of inquiry into culture. This message, we trust, is of interest to anyone who cares about the emergence and persistence of culture. In addition, the book reveals how the processes that govern individual cognition and behavior also ultimately have bigger, broader consequences on collective social structures. Thus, the ultimate consequences of psychological processes extend well beyond the disciplinary constraints of psychology. This message, we hope, is of interest to anyone who cares about the consequences of individual cognition and behavior.

We assume that many readers are unaware of all the existing theory and research that bears on the guiding questions about the psychological foundations of culture. This assumption is based on our own observations of existing literatures. Texts written for students of anthropology and sociology do not engage in the sort of detailed analysis of individual cognition and behavior necessary to study culture from a psychological perspective. Psychology texts rarely discuss the consequent impact of individuals' thoughts and behaviors on broader social structures. Cultural psychology books review psychological differences between cultures, but rarely address questions about the processes through which these cultural differences originate and evolve. Even texts in social psychology—in which the power of social norms is a defining principle—rarely discuss the processes through which those norms emerge in the first place or change over time. When they do, the discussions are brief and typically refer to research that is decades old or older (e.g., Jacobs & Campbell, 1961; Sherif, 1936).

This scarcity of coverage in existing texts does not properly measure how much we actually do know about the psychological foundations of culture. In recent years especially, there have emerged a number of research programs that address questions about the influence of psychological processes on the origins and evolution of all sorts of shared beliefs and other cultural structures. However, because these empirical inquiries often address very specific processes or specific examples of cultural norms, the intellectual linkages between these programs of research are not always obvious. These connections become clear when the different lines of theory and research are considered together. By providing this connecting context, We hope that this book reveals more substantially what we know about the many ways in which psychological processes influence the emergence and evolution of culture.

Just as importantly, we hope this book reveals that there is still plenty that we don't know. As exciting as we find the ideas, theories and phenomena summarized in these chapters, they merely scratch at the surface of what we can know, and will know. This book will have best achieved its goals if it inspires others to tackle the important questions raised about the psychological foundations of culture.

## THE PSYCHOLOGICAL FOUNDATIONS OF CULTURE: WHAT IT MEANS AND HOW IT CAN BE DONE

What does it mean to inquire into the psychological foundations of culture? Culture is a big broad construct; it transcends individuals, and doesn't lend itself easily to a psychological level of analysis. So, before proceeding further, it might be useful to consider in a bit more detail just how a psychological approach to the origins and evolution of culture might possibly proceed.

Let's begin with a bit of fun. You are probably familiar with a particular type of fill-in-the-blank analogy item that shows up on standardized academic achievement tests: The sort of items that fit the template "A is to B as blank is to D." Take a few seconds to answer these three:

1. An atom is to a substance as _____ is to a culture.
2. A gene is to a genome as _____ is to a culture.
3. A word is to a poem as _____ is to a culture.

In filling in those blanks, you may have generated three different answers, or you may have given the same answer across all three items. If you're like many people, you might have used words such as "person" to fill in one or more blanks. If you're like many other people, you might have used words such as "artifact," "ritual," "custom," "norm," "belief," or "behavior." If you're Richard Dawkins, you might have used the word "meme." There is, of course, no single best answer. The important point is that there *are* answers; virtually everyone finds some way of breaking the construct of culture down into smaller bits.

This little game illustrates a key assumption underlying inquiry into the psychological foundations of culture: Culture can be sensibly and fruitfully deconstructed. Just as physical substances are comprised of atoms, genomes are comprised of genes, and poems are comprised of words, the complex things that we perceive as "cultures" are, on closer inspection, comprised of some set of smaller units. Moreover, those basic building blocks of culture—whether they are considered persons, the rituals practiced by persons, or the beliefs held by persons—are things that are studied within the scholarly discipline of psychology.

This does not mean, of course, that culture can be appreciated only by studying the smaller units from which it emerges. Just as spices, species, and Spenserian sonnets can be described and appreciated without reference to the quanta of which they are comprised, so too culture can be described and studied without reference to psychological variables. Nevertheless, some study of those quanta is essential to a complete understanding of those more complex entitities. The meter and meaning of a rhyming couplet depend necessarily on the way specific words are assembled in its composition. So too, a complete understanding of culture requires some intellectual deconstruction and inquiry into those psychological things from which culture emerges.

Let's consider more formally just how culture might be sensibly deconstructed. To do so, we need to define what culture is. This isn't easy. If you asked 100 different people what culture is, you're likely to get 100 different answers, and none of them is likely to offer a fully satisfying definition to all interested parties. At a symposium on culture featured at the 1998 convention of the American Psychological Society, one speaker described culture in a manner that seemed perfectly reasonable to some listeners, but wildly off-target to others. (One member of the audience was overheard to mutter that it was the "wildest, wrongest definition of culture that I've ever heard.") Culture has been aptly characterized as an "elusive" concept (Pye, 1997). Nonetheless, it can be useful to sample a few of the many definitions one encounters.

Some of these definitions focus on the essential role of human influence on human physical and psychological reality. For example, the anthropologist Melville Herskovits (1948, p. 17) stated simply that culture is "the man-made part of the environment." Elaborating on this theme, the psychologist Harry Triandis (1994) wrote that "culture is a set of human-made objective and subjective elements that in the past have increased the probability of survival and resulted in satisfactions for the participants in an ecological niche, and thus became shared among those who could communicate with each other because they had a common language and they lived in the same time and place." Other definitions focus more explicitly on the collective nature of this human-made thing. The modern music composer John Adams (quoted in Ross, 2001, p. 42) said that culture is comprised of "the symbols that we share to understand each other." The anthropologist Geert Hofstede (1980, p. 21) wrote that culture is "the collective programming of the mind which distinguishes the members of one group from another." Margaret Mead, also an anthropologist, wrote that " 'Culture' . . . is an abstraction from the body of learned behavior which a group of people who share the same tradition transmit entire to their children, and, in part, to adult immigrants who become members of the society" (Mead, 1955, p. 12). Mead (1955, pp. 12–13) went on to note that the concept of culture "covers not only the arts and sciences, religions and philosophies . . . but also the system of technology, the political practices, the small intimate habits of daily life, such as the way of preparing or eating food, or of hushing a child to sleep, as well as the method of electing a prime minister or changing the constitution."

Considered together, these various definitions offer clues to an essential set of ingrediants that comprise culture.

As an important starting point, it's clear that culture is not a single observable thing, but is instead something of an abstraction inferred from the observation of many more specific things—beliefs, habits, actions, artifacts—that are more easily and directly observed.

It's also clear that in order for those more specific things to imply culture, they must be *shared*. Whether defined in terms of shared customs and rituals (Mead, 1955), shared symbols and meanings (Geertz, 1973), shared values (Schwartz & Bardi, 1997), or shared personality traits (Church, 2000), culture does not exist unless those customs, symbols, values, or traits are perceived to be relatively common across some population of individuals. This means that many of the things that imply cultures are those things that psychologists refer to collectively as "norms."

Lots of characteristics are relatively common across lots of people, but not all of them imply a culture. In order to contribute to the inferred presence of a culture, things that are shared must be shared only within some easily identifiable category of people. It is this *categorical identifiability*—defined most often by temporal, geographical, or demographic variables—that importantly differentiates cultural differences from other individual differences of the sort studied by personality psychologists. We rarely characterize the differences between introverts and extroverts as "cultural," but we do speak sensibly of cultural differences between the 1960s and the 1980s, between southern Europeans and Northern Europeans, between Japanese and Indians, between African-Americans and White Americans, between men and women, or between scientists and artists.

Not all shared features of identifiable populations define cultures. Culture-defining characteristics must be relatively common within some specific population while being relatively uncommon in others. This *differential commonality* is fundamental to the perception of culture. It means that norms imply the presence of culture only when those norms are bounded (temporally, geographically, demographically) rather than universal among human beings. The creation myths of the Haida peoples of the Northwest North American coast are cultural beliefs only because those same beliefs are uncommon among other peoples on the planet, whose own myths in turn help to define their own cultures.

The differential commonality of any one norm implies culture only when it coincides with the differential commonality of other norms as well. Culture is rarely implied by a single difference between populations; there must be *multiple differences* between two populations to imply the presence of two cultures. The northern United States would not be considered culturally different from the southern United States on the basis of linguistic accent alone, but because Northern and Southern accents are perceived to correlate with other things (different cuisines, different ways of responding to insults, different levels of enthusiasm for stock-car racing, and so on), the construct of culture is more readily perceived.

These considerations imply a sort of rudimentary recipe for culture. If some identifiable category of people is described by a cluster of norms that differ from the norms describing other categories of people, then that category of people is likely to be perceived as having a culture. The greater the number or more extreme the range of normative differences (in thoughts, actions, artifacts, language use, etc.), the more likely it is that one will perceive differences of culture.

By disassembling the slippery concept of culture in this manner, it becomes clearer how psychological inquiry into the emergence and evolution of culture can proceed. Psychological theories and research reveal how specific beliefs escape the bounds of individuals' heads and become shared across across enormous populations. Psychological theories and research identify the processes through which specific individuals' actions and behaviors influence the actions and behaviors of others, and so become norms, customs, and rituals. Psychological theories and research also help us understand how the specific clusters of thoughts and actions can become commonly shared among some populations while remaining uncommon among others. It is for this reason that it makes plenty of sense to characterize culture as an emergent property of psychological processes, along the lines of Sperber (1984, p. 42): "Culture is the precipitate of cognition and communication in a human population."

## THE SCOPE AND ORGANIZATION OF THIS BOOK

This book presents a set of theories, ideas and research findings that reveal in detail the ways in which psychological processes influence the things that constitute cultures. With a topic as large as this one, no single volume can be entirely comprehensive. One inevitably faces the trade-off between breadth and depth. If a book offers a sampling of different psychological approaches to the origins and persistence of culture—as this one does—then it cannot offer an extensive exploration of any single theoretical or methodological approach. Happily, there already exist some more narrowly focused and deeply explored books linking specific sets of processes to culture. For example, there are several books devoted specifically to the role of biological evolutionary processes in the emergence of culture (e.g., Barkow, Cosmides, & Tooby, 1992; Dunbar, Knight, & Power, 1999). There are several books also on the topic of "social representations," linking specific cognition and discourse processes to collective beliefs (e.g., Duveen & Lloyd, 1990; Farr & Moscovici, 1984). There are other books describing in detail the processes through which workgroups arrive at collective decisions and other shared perceptions (e.g., Thompson, Levine, & Messick, 1999; Witte & Davis, 1996). We don't wish to fish the same intellectual waters as these or other existing books, and so we've opted to cast a wider net. We offer this book instead as a sampler displaying a variety of different psychological ideas, theories, methods, and findings. And yet, as distinct as these approaches are from each other at a superficial level, they are bound together by a common theme: Each of them reveals how psychological processes ultimately influence the emergence, persistence, and change of culture.

The authors invited to contribute chapters to this book have been selected because they have done excellent and inspiring scholarly work that, in different ways, reveal the influence of psychological processes on the collective structures that define cultures. Across these chapters there is considerable intellectual diversity. Consequently, this book reveals how culture is influenced by processes operating at the individual level (e.g., cognitions, goals, information-processing strategies) as well as at the interpersonal level (e.g., communication, social influence). Through the diverse foci of the chapters, this book reveals the effects of these psychological processes on a wide variety of cultural customs, ritualized practices, shared mythologies, and other norms. Across these chapters, we witness the role of psychological processes on the evolution of culture in all sorts of different populations, ranging from small interacting groups to grand-scale masses of people occupying the same demographic or geographic category. This range of populations forcefully reminds us that the thing that we call culture can emerge—indeed, cannot fail to emerge—anywhere that there are people.

These chapters were crafted in such a way as to accomplish two important goals. Each chapter provides some conceptual overview, identifying a specific psychological process (or set of related processes) that can have predictable influences on cultural structures evolving over time within any human population. In addition, each chapter illustrates the general process with specific examples, showing how the underlying psychological process does indeed guide the shape of particular cultural structures within particular populations. The cumulative impact is a collection of chapters that covers a diverse set of specific topics, united by their pursuit of common intellectual goals. Together, the chapters summarize a coherent set of fundamental psychological processes whose impacts are revealed in differences between cultures, but that may potentially guide the emergence and development of any culture within any human population. Considered together, these processes reveal some of the deeper human universals that underlie cultural differences.

As with any edited volume, each chapter in this book is a coherent whole in its own right, so there is no need to read them in any specific order. Nevertheless, the chapters do focus on somewhat different questions, and it makes sense to lump them loosely together according to some broad organizational structure. The first section contains a set of chapters that review fundamental processes that help explain how and why cultures emerge at all. These chapters illustrate how the seemingly simple thoughts and local actions of individuals may craft culture. Chapters in the second section focus on why some shared beliefs and norms emerge rather than others, and illustrate these underlying processes through sustained analyses of specific domains of belief or normative behavior. Both the first and the second sections focus primarily on the emergence of cultural structures in the first place, whereas the third section contains chapters that explicitly address the persistence and change of cultures over time.

Inevitably, this organizational structure fails to do full credit to the multi-faceted contents of each chapter. Chapters that we have located in the first two sections certainly reveal implications not only for understanding the emergence of cultures, but also for the persistence and change of cultures. Processes reviewed in chapters that we have located in the third section are relevant to the origins, and not merely the persistence of cultures. Every one of the chapters, not just those in the middle section, illustrates the operation of psychological processes on some specific cultural beliefs and norms. Although the organizational structure imposed on this book is sensible, we are happy to remind readers that the simplicity of this structure is consistently repudiated by the richness of the chapters contained within.

The only chapter (other than this introductory one) that escapes our tripartite grouping of chapters is the last one. This "bookend" chapter casts a reflective eye on the preceding contents and on the topic of inquiry as a whole. It offers a set of critical, constructive comments for readers to consider when reflecting further on the legacy and promise of psychological inquiry into the foundations of culture.

## REFERENCES

Adamopoulos, J., & Kashima, Y. (1999). *Social psychology and cultural context.* Thousand Oaks, CA: Sage.

Barkow, J. H., Cosmides, L., & Tooby, J. (1992). *The adapted mind: Evolutionary psychology and the generation of culture.* New York: Oxford University Press.

Berry, J. W., et al. (1997). *Handbook of cross-cultural psychology.* Boston: Allyn & Bacon.

Brewer, M. B. (2003). Ethnocentrism and prejudice: A search for universals. In C. S. Crandall & M. Schaller (Eds.), *The social psychology of prejudice: Historical perspectives.* Seattle, WA: Lewinian Press.

Church, A. T. (2000). Culture and personality: Toward an integrated cultural trait psychology. *Journal of Personality, 68*, 651–703.

Dunbar, R., Knight, C., & Power, C. (1999). *The evolution of culture: An interdisciplinary view.* Edinburgh UK: Edinburgh University Press.

Duveen, G., & Lloyd, B. (1990). *Social representations and the development of knowledge.* New York: Cambridge University Press.

Farr, R. M., & Moscovici, S. (1984). *Social representations.* Cambridge, UK: Cambridge University Press;

Geertz, C. (1973). Religion as a cultural system. In C. Geertz (Ed.), *The interpretation of cultures.* New York: Basic Books., Harper Torchbooks.

Herkovits, M. J. (1948). *Man and his works: The science of cultural anthropology.* New York: Knopf.

Hofstede, G. (1980). *Culture's consequences: International differences in work-related values.* Beverly Hills, CA: Sage.

Jacobs, R. C., & Campbell, D. T. (1961). The perpetuation of an arbitrary tradition through several generations of a laboratory microculture. *Journal of Abnormal and Social Psychology, 62,* 649–658.

Levine, R. A. & Campbell, D. T. (1972). *Ethnocentrism.* New York: Wiley.

Mead, M. (1955). *Cultural patterns and technical change.* New York: Mentor Books.

Pye, L. W. (1997). Introduction: The elusive concept of culture and the vivid reality of personality. *Political Psychology, 18*, 241–254.

Ross, A. (2001, January 8). The harmonist. *New Yorker*, pp. 40–46.

Schwartz, S. H., & Bardi, A. (1997). Influences of adaptation to communist rule on value priorities in Eastern Europe. *Political Psychology, 18*, 385–410.

Sherif, M. (1936). *The psychology of social norms.* New York: Harper.

Sperber, D. (1984). The epidemiology of beliefs. In C. Fraser & G. Gaskell (Eds.), *The social psychological study of widespread beliefs* (pp. 25–44). Oxford, UK: Clarendon Press.

Sumner, W. G. (1906). *Folkways.* Boston: Ginn and Company.

Thompson, L. L., Levine, J. M., & Messick, D. M. (1999). *Shared cognition in organizations: The management of knowledge.* Mahwah, NJ: Lawrence Erlbaum Associates.

Witte, E. H., & Davis, J. H. (1996). *Understanding group behavior.* Mahwah, NJ: Lawrence Erlbaum Associates.

PART

# I

# HOW CULTURES EMERGE AT ALL

CHAPTER

# 2

# Human Awareness of Mortality and the Evolution of Culture

Sheldon Solomon
Skidmore College

Jeff Greenberg
University of Arizona

Jeff Schimel
University of Alberta

Jamie Arndt
University of Missouri–Columbia

Tom Pyszczynski
University of Colorado at Colorado Springs

> Culture and history and religion and science . . . [are] different from anything else we know of in the universe. That is a fact. It is as if all life evolved to a certain point, and then in ourselves turned at a right angle and simply exploded in a different direction. (Jaynes, 1976, p. 9)

> We know that virtually all of human behavior is transmitted by culture . . . The question is how biology and culture interact, and in particular how they interact across all societies to create the commonalities of human nature. (Wilson, 1998, p. 126)

What are the psychological foundations of culture? Authors tend to combine two perspectives when addressing this question. The first is an evolutionary perspective, which depicts *Homo sapiens* as animals who have evolved from earlier hominid species; cultures, as products of human thought and action, must therefore have resulted from adaptations over the course of evolution. The second is a cognitive science perspective, which depicts humans as information processing systems, a view that derives from the influential metaphor of the human mind as a computer.

Although our information-processing abilities cannot be denied, if we are animals, we cannot be computers; rather, the drives, desires, and processes by which we think, act, and create and perpetuate cultures must be those of an animal. In addition, despite the fact that social and natural scientists routinely tell people that humans are information-processing animals designed only to survive long enough to reproduce and care for their offspring before they die, people rarely if ever view themselves that way. People want to view themselves not as mere gene-conveying animals, but as beings who lead significant and enduring lives, and one critical function of culture is to help people accomplish that. To understand the psychological foundations of culture, then, we need a third complementary perspective that acknowledges that humans are animals with uniquely impressive intellectual capabilities, but with needs for meaning and value as well.

We think that the existential psychodynamic perspective provided by terror management theory does just that. In this chapter, we explain how this perspective provides novel insights that are necessary for any compelling account of the psychological foundations and functions of culture. The theory acknowledges the core animal drives and desires of humans as well as the intellectual advances which make us unique, especially the capacities for self-consciousness and temporal thought. It explains how the human needs for meaning and value emerge from this biological heritage and the role of culture in serving these needs. The theory is consistent with evolutionary principles, fits what we know about cultures past and present, and has generated a large body of empirical support within experimental social psychology.

## CONTEMPORARY EVOLUTIONARY THEORIZING ABOUT THE PSYCHOLOGY OF CULTURE

Prominent thinkers from a number of disciplines have noted that a theoretical account of culture—humanly created and transmitted beliefs about the nature of reality manifested through uniquely human institutions such as religion, art, and science—is a central problem in the study of mind (see e.g., Mithen, 1996; Pinker, 1997; Tooby & Cosmides, 1992; Wilson, 1998). In their seminal 1992 paper "The Psychological Foundations of Culture," John Tooby and Leda Cosmides proposed two critical epistemological prerequisites for addressing this problem. First, an adequate theory of culture must be *grounded in evolutionary biology*. Given the success of Darwin's theory of evolution by natural selection in accounting for the "fit" between physical characteristics of living organisms and their environments and how the physical attributes (within and between species) of populations change over time, all human behavioral and psychological propensities are presumably similarly best understood as consequences of evolutionary processes. Second, it must be *framed in terms of psychological processes*. Because all cultural affectations initially originated in minds of individuals, "*culture is the manufactured product of evolved psychological mechanisms situated in individuals living in groups*" (Tooby & Cosmides, 1992, p. 24). Consequently, all theoretical perspectives that presume the existence of culture without explaining its psychological underpinnings are epistemologically untenable (e.g., Durkheim, 1895/1962; Geertz, 1973; Miller, 1999; Shweder, 1990).

Despite this recognition of the importance of understanding the psychological underpinnings of culture, as well as the epistemological prerequisites for doing so, we believe that progress toward this goal has stalled for two reasons. First, discourse in evolutionary psychology regarding culture is currently dominated by an emphasis on cognitive information-gathering processes and adaptation to the physical environment in the service of enhancing reproductive fitness. For example, Tooby and Cosmides (1992) and Mithen (1996) view culture as a means to store and transmit useful information that facilitates effective exploitation of the physical environment. Similarly, Harris (1979) argues that cultural constructions developed as post hoc accommodations to material reality (e.g., prohibitions against eating pork developed in areas where raising hogs would be detrimental to survival relative to alternative means of sustenance). We have no quarrel with these assertions; clearly, culture facilitates the transmission of useful information and is a reflection of material conditions. However, following de Waal (2000, p. 25), we insist that a proper understanding of the nature and function of culture additionally requires an explicit consideration of nonmaterial, nonrational, non-information-processing psychological factors:

> Why can't evolutionary psychology put a little less evolution and a little more psychology into its thinking? We evolved a complex mental life that makes us act in all sorts of ways the sum of which should enhance reproductive success. But this strategy is by no means required for each and every behavior. To focus on just one, isolated from the rest of the package, is like seeking to understand why the kangaroo has such tiny front legs while ignoring what happened to its hind legs and tail.

Second, contemporary discourse in evolutionary psychology concerning the psychological functions of culture is generally uninformed by relevant ideas from psychoanalysis and experimental social psychology; the prototypic but by no means only example being Tooby and Cosmides's (1992) blanket condemnation of the social sciences lumped together under the caricature rubric of the Standard Social Science Model. E. O. Wilson (1998, p. 74) similarly disposes of more than a century of psychoanalytic thought in a few sentences—"Freud's conception of the unconscious, by focusing attention on hidden irrational processes of the brain, was a fundamental contribution to culture. It became a wellspring of ideas flowing from psychology into the humanities. But it is mostly wrong." Well, it is certainly partly wrong, but it is also partly right, and many of Freud's erroneous ideas have been refined and/or corrected by subsequent psychodynamic theorists (e.g., Becker, 1971; Brown, 1959; Horney, 1950; Rank, 1936). In addition, there is a burgeoning theoretical and empirical literature in support of many aspects of psychodynamic theories, including the existence of nonrational, nonconscious mental processes (see e.g., Erdelyi, 1985; Greenwald, 1980; Kunda, 1990; Pennebaker, 1990; Pyszczynski & Greenberg, 1987; Pyszczynski, Greenberg, & Solomon, 1999; Westen, 1998). Indeed, we now explain how a contemporary psychodynamic perspective and the research guided by it can facilitate a fuller understanding of the psychological underpinnings of culture.

## AN EXISTENTIAL PSYCHODYNAMIC ACCOUNT OF THE PSYCHOLOGICAL FOUNDATIONS OF CULTURE

> If therefore we are to discover in what form the destiny of the Western Culture will be accomplished, we must first be clear as to what culture is, what its relations are to visible history, to life, to soul, to nature, to intellect, what the forms of its manifestation are and how far these forms—peoples, tongues and epochs, battles and ideas, states and gods, arts and craft-works, sciences, laws, economic types and world-ideas, great men and great events—may be accepted and pointed to as symbols. (Spengler, 1926, pp. 3–4)

The quest to understand the psychological foundations of culture is not of recent origin; nor are evolutionary approaches to this question. Following Nietzsche (e.g., *The Gay Science,* 1887/1974; *Twilight of the Idols*, 1888/1998), Spengler's *The Decline of the West* (1926/1999) explicitly posed the question of what culture is and what functions it serves. His contemporary Freud was also interested in questions surrounding the nature of culture. Freud knew and respected Darwin's *The Origin of Species* (see, e.g., Newton, 1995), and genuinely believed that psychoanalytic theory was constructed from an explicitly evolutionary perspective. Indeed, Otto Fenichel (1945, p. 5) described the epistemological underpinnings of psychoanalytic inquiry this way:

> Scientific psychology explains mental phenomena as a result of the interplay of primitive physical needs—rooted in the biological structure of man and developed in the course of biological history (and therefore changeable in the

> course of further biological history)—and the influences of the environment on these needs.

Freud recognized the psychological foundations of culture as a central problem, and this was the primary focus of his later work, especially *The Future of an Illusion* (1928/1989) and *Civilization and Its Discontents* (1930/1989)—work that in turn influenced Hungarian psychoanalytic anthropologist Geza Roheim's *The Evolution of Culture* (1934) and *The Origin and Function of Culture* (1943).

Roheim (1943, p. 9) carefully considered the possibility that culture consists of accumulating accurate information about the nature of reality:

> . . . human beings living in a group, find a way to combine their energies in the struggle with the environment and . . . the most effective means are finally employed in this struggle. Variations in culture would in this case arise as variations in these means conditioned by a varying environment.

But he rejected this notion as "far from being true." Consistent with his psychoanalytic orientation, Roheim felt that culture was ultimately a product of the complex interplay of people's psychological needs, and that the need for accuracy was not the only need, or even the most important one, served by cultural conceptions of reality.

For Roheim, even a cursory examination of different cultures' fundamentally inconsistent and mutually exclusive cosmologies—accounts of the origin and structure of the universe and the role of human beings in it—renders the notion that culture serves a rational information-processing function providing accurate accounts of physical reality, at least highly suspect, if not patently absurd. As examples (reported in Langer, 1982), the Ainu, aboriginal people in northern Japan, believe in superhuman women with teeth in their vaginas who bear only female offspring after being impregnated by the wind; the Lugbara in northwestern Uganda and eastern Zaire describe God as a tall white man-like creature cut in half with one eye, ear, arm, and leg; in New Guinea, the Watut believe tadpoles gestated in the body of a boy killed by a ghost swim ashore and metamorphosize into girls and boys who take possession of the earth after spending their childhood years playing on the beach; in some parts of Borneo it is believed that humans descended from a sword handle that mated with a spindle. A bit closer to home, a substantial proportion of the population of the Western world believes that a large old bearded God created humankind in his image along with the rest of the inhabitants of the earth in six days before taking a well-deserved day of rest (Genesis), whereas highly successful and educated followers of the modern Western religion Scientology believe that "people are immortal spirits who have lived through many lifetimes after being banished to Earth 75 million years ago by an intergalactic ruler" (Frantz, 1998, p. A24).

Instead, citing examples from Melanesian folk-lore such as:

> A small bird invites all the animals to a great feast. Then he pulls mountain goats' fat out of his rectum with a hook and feeds them all. Raven boasts, "I can do the same." But when he tries only blood comes out of his intestines and he is put to shame before the guests.

Roheim (1943, p. 13) observed that all cultures are, in his words, "actuated" by phantastic beliefs about magical power employed to confer a sense of individual invincibility, from which he concluded that:

> The process of becoming civilized is ... not the direct result of adaptation to environment. ... It is through a series of complicated mechanisms of dealing with anxiety that our civilization has developed and is still developing. ... But these modifications are not due to the pressure of reality. ... The same environment ... did not compel the chimpanzee to modify its ego-structure. (Roheim, 1934, pp. 403, 416, 417)

What, then, is the nature of the uniquely human anxiety and the complicated mechanisms designed to reduce it that characterizes the development of culture?

## Consciousness: The Great Shift!

> Consciousness has developed only under the pressure of the need for communication; ... from the start it was needed and useful only between human beings (particularly between those who commanded and those who obeyed); and that it also developed only in proportion to the degree of this utility. Consciousness is really only a net of communication between human beings; it is only as such that it had to develop; a solitary human being who lived like a beast of prey would not have needed it. That our actions, thoughts, feelings, and movements enter our own consciousness–at least a part of them–that is the result of a "must" that for a terribly long time lorded it over man. As the most endangered animal, he needed help and protection, he needed his peers, he had to learn to express his distress and to make himself understood; and for all of this he needed "consciousness" first of all, he needed to "know" himself what distressed him, he needed to "know" how he felt, he needed to "know" what he thought. (Nietzsche, 1887/1974, p. 298)

Consciousness is the psychological attribute that renders us distinctly human, and makes culture both possible and necessary. Nietszche (1887/1974), Jaynes (1976), and Humphrey (1984) each independently hypothesized that consciousness evolved in humans in order to facilitate effective social interactions in groups arranged in dominance hierarchies–presumably because a person who knew how she or he felt would be in a better position to predict the behavior of others, which in turn conferred adaptive advantages to those in possession of such awareness. Consciousness is thus a fundamentally social (con-scious = to know with) and learned linguistic (and hence uniquely human) construction by which individuals conceive of themselves (I) as the principle characters in an ongoing narrative (Bruner, 1986, 1990) arranged in a three-dimensional spatialized mind-space (e.g., "I am looking forward to seeing you again soon" "I'll keep an eye out for you").

Consciousness is "intimately bound up with volition and decision" (Jaynes, 1976, p. 55); humans could delay behavior in novel situations long enough to ponder past experiences and, perhaps more importantly, envision the consequences of future actions, even those never previously undertaken: "Thus humans can learn from the past and plan for the future. And thus man is the historical mammal in that he can stand outside and look at his history; and thereby he can influence his development as a person, and . . . can influence the march of history in his nation and society as a whole" (May, 1953, p. 85). Consciousness allows human beings to contemplate that which does not yet exist and to transform the products of their imagination into physical reality. Only humans are truly creative–all other creatures must adapt to the physical universe as it is presented to them–human beings adapt the physical universe in accordance with their desires, making the unreal real (Rank, 1932). From an evolutionary perspective, then, consciousness evolved as we evolved into human beings because it was highly adaptive. However, consider the following.

## DREAM'S ENDING: THE TRAGIC VISION

> And with the rise and gradual conception of the "self" as the source of personal autonomy comes, of course, the knowledge of its limit–the ultimate prospect of death. The effect of this intellectual advance is momentous. . . . It is in a fairly recent phase of that evolutionary course that the realization of death as the inevitable finale of every life has overtaken mankind. . . . Its long preparation, however, has been as natural as the wholly unplanned developments which culminate in the peacock's ornamental tail or the beaver's landscape architecture. (Langer, 1982, pp. 90, 91, 103)

A conscious creature able to project him-/herself (I) throughout a linguistically constructed metaphorical universe of space and time was at an evolutionary advantage. The abilities to actively reflect on the past, to consider the possible consequences of a host of future potential courses of action, and to imagine novel possibilities that are then enacted in reality surely enhance inclusive fitness not only by allowing people to engage in a wide variety of actions in response to environmental conditions but also by allowing them to render environments suitable for their needs. As contemporary psychologists (e.g., Carver & Scheier, 1981; Duval & Wicklund, 1972) have argued, the capacity to reflect back on oneself allows the individual to strive toward and monitor progress toward long-term goals and thereby facilitates the attainment of such goals.

But as Rank (1936/1945) argued, consciousness is both a social and historical process, with increasing self-awareness over time, culminating in what Freud, Geza Roheim, Susanne Langer, Ernest Becker (1973), and others claimed is the most significant event in the evolutionary history of humankind: the explicit awareness of death as a natural and inevitable event, an awareness that threatened to undermine consciousness, intellectually and emotionally, as a viable form of mental organization. Intellectually, what an appalling and absolutely unacceptable affront for finely gene containers and conveyors (Dawkins, 1976) refined by billions of years of evolution developing a host of sophisticated physiological and behavioral strategies for keeping themselves alive, to learn by virtue of one of its most effective attributes (consciousness), that the most basic biological imperative on which individual life is organized (staying alive) is bound to be thwarted! Emotionally, the awareness that death is inevitable gives rise to the potential for debilitating anxiety:

> As a naked fact, that realization is unacceptable. . . . Nothing, perhaps, is more comprehensible than that people—savage or civilized—would rather reject than accept the idea of death as an inevitable close of their brief earthly careers. (Langer, 1982, pp. 87, 103)

Uniquely human awareness of mortality is thus a "natural" consequence of increasing self-consciousness, which otherwise provides human beings with remarkable adaptive advantages; however, conscious creatures encumbered with unbridled awareness of mortality would be crushed by both the weight of the logical paradox ("I am therefore I die?") and the emotional burden of death awareness—to the point of behavioral paralysis, in which case consciousness would no longer confer an adaptive advantage:

> For in much wisdom is much grief: and he that increaseth knowledge increaseth sorrow. . . . The wise man's eyes are in his head; but the fool walketh in darkness: and I myself perceived also that one event happeneth to them all. . . . For there is no remembrance of the wise more than of the fool for ever; seeing that which now is in the days to come shall all be forgotten. And how dieth the wise man? as the fool. (Ecclesiastes, or *The Preacher*)

It is at this point that evolutionary advantages emerged for cultural worldviews (and the people who adopted them) that could compellingly assuage the anxiety engendered by the uniquely human problem of death.

## A CENTRAL PSYCHOLOGICAL FOUNDATION OF CULTURE: THE DENIAL OF DEATH

> Man is the only being that knows death; all others become old, but with a consciousness limited to the moment. . . . Only fully-awakened man . . . whose understanding has been emancipated by the habit of language from dependence on sight, comes to possess the notion of transience, that is a memory of the past as past and an experiential conviction of irrevocability. . . . Here in the decisive moments of existence, when man first becomes man and realizes his immense loneliness in the universal, the world-fear reveals itself for the first time as the essentially human fear in the presence of death. . . . Here, too, the higher thought originates as meditation upon death. Every religion, every scientific investigation, every philosophy proceeds from it. (Spengler, 1926/1999, p. 166)

In the 1973 Pulitzer Prize-winning *The Denial of Death*, cultural anthropologist Ernest Becker argued that a close examination of seminal ideas from the natural and social sciences and the humanities converge on the notion that the denial of death is a dynamic force that instigates and directs a substantial proportion of human activity. Following Zilboorg (1943), Becker argued that fear of death is universal because it is the emotional manifestation of the biological predisposition toward self-perpetuation that we share with all living creatures (but that is known to be ultimately futile only by human beings). According to Becker, cultural worldviews are sets of beliefs about the nature of reality shared by groups of people that evolved to effectively manage the potential for debilitating terror resulting from the awareness of death; they do so through a host of elaborate social and psychological processes that serve to help us avoid thinking about dying and deny that death constitutes absolute annihilation.

The nature of cultural worldviews has thus been profoundly affected by the evolution of consciousness, self-consciousness and the consequent awareness of death:

> Death . . . posits the most terrifying threat to the taken-for-granted realities of everyday life. The integration of death within the paramount reality of social existence is . . . consequently, one of the most important fruits of symbolic universes. . . . All legitimations of death must carry out the same essential task—they must enable the individual to go on living in society after the death of significant others and to anticipate his own death with . . . terror sufficiently

> mitigated so as not to paralyze the continued performance of the routines of everyday life. . . . On the level of meaning, the institutional order represents a shield against terror. . . . The symbolic universe shelters the individual from ultimate terror by bestowing ultimate legitimation upon the protective structures of the institutional order. (Berger & Luckmann, 1966/1967, p. 101)

Culture accomplishes this goal by casting each of us as principle characters in an ongoing sacred narrative cosmological drama that imbues the world with meaning from which each one can derive a sense of value (self-esteem) and the consequent assurance that death can somehow be symbolically and/or literally transcended. This perspective then, helps explain why cultures have not evolved solely toward increasingly accurate accounts of the nature of reality, for example, as Tooby and Cosmides (1992) proposed:

> Information about adaptive courses of action in local conditions is difficult and costly to obtain by individual experience alone. Those who have preceded an individual in a habitat and social environment have built up in their minds a rich store of useful information. The existence of such information in other minds selected for specialized psychological adaptations that were able to use social observations to reconstruct some of this information within one's own mind. . . . By such reconstruction, one individual was able to profit from deducing what another already knew. (p. 119)

Our analysis also suggests that the emergence of culture and its various affectations—art, religion, music, philosophy, and so on—were not merely nonadaptive byproducts of mental processes designed to serve other purposes as Pinker (1997), among others, has declared: "Religion and philosophy are in part the application of mental tools to problems they were not designed to solve. . . . It is wrong to invent functions for activities that lack that design merely because we want to ennoble them with the imprimatur of biological adaptiveness" (p. 525). Rather, these aspects of culture are uniquely human, species-specific evolutionary adaptations, essential for sustaining consciousness as a viable form of mental organization in the wake of the explicit knowledge of death:

> In their developed forms, phantasy thinking and reality thinking are distinct mental processes, different modes of obtaining satisfaction. The fact that they have a distinct character when fully developed, however, does not necessarily imply that reality thinking operates quite independently of unconscious phantasy. It is not merely that they "blend and interweave"; their relationship is something less adventitious than this. On our view, reality-thinking cannot operate without concurrent and supporting unconscious phantasies. (Isaacs, 1948, p. 94)

The notion that culture, in all of its manifestations—religion, art, philosophy, science, politics, economics, and so on—serves an adaptive function by a creative misrepresentation of reality to preserve psychological equanimity in response to the uniquely human awareness of death (a by-product of the evolution of consciousness) is a proposition that we believe to be worthy of serious consideration for three reasons: (a) It follows from basic evolutionary principles; (b) it can account for what we know about past and present cultures; and (c) it is supported by a large body of empirical evidence.

## Convergence With Darwinian Principles

First, this explanation is entirely consistent with Darwin's original account of the mechanics of evolutionary change, as well as its more contemporary renderings: The psychological propensities of members of a given species are posited to be determined by the historical process of natural selection within particular environments. As Tooby and Cosmides (1992, p. 69) noted: "Organisms transact the business of propagation in specific environments, and the persistent characteristics of those environments. . . . Consequently, the structure of the environment causes corresponding adaptive organization to accumulate in the design of the organism." However, Tooby and Cosmides also recognized (p. 69) that evolution could proceed in response to the demands of internal organismic problems entirely independent of the demands of the external environment: "Obviously . . . adaptations may solve endogenous adaptive problems and may improve over evolutionary time without necessarily being driven by or connected to any change in the external environment." The notion that culture evolved to solve the "endogenous" problem engendered by the burgeoning awareness of the inevitability of death associated with human consciousness is thus completely consistent with an evolutionary point of view; indeed, this idea has been explicitly advanced by primatologist David Premack in E. O. Wilson's (1978) *On Human Nature*. In Wilson's words:

> If [for non-human primates] consciousness of self and the ability to communicate ideas with other intelligent beings exist, can other qualities of the human mind be far away? Premack has pondered the implications of transmitting the concept of personal death to chimpanzees, but he is hesitant. "What if like man," he asks, "the ape dreads death and will deal with this knowledge as bizarrely as we have? . . . The desired objective would be not only to communicate the knowledge of death but, more important, to find a way of making sure the apes' response would not be that of dread, which, in the human case, has led to the invention of ritual, myth, and religion. Until I can suggest concrete steps in teaching the concept of death without fear, I have no intention of imparting the knowledge of mortality to the ape." (p. 27)

### Convergence With Evidence From Past and Present Cultures

Second, this analysis can help account for much about what we know about past cultures from anthropological, archeological, and historical records, and what we know about contemporary cultures as well.

***In the Beginning Was the Word.*** Clearly death was a serious concern to our remote ancestors as evidenced by pit burials of Neanderthals, and simultaneous emergence of ritual burials and art in early *Homo sapiens* (see e.g., Mithen, 1996). Perhaps the ability to generate narrative accounts of death-transcending visions of reality (which in turn requires language) is the critical difference between *Homo sapiens* and at least 15 of closely related species of hominids that are no longer in existence (e.g., Donald, 1991; Tattersall, 2000). There is no evidence that these hominid species perished from physical deprivation or human predation; perhaps they died from fear in light of their burgeoning awareness of death, lacking the imaginative capability to generate death-denying and/or transcending cultural narratives.

How could they have died from fear? Most theorists would argue that the experience of fear would have been adaptive to the extent that it promoted effective survival skills, such as fleeing or fighting in the face of the danger. However, think of the old World War I cliché about there not being any atheists in foxholes. A creature with the dawning realization of its own mortality and no system of spiritual beliefs to quell the consequent fear would seem unlikely to venture forth and take the risks necessary for their own or their group's survival. Who will go out and risk life and limb to hunt down a woolly mammoth to replenish the group's food supply? Hominids with faith in some spiritual protection would be more bold and confident in engaging in the risky tasks necessary for survival in harsh dangerous environments. This suggests that with the dawn of awareness of mortality, hominid groups with particularly compelling spiritual beliefs and individuals particularly capable of sustaining faith in such beliefs would have had adaptive advantages; therefore such groups and individuals have thrived ever since.

But why might *Homo sapiens* have had more solidified spiritual beliefs than earlier human species? One possibility is that along with their increased cognitive capacity for symbolic thought came the ability for spoken language that surpassed that of their hominid cousins. Theoretical reconstructions of the soft tissue of the vocal tract of the Neanderthals and early hominids revealed that the larynx of these species would have been higher in the throat than that of modern humans, making only simple vocalizations possible (Laitman, Heimbuch, & Crelin, 1979). This evidence has led some anthropologists to the conclusion that even if early hominids had the cognitive capacity for language, their vocal apparatus left them with only a crude ability for verbal expression (Laitman, 1983; Laitman et al., 1979; Laitman & Heimbuch, 1982; Lieberman, 1985, 1989).

The linguistic prowess of *Homo sapiens* would have provided them with a heavy advantage over earlier hominids in activities that directly promote survival (e.g., sharing technology, coordinating hunting parties, etc.). However, the ability for a complex spoken language may have given *Homo sapiens* another, perhaps even more fundamental advantage. If *Homo sapiens* were able to contrive speech with syntax and grammar, then they may also have been able to develop a more sophisticated system of beliefs and narratives about death transcendence. For example, before venturing out on a hunt or exploring new territory, early *Homo sapiens* may have performed rituals and told stories about how the spirits would help them slay mammoths, leopards, and bears and would protect them from potential dangers in the physical world. The ability to produce spoken language would also have made it possible for modern humans to share their cultural reality with other members of their social group and build a strong consensus and sense of validity for their core beliefs. Without complex language, and therefore an adequate symbolic defense system to quell their fears, Neanderthals and early hominids may have been overcome by fear and unwilling to take on the necessary risks of hunting and exploration. When the surrounding land was no longer fecund, possibly because of harsh conditions or competition with *Homo sapiens*, Neanderthals and other hominids slowly died off.

> Thus, although language was first and foremost a social device, its initial utility was not so much in enabling a new level of collective technology or social organization, which it eventually did, or in transmitting skill, or in achieving larger political organizations, which it eventually did. Initially, it was used to construct conceptual models of the human universe. . . . The pre-eminence of myth in early human society is testimony that humans were using language for a totally new kind of integrative thought. Therefore, the possibility must be entertained that the primary human adaptation was not language *qua* language but rather integrative, initially mythical, thought. Modern humans developed language in response to pressure to improve their conceptual apparatus, not vice versa. (Donald, 1991, p. 215)

***Why Settle Down?*** This analysis may also provide a credible account of human beings' mysterious transition from small bands of seminomadic hunter-gatherers to larger groups of permanent town-dwellers. Many anthropologists and evolutionary psychologists argue that the development of agriculture (and domestication of animals) was responsible for this transition:

> Only ten thousand years ago, a tick in geological time, when the agricultural revolution began in the Middle East, in China, and in Mesoamerica, popula-

> tions increased in density tenfold over those of hunter-gatherer societies. Families settled on small plots of land, villages proliferated, and labor was divided. . . . The rising agricultural societies, egalitarian at first, became hierarchical. As chiefdoms and then states thrived on agricultural surpluses, hereditary rulers and priestly castes took power. (Wilson, 1998, p. 253)

Certainly, the discovery of agriculture made it possible for people to live together in larger groups. However, the notion that agriculture was the reason people originally came together is seriously undermined by the recent excavation (reported in Balter, 1998) of a settlement of approximately 10,000 people in Catalhoyuk, Turkey, occupied 9,000 years ago, a thousand years before any evidence of domestic agricultural activity. Archeologist Ian Hodder observed that "the rich wetland resources . . . would have been more easily exploited by a dispersed population in small settlements rather than by packing thousands of people into a village. . . . What you end up with is trying to understand why these people bothered to come together" (as quoted by Balter, 1998, p. 1445); other archaeologists agree that this settlement (and others like it) challenges "the long-held assumption that the first settlements and the transition from hunting and gathering to farming . . . were part of a single process," and raises the possibility that a "shared cultural revolution . . . preceded the rise of farming" (Balter, 1998, p. 1442).

We propose that the "shared cultural revolution" responsible for the transition to larger communities may have been an evolutionary change in human mentality with respect to managing the problem of death. This may have occurred for two reasons. First, humans who were like-minded with respect to spiritual beliefs and ideals naturally came together because greater consensus for such beliefs made these beliefs seem more "real" and thus more valid as fear-regulating psychological structures. Second, people may have formed more structured communities to become conscious (literally, to know with) of a historically unprecedented conception of God as an all-encompassing repository of wisdom and power, and to then "delegate all human power and all forces of nature to that supreme being, giving men an infinite reservoir of power on which they can draw by prayer" (Langer, 1982, p. 111) in exchange for lifelong prosperity, protection, and, ultimately, immortality. Thus, by coming together, people were able to create a shared meaning system, and then put a spiritual force at the helm of the community that allowed them to have ultimate power over nature, life, and death. This analysis reverses the order hypothesized by material accounts of the origin of social motives. Hierarchical social orders and deference to priestly authority were not engendered by an agricultural lifestyle. Rather, an agricultural lifestyle, and all that came afterward that we traditionally refer to as culture—such as history, art, science, and philosophy—were profoundly influenced by human beings' fantastically imaginative effort to overcome death by voluntarily relinquishing individual autonomy to delegated authority (the original "transference" according to Becker, 1975) through submission to supernatural spirits (the original "leap of faith"). This submission provided psychological equanimity through the belief that one is a valuable member of a meaningful universe and consequently eligible for immortality. Thus, although agriculture certainly made it more possible for larger groups of people to live together, the coming together of people was originally a solution to the problem of death.

Consistent with this explanation, the archaeologists at the Catalhoyuk excavation unearthed mass burials under the floors of houses, often in close physical proximity to painted murals of wild animals and hunting scenes. They speculated that "this close association between painting and burials is no coincidence" (Balter, 1998, p. 1445) and the function of art might be to control nature by symbolic representation. Jacques Cauvin of the Institute of Eastern Prehistory in France hypothesizes that such symbolic and religious pursuits instigated a "mental transformation" that allowed humans to see their environment differently and exploit it "more selectively and more actively" (as quoted by Balter, 1998, p.1445).

All subsequent human civilizations are clearly based on elaborate efforts to deny death. For example, in ancient Egypt:

> After a ruler died, his or her body was carefully treated and wrapped to preserve it as a mummy. According to ancient Egyptian belief, the pyramid, where the mummy was placed, provided a place for the monarch to pass into the afterlife. In temples nearby, priests performed rituals to nourish the dead monarch's spirit, which was believed to stay with the body after death. In the Old Kingdom (a period of Egyptian history from about 2575 BC to about 2134 BC), Egyptian artists carved hieroglyphs on the walls of the burial chamber, designed to safeguard the dead monarch's passage into the afterlife. . . . Sometimes, in addition to the burial chamber, there were storage chambers within the pyramid. These chambers held objects used in burial rituals as well as items for the deceased to use in the afterlife. (*Microsoft Encarta Encyclopedia*, CD ROM, 2000)

At the same time, in China, early emperors, following the Chinese proverb "Treat death as life," had their servants, artisans, concubines, and soldiers buried alive with them when they died (Mazzatenta, 1992). This tradition continued until 210 B.C., when Qin Shi Huang Di, the first emperor of unified China and builder of the Great Wall, sent a fleet of vessels with precious gifts in search of the Islands of Immortality. The expedition never returned, and the emperor continued what historian Li Yu-hing (quoted in Mazzatenta, 1996, p. 442) described as a "quest for immortality and eternal glory and power" by having himself buried with an entire army of life-sized and life-like terra cotta warriors, horses, and servants.

A century later, Jing Di, fifth ruler of the Han dynasty, was also entombed with a terra cotta army of one-third life-sized soldiers and horses. Summarizing archeologists' interpretations of these findings, Mazzatenta (1992) observed:

> Tomb excavations during the past 40 years are evidence of the Han belief that the afterlife was a prolongation of this life. Thus Jing Di's mausoleum, as his afterworld headquarters would have mirrored the magnificence of his residence on earth. The tombs of the rich were lavishly provisioned; goods brought along—everything from finely woven silks and musical instruments to food and drink—indicated life well lived. Whereas a common man might be buried with a miniature clay granary, the emperor got a full-size granary as well as his own army. (p. 120)

Back in the Near East, by 2000 B.C. there is evidence in Sumerian texts of the development of the Epic of Gilgamesh, the oral tradition that became the basis of the Old and New Testaments of the Bible and hence of the entire Judeo-Christian and Muslim traditions on which Western civilization was constructed and currently operates. In *The Cry for Myth*, Rollo May (1991; see also Gottsch, 2000, for a similar argument independently derived from an evolutionary perspective) notes that the story of Gilgamesh is a metaphor for the unique existential concerns of the human condition engendered by consciousness and the consequent awareness of death. In the story, Gilgamesh is overwhelmed with grief after the death of his best friend Enkidu, and becomes obsessed with the prospect of his own death: "When I die, shall I not be like unto Enkidu?" Gilgamesh then departs on a quest to obtain immortality, a Faustian voyage with no final destination that the human species has been pursuing from that time to the present day. And so we can see over the course of recorded history how the death denying ideologies of, for example, Judaism, Christianity, Islam, and Hinduism have spread and prospered over the many generations since those earlier conceptions of immortality.

And as we totter into the present millennium, secular nondenominational cultures, such as the United States, as well as explicitly atheistic communist (e.g., Russia and China) cultures continue to be constructed on the basic principle of death denial. In America, the back of the one-dollar bill says "In God We Trust," and just to the left is a picture of a pyramid (the ultimate immortality symbol) with a disembodied eyeball floating mysteriously above the pinnacle of the pyramid as if an all-encompassing power were shining his or her countenance on us. And indeed, according to Joseph Campbell (1988), this reflects the eye of God opening to us when we reach the top of the pyramid and attain immortality. Americans also go to great lengths to avoid direct contact with death: The average American has never seen a dead person and is loathe to live anywhere near people who are likely to die—that is, the sick and/or elderly stashed away in hospitals, nursing homes, and retirement communities in Florida, Arizona, and California. The average American goes to enormous lengths to retard and/or disguise the natural process of aging—hair replacement, hair removal, hair coloring, face lifts, tummy tucks, wrinkle removal, and so on.

In the former Soviet Union, thousands of people came to the Kremlin each day to see Lenin's body preserved for perpetuity in a glass tomb. Hitler was quite explicit in proclaiming that the Third Reich would endure long beyond his individual death; we can only be thankful that he was wrong about that. In communist China, a well-known party slogan is "May the Revolutionary Regime stay Red for ten thousand generations"—longer than the current age of the human race. In *Revolutionary Immortality: Mao Tse-Tung and the Chinese Cultural Revolution*, Robert Jay Lifton (1968) noted that all political revolutions are ultimately driven by concerns about death:

> Much of what has been taking place in China recently can be understood as a quest for revolutionary immortality. By revolutionary immortality I mean a shared sense of participating in permanent revolutionary fermentation, and of transcending individual death by "living on" indefinitely within this continuing revolution. Some such vision has been present in all revolutions and was directly expressed in Trotsky's ideological principle of "permanent revolution." ... Central to this point of view is the concept of symbolic immortality ... of man's need, in the face of inevitable biological death, to maintain an inner sense of continuity with what has gone on before and what will go on after his own individual existence. ... The revolutionary denies theology as such, but embraces a secular utopia through images closely related to the spiritual conquest of death and even to an afterlife. ... What all this suggests, then, is that the essence of ... all ... "power struggles," is power over death. (pp. 7–8)

The proposition that the course of cultural evolution was radically altered by the potential anxiety engendered by the "endogenous" problem of death is thus entirely consistent with archaeological findings, the historical record, and the nature of contemporary cultures.

## Convergence with Contemporary Research on the Role of Culture in Managing the Awareness of Mortality

There is also a large body of experimental evidence in accord with the notion that culture plays a primary role in a complex species-typical adaptation to the uniquely human awareness and denial of death. Following Rank (1931/1961, 1936), Zilboorg (1943), Roheim (1934, 1943), and especially Becker (1971, 1973, 1975), terror management theory (Greenberg, Pyszczynski, & Solomon, 1986; Solomon, Greenberg, & Pyszczynski, 1991) posits that the juxtaposition of an inclination toward self-preservation with the highly developed intellectual abilities that make humans aware of their vulnerabilities and inevitable death creates the potential for paralyzing terror. To allow people to function effectively in light of this realization, cultures evolved beliefs designed to help individuals manage the terror associated with this awareness of death. This has been accomplished primarily through the cultural mechanism of self-esteem, which consists of the belief that one is a valuable contributor to a meaningful universe. There are thus two basic components of what we refer to as the cultural anxiety buffer, both of which are necessary for effective *terror management*: (a) faith in a meaningful conception of reality that provides the possibility of death transcendence to those who meets the prescribed standards of value (the *cultural worldview*), and (b) the belief that one is meeting those standards of value (*self-esteem*). Because of the protection from the potential for terror that these psychological structures provide, people are motivated to maintain faith in their cultural worldviews and satisfy the standards of value associated with their worldviews.

Empirical research to assess the merits of terror management theory has been based on two broad hypotheses derived from the theory. First, if self-esteem serves an anxiety-buffering function, then high self-esteem (dispositional or temporarily elevated) should serve to reduce and/or eliminate negative affect, defensive responses, and physiological arousal engendered by stressful circumstances. Consistent with this proposition, high self-esteem has been shown to reduce: self-reported anxiety in response to gory death-related videos (Greenberg et al., 1992, Study 1); defensive distortions to deny vulnerability to early death (Greenberg et al., 1993); and, physiological arousal in response to threat of electrical shocks (Greenberg et al., 1992, studies 2 and 3).

Second, if cultural worldviews and self-esteem based on them serve a death-denying defensive function, then making mortality momentarily salient by asking people to ponder their own death should intensify allegiance to the worldview and striving to meet its standards of value. Over 90 experiments conducted in five different countries have provided support for mortality salience hypotheses: Mortality salience has been shown to lead to more negative evaluations and harsher punishments of moral transgressors and more favorable reactions and rewards to those who uphold moral standards (Florian & Mikulincer, 1997; Rosenblatt, Greenberg, Solomon, Pyszczynski, & Lyon, 1989), and more positive reactions to those who share one's religious or political beliefs, and correspondingly negative reactions to those with different beliefs (Greenberg et al., 1990). For example, mortality salience increases physical distancing from dissimilar others (Ochsmann & Mathy, 1994) and physical aggression toward them (McGregor et al., 1998). Mortality salience also increases perception of social consensus for one's attitudes (Pyszczynski et al., 1996) and discomfort when performing behavior counter to cultural norms (Greenberg, Simon, Porteus, Pyszczynski, & Solomon, 1995). In addition, recent evidence shows that mortality salience motivates bolstering for self-esteem as well as the worldview. For example, Taubman, Florian, and Mikulincer (1999) showed that Israeli soldiers who use driving ability as a basis for their self-worth drive more boldly after a reminder of death, and Goldenberg, McCoy, Pyszczynski, Greenberg, and Solomon (2000) demonstrated that people with high body self-esteem are more attentive to their bodies following a mortality salience induction.

Mortality salience effects have been obtained using open-ended questions about participants' own death, fear of death scales, gory accident footage, subliminal primes, and proximity to a funeral home. *Mortality salience effects are specific to thoughts of one's own death*; they are not produced by thoughts of other aversive or anxiety-provoking stimuli, such as thoughts of intense pain, paralysis, social exclusion, worries about life after college, giving a speech, failing an exam, or imagining the death of a loved one (see Greenberg, Solomon, & Pyszczynski, 1997). There is thus strong evidence that quite specific concerns about mortality influence a wide range of human social behavior in predictable ways.

Most recently, Pyszczynski et al. (1999) proposed a dual process theory to explicate the nature of the cognitive processes that underlie cultural worldview defense in response to mortality salience:

> Distinct defensive responses are activated by thoughts of death that are conscious and those that are on the fringes of consciousness (highly accessible but not in current focal attention). Proximal defenses entail the suppression of death-related thoughts or pushing the problem of death into the distant future by denying one's vulnerability to various risk factors. These defenses are rational, threat-focused, and are activated when thoughts of death are in current conscious attention. Distal terror management defenses entail maintaining self-esteem and faith in one's cultural worldview and serve to control the potential for anxiety resulting from awareness of the inevitability of death. These defenses are experiential, not related to the problem of death in any semantic or rational way, and are increasingly activated as the accessibility of death-related thoughts increases, up to the point at which such thoughts enter consciousness and proximal threat-focused defenses are initiated. (p. 835)

In support of this dual process conception, Greenberg, Arndt, Simon, Pyszczynski, and Solomon (2000) demonstrated that immediately after a mortality salience induction, people engage in proximal defenses (vulnerability-denying defensive distortions) but do not show evidence of distal defense (exaggerated regard and disdain for similar and dissimilar others respectively); as expected, distal defense was obtained after a delay, but proximal defenses were not. Additionally, defense of the cultural worldview does not occur when mortality is highly salient, or when people are forced to keep thoughts of death in consciousness following our typical subtle mortality salience manipulation (Greenberg, Pyszczynski, Solomon, Simon, & Breus, 1994), or when they are asked to behave "rationally" (Simon et al., 1997). We have also demonstrated that the accessibility of death-related thoughts is low immediately following mortality salience as a result of an active suppression of such thoughts, and that a delayed increase in the accessibility of death-related thoughts (presumably from relaxation of the suppression) is responsible for the delayed appearance of cultural worldview defense (Arndt, Greenberg, Solomon, Pyszczynski, & Simon, 1997). Heightened accessibility of death-related thoughts has been shown to be a necessary and sufficient condition to produce worldview defense following mortality salience (Arndt, Greenberg, Solomon, Pyszczynski, & Simon, 1997; Arndt, Greenberg, Pyszczynski, & Solomon, 1997), and cultural worldview defense serves to keep levels of death-thought accessibility low (Arndt, Greenberg, Solomon, Pyszczynski, & Simon, 1997; Harmon-Jones et al., 1997). See Fig. 2.1 for a graphic depiction of this dual defense process.

We agree with the Tooby and Cosmides (1992) assertion that "complex adaptations are usually species-typical; moreover, they are so well-organized and such good engineering solutions to adaptive problems that a

**THOUGHTS OF DEATH ENTER CONSCIOUSNESS**

V

**PROXIMAL DEFENSES: SUPPRESSION & RATIONALIZATION**

V

**INCREASE IN ACCESSIBILITY OF DEATH-RELATED THOUGHT OUTSIDE OF CONSCIOUSNESS**

V

**DISTAL TERROR MANAGEMENT DEFENSES:**
**WORLDVIEW DEFENSE AND SELF-ESTEEM BOLSTERING**

V

**DEATH THOUGHT ACCESSIBILITY IS REDUCED AND POTENTIAL TERROR IS AVERTED**

FIG. 2.1. Defensive processes activated by conscious and unconscious death-related thought (adapted from Pyszczynski, Greenberg, & Solomon, 1999).

chance coordination between problem and solution is ruled out as a plausible explanation" (p. 62). And it is in light of this claim that we would argue that the terror management process of sustaining self-esteem within the context of a cultural worldview qualifies as a species-typical evolutionary adaptation. Given the wide range of attitudes and behavior that are influenced by making one's own mortality salient, the complex interplay between conscious and nonconscious processes resulting from thoughts of death, and that all such defensive processes serve to reduce the accessibility of death-related thoughts, it seems highly unlikely that such an imaginative, sophisticated, elaborate, and highly organized system of death-denying psychological processes is the result of "chance coordination."

## SUMMARY AND CONCLUSIONS

> At first thought it seems strange, even fanciful, to regard a conceptual insight like the realization of natural mortality as a milestone on the road of man's evolutionary advance. On longer consideration, however, one can see many reasons to class it as such, both because of the conditions which its attainment has required and the influence it has had on the subjective and objective course of human life. . . . It marks no direct physical change, though indirectly and subtly it may produce many; its historical significance and its crucial function belong to the advance of mind, not of physique. (Langer, 1982, p. 89)

We agree with evolutionary psychologists such as Tooby and Cosmides that a psychological account of the underpinnings of culture is a central problem for the study of mind, and that credible theories should show "hallmarks of special design for proposed function," be "capable of generating specific and falsifiable empirical predictions," and "account for known data better than alternative hypotheses" (Buss, Haselton, Shackelford, Bleske, & Wakefield, 1998, p. 546). We propose that human awareness of death, as a result of the evolution of consciousness, instigated the construction of an elaborate host of psychological defenses in pursuit of immortality that are manifest in many important components of culture:

> Art: "The creative impulse . . . attempts to turn ephemeral life into personal immortality. In creation the artist tries to immortalize his mortal life" (Rank, 1932, p. 39).
>
> Economics: "The human animal is a beast that dies and if he's got money he buys and buys and buys and I think the reason he buys everything he can buy is that in the back of his mind he has the crazy hope that one of his purchases will be life ever-lasting" (Williams, 1955, p. 73).

> Science: "Fear—that is man's original and fundamental sensation; everything is explained by fear. . . . This protracted, ancient fear at length grown subtle, spiritual, intellectual—today, it seems to me, it is called: science" (Nietzsche, 1885/1982, p. 312).
>
> Religion: "All the teachings and training in Buddhism are aimed at that one single point: to look into the nature of the mind, and so free us from fear of death" (Rinpoche, 1994, pp. 51–52).

These culturally mediated responses to the fear of death operate at the individual level to minimize the accessibility of nonconscious thoughts of death by a complex interaction of conscious and nonconscious processes to sustain the belief that one is a valuable member of a meaningful universe.

Culture has thus been shaped in part to serve this species-specific evolutionary adaptation to the uniquely human awareness of death. This proposition is consistent with an evolutionary perspective; it can provide a compelling account of the archeological and historical record; and it is supported by an extensive empirical literature demonstrating the pervasive influence of intimations of mortality on a wide range of personal and interpersonal behaviors.

The psychological processes that use culture as a vehicle for death transcendence have been quite successful so far, as the burgeoning human population of over six billion attests. But will these modes of death transcendence continue to be viable human adaptations? As Becker (1975) noted rather somberly at the conclusion of *Escape from Evil*, an inevitable result of cultural worldviews serving a death-denying function may be the inability to tolerate those with different visions of reality, in that acceptance of the potential validity of alternative worldviews undermines the confidence with which one subscribes to one's own, and thus threatens to unleash the unmitigated terror ordinarily quelled by absolute faith in one's culture.

A host of compensatory processes are consequently instigated to restore psychological equanimity: derogating those who are different, pressuring them to dispose of their beliefs and convert to the dominant worldview (assimilation), incorporating neutered versions of their views into one's own (accommodation), and/or annihilating them to demonstrate that your vision of reality must have been "right" after all (Solomon et al., 1991). Prejudice, scapegoating, ideological fervor, and ongoing ethnic strife may thus be the psychological price to be paid for psychological equanimity via death-denying cultural worldviews. This has not been fatally problematic for the entire species as yet because for most of human history, there weren't as many people or cultures in close proximity or such destructive technologies so readily available. In contrast, the recent advent of powerful nuclear weapons in a culturally heterogeneous overpopulated world of limited physical resources makes human self-extermination a very real, albeit chilling, possibility.

We have argued elsewhere (Solomon et al., 1991) that the utility of any theory is determined not only by existing evidence and the nature of the questions generated by it, but also by the implications of the theory for constructive individual and social change. The psychodynamic perspective advanced here acknowledges the dynamic nature of change of over time—recall Fenichel's assertion, quoted earlier, that mental processes, as products of evolution, are "changeable in the course of further biological history," and Roheim's claim that civilization is still developing. Similarly, Jaynes (1976, p. 125) recognized that "it would be wrong to think that whatever the neurology of consciousness now may be, it is set for all time . . . the function of brain tissue is not inevitable . . . perhaps different organizations, given different developmental programs, may be possible." So perhaps all hope is not lost.

Roheim (1943, p.100) argued that culture "originates in delayed infancy and its function is security. It is a huge network of more or less successful attempts to protect mankind against the danger of object-loss, the colossal efforts made by a baby who is afraid of being left alone in the dark." On these grounds, he proposed that a viable future for our species will require that the human race "grow up"—to somehow squarely face up to and accept our vulnerabilities and mortality. Such a maturation process may require a profound transformation of the manner in which our uniquely human need for death transcendence is satisfied. We are hopeful that this chapter will contribute to a growing psychological discussion of the extent to which this is possible in the foreseeable future, and of precisely how it might be accomplished.

## REFERENCES

Arndt, J., Greenberg, J., Solomon, S., Pyszczynski, T., & Simon, L. (1997). Suppression, accessibility of death-related thoughts, and cultural worldview defense: Exploring the psychodynamics of terror management *Journal of Personality and Social Psychology, 73,* 5–18.

Arndt, J., Greenberg, J., Pyszczynski, T., & Solomon, S. (1997). Subliminal presentation of death reminders leads to increased defense of the cultural worldview. *Psychological Science, 8,* 379–385.

Balter, M. (1998). Why settle down? The mystery of communities. *Science, 282,* 1442–1445.

Becker, E. (1971). *The birth and death of meaning.* New York: Free Press.

Becker, E. (1973). *The denial of death.* New York: Free Press.

Becker, E. (1975). *Escape from evil.* New York: Free Press.

Berger, P. L., & Luckmann, T. (1966/1967). *The social construction of reality: A treatise in the sociology of knowledge.* Garden City, NY: Anchor Books.

Brown, N. O. (1959). *Life against death: The psychoanalytical meaning of history.* Middletown, CT: Wesleyan University Press.

Bruner, J. (1986). *Actual minds, possible worlds*. Cambridge, MA: Harvard University Press.

Bruner, J. (1990). *Acts of meaning*. Cambridge, MA: Harvard University Press.

Buss, D. M., Haselton, M. G., Shackelford, T. K., Bleske, A. L., & Wakefield, J. C. (1998). Adaptations, exaptations, and spandrels. *American Psychologist, 53*, 533–548.

Campbell, J. (1988). *The power of myth* (with Bill Moyers; B. S. Flowers, Ed.). New York: Doubleday.

Carver, C. S., & Scheier, M. (1981). *Attention and self-regulation*. New York: Springer-Verlag.

Dawkins, R. (1976). *The selfish gene*. Oxford: Oxford University Press.

de Waal, F. B. M. (2000, April 2). Survival of the Rapist. *New York Times Book Review*, pp. 24–25.

Donald, M. (1991). *Origins of the modern mind: Three stages in the evolution of culture and cognition*. Cambridge, MA: Harvard University Press.

Durkheim, E. (1962). *The rules of the sociological method*. Glencoe, IL: Free Press. (Original work published 1895)

Duval, S., & Wicklund, R. A. (1972). *A theory of objective self-awareness*. New York: Academic Press.

Erdelyi, M. H. (1985). *Psychoanalysis: Freud's cognitive psychology*. New York: W. H. Freeman.

Fenichel, O. (1945). *The psychoanalytic theory of neurosis*. New York: W. W. Norton.

Florian, V., & Mikulincer, M. (1997). Fear of death and the judgment of social transgressions: A multidimensional test of terror management theory. *Journal of Personality and Social Psychology, 73*, 369–380.

Frantz, D. (1998, February 13). Scientology's star roster enhances image. *New York Times*, pp. A1, A24.

Freud, S. (1989). *The future of an illusion*. New York: W. W. Norton. (Original work published 1928)

Freud, S. (1989). *Civilization and its discontents*. New York: W. W. Norton. (Original work published 1930)

Geertz, C. (1973). *The interpretation of cultures*. New York: Basic Books.

Goldenberg, J. L., McCoy, S. K., Pyszczynski, T. Greenberg, J., & Solomon, S. (2000). The body as a source of self-esteem: The effects of mortality salience on identification with one's body, interest in sex, and appearance monitoring. *Journal of Personality and Social Psychology, 79*, 118–130.

Gottsch, J. D. (2000). *Mutation, selection, and vertical transmission of theistic memes in religious canons*. Unpublished manuscript, Johns Hopkins University School of Medicine, Baltimore, MD.

Greenberg, J., Arndt, J., Simon, L., Pyszczynski, T., & Solomon, S. (2000). Proximal and distal defenses in response to reminders of one's mortality: Evidence of a temporal sequence. *Personality and Social Psychology Bulletin, 26*, 91–99.

Greenberg, J., Pyszczynski, T., & Solomon, S. (1986). The causes and consequences of a need for self-esteem: A terror management theory. In R. F. Baumeister (Ed.), *Public self and private self* (pp. 189–212). New York: Springer-Verlag.

Greenberg, J., Pyszczynski, T., Solomon, S., Pinel, E., Simon, L., & Jordan, K. (1993). Effects of self-esteem on vulnerability-denying defensive distortions: Further evidence of an anxiety-buffering function of self-esteem. *Journal of Experimental Social Psychology, 29*, 229–251.

Greenberg, J., Pyszczynski, T., Solomon S., Rosenblatt, A., Veeder, M., Kirkland, S., & Lyon, D. (1990). Evidence for terror management theory II: The effects of mortality salience on reactions to those who threaten or bolster the cultural worldview. *Journal of Personality and Social Psychology, 58*, 308–318.

Greenberg, J., Pyszczynski, T., Solomon, S., Simon, L., & Breus, M. (1994). Role of consciousness and accessibility of death-related thoughts in mortality salience effects. *Journal of Personality and Social Psychology, 67*, 627–637.

Greenberg, J., Simon, L., Porteus, J., Pyszczynski, T., & Solomon, S. (1995). Evidence of a terror management function of cultural icons: The effects of mortality salience on the inappropriate use of cherished cultural symbols. *Personality and Social Psychology Bulletin, 21*, 1221–1228.

Greenberg, J., Solomon, S., & Pyszczynski, T. (1997). Terror management theory of self-esteem and cultural worldviews: Empirical assessments and conceptual refinements. In M. Zanna (Ed.), *Advances in experimental social psychology* (Vol. 29, pp. 61–139). Orlando, FL: Academic Press.

Greenberg, J., Solomon, S., Pyszczynski, T., Rosenblatt, A., Burling, J., Lyon, D., & Simon, L. (1992). Assessing the terror management analysis of self-esteem: Converging evidence of an anxiety-buffering function. *Journal of Personality and Social Psychology, 63*, 913–922.

Greenwald, A. (1980). The totalitarian ego: Fabrication and revision of personal history. *American Psychologist, 35*, 603–618.

Harmon-Jones, E., Simon, L., Greenberg, J., Pyszczynski, T., Solomon, S., & McGregor, H. (1997). Terror management theory and self-esteem: Evidence that increased self-esteem reduces mortality salience effects. *Journal of Personality and Social Psychology, 72*, 24–36.

Harris, M. (1979). *Cultural materialism: The struggle for a science of culture*. New York: Random House.

Horney, K. (1950). *Neurosis and human growth: The struggle toward self-realization*. New York: W. W. Norton.

Humphrey (1984). *Consciousness regained*. Oxford, UK: Oxford University Press.

Isaacs, S. (1948). The nature and function of phantasy. *International Journal of Psycho-Analysis, XXIX*, 73–97.

Jaynes, J. (1976). *The origin of consciousness in the breakdown of the bicameral mind*. Boston: Houghton Mifflin.

Kunda, Z. (1990). A case for motivated reasoning. *Psychological Bulletin, 108*, 480–498.

Laitman, J. T. (1983). The evolution of the hominid upper respiratory system and implications for the origin of speech. In E. de Grolier (Ed.). *Clossogenetics: The origin and evolution of language* (pp. 63–90). Paris: Harwood Academic Press.

Laitman, J. T., & Heimbuch, R. C. (1982). The basicranium of plio-pleistocene hominids as an indicator of their upper respiratory systems 2. *American Journal of Physcial Anthropology, 59*, 323–343.

Laitman, J. T., Heimbuch, R. C., & Crelin, E. S. (1979). The basicranium of fossil hominids as an indicator of upper respiratory systems. *American Journal of Physical Anthropology, 51*, 15–33.

Langer, S. K. (1982). *Mind: An essay on human feeling*, (Vol. III). Baltimore, MD: Johns Hopkins University Press.

Lieberman, P. (1985). On the evolution of human syntactic ability: Its preadaptive bases—Motor control and speech. *Journal of Human Evolution, 14*, 657–668.

Lieberman, P. (1989). The origins of some aspects of human language and cognition. In P. Mellars & C. Stringer (Eds.) *The human revolution: Behavioral and biological perspectives on the origins of modern humans* (pp. 391–414). Edinburgh University Press.

Lifton, R. J. (1968). *Revolutionary immortality: Mao Tse-Tung and the Chinese Cultural Revolution*. New York: Random House.

May, R. (1953). *Man's search for himself*. New York: W. W. Norton.

May, R. (1991). *The cry for myth*. New York: Dell.

Mazzatenta, O. (1992). A Chinese emperor's army for an eternity. *National Geographic, 182*, 114–130.

Mazzatenta, O. (1996). China's warriors rise from the earth. *National Geographic, 190*, 68–85.

McGregor, H., Lieberman, J., Greenberg, J., Solomon, S., Arndt, J., Simon, L., & Pyszczynski, T. (1998). Terror management and aggression: Evidence that mortality salience promotes aggression toward worldview-threatening individuals. *Journal of Personality and Social Psychology, 74*, 590–605.

Miller, J. G. (1999). Cultural psychology: Implications for basic psychological theory. *Psychological Science, 10*, 85–91.

Mithen, S. (1996). *The Prehistory of the Mind: The cognitive origins of art, religion and science*. London, UK: Thames and Hudson.

Newton, P. M. (1995). *Freud: From youthful dream to mid-life crisis*. New York: Guilford Press.

Nietzsche, F. (1982). *Thus spoke Zarathustra*. New York: Penguin Books. (Original work published 1885)

Nietzsche, F. (1974). *The gay science*. New York: Vintage Books. (Original work published 1887)

Nietzsche, F. (1998). *Twilight of the idols*. Oxford: Oxford University Press. (Original work published 1888)

Ochsmann, R., & Mathy, M. (1994). *Depreciating of and distancing from foreigners: Effects of mortality salience*. Unpublished manuscript, Universitat Mainz, Mainz, Germany.

Pennebaker, J. (1990). *Opening up: The healing power of confiding in others*. New York: Morrow.

Pinker, S. (1997). *How the mind works*. New York: W. W. Norton.

Pyszczynski, T., & Greenberg, J. (1987). Toward an integration of cognitive and motivational perspectives on social inference: A biased hypothesis-testing model. In L. Berkowitz (Ed.), *Advances in experimental social psychology* (Vol. 20, pp. 297–340). Orlando, FL: Academic Press.

Pyszczynski, T., Greenberg, J., & Solomon, S. (1999). A dual process model of defense against conscious and unconscious death-related thoughts: An extension of terror management theory. *Psychological Review, 106*, 835–845.

Pyszczynski, T., Wicklund, R., Floresku, S., Gauch, G., Koch, H., Solomon, S., & Greenberg, J. (1996). Whistling in the dark: Exaggerated consensus estimates in response to incidental reminders of mortality. *Psychological Science, 7*, 332–336.

Rank, O. (1961). *Psychology and the soul*. New York: Perpetua. (Original work published 1931)

Rank, O. (1932). Art and artist: Creative urge and personality development. New York: Alfred A. Knopf.

Rank, O. (1945). *Will therapy and truth and reality*. New York: Alfred A. Knopf. (Original work published 1936)

Rinpoche, S. (1994). *The Tibetan book of living and dying*. New York: HarperCollins.

Roheim, G. (1934). The evolution of culture. *International Journal of Psycho-Analysis, XV*, 387–418.

Roheim, G. (1943). *The origin and function of culture*. Nervous and Mental Disease Monograph no. 69. New York: Nervous and Mental Disease Monographs.

Rosenblatt, A., Greenberg, J., Solomon, S., Pyszczynski, T., & Lyon, D. (1989). Evidence for terror management theory I: The effects of mortality salience on reactions to those who violate or uphold cultural values. *Journal of Personality and Social Psychology, 57*, 681–690.

Shweder, R. (1990). Cultural psychology: What is it? In J. U. Stigler, R. Shweder, & G. Gerdt (Eds.), *Cultural psychology* (pp. 1–43). Cambridge, UK: Cambridge University Press.

Simon, L., Greenberg, J., Harmon-Jones, E., Solomon, S., Pyszczynski, T., Arndt, J., & Abend, T. (1997). Terror management and cognitive-experiential self-theory: Evidence that terror management occurs in the experiential system. *Journal of Personality and Social Psychology, 72*, 1132–1146.

Solomon, S., Greenberg, J., & Pyszczynski, T. (1991). A terror management theory of social behavior: The psychological functions of self-esteem and cultural worldviews. In M. Zanna (Ed.), *Advances in experimental social psychology* (Vol. 24, pp. 91–159). Orlando, FL: Academic Press.

Spengler, O. (1999). *The decline of the West, Vol. 1: Form and actuality*. New York: Alfred A. Knopf. (Original work published 1926)

Tattersall, I. (2000). Once we were not alone. *Scientific American, 282*, 56–62.

Taubman, O., Florian, V., & Mikulincer, M. (1999). The impact of mortality salience on reckless driving: A test of terror management mechanisms. *Journal of Personality and Social Psychology, 76*, 35–45.

Tooby, J., & Cosmides, L. (1992). The psychological foundations of culture. In J. H. Barkow, L. Cosmides & J. Tooby (Eds.), *The adapted mind* (pp 19–136). New York: Oxford University Press.

Westen, D. (1998). The scientific legacy of Sigmund Freud: Toward a psychodynamically informed psychological science. *Psychological Bulletin, 124*, 333–371.

Williams, T. (1955). *Cat on a hot tin roof*. New York: New Directions Books.

Wilson, E. O. (1978). *On human nature*. Cambridge, MA: Harvard University Press.

Wilson, E. O. (1998). *Conscilience: The unity of knowledge*. New York: Alfred A. Knopf.

Zilboorg, G. (1943). Fear of death. *Psychoanalytic Quarterly, 12*, 465–475.

CHAPTER

# 3

# Cultural Elements Emerge From Dynamic Social Impact

Helen C. Harton
University of Northern Iowa

Martin J. Bourgeois
University of Wyoming

Imagine attending a small conference of relatively like-minded scientists. At the beginning of a talk, you're surprised to be handed a piece of paper. They apparently expect you to take a quiz! But you're a good sport, so you look down and circle your answer to the following analogy based on leaders in your field and quickly cover your paper: Serge Moscovici is to Stanley Schachter as Marilynn Brewer is to ... (A) Donald Campbell; (B) Leon Festinger; (C) Chuck Kiesler; (D) Thomas Ostrom; (E) Judith Rodin.

Then the person giving the talk asks you to discuss your answer with the people sitting to your left and right for about a minute. You compare your answers with the others, explaining the logic behind your choice: Perhaps you chose Campbell because of research connections or Rodin because of gender. When the minute is up, you are asked to answer the question again. What would the end distribution of answers look like?

We asked this exact question in demonstrations at eight conferences (Harton, Green, Jackson, & Latané, 1996). What we found, we argue here, was a slice of culture, an example of how cultures can emerge and persist through discussion. What follows is the distribution of responses before and after discussion for two analogies presented at one conference:

```
Analogy 1:  Before:  BADADEBAEBDBEEDBEE
            After:   BBDECBBBBBBBEEEEEE

Analogy 2:  Before:  EEABCCAECDAEBBBEBC
            After:   BBEBCCCEDDBBBBBEBD
```

People sometimes but not always yielded to their neighbors' arguments, resulting in a clear and nonrandom spatially distributed pattern of answers after discussion. In fact, people's answers after discussion were more similar to their neighbors than would be expected by chance. The reduction of independence from this clustering of responses led to associations between the answers. After discussion, people who chose answer E on the first analogy often chose answer B on the second. Even though there was no rational reason (such as similar arguments) to connect answers, the relations emerged simply because people became more similar to those they talked to on multiple issues. Minority viewpoints also decreased after discussion, as those who chose the initial majority answer gained converts. For example, in the first analogy, the two most popular answers initially, B and E, grew in popularity after discussion. Finally, despite this influence, diversity persisted, and likely would continue to persist, even if we had let the conferees continue to discuss their answers. In this same way, through day-to-day conversations about topics at local cafés, on street corners, and in office cubicles, culture is created and passed on through local social influence.

Schaller, Conway, and Crandall (chap. 1, this volume) define culture as a collection of elements that are shared by some definable set of people and differentiable from other sets. In our example just described, we could talk about a culture of people who chose answer E for the first analogy and answer B for the second and distinguish them from those who chose B/C. If these people continued to discuss other topics with those seated closest to them, we might also find that the E/B group became more similar in their beliefs about economics, their attitudes toward the death penalty, or even their personalities. These "cultures" in our example emerged in a matter of minutes. Imagine then how social influence has shaped culture over millennia, resulting in associated regional differences in food preferences, attitudes, and life outlooks!

We address the creation and persistence of culture in this chapter using dynamic social impact theory (DSIT; Latané, 1996a, 1996b), a dynamical systems approach to large scale influence that has received considerable empirical support. First we discuss what culture is, how it is formed, and how it changes over time. We link the answers to these questions to theoretical concepts from DSIT and provide both empirical and cultural examples of each concept. We then address two factors, involvement and heritability, that may limit influence, and describe other cultural elements that DSIT can help explain, such as attitudes toward ethnic groups, language, health-related attitudes and behaviors, and even human biology. We conclude by summarizing how DSIT helps us understand the formation and progression of culture.

## WHAT IS CULTURE?

Many psychological models of culture begin with the assumption that people living in disparate regions will differ from each other because of their socialization in a particular culture. Such top-down approaches do not attempt to explain the reasons for these cross-cultural differences, but simply document and describe the range of values for such psychological variables as self-concept, reasoning strategies, and relational behaviors to be expected between people from myriad cultures. Dynamic social impact theory (DSIT; Latané, 1996a, 1996b, 1996d; Nowak, Szamrej, & Latané, 1990) takes the opposite stance, explaining the emergence of cultural phenomena from the bottom up. DSIT adapts a theory of social influence among individuals (social impact theory; Latané, 1981) to explain how cultures varying in size from dyads and triads to countries and continents develop and change over time. We use the dynamical systems term *self-organization* to refer to this process of individual elements affecting each other to form patterns at the group level.

DSIT assumes that people influence and are influenced by others through the process of communication. When we talk about *communication*, we of course mean two-way face-to-face conversations, but we also mean the term more broadly, to indicate any type of social exchange of information. The observation that your neighbor cut his lawn yesterday is socially communicated information, as is hearing another neighbor derogate an ethnic group. Influence does not have to be intentional on the part of the actor or identified as a persuasion attempt by the target. It does not even have to be consciously noticed. For example, biological "communication" may occur through pheromones to affect body functions (Stern & McClintock, 1998).

DSIT posits that influence will occur whenever groups of people interact and on all socially influenceable attributes, from moods to clothing styles to opinions on abortion. It applies to both normative and informational influence and predicts conformity as well as compliance and obedience. DSIT states that influence will occur in proportion to three factors–strength, immediacy, and number–that form the basis for social impact theory (SIT; Latané, 1981).

The amount of influence, or social impact, a person has on another will be affected in part by individual differences in persuasiveness and supportiveness, or *strength*. Some people are more attractive, eloquent, rich, or educated than others, and those characteristics may lead them to have greater influence on those around them (see Petty & Wegener, 1998, for a review). Individuals also differ in their supportive strength. Some people, such as those who are low in need for closure (Richter & Kruglanski, chap. 5, this volume) or for whom the issue is highly important (Harton, 1998;

Krosnick & Petty, 1995; Sherif, Kelley, Rodgers, Sarup, & Tittler, 1973; Sherif, Sherif, & Nebergall, 1965) are more able to resist persuasive attempts and may provide greater support for like-minded colleagues. Persuasive and supportive strength may differ by issue and may be affected by the target's other characteristics. Although you might put more weight on your doctor's opinion about gene therapy than your gardener's, you would not necessarily be as convinced by the doctor's opinion on the best methods for growing geraniums. Likewise, a liberal would probably be more persuaded than a conservative by an American Civil Liberties Union opinion.

Influence will also increase as a function of closeness in physical or social space, or *immediacy*. Immediacy includes proximity, but is broader than mere closeness. For example, a person in a rural area may live a half mile from Neighbor Jones and a full mile from Neighbor Smith. Smith may in fact be higher in immediacy, however, if the road to her house is easier for the person to travel than the road to Jones is. Geographical features such as rutted roads, mountainous terrain, and bodies of water and social features such as differences in languages or worldviews affect the ease of communication and thus the degree of influence. But even in open societies with modern means of travel and communication, people still tend to interact most often with those who live closest to them (Latané, Liu, Nowak, Bonevento, & Zheng, 1995).

Finally, social impact depends on the number of others who share a particular attribute (Latané, 1981). You would be more likely to hang Christmas lights on your house after finding out that ten of your neighbors plan to hang lights than after knowing that only one does. Number also affects supportiveness. The more people who agree with your opinion, the less likely you will be to change it, independent of how many people try to convince you. As Asch (1955) showed, just having one fellow dissenter can reduce pressures to conform considerably. There are diminishing effects of number, however, with the first person having proportionally more influence than each coming after. The difference in impact between one person and two people will be much greater than the difference between 1,000 people and 1,001 people.

Social impact theory (Latané, 1981) is a parsimonious and well supported meta-theory that uses these three classes of variables to predict whether or not social influence will occur in any given situation. SIT assumes that one's moods, attitudes, and behaviors (and indeed, any attribute that is in part socially determined) will be influenced by others as a multiplicative function of the strength, immediacy, and number of sources and/or targets of social influence that are present. SIT is supported by a large body of experimental research on such phenomena as conformity, compliance, stage fright, helping, and obedience (e.g., Harkins & Latané,

1998; Harton & Latané, 1997b; Jackson & Latané, 1981; Latané, 1981; Latané & Harkins, 1976; Latané, Williams, & Harkins, 1979; Wolf & Latané, 1983).

So, people are more influenced by persuasive, close, and numerous others. How does that relate to culture? SIT itself is a static theory, one that makes predictions about the degree of social influence at any one time. If people are influenced and influence each other continuously in a spatially distributed environment (one where people have more access to some people than others), computer simulations have repeatedly shown that four phenomena consistently emerge (e.g., Latané & Bourgeois, 2001b; Latané & Nowak, 1997; Latané, Nowak, & Liu, 1994; Nowak & Latané, 1994; Nowak et al., 1990). These four phenomena–clustering, correlation, consolidation, and continuing diversity–form the predictions of dynamic social impact theory and describe a process for the creation and continuation of culture (Latané, 1996a, 1996b; Nowak et al., 1990). Clustering and correlation deal with how cultures are formed, whereas consolidation and continuing diversity address temporal change. Together, these four markers represent culture.

## HOW IS CULTURE FORMED?

Culture is formed through reciprocal and recursive individual social influence. This influence relies on communication at the local level and leads to an organization of associated beliefs (cultures) at the larger group level, whether the "larger group" is 10 people or 10 billion people. Clustering represents the fact that as people are influenced by those in their local area, pockets of shared opinions will form, leading to regional differences. One result of this clustering of opinion is that as multiple attitudes and attributes are influenced by the same people, overlapping clusters lead to associations or correlations between the socially influenced elements at the group level. These correlations of attributes can be thought of as ideologies (Lavine & Latané, 1996), social representations (Huguet & Latané, 1996), or stereotypes (Schaller & Latané, 1996).

### Clustering

DSIT's first prediction is that communication will lead to spatial clustering of attributes. In their classic study of social influence within a post-World War II married student housing complex, Festinger, Schachter, and Back (1950) found that people were much more likely to interact socially with close neighbors than with those living farther away. This immediacy principle (see also Latané et al., 1995) leads to the prediction that, over time, attitudes within a group should show regional clustering; that is, people will be increasingly likely to share similar attitudes with those living close to them. Such geographic clustering of attitudes was in fact observed in the Festinger et al. study. Local norms regarding a tenants' organization emerged within separate housing units, and people were much more likely to share attitudes with nearer neighbors than with those living farther away. It is important to note that in this housing complex people did not select their housing preferences based on common interests; rather, they were randomly assigned to apartments based on availability. Therefore, such clustering likely emerged from the day-to-day interactions of the residents.

Similar regional clustering of attitudes can be observed at various levels of resolution. For example, within the United States, maps could be drawn showing clusters of such attitudes and behaviors as Spam consumption (Weiss, 2000), expressions of prejudice (Pettigrew, 1986), and the appropriateness of violence to solve disagreements (Cohen & Nisbett, 1997; Vandello & Cohen, chap. 12, this volume). Michael Weiss's study of consumer attitudes (1994, 2000) shows that one can predict the product preferences of American citizens quite well based on where they live. On an even larger scale, the work of cross-cultural psychologists shows large psychological differences between people raised in different regions of the world on such traits as individualism versus collectivism.

Empirical research shows that these clusters can form quickly, simply on the basis of social influence. In one study, eight groups of 15 to 30 Introduction to Psychology students answered several multiple-choice questions on course material (Harton, Green, Jackson, & Latané, 1998). Then they discussed each answer for a minute with those people seated to their left and their right. Before discussion, choices were randomly distributed. But after discussion, students' answers were significantly more similar to their neighbors than would be expected by chance on all items. In only 1 minute, and on items that people should be motivated to learn because they might be tested on them, subcultures of belief emerged. Other face-to-face discussion studies have shown similar results, even on problems with a more demonstrably correct answer (Harton, Eshbaugh, & Binder, 2002; Rockloff & Latané, 1996).

A number of studies showing clustering of attitudes have been conducted using the Computer-Administered Panel Studies, or CAPS paradigm (Latané & Bourgeois, 2001). In this methodology, students communicate asynchronously over the computer for several sessions across 2 or 3 weeks. Students are randomly assigned codenames and "locations" in a 24-person group, but they only communicate with their four nearest "neighbors" in a communication geometry. These geometries model different aspects of real-world communication; individuals have more access to some people than to others. The particular communication geometry or pattern affects the degree of self-organization and where clusters form, but not whether they do (Latané & Bourgeois, 1996; Latané & L'Herrou, 1996; Latané & Nowak, 1997; Nowak, Latané, & Lewenstein, 1994).

Research using CAPS and other computer-administered discussion software has shown strong and consistent clustering for questions with correct answers (Latané & L'Herrou, 1996) as well as those without correct answers, such as social and political opinions (Bourgeois & Latané, 1996; Harton, Binder, & Russell, 2001; Huguet, Latané, & Bourgeois, 1998), jury decisions (Jackson, Bourgeois, & Latané, 2001), and definitions of aggression (Walker, 1999).

One of the most surprising studies, however, showed clustering of opinions about participants' own personalities (Latané & Bourgeois, 2000). Participants completed the NEO Five-factor Inventory (NEO-FFI; Costa & McCrae, 1992), a commonly used measure of the Big 5 personality traits of openness to experience, conscientiousness, extraversion, neuroticism, and agreeableness. Then they discussed three to six statements from one of the subscales with other participants. Even with personality, an ostensibly stable construct, perceptions self-organized. Participants became more similar to their neighbors by the final session simply as a result of short, asynchronous conversations with strangers. Of course, we do not believe that participants' personalities really changed vastly as a result of the study. Their perceptions of their personalities did converge, however, likely because of changing interpretations of items such as "I am not a worrier." As they discussed the items, participants began to reinterpret the items in a similar way to their neighbors, leading to shared representations of who they were.

The CAPS paradigm has also demonstrated clustering of behaviors. Latané and Bourgeois (2000a) exposed 15 groups of participants to a social dilemma; over five trials, group members were asked to choose whether to take $1.00 for themselves or to give 50 cents to each of four other group members. Between rounds, group members were told what their four neighbors in the computer network chose to do on the previous round. Again, group members were quite responsive to social influence, usually choosing to give if the majority of their neighbors gave and to take if most of their neighbors took. This positive social influence led to clear clusters of cooperators and competitors.

There is empirical evidence of clustering in real-world settings as well. In an initial field test of the predictions of DSIT, Bourgeois and Latané (1996) assessed clustering of attitudes within a high-rise 14-story dormitory on the campus of a southern university at the end of a school year. Students' attitudes, as reported on a 15-item questionnaire that assessed opinions about everything from drug and alcohol use to clothing and food preferences, were significantly more similar to students who lived on their floor than to students who lived on other floors. Of course, it is possible this effect was caused by residents being assigned to their living quarters based on common interests. Therefore, in a follow-up study, Bourgeois and Latané tracked the attitudes of students in the same building over time, measuring opinions at the beginning and end of a school year. If the attitude clustering is caused by communication, we would expect it to increase over the course of a school year. In fact, this is what happened; the clustering index increased on 13 of the 15 attitudes measured, and the overall increase was significant and quite large.

Across these and other studies (e.g., Bourgeois & Bowen, 2001; Bowen & Bourgeois, 2001), we have found that subcultures of beliefs and behaviors form reliably in a relatively short period of time on a variety of intellective and judgmental tasks. This reciprocal and simultaneous influence on a number of issues leads to another element of culture, correlation.

## Correlation

A second prediction of dynamic social impact theory is that attitudes that are originally unrelated across individuals within a group will become increasingly correlated over time. One reason for this prediction was articulated by Abelson (1979). To the extent that social subgroups within a population coincide with geographical distance, we would expect (as described earlier) more communication between neighbors who are closer to each other. People are more likely to come into contact with next door neighbors than with others living across town. As each subgroup converges on a local consensus on each issue, the degrees of freedom within the larger group essentially becomes reduced. That is, as regional clusters develop on each separate issue, individuals come to respond as members of their local subgroup instead of as individuals.

Cross-cultural differences (Brown, 1998) illustrate how attributes that are not related for any obvious reason may become correlated over time. People from Western countries tend to be more individualistic, more competitive, and more likely to emphasize what sets them apart from others than people from Eastern cultures. These differences in the self-concept overlap with differences in clothing style and diet between the two regions. Of course, there are individual differences within each region on each attribute, but if we were to look at correlations across such attributes, we would quite likely find that differences in the self-concept show large correlations with what people eat or wear. There is no logical link between food preferences and individualism/collectivism, yet one could probably predict food preferences quite well from information about a person's self-concept.

At the national level, Weiss's (1994) data on consumer attitudes show strong correlations between seemingly unrelated topics as a result of regional clustering in 211 marketing zones of the United States. For example, regions in which people buy more condoms have residents who are less likely to own a dog and less likely to support the death penalty (absolute value of *r*'s > .60). There are no obvious causal relationships between these variables (we will not even speculate as to what they could be), and DSIT shows us that there does not have to be. Correlations develop merely as a result of local social influence on a number of issues. This finding could explain how seemingly disparate beliefs, like being pro-life but pro-death penalty, can come to be related to each other and form ideologies even though there is no logical or causal relationship (or even an illogical one) between the beliefs.

These correlations can emerge in a very short period of time. Participants in a classroom setting answered five questions before and after discussion, three of which had good initial diversity (the initial majority was no greater than 70%; Harton et al., 1998). Across these three items and within each group of participants, the relationship between answers to pairs of questions increased significantly after discussion. These correlations were not due to particularly smart students getting each item correct and not-so-smart students getting them wrong; the percentage of students getting the items correct often did not increase after discussion. In fact, in no case did even 50% of the students get an item correct. The correlations were driven simply by local social influence on the separate items.

This is further illustrated by a study in which there was no possibility of logical linkages because the choices were completely arbitrary. In a CAPS study, participants tried to guess the majority opinion on several dichotomous choices such as the number *3* versus *8* or the color *red* versus *blue* (Latané & Bourgeois, 1996). In the last year of the study, 10 groups discussed six such issues. Before discussion, none of the responses were correlated. After discussion, a full 40% of them were significantly correlated, with an average absolute value correlation of .60.

In other cases, correlation can rise in part from a cognitive reorganization influenced by communication. In Huguet et al. (1998), 10 groups of 24 CAPS participants discussed human rights issues, whereas 5 other groups gave their opinions on the same items twice with no discussion. There were twice as many significant correlations after discussion than before between opinions on whether, for example, making a woman wear a veil when she goes in the street or forcing someone with a contagious disease to go to a hospital are violations of human rights. The number of significant correlations in the nondiscussion groups, meanwhile, decreased from the pretest to the posttest. Although part of these correlations was due to the loss of independence caused by clustering, changes in the ways people thought about and defined human rights (influenced by their communication partners) also seem to have played a role. The factor structure of items was stronger and closer to the way in which human rights experts had classified the items after discussion than before. This factor structure differed from group to group, illustrating slightly different "realities" that arose through social influence within communicators.

DSIT explains, and considerable anecdotal and empirical evidence supports, the creation of culture through communication. As people influence and are influenced by others in proportion to their strength, immediacy, and number in spatially distributed communication networks, attitudes and other socially influenceable attributes become regionally differentiated and linked to other attributes. Cultures are formed at least in part by local communication among individuals. This communication also leads to changes in culture over time. The other two markers of culture according to DSIT, consolidation and continuing diversity, deal with these temporal transformations.

## HOW DO CULTURES CHANGE OVER TIME?

Culture is not a static concept. Elements of culture change over time, as does the popularity of different cultural worldviews. Despite these changes, however, no one culture is likely to ever dominate the world. These aspects of culture are addressed by DSIT's phenomena of consolidation and continuing diversity. Consolidation shows how cultures change and majorities grow, but continuing diversity demonstrates that although some cultures may wax and others wane, differences will persist.

### Consolidation

Like all dynamical systems approaches, DSIT focuses on change over time. The distribution of opinions within a culture is not static, but rather constantly shifting. The third prediction of DSIT then is that attributes will consolidate, or decrease in diversity, as people influence each other over time.

The news media herald the latest opinion polls, illustrating daily (even hourly) shifts in public opinion. Such polls are undoubtedly influenced by a wide range of factors at the individual and group levels, including economic factors, the latest scandal, and international events. However, DSIT predicts that, other things being equal, diversity within groups becomes reduced over time. The majority tends to grow at the expense of minorities.

Noelle-Neumann (1984) provides many examples of such consolidation. Political races that seem fairly close before election time often result in landslides. Such a tendency toward consolidation may be seen on one level as a sheer mathematical probability. By definition, those holding minority opinions within a culture are more likely to be exposed to the viewpoints of others who disagree with them than are those in the majority. But another factor that may contribute to consolidation is Noelle-Neumann's concept of the spiral of silence. According to this model, when people believe they are in the minority within a culture, they are less willing to express their opinions out of fear of being isolated, rejected, or ridiculed. Both contact with majority members and the silence of minority members likely contribute to a reduction in minority sizes.

Religious beliefs provide another example of consolidation (Carroll, 2000; Halvorson & Newman, 1994). The largest American Protestant denomination, the Southern Baptist Convention, was born in the southeastern United States, but by 1990 it had spread to over 80% of the counties in the entire country. The denomination grew 133% in adherents from 1952 to 1990. At least part of this increase was at the expense of other, smaller denominations. For example, the number of members of the Episcopal Church decreased 5% during the same time period, despite a 65% growth in the United States' population (Halvorson & Newman, 1994).

Of course, consolidation within a group would not always be expected. The history of science presents many examples of ideas that began with a small minority that have proliferated within a culture, such as the theory of evolution. While some researchers have argued that minority influence is different than majority influence (Moscovici, 1985, 1994; but see the Wood, Lundgren, Ouellette, Busceme, & Blackstone 1994 meta-analysis that found no evidence of this), DSIT can account for both (Latané, 1996c; Latané & Wolf, 1981; Latané et al., 1994; Wolf & Latané, 1983). The opinions of minority factions are especially likely to prevail when their members are confident (Nemeth & Wachtler, 1974), when they appear flexible as opposed to rigid (Mugny, 1982), and when they offer compelling arguments against the majority position (Clark, 1990). In social impact theory terminology, minorities can be influential when their members are high in strength and/or immediacy.

Minorities must also be able to communicate their ideas effectively. Galileo was not the first person, or even the second, to promote the idea of a heliocentric universe. But one of the reasons why his view caught on, while Copernicus's was more or less ignored, was that Galileo's book was more interesting and readable and in the language of the people instead of in Latin (Hellman, 1998; see Crandall & Schaller, chap. 9, this volume). Having truth on one's side and being able to communicate that truth effectively can allow the minority to not only maintain its numbers, but to become the new majority. On balance, however, DSIT predicts consolidation within groups, other factors being equal.

Empirical evidence supports this growth of majorities. In the Harton et al. (1998) study, all eight groups also showed significant consolidation, as measured by a group-level index of diversity. The most popular answers, whether correct or not, grew in popularity, as those that were endorsed by few people lost support. This occurs with a variety of types of issues, from attitudes toward euthanasia to so-called “eureka” problems–logic problems with a demonstrable correct answer–to behaviors (Bourgeois & Latané, 1996; Harton et al., 2002; Jackson et al., 2002; Latané & Bourgeois, 2000a, 2001a; Latané & L'Herrou, 1996; Rockloff & Latané, 1996).

Discussion consistently leads to a reduction in diversity of opinion, whether the discussion takes place face-to-face, over a computer network, or in a more naturalistic setting. This consolidation is rarely total, however, which leads to our fourth marker of culture, continuing diversity.

## Continuing Diversity

Although consolidation leads to, in most cases, majority influence, this influence is not complete. Minority groups can and do remain and even thrive. Thus the final prediction of DSIT is that even though majority sizes will tend to increase, there will be continuing diversity. A wide variety of computer simulations using different programs and assumptions has shown that as long as there is some nonlinearity of attitude change (see section on involvement), there will not be total consensus (Latané & Nowak, 1997; Nowak et al., 1990). Because those holding minority opinions are largely insulated from dissent by others within their clusters who agree with them, they receive social support for maintaining their beliefs (Kameda & Sugimori, 1995).

Social critics in the 1950s warned of the homogenization of U.S. culture as a result of mass media. Because the production of television, movies, magazines, and newspapers was controlled by a small segment of the population, the concern was that regional differences would disappear. Yet it seems that there is even more diversity and disagreement today than 50 years ago. Regional accents persist despite decades of exposure to relatively accent-free television, and there is rarely national consensus on any important issue, as a recent U.S. Presidential election that ended in a virtual tie has shown.

Americans' responses to the terrorism attacks against the United States in September 2001 provide a seeming counterexample to continuing diversity. In the weeks and months after the attacks, the country seemed to come together, united in its support for the President and its opposition to terrorism. This apparent agreement, however, masked diversity on many other important issues, such as religion, homosexual rights, and gun control, on which the country is even more split than before (Lawrence, 2002). Beyond the level of the country, there are huge regional differences in the perceptions of the attacks, who did them, and whether the United States' reaction was justified (Benedetto, 2002).

Despite much consternation over the McDonald-ization of culture, a street in Miami looks very different from one in London or in New Delhi or even in Chicago. Where American institutions such as Wendy's, Pizza Hut, and Wal-Mart have spread, they have their own local flavor. You can get red wine with your giant smiling Mouse at that most American of icons, Disneyland Paris, but you must abstain at Disney World in Orlando. In the grocery section of a Chinese Wal-Mart, you can find live frogs and seafood, but you are unlikely to run across such delicacies stateside.

To the extent that a group segregates itself or is segregated by the majority culture, they close themselves off to influence from those outside their group. Their local majority can continue relatively uninfluenced, although the tradeoff for this protection is that they generally do not have much influence on the majority. An example is the Amish community in the United States. The Amish live much as their ancestors did at the turn of the last century, eschewing cars, telephones, and other modern conveniences. They are able to maintain this culture because they live in separate communities with their own schools and churches and mix with the "English" (non-Amish Americans) fairly infrequently. Those Amish who have ventured further into the majority culture, however, are more likely to be influenced by the things they see and the contacts they have. One group that ventures into local Iowa communities to do construction work does not use power tools or drive (they have a non-Amish driver ferry them to locations). But the Amish owner of the company uses a cell phone to make his business calls while on site, and the workers refresh themselves with Coke, Doritos, and Twinkies. Over time, those Amish who spend more time in contact with the majority culture may become more and more influenced by it.

Minority groups often realize that they and their children are influenced by their neighbors and that this influence can lead to the erosion of their culture. One jailer, cognizant of this trend, actually released several Amish youth from jail early because they liked it too much and he feared he was "ruining them" (Lynch, 1999). Once they experienced television, running water, and electric lights, they were less satisfied returning to their simpler lives. Some groups try to curtail or counteract this influence. For example, African American parents who live in mostly Caucasian suburbs are now joining "Jack and Jill" groups to give their children more contact with other African Americans and prevent assimilation (Edwards, 2001). Minority groups who have not taken these steps to protect their cultures have sometimes been completely integrated, as the cost of influence for minorities sometimes seems to be losing some of their own culture. To influence others, one must be open to influence oneself.

Continuing diversity has been demonstrated in several empirical investigations of social influence processes. In Harton et al. (1998), even though students were motivated to find the correct answer, in none of the eight groups did opinions converge on the items with good initial diversity. As long as no more than 70% of people initially agreed on a single answer, discussion never led to unity. This occurred not because individuals did not influence each other, but because those in local majorities provided support for each other, not realizing that they were in global minorities.

Even when there is a reward for consensus, spatially distributed communication networks can make it an elusive goal. In one version of the CAPS studies, students were rewarded with money for choosing the majority answer (Latané & L'Herrou, 1996). They only had information, however, about the choices of four of their neighbors. Despite their motivation, incomplete information about the larger group led people to believe they were choosing the majority answer when they were not, leading to continuing diversity. Similar results have been found in a number of other studies as well (Bourgeois & Latané, 1996; Harton et al., 2002; Jackson et al., 2002; Latané & Bourgeois, 2001a; Rockloff & Latané, 1996).

Cultures are changed, we argue, by the same processes through which they are formed: communication with others in one's local environment. Although influence usually allows majorities to grow, minorities sometimes gain converts as well, especially when they have "truth" on their side. Mutual and recursive influence among individuals leads to subtle and not-so-subtle changes in culture, but differences in persuasive and supportive strength, incomplete social networks, and nonlinear attitude change (as we discuss in the next section) prevent total consensus on most issues.

## WHICH ELEMENTS OF CULTURE ARE MORE LIKELY TO BE PASSED ON?

One thing we have learned from dozens of empirical tests of the predictions of DSIT is that people are much more willing to change their opinions on some issues than on others. Because all the forms of self-organization predicted by DSIT rely on social influence at the individual level, these differences should and do lead to different levels of self-organization. We next discuss two factors related to attitudes, involvement and heritability, which may affect the emergence of group-level properties predicted by DSIT.

### Involvement

Researchers have often assumed that attitudes change linearly, in proportion to information (Anderson, 1981). So, for example, if someone has a moderately positive attitude toward the death penalty, a few arguments against it should make the person a little less in favor, and a few arguments for it, a little more in favor. Both computer simulations (Latané & Nowak,

1997) and mathematical proofs (Abelson, 1964; Woelfel & Fink, 1980) have demonstrated that if people's attitudes do indeed change linearly, in a fully interconnected social system, eventually everyone will agree on some middle of the road position. Our examples in this chapter and observations in daily life, however, show that this just is not the case. For the regional differences in attitudes, languages, food preferences, and religions around us to have evolved, attitude change for at least some issues must be nonlinear.

An answer to this discrepancy between the treatment of individual attitudes by researchers as linear and what we know about group level attitudes being nonlinear is offered by the catastrophe theory of attitudes (CTA; Latané & Nowak, 1994). This theory suggests that sometimes attitude change will be linear and sometimes it will be nonlinear; the difference, or splitting factor, is involvement. Attitudes toward very uninvolving issues will tend to be neutral and change linearly, or in proportion to information. A few arguments in favor should make a person's attitude a little more positive; a few arguments against, a little more negative. As involvement (which can be operationalized as importance or personal relevance) increases, the degree of nonlinearity increases, so that for very involving issues, attitudes may be best represented as extreme categories rather than a continuum. On these issues, people will tend to be either positive or negative, without much middle ground. These attitudes will also be less susceptible to change, and when they do change, it will occur nonlinearly and in disproportion to the information. In other words, a few arguments against the death penalty are not likely to have much effect on a pro-death penalty advocate until some point when there are too many arguments to ignore and the attitude suddenly shifts to the other side.

Several studies have shown that more involving attitudes are more extreme than uninvolving attitudes (e.g., Harton, 1998; Harton & Latané, 1997a; Krosnick, 1988; Krosnick, Boninger, Chuang, Berent, & Carnot, 1993; Latané & Nowak, 1994; Liu & Latané, 1998a, 1998b; Raden, 1985). Highly involving attitudes are also more resistant to change (Krosnick & Petty, 1995; Sherif et al., 1965, 1973), and when they do change, this change occurs more suddenly than for less involving issues (Harton, 1998; Harton & Latané, 2002).

A diverse informational environment, communication, and nonlinear attitude change all are necessary for self-organization to occur. Without some degree of variation in information about the topic, there will be no diversity and thus no self-organization (see Harton & Latané, 2002). We have already discussed the importance of communication to social influence. Nonlinear change is also required, although it is somewhat confounded with communication. As CTA predicts, attitudes on involving or important topics show more nonlinear attitude change than attitudes on less involving topics (Harton & Latané, 2002). People also communicate more about important issues than unimportant ones (Binder, Russell, Sievers, & Harton, 2001), and this increased communication in turn leads to greater attributions of importance (Harton & Latané, 2002; Liu & Latané, 1998a). Thus, low involving issues are not likely to be discussed, but moderately involving issues may become more even more involving as a result of discussion.

Applied to our four markers of culture, CTA suggests that moderately involving attitudes should self-organize more than those that are low in involvement. Extremely uninvolving issues should either self-organize only temporarily, until everyone agrees on the average opinion, or, if they are not important enough to be discussed, not self-organize at all. Issues with some degree of involvement will both change nonlinearly and likely be communicated (see Schaller, Conway, & Tanchuk, 2002), leading to clustering and consolidation. At the very highest levels of involvement, attitudes will be more stable, which will result in less self-organization in the short term, as people are less responsive to influence. Over a period of years, however, the self-organization of these very involving issues may be as evident as for moderately involving issues, especially at the larger group levels. Although people are less likely to change their attitudes on these issues, change does still occur, and when it does, it will occur to a greater extent.

Empirical evidence supports this increase in clustering for involving attitudes. Huguet, Latané, and Michinov (1996) surveyed French naval recruits at the beginning and end of their required multiweek training camp on issues such as the quality of food at the naval camp and whether they wanted a land or sea assignment. Recruits were randomly assigned to their quarters, yet by the end of training there was a clear increase in clustering of attitudes by dorm for the most involving issues (with involvement measured in a relative rather than absolute sense). Clustering was not as great, but still significant, on moderately involving issues, and there was no clustering on the least involving topics. Presumably the highly involving issues were the issues they discussed most often and thus on which they were most influenced.

Involvement affects the likelihood of attitude change, the way (linear or sudden) it will change, and the likelihood of the attitude being communicated. Each of these factors, in turn, affects the degree of self-organization that will occur. Self-organization should be nonexistent or transient for very uninvolving issues, greater for moderately involving issues, and stable and relatively resistant to change for highly involving attitudes.

## Heritability

Although we typically think of attitudes as being learned (Eagly & Chaiken, 1993), many attitudes show a large genetic component (Eaves, Eysenck, & Martin, 1989; Olson, Vernon, Harris, & Jang, 2001). In fact, many attitudes show similar heritability coefficients to psychological constructs with a more generally accepted genetic basis, such as intelligence or psychopathology. This does not imply that there is a direct causal link from individual genes or groups of genes to specific attitudes; more likely, heritabilities are mediated by such factors as intelligence, temperament, global personality traits, or physical characteristics (Olson et al., 2001; Tesser, 1993). Tesser uses the example of the highly heritable attitude toward jazz music to illustrate these indirect effects. It is quite implausible to assume that there is a gene for jazz preference; however, the enjoyment of jazz is likely to be influenced by such heritable traits as temperament, personality (e.g., openness to experience), and the manner in which sensory systems are hard wired.

Because heritability is defined as the amount of variability within a group that can be explained by genetic differences, it stands to reason that attitudes with higher heritabilities should be less socially influenceable; to the extent that this is true, we would therefore expect less self-organization due to dynamic social impact. In fact, across three studies, Bourgeois (2002) found that attitude heritability does constrain self-organization. In a secondary analysis of data presented in Eaves et al. (1989), Bourgeois found that diversity of opinion at the population level was greater for higher heritability issues. This relationship was significant in each of six large sets of twins reported by Eaves et al. In a second study, Bourgeois pretested 84 students on 20 attitudes that varied widely in heritability. They then discussed within small groups two of these issues that were high in heritability, two that were moderate, and two that were low in heritability. Individuals were much less likely to change their opinions as heritability of the issue being discussed increased, and this led to less group-level consolidation on high-heritability issues. In a field study that measured attitudes varying in heritability within a campus housing complex, clustering of opinions by dorm floor was much less pronounced on higher heritability issues. Across all three studies, to the extent that genetic variation influenced attitudes at the individual level, the emergence of group-level elements of culture was constrained.

These heritability constraints may help researchers decide where to look for geographic variation in thoughts, feelings, and behaviors. To the extent that people from different cultures share common gene pools, we would expect to find less cross-cultural variation on psychological traits with a larger genetic component. These constraints may be shown at various levels of analysis, whether looking at cultural variations across different hemispheres, countries and continents, cities and states, or organizations, or simply different neighborhoods or floors within a campus housing complex.

## WHAT OTHER CULTURAL PHENOMENA CAN DSIT EXPLAIN?

DSIT predicts that all socially influenceable attributes should be subject to self-organization through communication. In this section, we discuss just a small subset of the cultural elements that can be better understood using DSIT: attitudes toward ethnic groups, language, health-related attitudes and behaviors, and biology.

### Attitudes Toward Ethnic Groups

Both our feelings about groups (prejudice) and our beliefs about the characteristics of these groups (stereotypes) are influenced by social information and interaction. Simply knowing that in-group members hold a more or less extreme view about a group can lead to changes in attitudes and behaviors toward that group that persist over time (Stangor, Sechrist, & Jost, 2001a, 2001b). Two-way verbal communication results in even greater consensus and extremity (Brauer, Judd, & Jacquelin, 2001; Schaller & Conway, 1999; Thompson, Judd, & Park, 2000). Discussions about a group will not take place unless there is something to talk about, however. There are very few Puerto Rican, South African, or Nepalese immigrants in Iowa or Wyoming, so it is probably not by chance that we do not often find ourselves talking about those groups. Without discussion, there is little reason for stereotypes to become shared (Schaller & Latané, 1996; Schaller et al., 2002).

These different clusters of opinion that form at the national, regional, and local levels will be determined by the strength, immediacy, and number of individuals promoting each viewpoint. Strength is in part related to group membership. In-group members' opinions about ethnic groups are more persuasive than the opinions of outgroup members (Stangor et al., 2001a), and knowledge that one shares a stereotype with in-group members leads to more resistance to change (Stangor et al., 2001a) and attitude-consistent behaviors (Sechrist & Stangor, 2001).

Personality characteristics may affect both persuasive and supportive strength. People who are high in authoritarianism and social dominance orientation are more prejudiced toward a number of groups than those lower in those characteristics (e.g., Altemeyer, 1998; Harton, Petersen, & Schwab, 2001; McFarland, 2001; Pratto, Sidanius, Stallworth, & Malle, 1994; Whitley, 1999). Given that more involving and extreme attitudes are more stable (Harton & Latané, 2002), those who are very high or very low in authoritarianism or social dominance may therefore be particularly stubborn in their attitudes toward other groups. Individual differences in need for closure can also affect openness to influence (Richter & Kruglanski, chap. 5, this volume).

Immediacy affects the potential spreading of the attitude. For example, it is harder for the Mexican stereotype of Americans to spread to Kenya than to Costa Rica because of the physical and social distances between the countries. People who are less immediate, either because they live farther away or are not directly communicated with (e.g., seen over television rather than in person) will be less persuasive. As influence spreads beyond primary sources, the information becomes degraded (Thompson et al., 2000) and more consistent with cultural stereotypes (Lyons & Kashima, 2001), leading to less direct influence.

Influence will manifest itself in increased consensus in attitudes within a communicating group (Schaller & Conway, 1999; Schaller et al., 2002; Thompson et al., 2000), but it will also lead to regional differences in attitudes at the larger group level. Research on the social influence of prejudice and stereotypes has generally focused on agreement across groups rather than disagreements within groups, however, the latter likely exists as well. Even relatively homogeneous groups of college students discussing the same information about a target group do not come to 100%, or even 85%, agreement on elements of a stereotype (Haslam et al., 1998; Haslam, Oakes, Reynolds, & Mein, 1999). In the "real-world" situation where people may have very different initial pools of information and where communication is more sporadic and incomplete (everyone does not communicate with everyone else), there should be even greater between-group differences.

These regional differences in degree and content can be seen in prejudiced attitudes across regions of the United States. Both attitudes about African Americans and opinions about race-related policies differ by region of the United States, and when a person moves from one region to another, his or her attitudes change to more closely fit the local culture (Glaser & Gilens, 1997). The content of prejudices toward African Americans also varies across regions. Anecdotally, Southerners have more negative attitudes toward African Americans as a category, although they may have African American coworkers and friends who they like and interact with. Northerners, on the other hand, may have more positive attitudes toward the category of African Americans than Southerners but feel more uncomfortable in interactions with individual African Americans.

Regional differences in stereotypes also spread through communication. Stereotypes that are talked about more often are more consensually shared (Schaller & Conway, 1999; Schaller et al., 2002). One could find places relatively easily where there is no stereotype of Icelanders, Bulgarians, or Chileans. There are probably very few places one could go, however, where people do not have a stereotype of Americans, because of the influence of the United States on world economy and culture. But even with all the world discussing the United States and continuing coverage of the country on CNN reaching the most remote tents in Tanzania, there is no world consensus on the "typical" American. Australians believe that Americans are nationalistic, arrogant, talkative, and tradition-loving (Haslam et al., 1998). Americans see themselves in some of the same ways (although of course they use the terms "patriotic," "proud," and "outgoing"), but they do not describe themselves as tradition-loving (Stephan et al., 1993). Russians see Americans as ambitious, competent, and spontaneous (Stephan et al., 1993), whereas representatives from six African nations characterized Americans as modern, polite, and aggressive (McAndrew & Akande, 1995). Within each region, different aspects of the stereotype are likely to be talked about, as, for example, Americans' "aggressiveness" has more implications for some countries than others. Contrasts with the host culture also determine what is discussed and thus become part of the stereotype, so that Australians characterize Americans as traditional whereas Africans characterize Americans as modern.

People influence and are influenced by those around them on a number of attributes, from the type of racism they practice to the type of food they eat. This simultaneous influence leads to correlation, as people become similar to their neighbors on several characteristics, leading to overlapping clusters of opinion. For example, the term *redneck racism* that has sometimes been used for the blatant form of racism (Gaertner & Dovidio, 1986) reflects a stereotype that may be a result of a bottom-up (simultaneous social influence) rather than a top-down (logical linkages) process. The term *redneck* likely derives from the red necks that farmers often got from working out in the sun, particularly in the southern United States (Hendrickson, 1993), and its use with regard to racism implies that poor, White, rural Southerners are more likely to be blatantly racist than are other groups. There are, in fact, relationships between education level (Burns & Gimpel, 2000; Jenssen & Engesbak, 1994) and region of the country (Glaser & Gilens, 1997) and reported prejudice, which have generally been explained in terms of group threat and a segregationist past. It is also possible, however, that at least part of these correlations is due to local social influence. As people talk to those around them (who tend to share their educational backgrounds because of economic segregation in the United States), they influence each other. Similar correlations could probably be found between desire for grits for breakfast or love of sweet iced tea and racism in the Caucasian population, but this does not mean that disliking African Americans leads one to choose white foods or crave sugar. The correlations can come about merely because both attitudes have been influenced locally, through daily communication.

Stereotypes themselves represent correlations, as individual beliefs about a group come to be associated. Separate beliefs of a group as "aggressive" and "intelligent," influenced through individual discussions about group members' behaviors, can over time lead to linkages between the traits as they form a stereotype of the group (Schaller & Latané, 1996). Those aspects of a person that are most stereotypical are more likely to be discussed (Lyons & Kashima, 2001), further perpetuating the stereotype.

Consolidation is illustrated by how these attitudes have changed over time. Many researchers have documented a change in the form of racism over the years, from the more blatant discrimination and segregation of the early 1900s to a more subtle or modern racism today (Dovidio & Gaertner, 1998; McConahay, 1986; Sears, 1998). Although some "old-fashioned" racists still exist, societal norms rejecting overt prejudice have led to a more indirect and socially desirable method of expressing negative affect toward minorities. A modern racist might express his negative attitudes by denying that racism is a problem or citing the unfairness of Affirmative Action policies. Group norms such as these affect not only the way individuals show prejudice, but also the groups toward which they express it. Crandall, Eshleman, and O'Brien (2002) found a very strong relationship between people's views on the acceptability of prejudice toward certain groups and the amount of prejudice they themselves reported toward those targets.

Stereotypes of African Americans have also changed over time. For example, 84% of respondents in a 1933 survey characterized African Americans as superstitious (Katz & Braly, 1933), but this percentage fell to 41% in 1951 (Gilbert, 1951), and 1% in 1993 (Dovidio, Brigham, Johnson, & Gaertner, 1996). Other stereotypes, such as "musical," remain, and still other new ones such as "aggressive" have appeared (Krueger, 1996). Schaller et al. (2002) linked these changes in stereotypes to the degree to which the elements are communicable. For a stereotype to persist, it must be communicated to others. For populous groups (those that people talk about regularly), those traits that are more easily communicated are more likely to persist as part of the stereotype of that group. Discussion also leads to greater consensus in stereotypes (Haslam et al., 1998; Schaller & Conway, 1999; Thompson et al., 2000) as the majority influences the minority.

Despite the influence and increasing consensus caused by discussion, however, diversity persists and will continue to persist. More than 100 years after the Civil War, attitudes toward African Americans across the United States may have changed, but different opinions and beliefs abound, often regionally differentiated. European Americans do not agree on their attitudes toward African Americans, Mexicans, or Filipinos, nor do they agree on the level or types of racism they exhibit toward these groups (see Nail, Harton, & Decker, in press).

Thus, attitudes about ethnic groups are socially influenced, and this influence seems to be proportional to the strength, immediacy, and number of individuals doing the influencing. Communication drives this process, which has resulted in regional differences, correlation with other aspects of culture, changes over time, and continuing diversity.

## Language

Languages are another socially spreadable element of culture. Some influences on language are intentional, such as when a ruler declares an official language, whereas others occur less purposefully, like subtle changes in pronunciations that result in regional accents. No language has an inherent advantage over others (Lieberson, 1982). They spread as a function of the same types of variables as other socially influenceable attributes we have discussed: strength, immediacy, and number.

The languages spoken by powerful groups are more likely to proliferate than those spoken by relatively powerless groups. When speakers of a language are more involved in international banking, trade, or politics or when speakers are influential religiously or militarily, those languages will be advantaged compared to others (Lieberson, 1982). For example, the international importance of the English language was boosted by the military success of Great Britain and the United States in World War I. President Wilson's central role at the peace talks after the war largely determined that the Treaty of Versailles be written in English as well as French. This decision made English an official language of the League of Nations (even though the United States never ended up joining) and contributed to French's demise as the main language of diplomatic discourse (Lieberson, 1982).

"Negative" strength factors (a desire to distance oneself from a group or individual) can also lead to language shifts. One of the major newspapers in Postville, Iowa, was published entirely in German until 1917, when it switched its name to the Postville Herald and began publishing in English. At about the same time, the large German church in town quit holding services in the German language (S. Schroeder, personal communication, February 25, 2002). Apparently the desire to distance themselves from the United States' enemy, Germany, and to make themselves more acceptable to other Americans was sufficient to effect the switch in language. In fact, Iowa's governor during World War I issued a proclamation banning the speaking of foreign languages (especially German) in all public places in the state of Iowa, even though German Americans were Iowa's largest ethnic group at the time (Schweider, 1996). These changes certainly contributed to a decrease in German speakers in Iowa, although there is at least one church in Iowa that still holds regular German-language services today. Other countries such as France, Japan, and Tanzania have reacted in a similar way against English by forming agencies to protect their languages from English encroachment (Wardhaugh, 1987).

One of the most important factors affecting language spread is number. The more people who speak a language, the more likely that language is to survive and grow (Lieberson, 1982; Wardhaugh, 1987). Beyond sheer number, however, the geographic placement of these people is critical. For example, Chinese and Hindi are spoken by millions of people, yet these languages have not proliferated as much as English, in part because of their geographic concentration of speakers in one area. The more geographically dispersed the speakers of a language are (given a sufficient number of speakers to maintain themselves), the more that language will spread. Ease of transportation and communication also facilitate language spread, whereas religious, geographical, and social boundaries discourage it. There are some regions in the Appalachian mountains on the East Coast of the United States where, because of geographic isolation, English has evolved differently than in other parts of the country (Hazen & Fluharty, in press). Although the common perception of Elizabethan English being spoken in remote mountains areas is a romantic myth, there are some older pronunciations, words, and verb forms that have survived in these regions that long died out elsewhere in the country (Wolfram & Christian, 1976; Wolfram & Fasold, 1974). For example, Shakespeare and many Appalachians alike would be insulted to be called a *moldwarp* (a stupid person), whereas most contemporary Americans would just be confused (Metcalf, 2000).

Influence leads to obvious regional differences in languages at the levels of continents, countries, and provinces. The Portuguese, Spanish, French, and Italian speak different languages, but these neighboring countries speak languages that are more similar to each other than any are to Chinese or Japanese. Many countries, such as Switzerland, are divided linguistically, with other regional differences overlapping the language ones. Even within Iowa, a relatively homogeneous state in the middle of an English-speaking country, pockets of other languages survived in areas for decades. In the small town of Decorah, Iowa, there was a Norwegian language newspaper published until 1972 (*Ayer Directory*, 1973) and regular Norwegian language church services through 1959 (Rod Library reference staff, personal communication, February 26, 2002).

There are regional differences within languages as well. British English is very different from American English in pronunciations, spellings, and the meanings of words (as an American friend found out when she loudly begged a friend to show her how to *shag* on the London tube). Metcalf (2000) provides the following example: An American might ride in an *elevator* with a *flashlight* and a *wrench*; a British person would ride in a *lift* with a *torch* and a *spanner*. Different verb forms have evolved in the two countries as well. Complete the sentence: Today I dive; yesterday I ____. The word that you use to complete the blank is probably influenced by where you live. Americans prefer "dove" as the past tense of dive, whereas the British say "dived" (Pinker, 1999). Even two Americans from Brooklyn, New York, and Charleston, South Carolina, would have some difficulty understanding each other because of vast differences in pronunciations and usages of words.

Other cultural differences, from responses to violence (Vandello & Cohen, chap. 12, this volume) to television viewing habits (Weiss, 1994) to preferences in nail polish (Harton & Latané, 1997c) have developed alongside languages and accents, leading to discernable cultural identities. Simply noting the pronunciations as someone says "the car should be washed next to the house at high tide" can give you a wealth of information about her likely hobbies, attitudes, and clothing preferences.

Languages are also consolidating. Of the at least 15,000 languages that existed in the 15th century, only 6,800 are still spoken, and the rate of homogenization is increasing, with a current rate of about one language death every 2 weeks (Sampat, 2001). Half of the world's population speaks one of the 15 most popular languages as a first language, and 90% of people speak one of the top 100. Many of the languages that are spoken by fewer than 100,000 people have held on for as long as they have because of geographic restrictions that limited contact with, and therefore influence from, outsiders (contact that is rapidly increasing in most cases). For example, on the island of Janitzio in Central Mexico, Purepuca Indians spoke their native language Tarasco for years. As the island has come into more contact with the mainland, however, use of the native language has decreased and Spanish has become the dominant language of the population. Fewer than 60,000 people in Mexico now speak Tarasco (Grimes, 1992). English, meanwhile, has developed from a language spoken by a few people on a relatively small island to one of the world's most dominant languages, with more than a quarter of a billion people learning it as their first language and many more learning it as a second or third language (Roberts, 1999).

Languages evolve within themselves over time as well. Words that are not often used fall from the vernacular, and new terms take their place. Slang terms are particularly quick to change, as yesterday's *dweeb* becomes today's *dork*. Children try to make sense of what they hear, and the small changes they make shape language, words as well as verb forms, over time (Pinker, 1999). All of English's irregular verbs were once regular verbs—following rules that are now forgotten or that are no longer applicable because of changes in spelling and pronunciation. In Old and Middle English, there were separate verb forms for different persons (I, you singular, he, we, you plural) in the past tense (Pinker, 1999) much as there is today in Spanish. Meanwhile, Spanish has suffered a reduction in verb forms as well, with the familiar plural "vosotros" term now common in few countries besides Spain.

But despite this influence, it is not likely that the world will soon all speak one language (notwithstanding what appears to be the case on *Star Trek*). The number of languages may continue to decline as communication across geographical constraints becomes easier, but regional differences within and between languages will persist. Even within relatively small areas, distinct accents can be differentiated. In North Carolina, residents can easily distinguish between someone who lives on the coast versus the piedmont versus the mountains simply by how they pronounce certain words.

Language is an important element of culture, one that is formed and changed through the kinds of bottom-up processes we have described here. But it is neither synonymous with nor unaffected by culture. The Irish language is essentially lost from the Irish people, yet the Irish culture remains distinct from that of England, Scotland, or any other country. Likewise, most Basques no longer speak Basque, but they definitely do not consider themselves to be Spaniards (Wardhaugh, 1987). Languages influence how people interpret and communicate about events. This communication then affects people's social representations and other cultural elements (Lau, Lee, & Chiu, chap. 4, this volume), as well as the language itself.

Thus languages ebb and flow, and these evolutions are determined by the strength, immediacy, and number of speakers of the languages. Within languages, regional accents and word usages develop, and over time, the language changes. These changes occur in geographical clusters, and they are correlated with other elements of culture. The number of languages is decreasing, yet it is very unlikely that the world will ever sing with one voice or even one language.

### Health-Related Attitudes and Behaviors

There are many health-related attitudes and behaviors that are socially influenced, as studies of contagion have shown. Both alcohol-related attitudes and students' beliefs about the alcohol attitudes of other students cluster by floor and building in college dorms (Bourgeois & Bowen, 2001). In younger adolescents, crowd affiliations (e.g., "Jocks," "Brains") predict alcohol use and sexual behavior, even after controlling for demographic variables and self-esteem (Dolcini & Adler, 1994). Popular and older children who are higher in "strength" seem to lead the adoption of some of these lifestyle attitudes (Harton & Latané, 1997b).

Crandall (1988) showed that binge eating behavior in sorority women also clusters. Not only did different norms for the "appropriate" amount of bingeing develop in the two sororities he surveyed, but popularity within the group was related to adherence to the group norm. Women became more similar to their friends over time in their levels of binge eating, showing that influence rather than selection drove at least part of these differences. These bulimic norms likely correlated with other differences (e.g., in study behaviors, drinking, and clothing style) between the sororities, leading to the establishment of a sorority culture that would be recognized by those outside the sorority as well as those in it.

Depression is another socially contagious attribute. Nondepressed students randomly assigned to live with a depressed roommate become more depressed themselves over time (Howes, Hokanson, & Loewenstein, 1985), and this influence occurs even when controlling for negative life events and anxiety (Joiner, 1994). Married couples are also similar in negativity affectivity (a combination of depression and neuroticism; Karney, Bradbury, Fincham, & Sullivan, 1994). A meta-analysis of these and other studies has suggested that depressive symptoms and mood may be contagious among close adults (Joiner & Katz, 1999). Children are not immune to this influence either. At least two studies have shown that they tend to be more similar to their friends in depression as well (Haselager, Hartup, van Lieshout, & Riksen-Walraven, 1998; Mariano & Harton, 2002).

Once again, these examples are consistent with our argument that individual social influence, weighted by the strength, immediacy, and number of persuaders, leads to the development of behavioral norms. These norms are regionally differentiated, likely correlated with other attributes, and open to change over time. They occur for both positive (e.g., responsible alcohol use) and negative (e.g., binge eating) behaviors.

## Biology

Attitudes and behaviors do not have to be conscious or even in a person's awareness to be affected by these social influence processes. People may also be affected by each other's biology, communication that is passed through pheromones (Stern & McClintock, 1998) or other scents (Thornhill & Gangestad, 1999). For example, Jorgensen et al. (2001) recently showed that there are regional differences in men's sperm production and mobility. They dismissed genetics as a likely cause and suggested environmental or lifestyle influences as more probable. These lifestyle differences, such as food preferences, alcohol consumption, and sports participation, are at least in part socially influenced. But there may be other, more direct social influences on sperm quality that have led to these regional differences as well. For example, if one man is a strong sperm producer, other men in direct competition with this man for mates (those men in the same geographical area) could increase their sperm production as a mating strategy.

There is other evidence that men's levels of sperm production are affected by social interactions (beyond the obvious ones). Baker and Bellis (1995) found a social influence on sperm production in a study in which couples recorded their interactions and provided ejaculate from their lovemaking sessions. The more time a woman spent away from her partner, the higher his sperm count during their next sexual encounter, independent of whether he had masturbated since he was last with her. This may be an evolutionary strategy to protect against mate poaching—if the partner has had an affair while she was away, the increased sperm will reduce the likelihood that she could become impregnated by the other man. Although these strategies are not conscious, they are still socially influenced because they vary based on social interactions with others.

Female physiology is also socially influenced. The ovulation cycles of humans, along with animals such as rats, lemurs, hamsters, bats, and chimpanzees, are affected by the social contacts the creatures have with other females (McClintock, 1971, 1978, 1983, 1998; Wallis, 1985; Weller & Weller, 1997). After publication of McClintock's 1971 study in which female roommates became more similar in their ovulation cycles over time, menstrual synchronicity in humans became known as almost "fact." Further research has shown, however, that the relationship is not so simple. Sometimes females' ovulation becomes more similar to those of women with whom they are in close contact, but at other times dissynchronicity or another type of entrainment occurs (McClintock, 1998). In any case, the ovulation cycle is being influenced, but the direction of the influence may depend on factors such as age, competition for mates, or environmental conditions. These different patterns of influence are completely consistent with DSIT. Although most of our examples in this chapter have dealt with positive social influence, where people are influenced to agree with others, negative "strength" in the model actually predicts anticonformity, or a movement away from the attitude of others (Nail, MacDonald, & Levy, 2000). In situations where it is evolutionarily advantageous, such as when women may be well served by giving birth simultaneously, women may influence each other's cycles into synchronicity. When there is a paucity of available mates, on the other hand, women's cycles may become dissynchronous so that each one's chances of reproduction may be heightened.

Research on social influences on biology is still relatively new, but several evolutionary scientists have noted other interactions between the biological and social. For example, women who are in the most fertile phase of the menstrual cycle seem to be more attracted to the scents of more symmetrical men (Thornhill & Gangestad, 1999), who other research suggests may be better genetic partners (Gangestad & Thornhill, 1997). Women who are not in their fertile phase do not differentiate between the scents of relatively symmetrical and asymmetrical men. This example does not illustrate regional differences or some of the other effects we have discussed in this chapter (although there could be intragender influence on scents or the effects of scents as well), but is consistent with the idea that people communicate with each other in ways that have real consequences for those involved without their having any awareness of it. This communication is likely affected by strength, immediacy, and number cues, and may have far-reaching effects on our culture through our biology. Further exploration of these relationships may be a step toward integrating the meta-theory of dynamical systems with that of evolutionary psychology (see Kenrick, 2001; Kenrick, Li, & Butner, 2003).

## CONCLUSIONS

In this chapter, we have shown how culture can be created from the bottom up, through individual social influence occurring reciprocally and recursively. As people influence those around them on multiple preferences, beliefs, and behaviors, four phenomena predicted by dynamic social impact theory emerge. These are *clustering*, whereby people become more similar on these attributes to those around them; *correlation*, in which influence on multiple attributes leads to linkages or correlations among them; *consolidation*, or a reduction in minority sizes over time; and *continuing diversity*, whereby the minority attributes, although decreased in size, persevere. Involvement and heritability, two factors that limit attitude change, constrain the development of these phenomena, which are reflected in cultural elements including prejudice, language, health attitudes, and biology.

Cultures are formed and changed through daily communication, as overlapping regional differences in attributes lead to identities. Without necessarily even being aware of it, individuals act to perpetuate their cultural present and help to define their future, simply as a result of going about their days.

## ACKNOWLEDGMENTS

We thank Jerry Cullum, Frank Fernandez, Nick Schwab, and Krista Van Hooser for their helpful comments on previous versions of this chapter.

## REFERENCES

Abelson, R. P. (1964). Mathematical models of the distribution of attitudes under controversy. In N. Fredericksen & H. Gullicksen (Eds.), *Contributions to mathematical psychology* (pp. 142–160). New York: Holt, Rinehart, & Winston.

Abelson, R. P. (1979). Social clusters and opinion clusters. In P. W. Holland & S. Leinhardt (Eds.), *Perspectives in social network research* (pp. 239–256). Reading, MA: Addison-Wesley.

Altemeyer, B. (1998). The other "authoritarian personality." In M. P. Zanna (Ed.), *Advances in experimental social psychology* (Vol. 30, pp. 48–92). New York: Academic Press.

Anderson, N. H. (1981). *Foundations of information integration theory*. New York: Academic Press.

Asch, S. E. (1955). Opinions and social pressure. *Scientific American, 193*, 31–35.

*Ayer directory of publications*. (1973). Philadelphia: Ayer Press.

Baker, R. R., & Bellis, M. A. (1995). *Human sperm competition: Copulation, masturbation, and infidelity*. London: Chapman and Hall.

Bendetto, R. (2002, March 5). Great divide splits U.S., Islamic cultures, poll finds. *USA Today*. Available at: http://www.usatoday.com, accessed March 5.

Binder, D., Russell, E., Sievers, A., & Harton, H. C. (2001, February). *Clustering, consolidation, and personality in electronic discussions: A test of dynamic social impact theory*. Poster presented at the meeting of the Society for Personality and Social Psychology, San Antonio, TX.

Bourgeois, M. J. (2002). Heritability of attitudes constrains dynamic social impact. *Personality and Social Psychology Bulletin, 28*, 1063–1072.

Bourgeois, M. J., & Bowen, A. M. (2001). Self-organization of alcohol-related attitudes and beliefs in a campus housing complex: An initial investigation. *Health Psychology, 20*, 434–437.

Bourgeois, M. J., & Latané, B. (1996, June). *Self-organization in a high rise college dormitory*. Paper presented at Nag's Head Conference on Groups, Networks, & Organizations, Boca Raton, FL.

Bowen, A. M., & Bourgeois, M. J. (2001). The contribution of pluralistic ignorance, dynamic social impact, and contact theories to attitudes toward lesbian, gay, and bisexual college students. *Journal of American College Health, 50*, 91–96.

Brauer, M., Judd, C. M., & Jacquelin, V. (2001). The communication of social stereotypes: The effects of group discussion and information distribution on stereotypic appraisals. *Journal of Personality and Social Psychology, 81*, 463–475.

Brown, J. D. (1998). *The self*. Boston: McGraw-Hill.

Burns, P., & Gimpel, J. G. (2000). Economic insecurity, prejudicial stereotypes, and public opinion on immigration policy. *Political Science Quarterly, 115*, 201–225.

Carroll, B. E. (2000). *The Routledge historical atlas of religion in America*. New York: Routledge.

Clark, R. D. III. (1990). Minority influence: The role of argument refutation of the majority position and social support for the minority position. *European Journal of Social Psychology, 20*, 489–497.

Cohen, D., & Nisbett, R. E. (1997). Field experiments examining the culture of honor: The role of institutions in perpetuating norms about violence. *Personality and Social Psychology Bulletin, 23*, 1188–1199.

Costa, P. T., Jr., & McCrae, R. R. (1992). *Revised NEO Personality Inventory (NEO-PI-R) and NEO Five-factor Inventory (NEO-FFI) professional manual*. Odessa, FL: Psychological Assessment Resources.

Crandall, C. S. (1988). Social contagion of binge eating. *Journal of Personality and Social Psychology, 55*, 588–598.

Crandall, C. S., Eshleman, A., & O'Brien, L. (2002). Social norms and the expression and suppression of prejudice: The struggle for internalization. *Journal of Personality and Social Psychology, 82*, 359–378.

Dolcini, M. M., & Adler, N. E. (1994). Perceived competencies, peer group affiliation, and risk behavior among early adolescents. *Health Psychology, 13*, 496–506.

Dovidio, J. F., Brigham, J. C., Johnson, B. T., & Gaertner, S. L. (1996). Stereotyping, prejudice, and discrimination: Another look. In N. Macrae, C. Stangor, & M. Hewstone (Eds.), *Foundations of stereotypes and stereotyping* (pp. 276–319). New York: Guilford.

Dovidio, J. F., & Gaertner, S. L. (1998). On the nature of contemporary prejudice: The causes, consequences, and challenges of aversive racism. In J. L. Eberhardt & S. T. Fiske (Eds.), *Confronting racism: The problem and the response* (pp. 3–32). Thousand Oaks, CA: Sage.

Eagly, A. H., & Chaiken, S. (1993). *The psychology of attitudes*. New York: Harcourt, Brace, Jovanovich.

Eaves, L. J., Eysenck, H. J., & Martin, N. G. (1989). *Genes, culture, and personality: An empirical approach*. London: Academic Press.

Edwards, T. M. (2001, July 2). A twist on Jack and Jill. *Time*. Available at http://www.time.com, accessed January 12, 2002.

Festinger, L., Schachter, S., & Back, K. (1950). *Social pressures in informal groups: A study of human factors in housing*. New York: Harper and Brothers.

Gaertner, S. L., & Dovidio, J. F. (1986). The aversive form of racism. In J. F. Dovidio & S. L. Gaertner (Eds.), *Prejudice, discrimination, and racism* (pp. 61–90). New York: Academic Press.

Gangestad, S. W., & Thornhill, R. (1997). Human sexual selection and developmental stability. In J. A. Simpson & D. T. Kenrick (Eds.), *Evolutionary social psychology* (pp. 169–195). Mahwah, NJ: Lawrence Erlbaum Associates.

Gilbert, G. M. (1951). Stereotype persistence and change among college students. *Journal of Abnormal and Social Psychology, 46*, 245–254.

Glaser, J. M., & Gilens, M. (1997). Interregional migration and political resocialization: A study of racial attitudes under pressure. *Public Opinion Quarterly, 61*, 72–86.

Grimes, B. F. (Ed.). (1992). *Ethnologue: Languages of the world* (12th ed.). Dallas: Summer Institute of Linguistics.

Halvorson, P. L., & Newman, W. M. (1994). *Atlas of religious change in America, 1952–1990*. Atlanta, GA: Glenmary Research Center.

Harkins, S. G., & Latané, B. (1998). Population and political participation: A social impact analysis of voter responsibility. *Group Dynamics, 2*, 192–207.

Harton, H. C. (1998). *The dynamics of attitudes: Individual beliefs to cultural norms*. Unpublished doctoral dissertation, Florida Atlantic University, Boca Raton, FL.

Harton, H. C., Binder, D., & Russell, E. (2001). *Clustering and consolidation in real time computer discussions*. Unpublished manuscript, University of Northern Iowa, Cedar Falls.

Harton, H. C., Eshbaugh, E. M., & Binder, D. (2002). *Group discussion and question type*. Unpublished manuscript, University of Northern Iowa, Cedar Falls.

Harton, H. C., Green, L. R., Jackson, C., & Latané, B. (1996, June). *An effective classroom demonstration of dynamic social impact.* Poster presented at the meeting of the American Psychological Society Institute on the Teaching of Psychology, San Francisco, California.

Harton, H. C., Green, L. R., Jackson, C., & Latané, B. (1998). Demonstrating dynamic social impact: Consolidation, clustering, correlation, and (sometimes) the correct answer. *Teaching of Psychology, 25*, 31–34.

Harton, H. C., & Latané, B. (1997a). Information- and thought-induced polarization: The mediating role of involvement in making attitudes extreme. *Journal of Social Behavior and Personality, 12*, 271–299.

Harton, H. C., & Latané, B. (1997b). Social influence and adolescent lifestyle attitudes. *Journal of Research on Adolescence, 7*, 197–220.

Harton, H. C., & Latané, B. (1997c). The social self-organization of culture. In F. Schweitzer (Ed.), *Self-organization of complex structures: From individual to collective dynamics* (pp. 355–366). London: Gordon and Breach.

Harton, H. C., & Latané, B. (2002). *The catastrophe theory of attitudes: A dynamic model of attitude structure and change*. Unpublished manuscript, University of Northern Iowa.

Harton, H. C., Petersen, A. K., & Schwab, N. (2001). *Prejudice in the Heartland: Attitudes toward Mexican immigrants, Bosnian refugees, and African-Americans*. Manuscript submitted for publication.

Haselager, G. J. T., Hartup, W. W., van Lieshout, C. F. M., & Riksen-Walraven, J. M. A. (1998). Similarities between friends and nonfriends in middle childhood. *Child Development, 69*, 1198–1208.

Haslam, S. A., Oakes, P. J., Reynolds, K. J., & Mein, J. (1999). Rhetorical unity and social division: A longitudinal study of change in Australian self-stereotypes. *Asian Journal of Social Psychology, 2*, 265–280.

Haslam, S. A., Turner, J. C., Oakes, P. J., Reynolds, K. J., Eggins, R. A., Nolan, M., & Tweedie, J. (1998). When do stereotypes become really consensual? Investigating the group-based dynamics of the consensualization process. *European Journal of Social Psychology, 28*, 755–776.

Hazen, K., & Fluharty, E. (in press). Defining Appalachian English: West Virginia and beyond. In M. Bender (Ed.), *Linguistic diversity in the South: Changing codes, practices, and ideologies*. Athens: University of Georgia Press.

Hellman, H. (1998). *Great feuds in science: Ten of the liveliest disputes ever.* New York: Wiley and Sons.

Hendrickson, R. (1993). *Whistlin' Dixie: A dictionary of Southern expressions.* New York: Facts on File.

Howes, M. J., Hokanson, J. E., & Loewenstein, D. A. (1985). Induction of depressive affect after prolonged exposure to a mildly depressed individual. *Journal of Personality and Social Psychology, 49,* 1110–1113.

Huguet, P., & Latané, B. (1996). Social representations as dynamic social impact. *Journal of Communication, 46,* 57–63.

Huguet, P., Latané, B., & Bourgeois, M. J. (1998). The emergence of a social representation of human rights via interpersonal communication: Empirical evidence for the convergence of two theories. *European Journal of Social Psychology, 28,* 831–846.

Huguet, P., Latané, B., & Michinov, N. (1996, June). *Clustering and correlation in the French Navy: Further evidence for dynamic social impact theory.* Paper presented at the Nags Head Conference on Groups, Networks, and Organizations, Highland Beach, FL.

Jackson, C., Bourgeois, M. J., & Latané, B. (2002). *Dynamic social impact theory on trial: Consolidation, clustering, and continuing diversity in electronic juries.* Unpublished manuscript, Florida Atlantic University, Boca Raton, FL.

Jackson, J. M., & Latané, B. (1981). All alone in front of all those people: Stage fright as a function of number and type of co-performers and audience. *Journal of Personality and Social Psychology, 40,* 73–85.

Jenssen, A. T., & Engesbak, H. (1994). The many faces of education: Why are people with lower education more hostile towards immigrants than people with higher education? *Scandinavian Journal of Educational Research, 38,* 33–50.

Joiner, T. E., Jr. (1994). Contagious depression: Existence, specificity to depressed symptoms, and the role of reassurance seeking. *Journal of Personality and Social Psychology, 67,* 287–296.

Joiner, T. E., Jr., & Katz, J. (1999). Contagion of depressive symptoms and mood: Meta-analytic review and explanations from cognitive, behavioral, and interpersonal viewpoints. *Clinical Psychology: Science and Practice, 6,* 149–164.

Jorgensen, N., Andersen, A., Eustache, F., Irvine, D. S., Suominen, J., Petersen, J. H., Andersen, A. N., Auger, J., Cawood, E. H. H., Horte, A., Jensen, T. K., Jouannet, P., Keiding, N., Vierula, M., Toppari, J., & Skakkebaek, N. E. (2001). Regional differences in semen quality in Europe. *Human Reproduction, 16,* 1012–1019.

Kameda, T., & Sugimori, S. (1995). Procedural influence in two-step group decision making: Power of local majorities in consensus information. *Journal of Personality and Social Psychology, 69,* 865–876.

Karney, B. R., Bradbury, T. N., Fincham, F. D., & Sullivan, K. T. (1994). The role of negative affectivity in the association between attributions and marital satisfaction. *Journal of Personality and Social Psychology, 66,* 412–424.

Katz, D., & Braly, K. (1933). Racial stereotypes of one hundred college students. *Journal of Abnormal and Social Psychology, 28,* 280–290.

Kenrick, D. T. (2001). Evolutionary psychology, cognitive science, and dynamical systems: Building an integrative paradigm. *Current Directions in Psychological Science, 10,* 13–17.

Kenrick, D. T., Li, N. P., & Butner, J. (2003). Dynamical evolutionary psychology: Individual decision-rules and emergent social norms. *Psychological Review, 110,* 3–28.

Krosnick, J. A. (1988). The role of attitude importance in social evaluation: A study of presidential candidate evaluation, policy preferences, and voting behavior. *Journal of Personality and Social Psychology, 55,* 196–210.

Krosnick, J. A., Boninger, D. S., Chuang, Y. C., Berent, M., & Carnot, C. G. (1993). Attitude strength: One construct or many related constructs? *Journal of Personality and Social Psychology, 65,* 1132–1151.

Krosnick, J. A., & Petty, R. E. (1995). Attitude strength: An overview. In R. E. Petty & J. A. Krosnick (Eds.), *Attitude strength: Antecedents and consequences* (pp. 1–24). Hillsdale, NJ: Lawrence Erlbaum Associates.

Krueger, J. (1996). Personal beliefs and cultural stereotypes about racial characteristics. *Journal of Personality and Social Psychology, 71*, 536–548.

Latané, B. (1981). The psychology of social impact. *American Psychologist, 36*, 343–356.

Latané, B. (1996a). Dynamic social impact: Robust predictions from simple theory. In R. Hegselmann, U. Mueller, & K. Troitzsch (Eds.), *Modelling and simulation in the social sciences from the philosophy of science point of view* (pp. 287–310). Dordrecht, the Netherlands: Kluwer.

Latané, B. (1996b). Dynamic social impact: The creation of culture by communication. *Journal of Communication, 46*, 13–25.

Latané, B. (1996c). Strength from weakness: The fate of opinion minorities in spatially distributed groups. In E. Witte & J. H. Davis (Eds.), *Understanding group behavior: Consensual action by small groups* (pp. 193–220). Hillsdale, NJ: Lawrence Erlbaum Associates.

Latané, B. (1996d). The emergence of clustering and correlation from social interaction. In R. Hegselmann & H. O. Peitgen (Eds.), *Order and chaos in nature and society* (pp. 79–104). Vienna: Holder-Pichler.

Latané, B., & Bourgeois, M. J. (1996). Experimental evidence for dynamic social impact: The emergence of subcultures in electronic groups. *Journal of Communication, 46*, 35–47.

Latané, B., & Bourgeois, M. J. (2001a). Dynamic social impact and the consolidation, clustering, correlation, and continuing diversity of culture. In M. A. Hogg & R. S. Tindale (Eds.), *Blackwell handbook of social psychology: Group processes* (pp. 235–258). Oxford: Blackwell.

Latané, B., & Bourgeois, M. J. (2001b). Successfully simulating dynamic social impact: Three levels of prediction. In J. Forgas & K. Williams (Eds.), *Social influence: Direct and indirect processes. The Sydney Symposium on Social Psychology* (pp. 61–76). Philadelphia, PA: Psychology Press.

Latané, B., & Harkins, S. (1976). Cross-modality matches suggest anticipated stage fright a multiplicative power function of audience size and status. *Perception and Psychophysics, 20*, 482–488.

Latané, B., & L'Herrou, T. (1996). Spatial clustering in the conformity game: Dynamic social impact in electronic groups. *Journal of Personality and Social Psychology, 70*, 1218–1230.

Latané, B., Liu, J. H., Nowak, A., Bonevento, M., & Zheng, L. (1995). Distance matters: Physical space and social impact. *Personality and Social Psychology Bulletin, 21*, 795–805.

Latané, B., & Nowak, A. (1994). Attitudes as catastrophes: From dimensions to categories with increasing importance. In R. Vallacher & A. Nowak (Eds.), *Dynamical systems in social psychology* (pp. 219–249). New York: Academic Press.

Latané, B., & Nowak, A. (1997). Self-organizing social systems: Necessary and sufficient conditions for the emergence of consolidation and clustering. In G. Barnett & F. Boster (Eds.), *Progress in communication sciences: Persuasion* (pp. 43–74). Norwood, NJ: Ablex.

Latané, B., Nowak, A., & Liu, J. H. (1994). Measuring emergent social phenomena: Dynamism, polarization, and clustering as order parameters of social systems. *Behavioral Science, 39*, 1–24.

Latané, B., Williams, K., & Harkins, S. (1979). Many hands make light the work: The causes and consequences of social loafing. *Journal of Personality and Social Psychology, 37*, 822–832.

Latané, B., & Wolf, S. (1981). The social impact of majorities and minorities. *Psychological Review, 88*, 438–453.

Lavine, H., & Latané, B. (1996). A cognitive-social theory of public opinion: Dynamic impact and cognitive structure. *Journal of Communication, 46*, 48–56.

Lawrence, J. (2002, February 18). Special report: Behind its united front, nation divided as ever; Terror attacks changed USA's mood, but not its attitudes. *USA Today*, p. A1.

Lieberson, S. (1982). Forces affecting language spread: Some basic propositions. In R. L. Cooper (Ed.), *Language spread: Studies in diffusion and social change* (pp. 37–62). Bloomington, IN: Indiana University Press.

Liu, J. H., & Latané, B. (1998a). Extremitization of attitudes: Does thought- and discussion-induced polarization cumulate? *Basic and Applied Social Psychology, 20*, 103–110.

Liu, J. H., & Latané, B. (1998b). The catastrophic link between the importance and extremity of political attitudes. *Political Behavior, 20*, 105–126.

Lynch, J. Q. (1999, August 27). Amish vandals freed—From jail's luxuries. *Cedar Rapids Gazette*, p. 1A.

Lyons, A., & Kashima, Y. (2001). The reproduction of culture: Communication processes tend to maintain cultural stereotypes. *Social Cognition, 19*, 372–394.

Mariano, K. A., & Harton, H. C. (2002). *Similarities in aggression, inattention/hyperactivity, depression, and anxiety in middle childhood friendships*. Manuscript submitted for publication.

McAndrew, F. T., & Akande, A. (1995). African perceptions of Americans of African and European descent. *Journal of Social Psychology, 135*, 649–655.

McClintock, M. K. (1971). Menstrual synchrony and suppression. *Nature, 229*, 244–245.

McClintock, M. K. (1978). Estrous synchrony and its mediation by airborne chemical communication (*Rattus norvegicus*). *Hormones and Behavior, 10*, 264–276.

McClintock, M. K. (1983). Pheromonal regulation of the ovarian cycle: Enhancement, suppression and synchrony. In J. G. Vandenbergh (Ed.), *Pheromones and reproduction in mammals* (pp. 13–149). New York: Academic Press.

McClintock, M. K. (1998). Whither menstrual synchrony? In R. C. Rosen (Ed.), *Annual review of sex research* (Vol. 9, pp. 77–95). Mount Vernon, IA: Society for the Scientific Study of Sexuality.

McConahay, J. B. (1986). Modern racism, ambivalence, and the modern racism scale. In J. F. Dovidio & S. L. Gaertner (Eds.), *Prejudice, discrimination and racism* (pp. 91–125). Orlando, FL: Academic Press.

McFarland, S. (2001). *Prejudiced people: Individual differences in explicit prejudice*. Manuscript submitted for publication.

Metcalf, A. (2000). *How we talk: American regional English today*. New York: Houghton Mifflin.

Moscovici, S. (1985). Social influence and conformity. In G. Lindzey & E. Aronson (Eds.), *Handbook of social psychology* (3rd ed., Vol. 2, pp. 347–412). New York: McGraw-Hill.

Moscovici, S. (1994). Three concepts: Minority, conflict, and behavioral style. In S. Moscovici, A. Muchi-faina, & A. Maass (Eds.), *Minority influence* (pp. 233–251). Chicago: Nelson-Hall.

Mugny, G. (1982). *The power of minorities*. New York: Academic Press.

Nail, P. R., Harton, H. C., & Decker, B. P. (in press). Political orientation and modern versus aversive racism: Tests of Dovidio and Gaertner's integrated model. *Journal of Personality and Social Psychology*.

Nail, P. R., MacDonald, G., & Levy, D. A. (2000). Proposal of a four-dimensional model of social response. *Psychological Bulletin, 126*, 454–470.

Nemeth, C. J., & Wachtler, J. (1974). Creating perceptions of consistency and confidence: A necessary condition for minority influence. *Sociometry, 37*, 529–540.

Noelle-Neumann, N. (1984). *The spiral of silence: Public opinion, our social skin*. Chicago: University of Chicago Press.

Nowak, A., & Latané, B. (1994). Simulating the emergence of social order from individual behavior. In N. Gilbert & J. Doran (Eds.), *Simulating societies: The computer simulation of social processes* (pp. 63–84). London: University College Press.

Nowak, A., Latané, B., & Lewenstein, M. (1994). Social dilemmas exist in space. In U. Schulz, W. Albers, & U. Mueller (Eds.), *Social dilemmas and cooperation* (pp. 269–289). Berlin: Springer.

Nowak, A., Szamrej, J., & Latané, B. (1990). From private attitude to public opinion: A dynamic theory of social impact. *Psychological Review, 97*, 362–376.

Olson, J. M., Vernon, P. A., Harris, J. A., & Jang, K. L. (2001). The heritability of attitudes: A study of twins. *Journal of Personality and Social Psychology, 80*, 845–860.

Pettigrew, T. F. (1986). *Racially separate or together?* New York: McGraw-Hill.

Petty, R. E., & Wegener, D. T. (1998). Attitude change: Multiple roles for persuasion variables. In D. T. Gilbert, S. T. Fiske, & G. Lindzey (Eds.), *The handbook of social psychology* (Vol. 1, 4th ed., pp. 323–390). Dubuque, IA: McGraw-Hill.

Pinker, S. (1999). *Words and rules: The ingredients of language*. New York: Basic Books.

Pratto, F., Sidanius, J., Stallworth, L. M., & Malle, B. F. (1994). Social dominance orientation: A personality variable predicting social and political attitudes. *Journal of Personality and Social Psychology, 67*, 741–763.

Raden, D. (1985). Strength-related attitude dimensions. *Social Psychology Quarterly, 48*, 312–330.

Roberts, P. (1999). Something about English. In S. Hirschberg & T. Hirschberg (Eds.), *Reflections on language* (pp. 316–325). New York: Oxford University Press.

Rockloff, M. J., & Latané, B. (1996). Simulating the social context of human choice. In U. M. K. G. Troitzsch, G. N. Gilbert & J. E. Doran (Ed.), *Social science microsimulation* (pp. 359–377). Berlin: Springer-Verlag.

Sampat, P. (2001, May/June). Last words. *World Watch*, pp. 34–40.

Schaller, M., & Conway, L. G. III. (1999). Influence of impression-management goals on the emerging contents of group stereotypes: Support for a social-evolutionary process. *Personality and Social Psychology Bulletin, 25*, 819–833.

Schaller, M., Conway, L. G. III, & Tanchuk, T. L. (2002). Selective pressures on the once and future contents of ethnic stereotypes: Effects of the communicability of traits. *Journal of Personality and Social Psychology, 82*, 861–877.

Schaller, M., & Latané, B. (1996). Dynamic social impact and the evolution of culture: A natural history of stereotypes. *Journal of Communication, 46*, 64–72.

Schwieder, D. (1996). *Iowa: The middle land*. Ames: Iowa State University Press.

Sears, D. O. (1998). Racism and politics in the United States. In J. L. Eberhardt & S. T. Fiske (Eds.), *Confronting racism: The problem and the response* (pp. 76–100). Thousand Oaks, CA: Sage.

Sechrist, G. B., & Stangor, C. (2001). Perceived consensus influences intragroup behavior and stereotype accessibility. *Journal of Personality and Social Psychology, 80*, 645–654.

Sherif, C. W., Kelley, M., Rodgers, H. L., Sarup, G., & Tittler, B. I. (1973). Personal involvement, social judgments, and action. *Journal of Personality and Social Psychology, 27*, 311–328.

Sherif, C. W., Sherif, M., & Nebergall, R. E. (1965). *Attitude and attitude change: The social judgment-involvement approach*. Philadelphia: Saunders.

Stangor, C., Sechrist, G. B., & Jost, J. T. (2001a). Changing racial beliefs by providing consensus information. *Personality and Social Psychology Bulletin, 27*, 486–496.

Stangor, C., Sechrist, G. B., & Jost, J. T. (2001b). Social influence and intergroup beliefs: The role of perceived social consensus. In J. P. Forgas & K. D. Williams (Eds.), *Social influence: Direct and indirect processes: The Sydney symposium of social psychology* (pp. 235–252). Philadelphia: Psychology Press.

Stephan, W. G., Ageyev, V., Stephan, C. W., Abalakina, M., Stefanenko, T., & Coates-Shrider, L. (1993). Measuring stereotypes: A comparison of methods using Russian and American samples. *Social Psychology Quarterly, 56*, 54–64.

Stern, K., & McClintock, M. K. (1998). Regulation of ovulation by human pheromones. *Nature, 392*, 177–179.

Tesser, A. (1993). The importance of heritability in psychological research: The case of attitudes. *Psychological Review, 100*, 129–142.

Thompson, M. S., Judd, C. M., & Park, B. (2000). The consequences of communicating social stereotypes. *Journal of Experimental Social Psychology, 36*, 567–599.

Thornhill, R., & Gangestad, S. W. (1999). The scent of symmetry: A human sex pheromone that signals fitness? *Evolution and Human Behavior, 20*, 175–201.

Walker, S. (1999). *Linking dynamic social impact theory to social representations theory: The emergence of social representations of aggression through electronic communication*. Unpublished doctoral dissertation, Florida Atlantic University, Boca Raton.

Wallis, J. (1985). Synchrony of estrous swelling in captive group living chimpanzees (Pan troglodytes). *International Journal of Primatology, 6*, 335–350.
Wardhaugh, R. (1987). *Languages in competition: Dominance, diversity, and decline*. New York: Basil Blackwell.
Weiss, M. J. (1994). *Latitudes & attitudes : An atlas of American tastes, trends, politics, and passions from Abilene, Texas to Zanesville, Ohio*. Boston: Little, Brown.
Weiss, M. J. (2000). *The clustered world: How we live, what we buy, and what it all means about who we are*. Boston: Little, Brown.
Weller, A., & Weller, L. (1997). Menstrual synchrony under optimal conditions: Bedouin families. *Journal of Comparative Psychology, 111*, 143–151.
Whitley, B. E., Jr. (1999). Right-wing authoritarianism, social dominance orientation, and prejudice. *Journal of Personality and Social Psychology, 77*, 126–134.
Woelfel, J., & Fink, E. L. (1980). *The measurement of communication processes: Galileo theory and method*. San Diego, CA: Academic Press.
Wolf, S., & Latané, B. (1983). Majority and minority influences on restaurant preferences. *Journal of Personality and Social Psychology, 45*, 282–292.
Wolfram, W., & Christian, D. (1976). *Appalachian speech*. Arlington, VA: Center for Applied Linguistics.
Wolfram, W., & Fasold, R. W. (1974). *The study of social dialects in American English*. Englewood Cliffs, NJ: Prentice Hall.
Wood, W., Lundgren, S., Ouellette, J. A., Busceme, S., & Blackstone, T. (1994). Minority influence: A meta-analytic review of social influence processes. *Psychological Bulletin, 115*, 323–345.

CHAPTER

# 4

# Language, Cognition, and Reality: Constructing Shared Meanings Through Communication

Ivy Y.-M. Lau
Sau-lai Lee
Chi-yue Chiu
University of Hong Kong

The relation of language and thought has occupied the center stage in many theoretical discussions on the psychological foundation of culture. One of the most controversial views is embodied in the Whorfian hypothesis, which holds that the grammatical structures of markedly different languages cause their speakers to develop markedly different cultural representations of the reality. Reviews of the Whorfian hypothesis (e.g., Brown, 1976; Glucksberg, 1988; Pinker, 1994; Rosch, 1987) find little support for linguistic determinism. However, recent advances in cognitive psychology and cultural studies reveal that the use of language in human interaction may play an important role in the evolution and maintenance of cultural representations. In this chapter, we propose a model to describe the relationships between culture, language, communication, and shared cognitions. Figure 4.1 illustrates the cyclical relation among the four variables in the model. It assumes that:

- Language is a carrier of cultural meanings.
- Cultural meanings are evoked when language is used in interpersonal communication.
- The use of language in communication will increase the accessibility of existing shared representations in the culture. In addition, through communication, private, idiosyncratic representations will be transformed

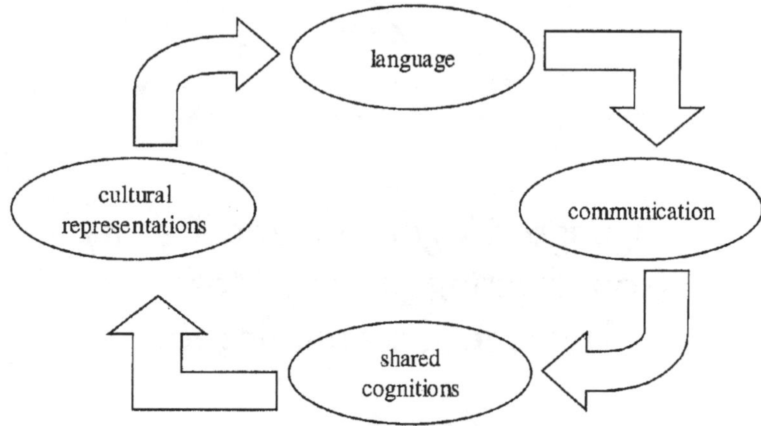


FIG. 4.1. A model of the reciprocal relationship between language, communication, shared cognitions, and culture.

into public, shared representations, which in turn form the cognitive foundation of culture.

- Evolved shared representations would then be encoded into the language and the cycle continues.

We begin this chapter with a review of some provocative claims in the Whorfian hypothesis, which has motivated the construction of the proposed model. Next, we review the evidence for the proposed model and conclude by discussing the model's implications for the construction of a dynamic constructionist approach to cultural psychology.

## THE WHORFIAN HYPOTHESIS

Arguments dating back at least to the 18th century suggest a symbiotic relation between language and thought. Johann Gottfried von Herder, an 18th-century German philosopher, argued that because people come to know ideas through language, its characteristics help to shape experience for its speakers; thus, language is closely tied to a culture's character (Code, 1980). Other 18th- and early 19th-century German thinkers, such as Johann Georg Hamann and Wilhelm von Humboldt, also insisted that language is not merely a vehicle for the expression of thought; instead, thought and language are interdependent (Stam, 1980). When discussing the influence of language on thought, von Humboldt stated that the diversity of language "is not one of sounds and signs, but a diversity of the world-views themselves" (cited in Stam, 1980, p. 245). The Humboldtian tradition was continued by anthropologists, most notably Franz Boas, who claimed that linguistic inquiry provided the information necessary to reveal the psychology of the people of the world (Boas, 1911/1966), and Sapir, who believed that language was the means by which humans structure and organize their environment (Sapir, 1912).

It was Benjamin Lee Whorf, an amateur ethnolinguist, who brought the idea of linguistic relativity to the attention of a formative generation of American researchers interested in language and thought. Like Boas and Sapir, Whorf claimed that language embodies a world view (or *Weltanschauung*) and shapes individual cognition. In essence, the linguistic relativity hypothesis states that a language's grammar constrains the way its speakers perceive external information and shapes their mental representations of the information. Whorf submitted that the use of language to code experiences would eventually create a correspondence between linguistic patterns and mental representations:

> We dissect nature along lines laid down by our native languages . . . the world is presented in a kaleidoscopic flux of impressions which has to be organized by our minds—and this means largely by linguistic systems in our minds. We cut nature up, organize it into concepts, and ascribe significances as we do, largely because we are parties to an agreement to organize it in this way—an agreement that holds throughout our speech community and is codified in the patterns of our language. The agreement is, of course, an implicit and unstated one, BUT ITS TERMS ARE ABSOLUTELY OBLIGATORY; we cannot talk at all except by subscribing to the organization and classification of data which the agreement decrees. (Whorf, 1956, pp. 213–214)

Because of such linguistic organization of our perception of the environment, speakers of markedly different languages will come to represent physically similar information differently in their mind:

> Users of markedly different grammars are pointed by their grammars toward different types of observations and different evaluations of externally similar acts of observation, and hence are not equivalent as observers but must arrive at somewhat different views of the world. (Whorf, 1956, p. 221)[1]

Whorf illustrated these points by comparing mental representations of time and space shared among Hopis and those shared among speakers of

---

[1]The linguistic relativity hypothesis does not imply that individuals who speak different languages *cannot* understand the thoughts of one another. Rather, it submits that speakers of markedly different languages may have different *habitual* ways of thinking. Whorf also did not think that all thoughts are linguistic. According to him, only the linguistic elements of thoughts are linguistically determined (see Whorf, 1956, p. 66, footnote 2).

standard average European (SAE) languages. SAE languages differ from Hopi languages in that in SAE languages, there are no formal markers between real plurals (seven dogs) and imaginary plurals (seven days). Consequently, a speaker of SAE languages may habitually assume that imaginary plurals are just as much countable as are real plurals. Whorf believed that this is an objectification of the referent: Concepts of time are dissociated with the subjective experience of "becoming later" and are objectified as counted *quantities*. Another example is the three-tense system of SAE verbs, which, Whorf contended, disposes a SAE language speaker to "CONSTRUCT AND CONTEMPLATE IN THOUGHT a system of past, present, future, in the objectified configuration of points on a line" (Whorf, 1956, p. 144).

Furthermore, language constrains development of non-linguistic cultural norms. Whorf (1956) posited that a vast amount of culture "is not linguistic but yet shows the shaping of influence of language" (p. 147). An example of this is that because time can be counted as quantities, it can be spent and saved. Because time is important, hence the SAE language speakers' emphasis on saving time. Regarding the development of cultural norms concerning time, Whorf (1956) observed that:

> No doubt this vast system, once built, would continue to run under any sort of linguistic treatment of time; but that it should have been built at all, reaching the magnitude and particular form it has in the Western world, is a fact decidedly in consonance with the patterns of the SAE languages. (p. 154)

Whorf did not overlook culture's influences on language use. However, he submitted that such influences were weak when compared to the causal effects of language on cultural evolution:

> How does such a network of language, culture, and behavior come about historically? Which was first: the language patterns or the cultural norms? In main they have grown up together, constantly influencing each other. But in this partnership, the nature of the language is the factor that limits free plasticity and rigidifies channels of development in the more autocratic way. (Whorf, 1956, p. 156)

According to Whorf, the language of a culture carries a shared worldview. Markedly different languages evoke in the mind of their speakers different mental images of physically similar events. Furthermore, some cultural norms in a linguistic community are constrained by the structure of the language used in that community. In summary, Whorf maintained that the use of language to code experiences lays the foundation of cultural evolution.

### Challenges to Linguistic Determinism

There are two strong assumptions in the Whorfian hypothesis:

1. In every language, there is an integrated "fashion of speaking." This fashion of speaking cuts across the typical grammatical classifications and includes lexical, morphological, syntactic and other systematically diverse means "coordinated in a certain frame of consistency" (Whorf, 1956, p. 158).
2. It is this fashion of speaking (or cryptotype) that affects thinking.

There is little empirical support for linguistic determinism of cognitive functioning. First, referent codability was found to have little effect on referent memory. For example, Americans have 11 basic color terms, whereas the Dani (a Stone Age tribe from Indonesian New Guinea) have only two achromatic terms for color. However, these two language groups do not differ in color memory (Heider & Olivier, 1972).[2] Second, in the grammar of the Navaho language, different verb stems are required depending on whether the subject or object in the sentence refers to a "long" object or to a "round" object. Despite this grammatical pattern for object categorization, compared to English-speaking children, who did not have this implicit marking in their language, Navaho-speaking children did not have a greater tendency to organize their perceptual world by shapes (Carroll & Casagrande, 1958). Finally, unlike English, Chinese lacks a formal grammatical marking for counterfactuals. The structure of Chinese grammar also does not facilitate entification of conditions or events. Bloom (1981) submits that these characteristics of the Chinese language may lower Chinese speakers' ability to engage in abstract, theoretical thinking.[3] This claim was disconfirmed in cross-cultural studies that compared the abilities of Chinese and Americans to engage in counterfactual thinking and to understand entifications of conditions and events (Au, 1983, 1984; Liu, 1985; Takano, 1989).

---

[2]Color codability studies were popular because they seem to meet the criteria thought to be necessary to test the "Whorfian hypothesis" (see Rosch, 1987): First, variations in color vocabulary can be readily found in natural languages. Second, investigators can measure the physical units of colors (e.g., wavelength) independent of how colors are coded in different languages. Third, members in different language communities should have more or less equivalent experiences with colors. Finally, nonlinguistic measures of color cognition—color perception, color memory—are available. However, human color perception is limited by specific neural–physiological mechanisms (Kay & McDaniel, 1978). Accordingly, any linguistic effects would be bound by our physiological capacity to perceive and distinguish different areas on the color spectrum (Heider, 1972). Therefore, if anything, color perception is an area that linguistic influence would be relatively weak.

[3]Whorf noted that standard average European languages tend to objectify conditions and events. In direct contradiction to Bloom's claim, Whorf believed that this fashion of speech would hinder abstract scientific thinking among SAE speakers.

The lack of evidence for the two strong assumptions in the Whorfian hypothesis has led some writers to the conclusion that "there is no scientific evidence that languages dramatically shape their speakers' ways of thinking" (Pinker, 1994, p. 12). The demise of the Whorfian hypothesis is accompanied by a decrease in enthusiasm for investigating the linguistic foundation of culture. As Chomsky (1992) argued, "The computational system of language that determines the forms and relations of linguistic expressions may indeed be invariant; in this sense, there is only one human language, as a rational Martian observing humans would have assumed" (p. 50). With such overriding concern with language universals, deep differences in human cognitions between language groups are not to be expected.

## WHORFIAN HYPOTHESIS: A NEW LOOK

The Whorfian hypothesis focuses on differences in structural characteristics between languages, and on how such differences constrain thoughts. Chomsky (1992) may well have been correct that the deep structures that give rise to surface forms may be invariant across languages. However, how the same state of affairs is referred to may vary markedly across language groups. Structural characteristics of a language may not rigidly determine its speakers' way of thinking. However, language may, as Whorf submitted, carry shared representation of the reality, which will be evoked when language is *used* in human interactions. We contend that when the two strong assumptions in the Whorfian hypothesis are relaxed, there may be support for some of the cognitive processes implicated in Whorf's ideas. Specifically, we agree with Whorf that (a) language is a carrier of shared meanings, and (b) when language is used in human communication, the shared meanings carried in the language are evoked to guide perceptions and interpretations of the reality. In addition, we contend that (c) activation of shared meanings in communication will further increase the cognitive accessibility of shared meanings in the communicators, and (d) through communication, private cognitions of the participants can be made and directed toward a shared representation (Krauss & Chiu, 1998). In this formulation, language is not a causal variable in the strict sense, but one that interacts with and bears a mutually influential relation with shared representations. We review the evidence for these contentions, which, as we argue, provide a new approach to understanding the linguistic foundation of culture.

### Language as a Carrier of Cultural Meanings

What is the basis for language rendering culturally shared meanings? The "tool and tool use model" (TATUM; Semin, 1998) offers a useful framework to conceptualize the role of language as a carrier of shared meanings. In

TATUM, language is compared to a set of tools. Each tool has its properties and is best suited for certain tasks. However, whether a particular tool would be used, when it is used, and what it would be used for depends on the goal and motivation of the tool user.

Following the tool analogy, it is reasonable to assume that a tool could be structured somewhat differently in different environments. For example, the eating tool could take different forms, such as that of a pair of chopsticks or a fork and a knife. The differences probably are at least partly due to certain material and cultural characteristics of the environment that provide for the development of the tool. For example, an abundance of bamboo and the cultural practice of not cutting up food at the dinner table could very likely have contributed to the use of chopsticks. In this sense, a tool embodies material and cultural characteristics of its usage environment. Given that all humans are endowed with the same linguistic physiological materials, it is reasonable to argue that linguistic tools carry mainly, if not only, cultural meanings.

Conceptually, the relation between language and shared meanings could be studied both intralinguistically and cross-linguistically. Evidence from both types of research using different levels of linguistic analysis attests to the capacity of language rendering socially shared meanings.

***Linguistic and Psychological Gender.*** As an illustration, consider the case of linguistic and psychological gender. Psychological gender refers to person categories based on social conceptualization of human sexuality. Linguistic, or grammatical, gender refers to formal categories, the basis for which is "partly arbitrary but also partly based on distinguishable characteristics (as shape, social rank, manner of existence, or sex) and (determine) agreement with and selection of other words or grammatical forms" (*Webster's Ninth New Collegiate Dictionary*, 1987). As stated in the definition, linguistic gender is only partly determined by the sex of the referent. In some European languages, all nouns are inflected (with the appropriate form or article) for gender on an arbitrary basis. For example, in French, the term for "the moon" is feminine (*la lune*) and the term for "the sun" is masculine (*le soleil*). On the other hand, in German, "the moon" is masculine (*der Mond*) and "the sun" is feminine (*die Sonne*). Would users of a language infer psychological gender properties from gender inflections of nouns? For example, would French speakers conceptualize the moon in more psychologically feminine ways and the sun in more psychologically masculine ways than would German speakers?

To attempt to answer these questions, one may soon run into difficulties stemming from the voluminous literary works in relation to the sun and the moon in both languages. Any feminine or masculine conceptualization of the two celestial bodies could be due to what has already been written on or about them, rather than associations with psychological gender (see Konishi, 1993). To make a clear case for psychological inferences based on linguistic gender would require studies using words that have no prior semantic or literary association, words that are completely new. One category of words that satisfy this requirement is nonsense words. When prior associations are controlled for, Italian speakers who were showed Italianate nonsense words with either masculine (*-o*) or feminine (*-a*) endings made semantic judgments similar to those for the words "men" and "women," respectively (Ervin, 1972).

Extending research on linguistic gender to the Chinese language, Tong, Chiu, and Fu (2001) examined the effect of gendered radicals of nonsense Chinese characters on estimation of the characters' connotations. Chinese is written in the form of characters and each character is by itself a morpheme (unit of meaning). Although most Chinese characters are not inflected for gender, the unique morphological construction of Chinese characters offers a good opportunity to study the relationship of linguistic and psychological gender. About 80% to 90% of the characters in modern Chinese are composed of two components: the radical and the stem (Hoosain, 1991). Both the radical and the stem may also be a morpheme. For example, the character for "drink" (喝) and "sing" (唱) share the radical "mouth" (口), and both characters involve oral activities. The stem may offer a phonetic clue to the character's pronunciation (e.g., 昌 in 唱) or a semantic clue to the character's meaning (e.g., "bird" [鳥] in "the humming of birds" [鳴]). Research has shown that a character's radical can affect its connotation. For example, when making judgments about whether the referent of a character is female or male, people are faster when the gender inferred from the radical (e.g., "woman" [女]) is consistent with the gender of the referent (e.g., "sister" [妹]) than when it is not (e.g., "son-in-law" [婿]) (Zhang, Zhang, & Peng, 1990). Prior associations, however, cannot be ruled out as an explanation for the observed results.

In the study by Tong et al. (2001), participants rated nine nonsense Chinese characters on semantic differential scales tapping evaluation (very good–very bad), potency (very strong–very weak), and activity (very active–very passive). The characters were formed by combining three radicals ("woman," "human," or "cow") with three stems ("benefit," "tongue," or "harm"). Participants' ratings were clearly affected by the radical of the nonsense characters. Nonsense characters with the radical "woman" were rated to be less active and less potent than nonsense characters with the other radicals. Furthermore, ratings for the nonsense characters were consistent with participants' ratings for the real character "woman." The results indicated that the nonsense characters with the radical "woman" may have activated the cultural representation of woman, and therefore were rated as less potent and less active. Taken together, research findings of studies on the relation between linguistic and psychological gender indicate that linguistic genders encode and reflect shared social evaluation of psychological genders.

***Pronoun Drop and Cultural Individualism.*** The cultural dimension of individualism–collectivism has received considerable theoretical and empirical attention (e.g., Bond & Smith, 1996; Hofstede, 1980; Kashima & Kashima, 1998; Markus & Kitayama, 1991; Ng, Loong, He, Liu, & Weatherall, 2000; Singelis, Triandis, Bhawuk, & Gelfand, 1995; Triandis, 1990). Individualism stresses the desirability of being independent from people around us and to express the inner set of attributes and abilities. Collectivism stresses the importance of being interdependent with the social world, maintaining good relationship and fitting in. In individualistic cultures, where individual uniqueness is valued, the individual is expected to be distinct from the context of the situation. By contrast, the individual in collectivistic cultures is expected to be part of the social context.

The linguistic system of pronoun encodes conceptions of the social self in the culture. The choice of pronouns in some languages (e.g., *vous* vs. *tu* in French) is indicative of the perceived relationship between the speaker and the addressee. Furthermore, the use of pronouns sustains attention on the referent of the pronoun, bringing the person out from the conversational background. Pronouns, such as "I" and "you" in English, are used to refer to persons or things named or understood within a particular context. Thus, the tolerance for pronoun drop is suggestive of the psychological differentiation between the speaker and the speech context. In some languages (e.g., English), the use of the pronoun is grammatically obligatory. In other languages (e.g., Spanish), the subject pronoun can be dropped because the referent can be recovered from the verb inflections. There are some languages (e.g., Chinese) in which the subject pronoun can be dropped even though there is neither verb inflection nor the subject–verb agreement rule. The grammatical obligatory use of the first-person pronoun maximally distinguishes the speaker's self. Similarly, obligatory use of the second-person pronoun maximally distinguishes the addressee(s). The omission of either one or both of the two classes of pronouns deemphasizes the salience of their corresponding referent(s).

To examine the relation between individualism, collectivism, and pronoun use, Kashima and Kashima (1998) correlated the grammatical tolerance for pronoun drop with different cultural-linguistic groups' emphasis on individualism–collectivism. Cultural scores of 76 countries from prior major cultural surveys were reanalyzed. Languages spoken in these countries were scored for whether pronoun drop was grammatically licensed. As expected, low individualism score, originally obtained by Hofstede (1980, 1991), correlated significantly with pronoun drop ($r = .64$, $p < .01$).

***Referent Codability.*** Referent codability in a language refers to the availability of a linguistic code in that language that will allow its referent to be expressed easily, rapidly, briefly, and uniformly. Although color memory studies have failed to reveal reliable effects of color codability on color recognition, results from one study seem to contradict this general conclusion. Hoffman, Lau, and Johnson (1986) investigated possible social cognitive effect of differential codification of personality traits in English versus Chinese. The researchers identified English-language and Chinese-language personality adjectives that have no economical equivalent in the other language. For example, there is no single English term equivalent in meaning to the Chinese personality adjective *shì gu*, which depicts a person who, among other things, is worldly, experienced, socially skillful, and somewhat reserved. On the other hand, there is no single Chinese adjective for someone who has artistic skills and interests, an "artistic" cognitive style and temperament, and leads a "bohemian" lifestyle. The appropriate English term is *artistic* (or, better, the *artistic type*).

There were three groups of participants in their study: a group of English monolinguals, a group of Chinese–English bilinguals who processed the information in English, and a group of Chinese–English bilinguals who processed the information in Chinese. (By including two bilingual groups with comparable cultural backgrounds, except for the language used in the experiment, it is possible to control for cultural variables to a certain extent. Differences between the two bilingual groups can be more clearly attributed to linguistic effects.) Participants read a set of concrete behavioral descriptions of four fictitious characters, either in English or in Chinese. Two of the characters exemplified personality schemas with economical labels in Chinese but not in English (the Chinese-specific adjectives) and the other two characters exemplified personality schemas with economical labels in English but not in Chinese (the English-specific adjectives).

Of main interest in the study was the interaction of language and schematic thinking. Indications of schematic processing include going beyond the information given to infer schema-congruent attributes not found in the original description, and memory biased in the direction of the schema. It was found that participants processing the character descriptions in English showed greater evidence of schematic thinking in the case of the two characters exemplifying the personality types with English-specific labels, whereas those processing the descriptions in Chinese showed greater evidence of schematic thinking in the case of the two characters exemplifying the personality types with Chinese-specific labels.

In short, the findings just reviewed showed that different aspects of language, from individual personality adjectives to grammatical gender and pronoun use, are saturated with culturally shared meanings.

## Language and Thought

The strong assumptions of the Whorfian hypothesis argue that the shared meanings carried in a language will invariably affect the language users' cognitive representations of the reality. However, as suggested by the tool metaphor, tool use depends on the usage context. Therefore, linguistic rendering of shared meanings does not imply that those meanings will always be evoked and influence speakers' thought and behavior. A series of cross-language studies (Kay & Kempton, 1984) provided good illustrations of this point. Unlike English, which has distinct terms for "green" and "blue," Tarahumara (a Uto-Aztecan language of northern Mexico) does not make a lexical distinction between these two color categories. The stimuli in the studies consisted of triads of greenish-blue or blueish-green color chips. Within each triad (chips A, B, and C), the researchers varied the difference in wavelength between pairs of colors. For example, the distance between A and B could be greater than, smaller than, or equal to that between A and C or B and C. Furthermore, the specific wavelength corresponding to the blue–green lexical boundary in English was located between different pairs of colors across triads. Native speakers of either language were asked, in their respective languages, to judge which one of the three colors was most different from the other two. Participants' judgments reflected their judgments of the distance between the colors. When the participants' subjective judgments were compared to the physical distance of the stimuli, the English-speaking participants, but not Tarahumara-speaking participants, systematically overestimated the distance between two colors when the green–blue color boundary passed between them. Kay and Kempton reasoned that the English-speaking participants might have used a naming strategy when they performed the task. For instance, they might have labeled the two colors left of the green–blue lexical category boundary "green" and the color right of the boundary "blue." As a consequence, they overestimated the perceptual distance between the first two colors and the third color. However, the Tarahumara-speaking participants did not enjoy the "convenience" of this naming strategy and their judgments were in overall agreement with the actual differences in wavelength.

In a second study, the researchers introduced a judgment task that was ostensibly different from, but logically equivalent to, the one used in the first study. The investigators eliminated the naming effects among the English-speaking participants by inducing them to use both verbal labels ("blue" and "green") to encode the same color. First, they paired the target color with a greener color chip and led the participants to encode the target color as the "bluer" color. Then, they paired the target color with a bluer color and led the participant to encode the target color as the "greener" color. Following this, the participants were asked to contrast the size of the difference in hue between the pairs of chips (i.e., to compare the difference in greenness or blueness). Under this condition, the English-speaking participants' perceptual judgments agreed with those of their Tarahumara-speaking counterparts. The color labels of "green" and "blue" provided English speakers with a cognitive tool to carve the continuous color spectrum into discrete categories. In most circumstances, the availability of these categories simplifies perceptual judgments, but with the consequence of sometimes biasing them. However, when this tool was made temporarily obsolete, its effects on perception vanished.

In summary, regardless of how loaded with shared meanings different linguistic forms or expressions are, they would not have any effect on our construal of reality if they remain dormant in our conceptual reservoir. By the same argument, when shared meanings carried in different linguistic tools are activated, they could induce cognitive and behavioral consequences.

***Memory Effects of Language Use.*** It is well established that linguistic encoding of a visual stimulus distorts memory of the stimulus in the direction of the linguistic label (Carmichael, Hogan, & Walter, 1932; Daniel, 1972; Loftus, 1977; Loftus & Palmer, 1974; Ranken, 1963; Santa & Baker, 1975; Thomas & DeCapito, 1966). Studies using social stimuli such as emotional expressions (Woll & Martinez, 1982) and person information (Bellezza & Bower, 1981; Cohen, 1981; Snyder & Uranowitz, 1978) have yielded similar results. Schooler and Engstler-Schooler (1990) provided a cognitive account of language encoding: "Verbalizing a memory may produce a verbally-biased memory representation that can interfere with the application of the original visual memory" (p. 36). Accordingly, once the implicit, shared meanings encoded in language are evoked, they may produce relatively durable cognitive effects (Chiu, Krauss, & Lau, 1998).

The cognitive effects of linguistic encoding are particularly pronounced when the stimuli have low referent codability (see Chiu et al., 1998), and when figural versus literal labels (e.g., "It looks like a baseball" versus "It is a sphere") are used to encode the stimuli (see Lau, Chiu, & Lee, 2001). In daily communication, speakers' goals and motivations help to decide whether the evoked shared meanings would be utilized in subsequent cognitive tasks (see Chiu, Morris, Hong, & Menon, 2000). A case in point is the use of personality schemas. The leading effect of codable schemas on person perception (Hoffman et al., 1986) can be attenuated when people are held responsible for their impressions, that is, when people are motivated to rely on received information and not schema-based inferences (Lau & Hoffman, 2000).

## Communication and Shared Cognitions

Thus far, we have argued that culturally shared meanings are encoded in language. When language is used to encode a state of affairs, a linguistic representation of that state of affairs will be created or evoked, which will in turn overshadow the perceptual information in the direction of the linguistic label. If a speaker's description of a state of affairs conforms to the conventional conception of that state of affairs, the person's subsequent representation is likely to be in line with the cultural convention, and the speaker would internalize the conventional perception of that state of affairs.

The foregoing discussion pertains to some of the potentials for linguistic effects on cognition. However, for language to exert its influence, it has to be used. A major function of language is communication. Bruner (1990) highlighted the importance of communication for the psychological foundation of culture when he commented that "By virtue of participation in culture, meaning is rendered *public* and *shared*. Our culturally adapted way of life depends upon shared meanings and shared concepts and depends as well upon shared modes of discourse for negotiating differences in meaning and interpretation" (pp. 12–13).

Within a language, people can express their thoughts in many different ways. Moreover, language can be used to express both culturally shared cognitions and relatively idiosyncratic thoughts. Why should people draw on culturally shared knowledge when they speak? When there are alternative ways to refer to a particular state of affairs, communicators would assess what the communication partners mutually know and formulate a message that can be understood within the estimated common ground of knowledge. Research showed that people are remarkably sensitive to the relative distribution of knowledge in their linguistic community: They know what most people in their community would know and what they would not know (Fussell & Krauss, 1991, 1992; Lau, Chiu, & Hong, 2001). In addition, people also utilize the estimated social distribution of knowledge when they formulate a message for their communication partner (Lau & Chiu, 1999). In one study (Lau et al., 2001, Experiment 1), participants, who were Hong Kong residents, estimated other Hong Kong residents' knowledge of specific landmarks in Hong Kong, Macau, and New York City, and identified the landmarks themselves. Identification of landmarks provided a direct estimation of the proportion of people who would know the landmarks in question. In general, although participants tended to overestimate knowledge of landmarks they themselves knew, they were sensitive to the relative distribution of knowledge of the landmarks. Their estimation of the percentage of people who could identify the landmarks correlated very highly with the actual percentage of people who could correctly identify the landmarks ($r = .94$).

In another experiment (Lau et al., 2001, Experiment 2), participants, all Hong Kong residents, described pictures of 30 specific landmarks in Hong Kong, Macau, or New York City, so that another Hong Kong resident could identify from the description which of the 30 landmarks was being referred to in each description. When the target stimuli were judged to have relatively low recognizability (in Lau et al., 2001, Experiment 1), speakers provided more information in their description (Kingsbury, 1968) and were less likely to mention the names of the stimuli (see Isaacs & Clark, 1987). Furthermore, it has been shown that when addressees decode a communicative message, they also estimate how most people in the community would interpret a message, and are more ready to accept a popular interpretation than an unpopular one (Yeung, 2000). In short, whenever people encode or decode a message, they would assess what most people in the relevant community know and do not know.

As noted, communicators would choose expressions that the addressee is expected to know, that is, expressions that can be understood within a common ground of knowledge. Relatively idiosyncratic knowledge or expressions are likely to be excluded. In one study, Krauss, Vivekananthan, and Weinheimer (1968) had participants in the first experimental session name color chips in a way that would enable themselves or another participant to identify the color chips at a later time. Compared to messages intended for the self, messages intended for others contained a less diverse vocabulary and words of higher frequency. In the second experimental session, the same group of participants identified the colors referred to in their own messages or in another participant's messages. Not surprisingly, the participants were best able to identify the referents of their own messages. When participants were asked to identify the referents of another participant's messages, identification accuracy was higher for the messages intended for others than those intended for self.

In referring to a state of affairs, communicators with divergent perspectives often collaborate to construct a shared representation of the topic of communication. A study reported by Wilkes-Gibbs and Kim (1991) illustrated this point. In the study, participants were presented with a list of 12 ambiguous drawings, each of which could be encoded by one of two alternate labels (e.g., "Viking ship" vs. "person swimming"). The participants in one condition were led to encode the drawings by one set of labels and the remaining participants were led to encode the drawings by another set. Next, the participants engaged in a communication task. Each participant was paired with another participant who either used the same (matched code condition) or a different set of labels (mismatched code condition) to encode the drawings. Each pair conversed to arrange the 12 drawings in identical orders without being able to see each other. All participants were later asked to reproduce and to recognize the drawings they saw.

As expected, participants in the matched code condition took less time than participants in the mismatched code condition to finish the communication task. However, by the sixth trial, participants in both conditions had established a common way of referring to the drawings. More interestingly, during the conversation, when the drawings were referred to, participants in the matched code condition exclusively used the same labels they had used to encode the drawings, whereas participants in the mismatched code condition had a greater tendency to jointly generate new and novel labels. These findings are consistent with the idea that, through the communication processes, the communicators, regardless of how they encode the information initially, will move toward a common way of naming a referent.

In addition, mental representations of the referents were distorted in the direction of the established references. First, participants in the matched code condition reproduced inaccurate drawings biased in the direction consistent with the labels used to encode the drawings. In contrast, participants' reproductions in the mismatched code condition were more neutral and accurate. Furthermore, when the established common labels matched the participants' initial labels, participants displayed systematic memory errors in the direction consistent with the initial labels. For example, the ambiguous drawing initially labeled as "a Viking ship" now looked more like a Viking ship in these participants' mind. In contrast, when the established common labels did not match the participants' initial labels, the initial labels had little effect on memory for the drawings.

Analogous effects were also found when social information was communicated. In one study (McCann, Higgins, & Fondacaro, 1991), participants read ambiguous descriptions about a target person that were equally likely to elicit positive or negative trait labels (e.g., "adventurous" vs. "reckless"). They then formulated a message for an audience who they believed either liked or disliked the target. After this task, the participants either waited for 15 minutes or returned 1 week later to formulate a second message for another audience who either liked or disliked the target. One week after they had formulated the second message, they were asked to describe their impression of and attitude toward the target. Most pertinent to the present discussion is the finding that participants generally produced messages that were consistent with their audience's attitude toward the target. Furthermore, participants' own impressions of the target were evaluatively consistent with one of their audience's attitude toward the target, depending on the amount of delay.

Our review illustrated the operation of the processes implicated in Bruner's (1990) comment on the psychological foundation of culture. When people communicate to members of their culture, they assess what most members in the culture know and do not know (Fussell & Krauss, 1992; Lau et al., 2001). Speakers avoid using idiosyncratic expressions and low-frequency words to help the addressee to accurately decode the intended meaning of communicative message (Krauss et al., 1968). Addressees give primary considerations to the most popular interpretation of an utterance in the culture when they decode a message's intended meaning (Yeung, 2000). In doing so, socially shared representations in the culture are evoked to guide message production and comprehension. In addition, communicators with initial divergent perspectives collaborate to establish mutually acceptable referring expressions (Wilkes-Gibbs & Kim, 1991). They also modify their expressions in the direction of their addressee's attitudes (McCann et al., 1991). Finally, the shared linguistic representation established in communication overshadows the original representation of the object of conversation. Through these processes, the communicators are cognitively committed to the shared linguistic representations established in communication.

The foregoing analysis implies that:

1. In both message production and comprehension, communicators are more likely to evoke existing shared representations in the culture than representations that are not. As noted, speakers would avoid idiosyncratic expressions and low frequency words in their messages. Such practice contributes to the maintenance of shared representations. In several studies of serial reproduction of stories that contained both stereotype consistent and inconsistent information (Kashima, 2000), information that was inconsistent with cultural stereotypes was retained proportionately more than consistent information at the beginning of the chain. However, as the chain of reproductions continued, inconsistent information began to drop off drastically, leaving the consistent information to dominate the last reproductions. Thus, stereotypes are maintained through the chain of reproductions.

2. When the shared linguistic representation established in communication is the same as the communicators' initial representation (as in the matched code condition in the Wilkes-Gibbs & Kim, 1991, experiment), the initial representation will be maintained. As Sperber (1996) put it, "Those representations which are repeatedly communicated *and* minimally transformed in the process will end up belonging to the culture" (p. 88).

3. The same psychological principle can be applied to explain cultural changes. Shared representations are products of cumulative experiences in social interactions. Once constructed, a representation is stored in memory. With new communication experiences, a new representation will be constructed and superimposed on the pre-existing representation. To the extent that differences in the relevant dimensions occur, the representation in question is changed.

4. As a series of related communications occurs over time, the representation slowly evolves (Kashima, 1999, 2000; Kashima & Kerekesh, 1994). That is, persistent outcomes of representational evolution are fortified cogni-

tively by linguistic influences. The cycle of mutual causality between language and shared representation portrayed in Fig. 4.1 perpetuates.

## TOWARD A DYNAMIC CONSTRUCTIONIST APPROACH TO CULTURAL PSYCHOLOGY

Collective construction of socially shared knowledge and beliefs (i.e., social representations) is central to understanding the psychological foundation of culture. Some writers believe that to be culturally influential, a social representation has to be "widely and durably distributed in a social group" (Sperber, 1996, p. 49). Most research in cross-cultural and cultural psychology has sought to document stable, deep cultural differences in meaning construction (e.g., Menon, Morris, Chiu, & Hong, 1999; Morris & Peng, 1994; Peng & Nisbett, 1999). However, relatively little attention has been given to when and how such differences in meaning construction would emerge (see Chiu et al., 2000; Hong, Morris, Chiu, & Benet-Martinez, 2000). How shared representations spread geographically and develop over time is also under-investigated (see Kashima, 2000; Latané, 1996). One way to understand how shared representations spread and evolve, as Sperber (1996) suggests, is to examine how shared representations "are cognized by individuals and how they are communicated within a group" (p. 97). We have described how shared representations are created, evoked, maintained and changed in the communication process. We believe that the same interpersonal processes in communication may account for two other important cultural processes: (a) spatial distribution of shared cognitions, and (b) development of culture-specific cognitive style.

### Spatial Distribution of Shared Cognitions

Thus far, our analysis has been restricted to dyadic communication. Yet there are reasons to believe that dyadic communication within a collective could result in systematic spatial distribution of shared representations, which will ultimately lead to formation of complex systems of social representations often referred to as cultures (Latané, 1996). In general, the opportunity to communicate increases with physical proximity. People are more likely to communicate with people in the same neighborhood or workplace than with people living far away. When people communicate with others, shared representations are established. As communication continues, there is a tendency for sets of beliefs, values, and practices to become spatially differentiated (or clustered). In addition, previously unrelated beliefs, values, or practices would become strongly associated (or correlated) and relatively homogeneous (or consolidated). Although consolidation could ultimately result in complete amalgamation, clustering protects minorities from majority influence, thus ensuring continuing diversity.

Latané and his colleagues (Huguet, Latané, & Bourgeois, 1995; Latané & Bourgeois, 1996; Latané & L'Herrou, 1996) simulated these processes of culture formation in a series of computer-mediated human communication games using the electronic mailing system. They organized participants in these studies into groups of 24 and informed them of the majority opinions. Each participant could communicate with only a fixed number of individuals (approximating physical constraints in real life). Over a number of electronic sessions, clusters of opinions were formed along group boundary. Within each communication group, opinions were more homogeneous and previously uncorrelated issues were correlated. However, at the end of the studies, even with incentives to agree with the opinions of the majority, there still remained pockets of different opinions.

Similar results were obtained in a 3-year longitudinal study of political socialization of business and social science students (Guimond & Palmer, 1996). In this study, over time, social sciences students became more likely than business students to attribute poverty and unemployment to systemic factors. Furthermore, beliefs about different causes of poverty that were unrelated in the first year became related in the third year. Toward the end of their studies, students developed social representations that are more structured and typical of their counterparts in their respective academic areas.

Spatial distribution of shared representation not only is observed within the realm of attitude but also has behavioral manifestation. Crandall (1988) found evidence for shared representation of the suboptimal behavior of binge eating within college sororities. Relative to responses collected at the beginning of a semester, participants' binge eating behavior was found to be more like that of their friendship group by the end of the semester, after prolonged and intense contact for 7 months. Furthermore, each of the sororities had its own distinct pattern of binging, and residents were sanctioned for not sharing the "binging standard."

In short, these studies illustrated how interpersonal communication could contribute to spatial distribution of shared representations and formation of "cultures."

## Development of Culture-Specific Cognitive Differentiation

Recall the unsuccessful attempts to relate color codability to color memory. Lantz and Stefflre (1964) have criticized the codability research for its sole emphasis on the role of dictionary words and/or grammatical categories and for its negligence of the productivity of language. They submitted that color codability will predict differential color memory only when the former "reflects communication differences" (p. 480). To test this idea, they correlated color recognition memory of one group of participants with communication accuracy, color-naming agreement, and brevity of descriptions established with other groups of participants. Communication accuracy was established by first asking a group of encoders to name an array of colors so that a friend can pick out the colors later. Then another group of participants were shown the naming messages and asked to pick out the target colors. A communication accuracy score for each color was derived from how well the naming messages can accurately communicate the color to the decoders. In a second experiment, participants were asked to perform a color recognition memory task. As expected, recognition performance was most significantly and positively correlated with communication accuracy. Later studies found that a color's communicability affects its recognizability independent of its focality (Garro, 1986; Lucy & Shweder, 1979, 1988). These findings highlight people's better memory for referents that can be communicated accurately.

Recall that in the Krauss et al. (1968) experiment, when participants described a color to another person, they tended to use high-frequency words and avoid idiosyncratic expressions. In other words, they tended to use expressions that were widely shared in the culture. That is, reliance on culturally shared representations facilitate communication accuracy.

When people communicate about a particular state of affairs frequently, the communication process would entail an eventual establishment of shared representations of that state of affairs. Schaller, Conway, and Tanchuk (2002) demonstrated the close relation between communicability and shared representations (stereotypes) of African Americans. Using as their basis stereotype studies conducted over six decades, Schaller et al. (2002) calculated the extent to which specific traits persisted as stereotypic over time. It was found that the likelihood of a target trait being used in communication (an index of communicability) predicted persistence. We contend that established shared representation, in turn, would aid communication accuracy and efficiency. In addition, people would also develop better memory for that state of affairs, and hence the positive correlation between communication accuracy and memory.

Cultures may very well differ in how frequently a particular state of affairs is communicated. If frequency of communication is indeed linked to communication accuracy and memory, cultures may differ in how well a particular state of affairs can be accurately communicated and memorized. Because there is no basis for expecting that the positive relation between communication accuracy and referent memory to be different cross-culturally, different cultures should find different representations of the environment more, or less, easy to communicate and less, or more, difficult to memorize.

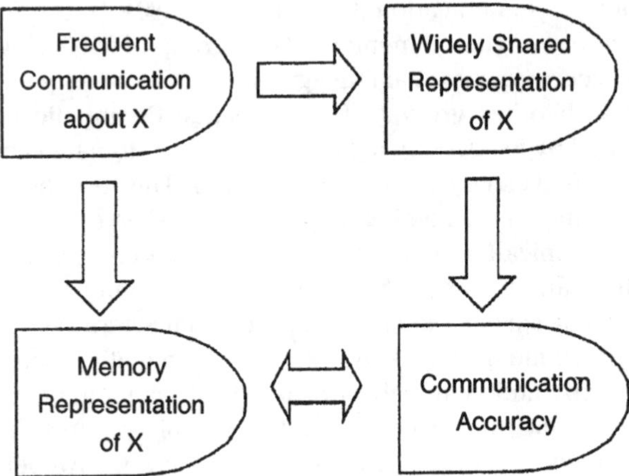


FIG. 4.2. Communication and development of cognitive traits.

A cross-language study reported by Stefflre, Vales, and Morley (1966) provided evidence for these expectations. The investigators collected communication accuracy and recognizability data for a set of color chips from native Spanish speakers and native speakers of Yucatec (a Mayan language). The correlation between communication accuracy and recognition accuracy was .45 in the Yucatec-speaking sample and .59 in the Spanish-speaking sample. Both correlations were statistically reliable. However, the correlation between communication accuracy in Spanish and communication accuracy in Yucatec was insignificant. That is, speakers of different languages remembered different colors better.

In short, the evidence is consistent with the idea, which is summarized in Fig. 4.2, that frequency of communication may contribute to the emergence of culture-specific cognitive differentiation of the "kaleidoscopic flux of impressions."

## CONCLUSION

We began this chapter by introducing the provocative ideas contained in the Whorfian hypothesis. By linking culture to static features of languages, Whorf espoused a deterministic view of culture. In other words, each culture is determined by the language its members speak to represent the reality in a particular manner. As Whorf (1956) put it:

> Every language is a vast pattern-system, different from others, in which are culturally ordained the forms and categories by which the personality not only communicates, but also analyzes nature, notices or neglects types of re-

lationship and phenomena, channels his reasoning, and builds the house of his consciousness. (p. 252)

Similar rhetoric is often found in contemporary cultural psychological research, which seeks to locate the origin of cultural differences in meaning construction in some static, essential qualities of cultures (e.g., thinking style, core values). In this chapter, we present a different approach to the psychological foundation of culture, which emphasizes the interpersonal processes that create, activate, maintain, and modify the shared representations. In this approach, culture is shared, evolving, and spreading. We hope that this approach will provide a new direction to explore the social psychological processes that give rise to these dynamic qualities of culture.

## ACKNOWLEDGMENT

Preparation of this manuscript was supported by a grant awarded to the third author by the Research Grants Council, HKSAR.

## REFERENCES

Au, T. (1983). Chinese and English counterfactuals: The Sapir–Whorf hypothesis revisited. *Cognition, 15*, 155–187.

Au, T. (1984). Counterfactuals: In reply to Alfred Bloom. *Cognition, 17*, 289–302.

Bellezza, F. S., & Bower, G. H. (1981). Person stereotypes and memory for people. *Journal of Personality and Social Psychology, 41*, 856–865.

Boas, F. (1966). Introduction. In F. Boas & J. W. Powell (Eds.), *Handbook of American Indian languages* (pp. 1–79). Lincoln: University of Nebraska Press. (Original work published 1911)

Bloom, A. H. (1981). *The linguistic shaping of thought: A study in the impact of language on thinking in China and the West.* Hillsdale, NJ: Lawrence Erlbaum Associates.

Bond, M. H., & Smith, P. B. (1996). Cross cultural social and organizational psychology. *Annual Review of Psychology, 47*, 205–235.

Brown, R. (1976). Reference: In memorial tribute to Eric Lenneberg. *Cognition, 4*, 125–153.

Bruner, J. (1990). *Act of meaning.* Cambridge, MA: Harvard University Press.

Carmichael, L., Hogan, H. P., & Walter, A. A. (1932). An experimental study of the effect of language on the reproduction of visually perceived form. *Journal of Experimental Psychology, 15*, 73–86.

Carroll, J. B., & Casagrande, J. B. (1958). The function of language classifications in behavior. In E. E. Maccoby, T. M. Newcomb & E. L. Hartley (Eds.), *Readings in social psychology* (3rd ed., pp. 18–31). New York: Holt, Rinehart & Winston.

Chiu, C. Y., Krauss, R. M., & Lau, I. (1998). Some cognitive consequences of communication. In S. R. Fussell & R. J. Kreuz (Eds.), *Social and cognitive approaches to interpersonal communication* (pp. 259–276). Mahwah, NJ: Lawrence Erlbaum Associates.

Chiu, C., Morris, M., Hong, Y., & Menon, T. (2000). Motivational cultural cognition: The impact of implicit cultural theories on dispositional attribution varies as a function of need for closure. *Journal of Personality and Social Psychology, 78*, 247–259.

Chomsky, N. (1992). *Language and thought.* Wakefield, RI: Moyer Bell.

Code, L. (1980). Language and knowledge. *Words, 31*, 245–258

Cohen, C. E. (1981). Person categories and social perception: Testing some boundaries of the processing effects of prior knowledge. *Journal of Personality and Social Psychology, 40*, 441–452.

Crandall, C. S. (1988). Social contagion of binge eating. *Journal of Personality and Social Psychology, 55*, 588–598.

Daniel, T. C. (1972). Nature of the effect of verbal labels on recognition memory for form. *Journal of Experimental Psychology, 96*, 152–157.

Ervin, S. M. (1972). The connotations of gender. *Word, 18*, 249–261.

Fussell, S. R., & Krauss, R. M. (1991). Accuracy and bias in estimates of others' knowledge. *European Journal of Social Psychology, 21*, 445–454.

Fussell, S. R., & Krauss, R. M. (1992). Coordination of knowledge in communication: Effects of speakers' assumptions about others' knowledge. *Journal of Personality and Social Psychology, 62*, 378–391.

Garro, L. (1986). Language, memory, and focality: A reexamination. *American Anthropologist, 88*, 128–136.

Glucksberg, S. (1988). Language and thought. In R. S. Sternberg & E. E. Smith (Eds.), *The psychology of human thought* (pp. 214–241). New York: Cambridge University Press.

Guimond, S., & Palmer, D. L. (1985). The political socialization of commerce and social science students: Epistemic authority and attitude change. *Journal of Applied Social Psychology, 26*, 1985–2013.

Heider, E. R. (1972). Universals in color naming and memory. *Journal of Experimental Psychology, 93*, 10–20.

Heider, E. R., & Olivier, D. C. (1972). The structure of the color space in naming and memory for two languages. *Cognitive Psychology, 3*, 337–354.

Hoffman, C., Lau, I., & Johnson, D. R. (1986). The linguistic relativity of person cognition: An English-Chinese comparison. *Journal of Personality and Social Psychology, 51*, 1097–1105.

Hofstede, G. (1980). *Culture's consequences: International differences in work-related values.* Beverly Hills, CA: Sage.

Hofstede, G. (1991). *Culture and organizations: Software of the mind.* London: McGraw-Hill.

Hoosain, R. (1991). *Psycholinguistic implications for linguistic relatively: A case study of Chinese.* Hillsdale, NJ: Lawrence Erlbaum Associates.

Hong, Y., Morris, M., Chiu, C., & Benet-Martinez, V. (2000). Multicultural minds: A dynamic constructivist approach to culture and cognition. *American Psychologist, 55*, 709–720.

Huguet, P., Latané, B., & Bourgeois, M. J. (1995, July). *A social representation emerges from communication.* Poster presented at the annual meetings of the American Psychology Society, New York.

Isaacs, E. A., & Clark, H. H. (1987). References in conversation between experts and novices. *Journal of Experimental Psychology: General, 116*, 26–37.

Kashima, Y. (1999). Tensor product model of exemplar-based category learning. In J. Wiles & T. Dartnall (Eds.), *Perspectives on cognitive science: Theories, experiments, and foundations* (Vol. 2, pp. 191–203). Stamford, CT: Ablex.

Kashima, Y. (2000). Maintaining cultural stereotypes in the serial reproduction of narratives. *Personality and Social Psychology Bulletin, 26*, 594–604.

Kashima, Y., & Kashima, E. (1998). Culture and language: The case of cultural dimensions and personal pronoun use. *Journal of Cross-Cultural Psychology, 29*, 461–486.

Kashima, Y., & Kerekesh, A. R. Z. (1994). A distributed memory model of averaging phenomena in person impression formation. *Journal of Experimental Social Psychology, 30*, 407–455.

Kay, P., & Kempton, W. (1984). What is the Sapir–Whorf hypothesis? *American Anthropologist, 86*, 65–79.

Kay, P., & McDaniel, C. K. (1978). The linguistic significance of the meanings of basic color terms. *Language, 54*, 610–646.

Kingsbury, D. (1968). *Manipulating the amount of information obtained from a person giving directions.* Unpublished honors thesis, Harvard University, Department of Social Relations, Cambridge, MA.

Konishi, T. (1993). The semantics of grammatical gender: A cross-cultural study. *Journal of Psycholinguistic Research, 22*, 519–534.

Krauss, R. M., & Chiu, C. (1998). Language and social behavior. In D. T. Gilbert, S. T. Fiske, & G. Lindzey (Eds.), *The handbook of social psychology* (4th ed., Vol. 2, pp. 41–88). New York: McGraw-Hill.

Krauss, R. M., Vivekananthan, P. S., & Weinheimer, S. (1968). "Inner speech" and "external speech". *Journal of Personality and Social Psychology, 9*, 295–300.

Lantz, D., & Stefflre, V. (1964). Language and cognition revisited. *Journal of Abnormal and Social Psychology, 69*, 472–481.

Latané, B. (1996). Dynamic social impact: The creation of culture by communication. *Journal of Communication, 46*, 13–25.

Latané, B., & Bourgeois, M. J. (1996). Experimental evidence for dynamic social impact: The emergence of subcultures in electronic groups. *Journal of Communication, 46*, 35–47.

Latané, B., & L'Herrou, T. (1996). Spatial clustering in the conformity game: Dynamic social impact in electronic groups. *Journal of Personality and Social Psychology, 70*, 1218–1230.

Lau, I., & Chiu, C. Y. (1999). Review of "Referential communication tasks." *Journal of Language and Social Psychology, 18*, 328–336.

Lau, I., Chiu, C. Y., & Hong, Y. Y. (2001). I know what you know: Assumptions about others' knowledge and their effects on message construction. *Social Cognition, 19*, 587–600.

Lau, I., Chiu, C. Y., & Lee, S. L. (2001). Communication and shared reality: Implications for the psychological foundations of culture. *Social Cognition, 19*, 350–371.

Lau, I., & Hoffman, C. (2000). *Accountability, cognitive busyness and the linguistic relativity hypothesis: Attentional and motivational effects on the linguistic shaping of thought.* Unpublished manuscript. Hong Kong: University of Hong Kong.

Liu, L. G. (1985). Reasoning counterfactually in Chinese: Are there any obstacles? *Cognition, 21*, 239–270.

Loftus, E. F. (1977). Shifting human color memory. *Memory and Cognition, 5*, 696–699.

Loftus, E. F., & Palmer, J. C. (1974). Reconstruction of automobile destruction: An example of the interaction between language and memory. *Journal of Verbal Learning and Verbal Behavior, 13*, 585–589.

Lucy, J. A., & Shweder, R. A. (1979). Whorf and his critics: Linguistic and nonlinguistic influences on color memory. *American Anthropologist, 81*, 581–615.

Lucy, J. A., & Shweder, R. A. (1988). The effect of incidental conversation on memory for focal colors. *American Anthropologist, 90*, 923–931.

Markus, H. R., & Kitayama, S. (1991). Culture and the self: Implications for cognition, emotion, and motivation. *Psychological Review, 98*, 224–253.

McCann, C. D., Higgins, E. T., & Fondacaro, R. A. (1991). Primacy and recency in communication and self-persuasion: How successive audiences and multiple encodings influence subsequent evaluative judgments. *Social Cognition, 9*, 47–66.

Menon, T., Morris, M. W., Chiu, C., & Hong, Y. (1999). Culture and the construal of agency: Attribution to individual versus group dispositions. *Journal of Personality and Social Psychology, 76*, 701–717.

Morris, M. W., & Peng, K. (1994). Culture and cause: American and Chinese attributions for social and physical events. *Journal of Personality and Social Psychology, 67*, 949–971.

Ng, S. H., Loong, C. S. F., He, A. P., Liu, J. H., & Weatherall, A. (2000). Communication correlates of individualism and collectivism: Talk directed at one or more addresses in family conversations. *Journal of Language and Social Psychology, 19*, 26–45.

Peng, K., & Nisbett, R. E. (1999). Culture, dialectics, and reasoning about contradiction. *American Psychologist, 97*, 185–200.

Pinker, S. (1994). *The language instinct.* New York: William Morrow.

Ranken, H. B. (1963). Language and thinking: Positive and negative effects of naming. *Science, 141*, 48–50.

Rosch, E. (1987). Linguistic relativity. *Etc., 44*, 254–279.

Santa, J. L., & Baker, L. (1975). Linguistic influences on visual memory. *Memory and Cognition, 3*, 445–450.

Sapir, E. (1912). Language and environment. *American Anthropologist, 14*, 226–242.

Schaller, M., Conway, L. G. III, & Tanchuk, T. L. (2002). Selective pressures on the once and future contents of ethnic stereotypes: Effects of communicability of traits. *Journal of Personality and Social Psychology, 82*, 861–877.

Schooler, J. W., & Engstler-Schooler, T. Y. (1990). Visual overshadowing of visual memories: Some things are better left unsaid. *Cognitive Psychology, 22*, 36–71.

Semin, G. R. (1998). Cognition, language, and communication. In S. R. Fussell & R. J. Kreuz (Eds.), *Social and cognitive approaches to interpersonal communication* (pp. 229–257). Mahwah, NJ: Lawrence Erlbaum Associates.

Singelis, T. M., Triandis, H. C., Bhawuk, D., & Gelfand, M. J. (1995). Horizontal and vertical dimensions of individualism and collectivism: A theoretical and measurement refinement. *Cross Cultural Research: The Journal of Comparative Social Science, 29*, 240–275.

Snyder, M., & Uranowitz, S. W. (1978). Reconstructing the past: Some cognitive consequences of person perception. *Journal of Personality and Social Psychology, 36*, 941–950.

Sperber, D. (1996). *Explaining culture: A naturalistic approach.* Oxford, England: Blackwell.

Stam, H. J. (1980). An historical perspective on linguistic relativity. In R. Rieber (Ed.), *Psychology of language and thought* (pp. 239–262). New York: Plenum Press.

Stefflre, V., Vales, V. C., & Morley, L. (1966). Language and cognition in Yucatan: A cross-cultural replication. *Journal of Personality and Social Psychology, 4*, 112–115.

Takano, Y. (1989). Methodological problems in cross-cultural studies of linguistic relativity. *Cognition, 31*, 141–162.

Thomas, D. R., & DeCapito, A. (1966). Role of stimulus labeling in stimulus generalization. *Journal of Experimental Psychology, 71*, 913–915.

Tong, Y., Chiu, C., & Fu, H. (2001). Linguistic gender is related to psychological gender: The case of "Chinese characters." *Journal of Psychology in Chinese Societies, 2*, 107–117.

Triandis, H. C. (1990). Cross-cultural studies of individualism and collectivism. In J. Berman (Ed.), *Nebraska Symposium on Motivation, 1989* (pp. 41–133). Lincoln: University of Nebraska Press.

*Webster's Ninth New Collegiate Dictionary*. (1987). Markham, Ontario: Thomas Allen & Son.

Whorf, B. L. (1956). *Language, thought, and reality: Selected writings of Benjamin Lee Whorf.* New York: Wiley.

Wilkes-Gibbs, D., & Kim, P. H. (1991, November). *Discourse influences on memory for visual forms.* Paper presented at the 1991 meeting of the Psychonomic Society, San Francisco, CA.

Woll, S. B., & Martinez, J. M. (1982). The effects of biasing labels on recognition of facial expressions of emotion. *Social Cognition, 1*, 70–82.

Yeung, W. L. (2000). *The importance of consensus assessment in speech act comprehension.* Unpublished master's thesis, Department of Psychology, University of Hong Kong, Hong Kong.

Zhang, J. J., Zhang, H. C., & Peng, D. L. (1990). The recovery of the meaning of Chinese characters in the classifying process. *Acta Psychologica Sinica, 22*, 397–405.

CHAPTER

# 5

# Motivated Closed Mindedness and the Emergence of Culture

Linda Richter
Columbia University

Arie W. Kruglanski
University of Maryland

In recent years, there has been growing interest in the link between culture and human cognition. For the most part, this research has focused on the various ways in which culture, or specific aspects of cultural knowledge, affects cognition and the different meanings one may draw from surrounding physical and social stimuli depending on one's cultural perspective (Hong, Morris, Chiu, & Benet-Martinez, 2000; Miller, 1999; Tomasello, 2000). What has received less attention, however, is the ways in which human cognition, and motivational effects on cognition in particular, influence the formation of cultures and the perpetuation of particular cultural norms or patterns.

*Merriam-Webster's Collegiate Dictionary* (1998) defines *culture* as "the customary beliefs, social forms, and material traits of a racial, religious, or social group." Similarly, culture can be defined as "the shared beliefs, values, traditions, and behavior patterns of particular groups" (Berry, Poortinga, Segall, & Dasen, 1992). In many cases, the group is reciprocally defined by the culture such that it is characterized by the shared knowledge, shared set of assumptions, and fundamental beliefs that the members of the group hold in common.

There exists a fundamental connection between culture and the human *need to know*, or to possess a set of valid opinions, attitudes, or beliefs. According to Leon Festinger (1954), physical reality rarely affords objective standards for validating one's personal opinions, beliefs, and attitudes. Therefore, people attempt to obtain validation by comparing and adjusting their personal opinions, beliefs, and attitudes to those of others. This adjustment often can be seen among recent immigrants who try to fit in and make sense of their new environment by absorbing or adopting, at least to some extent, the norms and values of the new land. This quest for a "social reality" (Festinger, 1950) promotes a general uniformity, or interpersonal consistency, in the basic beliefs and norms among members of a particular community.

Indeed, human beings are social in their very essence and, therefore, all human knowledge is essentially shared, or socially constructed, knowledge. The values, attitudes, beliefs, and behavioral norms shared by members of a cultural group derive from basic social processes, such as social comparison, attempts to influence others, or, in some cases, the readiness to be influenced by others. As the Asch (1956) conformity experiments demonstrate, when faced with disagreement from others, an individual's own judgments about what appears to be obvious can often be shaken. Similarly, anecdotal evidence suggests that in totalitarian states (like the former Soviet Union or Nazi Germany) that engulf the populace with propagandist messages, many citizens soon begin to question their once deeply ingrained notions and begin to espouse the beliefs and values that the state makes so accessible and compelling. Thus, fundamental socio-psychological processes such as social influence, social comparison, or the pressures toward opinion uniformity may drive the development of shared beliefs, values, and traditions that culture consists of. The extent of their impact and the rate at which a homogeneous culture may develop would depend on the cognitive needs of members of a particular collectivity at a given time.

## NEED FOR COGNITIVE CLOSURE

A motivational construct of potential relevance to the psychological process underlying the development of culture is the need for cognitive closure (Kruglanski, 1989; Kruglanski & Webster, 1996; Webster & Kruglanski, 1998). This particular need has been defined as a desire for "an answer to a question on a given topic, any answer, . . . compared to confusion and ambiguity" (Kruglanski, 1990, p. 337).

The *need for closure* differs from the more general *need to know*, mentioned earlier, in that the latter seeks to attain a set of valid opinions, attitudes, or beliefs, whereas the former merely seeks to attain an answer that will reduce ambiguity or uncertainty. That is, the validity or accuracy of what is "known" when one seeks to satisfy a need for closure is secondary to the more pressing goal of being able to stop thinking about the issue. In fact, the concern for veridicality or the "fear of invalidity," as it has been called (Kruglanski, 1989), is known as one of the major factors that may lower the need for closure (cf. Kruglanski & Freund, 1983).

The need for closure is assumed to vary on a continuum from a strong desire for closure to a strong wish to avoid closure. The desire to attain cognitive closure is assumed to arise when extended information processing is subjectively costly, or when the perceived benefits of possessing closure are high. For instance, a lack of closure may connote the necessity to process information further, and this may be seen as costly under certain circumstances, such as when an individual is subjected to time pressure (Heaton & Kruglanski, 1991; Kruglanski & Freund, 1983; Richter & Kruglanski, 1998) or environmental noise (Kruglanski & Webster, 1991; Kruglanski, Webster, & Klem, 1993), when he or she anticipates a more alluring task (Webster, 1993), or when he or she is fatigued (Webster, Richter, & Kruglanski, 1996). Consequently, this need may be subject to a host of situational influences, as well as representing a stable dimension of individual differences stemming from the tendency to generally value closure (i.e., perceive it as highly advantageous) and to find its absence aversive. The presence of stable individual differences in the need for closure has been assessed by the Need for Closure Scale (Webster & Kruglanski, 1994); scores on this instrument cross-validated the situational inductions of this need across a variety of cognitive and social tasks (for reviews see Kruglanski et al., 1997; Kruglanski & Webster, 1996; Webster & Kruglanski, 1998). The Need for Closure Scale has been translated into several European and Asian languages and was shown to exhibit comparable psychometric properties across its various translations (Mannetti, Pierro, Kruglanski, Taris, & Beznovic, 2000).

The need to avoid closure is assumed to arise when the perceived costs of closure or cognitive commitment are high, for example, when there are perceived benefits to delaying decisions or judgments or disadvantages to arriving at erroneous conclusions. For example, the need to avoid closure would arise when an individual experiences evaluation apprehension, feels accountable for a decision, has a strong motivation to be accurate, is anticipating an imminent unpleasant task, or when the suspension of judgment may appear to be the most desirable option under the circumstances (Kruglanski & Freund, 1983; Kruglanski & Webster, 1996; Richter & Kruglanski, 1997, 1998; Webster, 1993; Webster et al., 1996).

According to need for closure theory, individuals high in the need for closure have a tendency to seek immediate and permanent answers, desiring not only to form judgments urgently, but also to attain transsituationally stable rather than transitory answers (Kruglanski & Webster, 1996). Therefore, the need for closure may elicit premature "seizing" and "freezing" on the most accessible cues or information, and the tendency to underadjust one's judgments based on less accessible, albeit still relevant, cues or information. Thus, a motivation for cognitive closure may increase a person's tendency to encode situational information in terms of momentarily accessible inference rules, and reduce the tendency to search for alternative relevant constructs (Kruglanski, 1989, 1990). Moreover, the need for closure may induce a bias toward *permanent knowledge*. This may induce a preference for *abstract knowledge* that affords permanence (or consistency) across situations, and for *consensual knowledge* exhibiting stability or consistency across persons.

The need for closure plays a major role in knowledge formation processes in that it brings to a halt the (potentially endless) cycle of doubt involving the generation of hypotheses that compete with one's current assumption and their testing against relevant data. If culture essentially consists of shared knowledge (on matters of values, customs, and world beliefs), the need for closure should form a key factor in the formation of culture as well.

The epistemic goal of cognitive closure is relevant to culture in two major ways. First, it sets in motion the processes of culture building, or the construction of common social realities that provide epistemic stability for members of a group. Research examining the antecedents and consequences of the need for closure has highlighted the effects of epistemic goals on numerous interpersonal processes that relate to the emergence of culture, including majority and minority group behavior, social influence, political ideology, and interpersonal communication. The need for closure, however, not only plays a role in the formation or emergence of cultures, but also constitutes a dimension along which cultures may differ in a manner that affects both their inner workings and their relations to other cultures. That is, the need for closure has an impact on the perpetuation of cultural norms or patterns over time within and between particular cultural groups. This chapter discusses both types of relevance of need for closure to culture, drawing on examples and research findings from our past and recent work.

## THE DEVELOPMENT OF CULTURE: NEED FOR CLOSURE AND CONSENSUS STRIVINGS

Perhaps of most immediate relevance to the formation and perpetuation of culture is our research indicating that a heightened need for closure induces in individuals the quest for consensus. Active engagement in consensus building with regard to a group's basic attitudes, beliefs, values, or principles is one of the primary forces behind the emergence of culture. Our experimental research indicates that the need for closure contributes significantly to the pursuit of group consensus.

## Consensus Building

Participants in a series of experiments by Kruglanski et al. (1993) demonstrated a greater desire for consensus with their partner regarding a verdict on a legal case when they were either dispositionally high (vs. low) in the need for closure or when they were situationally placed under high (vs. low) need for closure via the presence (vs. absence) of ambient noise. In some cases, attaining consensus compelled the participant to exert influence over the partner, and in other cases, the participant allowed him- or herself to be so influenced. That is, the way participants went about forming consensus varied depending on whether or not they initially had a sufficient informational base on which to "seize" and "freeze" prior to engaging in deliberation with their partner. Those who did not have a prior crystallized opinion were more amenable to their partner's arguments and ready to shift their own verdict when under high (vs. low) need for closure, whereas those who did have prior crystallized opinion were more resistant to changing their verdict. Thus, a high need for closure in some cases influenced participants' openness to persuasion and in other cases induced greater persuasion attempts directed at the partner, both in the interest of forming a strong and reliable consensus.

The attainment of shared values, attitudes, beliefs, and behavioral norms characteristic of a cultural group is driven in large part by these types of subtle pressures among group members to attain consensus on key issues central to the cultural identity. For example, cultures with a distinct religious foundation exemplify this tendency by valuing those who take on an active role in persuading other group members to subscribe to the basic tenets of the faith, by either serving as role models (e.g., a nun or monk), actively imparting these principles to others (e.g., parochial school teacher), or doling out judgments or punishments to those who do not abide by the values or beliefs central to that culture (e.g., a priest, a religious court).

Even beyond the self- and community-appointed deliverers of cultural messages, the increased attempts at persuasion that can be seen among groups high in the need for closure may contribute, in part to the development of localized patterns of consensus in attitudes, values, practices, and identities, which ultimately become interpreted as subcultures. According to Latané's dynamic social impact theory (1996), individuals located in a particular space reciprocally and recursively influence one another through communication processes. Ultimately, such processes help form self-organized subcultures consolidated around a set of cohesive social attributes and correlated attitudes, values, and norms that become the "general public opinion" of the larger social system (Lavine & Latané, 1996). According to the present analysis, the need for closure may contribute to the formation of such subcultures.

### Eliminating Obstacles to Consensus

When neither changing one's own opinion nor changing the opinion of the other appears desirable or possible, groups under high need for closure may redefine the group boundaries by rejecting the opinion deviates (Festinger, 1950; Schachter, 1951), thereby attaining consensus by exclusion. If the desire for consensus is augmented by the need for closure, so should be the tendency to expel and/or downgrade dissenters from the common view. Kruglanski and Webster (1991) conducted a series of experiments examining this issue and found, indeed, that group members whose need for closure was experimentally heightened (via time pressure or a noisy environment) tended to denigrate opinion deviates and positively evaluate the conformists who contributed through their activities to the emergence of a group consensus. In real-world cultural groups, such as certain religious cultures, rejection of the opinion deviate can occur via subtle ignoring, denunciation, or more blatant ostracism or excommunication from the group.

## THE PERPETUATION OF CULTURE: NEED FOR CLOSURE AND THE MAINTENANCE OF CONSENSUS

Once a certain degree of consensus has been attained within a particular group or community and the essential identifying components of the culture have been established, a number of intrapersonal, interpersonal, and intergroup processes come into play to help ensure the perpetuation of those established cultural norms. The need for cognitive closure may affect these processes as well.

### In-Group Favoritism

The desire for consensus among persons high in the need for closure invests the in-group with particular value as a source of closure (after all, one cannot have consensus with all of the people, hence the delimitation of one's reference group is a practical inevitability). If so, one may expect that persons high (vs. low) in the need for closure will manifest a particularly pronounced degree of in-group favoritism. Similarly, to the extent that the out-group is contrasted to the in-group, high (vs. low) need for closure individuals may manifest a particularly pronounced degree of out-group derogation.

In support of this contention, Shah, Kruglanski, and Thompson (1998) found in a series of experiments a more pronounced in-group bias and more pronounced out-group derogation among groups high in the need for closure (as measured by the Need for Closure Scale and manipulated via time pressure). These tendencies were manifested both in enduring "real-world" groups (participants' ethnic group memberships) and in "artificial" groups created in the laboratory. The Shah et al. (1998) findings were recently replicated in an additional set of five studies drawing on various real-world groups in the United States and Italy (Kruglanski, Shah, Pierro, & Mannetti, 2001).

The mere experience of inclusion in one group and exclusion from another, no matter how baseless or insignificant, is often sufficient to induce the in-group bias phenomenon (Allen & Wilder, 1975; Tajfel, Billig, Bundy, & Flament, 1971). Indeed, the in-group bias is so highly pervasive that it can be considered a fundamental social component of almost any type of group. Although its strength may vary across cultural settings (Bond, 1988), its presence appears practically universal (Smith & Bond, 1993; Stephan & Stephan, 1996). The findings of Shah et al. (1998) and Kruglanski et al. (2001) suggest that at least one source of the ubiquitous in-group bias is the fundamental importance of in-groups as a source of social reality for their members, whose value is augmented as a function of members' need for cognitive closure.

## The Allure of Self-Resembling and Homogeneous Groups

Building on our earlier findings, further research examining the in-group bias demonstrated that its occurrence depends to some extent on the nature of the in-groups and the out-groups and in particular on the degree to which membership of these groups appears to be self-resembling and homogeneous. Self-resembling groups may be perceived as particularly likely providers of consensus and hence they should be appealing to high need for closure members (Kruglanski et al., 2001). Because in-groups are typically perceived as more self-resembling than out-groups, it is possible that the greater in-group favoritism and out-group derogation manifested by high (vs. low) need for closure individuals is in part due to their differential self-resemblance. Data from the Kruglanski et al. (2001) research are consistent with this implication. In this research, once the differential self-resemblance of in-groups versus out-groups was controlled for, the extent of in-group favoritism/out-group derogation was significantly attenuated.

Furthermore, because diversity (in personal characteristics, ethnic group membership, etc.) may bode ill for the likelihood of attaining and maintaining consensus within a group, members with a heightened need for closure not only may be less favorably disposed to in-groups whose composition is diverse, but also less adversely disposed to homogeneous out-groups. That is, an out-group with a high internal similarity of opinions would appear more attractive and derogated less by individuals high (vs.

low) in the need for closure. Kruglanski et al. (2001) found consistent support for this proposition in a series of studies conducted with various natural groups in the United States and Italy.

## Need for Closure and the Homogenization of Culture

The heightened in-group favoritism and out-group derogation commonly found in emerging subcultures serves to solidify the group consensus and establish a homogenized culture that is secure, and thus appealing, to the group members who are high in the need for closure. Specifically, a heightened need for closure promotes a tendency to "seize" on one's most highly accessible cognitive constructs and then "freeze" on these constructs in order to cease the unsettling and often effortful attempts to process novel information in the face of uncertainty. When a group is under a high need for closure, collective adherence to the most accessible constructs may lead to homogenization of the culture around pervasively accessible cultural norms and ideals.

Consistent with this implication, Kruglanski and Freund (1983) found that the tendency to adhere to cultural stereotypes (i.e., regarding the characteristics of Sephardi vs. Ashkenazi Jews) is augmented under a need for closure induced by time pressure. According to the present perspective, stereotypes are highly accessible constructs that can be readily applied to an individual fitting any of the stereotyped group's characteristics without having to expend the effort that is required when attending to individuating characteristics. In support of this, Schaller, Boyd, Yohannes, and O'Brien (1995) observed that the need for closure (as assessed by the Personal Need for Structure measure; Neuberg & Newsom, 1993) increases the tendency to form stereotypes on the basis of false information. An interesting implication of this finding is that when a group judges out-group members predominantly on the basis of stereotypes, it not only creates a perceived homogenization of the out-group (because all out-group members are thought to share common characteristics), but a homogenization of the in-group as well. That is, to the extent that all group members view individuals outside of their group in a similar way and in accordance with an agreed-on set of characteristics, diversity in views, beliefs, attitudes, and opinions within the in-group is virtually eliminated.

Beyond stereotyping, the tendency to "seize" and "freeze" on highly accessible information and insufficiently adjust judgments to take into account less accessible, although quite relevant evidence, also has been demonstrated in studies that have shown more pronounced primacy effects in impression formation (Heaton & Kruglanski, 1991; Kruglanski & Freund, 1983; Webster et al., 1996), and a greater likelihood of committing the "fundamental attribution error" (Webster, 1993) among individuals high in the need for closure. Each of these phenomena increases the likelihood that individuals in one cultural group will make simplified judgments of members of other cultural groups, whether in relying on first impressions, in judging others on the basis of group-stereotypes rather than individuating information, or in attributing others' actions to inherent personal traits rather than situational circumstances. Thus, relying on culturally accessible constructs and simplified stereotypes in forming impressions of others helps contribute to the derogation of out-groups and the evolution of a relatively homogeneous in-group culture with high internal consensus and limited ambiguity or uncertainty.

### Need for Closure and the Affirmation of Cultural Values: Terror Management Effects

To the extent that a group can derogate the norms, attitudes, and beliefs of out-groups, the greater the assurance in-group members will have regarding the value of their own cultural group and its associated beliefs, attitudes, and norms. One of the most interesting findings in recent social psychological research is the effect of mortality salience on the affirmation of one's own cultural values, often at the expense of the beliefs of other cultural groups. Working under the aegis of terror management theory, Rosenblatt, Greenberg, Solomon, Pyszczynski, and Lyon (1989), for example, proposed that the abject terror evoked by the sheer prospect of one's own mortality increases the need to perceive one's existence as meaningful and hence to increase the degree to which one upholds and glorifies one's cultural values (as a source of "meaning"). It is plausible to assume, moreover, that mortality salience increases one's existential uncertainty, which in turn may heighten one's need for closure. Thus, the increased adherence to one's cultural values under mortality salience may represent not only the need to perceive one's existence as meaningful, but also a defense against uncertainty and the tendency to embrace culturally shared realities. Indeed, similar to the rejection of deviates observed under high need for closure (Kruglanski & Webster, 1991), Rosenblatt and colleagues (1989) demonstrated that mortality salience increases the intolerance and hostility toward those who threaten one's cultural values or worldviews.

### Need for Closure Magnifies Cross-Cultural Differences

The adherence of high need for closure persons to their accessible conceptions, values, and ideals may magnify the differences among cultures beyond the extent to which they initially existed. A series of studies on this issue was recently conducted building on the notion that North Americans and Chinese persons possess differing implicit social theories, such that the

North Americans conceive of *individuals* as autonomous agents and the Chinese tend to conceive of *groups* as autonomous agents (Chiu, Morris, Hong, & Menon, 2000). The experimental findings indicated that a high need for closure (as measured by the Need for Closure Scale or manipulated via time pressure) caused participants to rely more on implicit theories derived from acculturation, such that North American participants under high (vs. low) need for closure increased their attributions to personal but not group dispositions, whereas Chinese participants under high (vs. low) need for closure increased attributions to group but not personal dispositions. Thus, need for closure was found to polarize or make more extreme the differences among cultural viewpoints, as persons under high (vs. low) need for closure were found to become more prototypical of their cultural modes of thought and judgment.

## Need for Closure and Communication Between Cultures

The tendency induced by a high need for closure to adhere to one's cultural viewpoints may pose obstacles to effective communication insofar as the latter requires appreciation of one's conversation partner's perspectives. In communication theory, this is known as "audience design" and the establishment of "common ground" with one's communication partners (Clark, 1985; Clark & Murphy, 1982; Krauss & Fussel, 1996). If one is too enmeshed in one's own point of view, or is too communicatively "autistic," the message will fall flat and fail to register with the listener. We (Richter & Kruglanski, 1999) recently conducted an experiment in which these notions were submitted to an empirical test. We employed a referential task in which participants were given a set of abstract figures and were asked to describe them so that either they themselves (in the nonsocial condition) or another person (in the social condition) will be able later to match the figures to the descriptions. Although no differences due to need for closure appeared in the nonsocial condition, they did significantly emerge in the social condition. Specifically, other-directed messages produced by high (vs. low) need for closure individuals (measured by the Need for Closure Scale) were briefer and more idiosyncratic (or figurative). As a consequence, they were less successfully decoded by their recipients. These findings support the notion that need for closure may impede effective communication in situations where the conversation partners depart from different perspectives on a given subject matter. When under a high need for closure, speakers may tend to "seize" and "freeze" on their own views and perspectives, exhibiting a self-centered bias, such that they fail to sufficiently modify their communications to suit the divergent perspectives of their audience. This may produce communication failure, culminating in serious misunderstandings, perpetuation of conflict, and ultimate alienation of outside groups.

In the same vein, a high need for closure can produce difficulties in negotiation attempts. This was demonstrated in a series of experiments by de Dreu, Koole, and Oldersma (1999), who found that dispositionally high (vs. low) need for closure negotiators were more likely to "seize" and "freeze" on key focal points in the topic of negotiation and on stereotypic information when discussing the possibility of making concessions. Thus, even when a cultural group is motivated to open communications with an outgroup, the effectiveness of such attempts might be limited by a high need for closure.

An example of this can be seen in the recent Middle East peace talks where the negotiating parties come from disparate cultural backgrounds and worldviews. The political climate surrounding the negotiations undoubtedly has a sense of urgency, placing the negotiating parties under a heightened need for closure. Indeed, despite numerous attempts to attain concessions acceptable to all involved, the progress of the negotiations has been stymied by long-held stereotypes and an inability to move beyond the attitudes, beliefs, and perspectives upon which the negotiators' cultures have been "frozen" for many decades.

Indeed, efforts to reduce intergroup prejudice occasionally involve the bringing together of conflicted parities in a stress-free environment that would allow them to communicate more effectively and ultimately gain an appreciation for each other's beliefs, customs, and values. To this end, the Seeds of Peace program brings together Palestinian and Israeli teenagers each summer in a neutral camp setting in Maine to allow them to get to know one another in a manner that supercedes the common stereotypic descriptions that each group has grown up believing. Without such efforts, ignorance, hostility, lack of appreciation for alternative cultures, and ineffective communication, all brought on by fear of uncertainty and of the unfamiliar, may perpetuate the gap between different cultural groups, and hinder the resolution of conflicts.

## NEED FOR CLOSURE AND THE EMERGENCE OF PARTICULAR CULTURAL PATTERNS

The desire of groups with a heightened need for closure to attain consensus may express itself in certain systematic ways that not only contribute to the emergence of a unique culture, but also play a defining role in the specific patterns a particular culture may assume. That is, a sense of uncertainty or instability stemming from a group's unique circumstances may motivate members of a cultural group to limit their openness to diverse views and opinions that might threaten their sense of certainty. For example, members of a cultural group functioning in a state of motivated closed mindedness that derives from a high need for closure tend to succumb to autocratic leadership, lean toward conservative points of view, and promote collectivist (vs. individualistic) attitudes and behaviors.

## Motivated Closed Mindedness and the Emergence of Autocracy

Because consensus is at a particular premium under a heightened need for closure and the fear of uncertainty is so strong, one may expect the emergence of high authoritarianism among members of a cultural group who are high in the need for closure. Indeed, research suggests that stress (a condition that often brings on a sense of uncertainty and thus a need for closure) is related to higher levels of authoritarianism (Korten, 1962). Rosenbaum and Rosenbaum (1971) demonstrated that subjects attempting to complete a task under stressful conditions performed best under authoritarian (vs. democratic) leadership and enjoyed the task more when it was structured (vs. unstructured).

Group members living under stressful circumstances and thus hungering for a sense of certainty will be more willing to give over their freedoms to an autocratic leadership. This is because an autocratic leadership and decision structure in a group may contribute to the quick emergence of consensus (consisting, simply, of the acceptance of a leader's opinion). Because of the extensive discussion and debate characteristic of egalitarian or democratic structures, they may be characterized by a lack of consensus or a stable social reality; they may be more open to innovation and to change that may constitute a threat to high need for closure persons.

Recent experimental research supports this notion by demonstrating that groups whose members are under a heightened need for closure (either dispositionally or when manipulated via time pressure) tend to be more authoritarian and more likely to allow for the development of an autocratic decision-making structure (Pierro, Mannetti, De Grada, Levi, & Kruglanski, 2000). This is evidenced in groups whose members are high in the need for closure by greater asymmetry in members' tendency to control or dominate the group discussion and the greater perception among group members that these dominating individuals exerted the greatest influence over the group's decision. Specifically, in-groups whose members were high (vs. low) in the need for closure with an autocratic interaction style were more conversationally dominant as well as influential than less autocratic members. In addition, groups under high (vs. low) need for closure showed greater asymmetry among members in the degree of centrality of certain members within the group, the degree to which they participated in the group process and were accorded attention or prestige. That is, in high (vs. low) need for closure groups, certain members were more likely to become the centers of in-going and out-going communications than were others. Furthermore, in a study examining the effect of the need for cognitive closure on group interaction during collective negotiations, dispositionally high (vs. low) need for closure groups demonstrated greater uniformity pressures and less egalitarian group participation (De Grada, Kruglanski, Mannetti, & Pierro, 1999). Briefly then, under conditions where group members were high in the need for closure, they demonstrated behaviors that seemed to encourage the emergence of an autocratic or hierarchical leadership.

The presumed high need for closure and tendency toward authoritarianism in German society in the earlier part of the 20th century, and the subsequent rise to power of Hitler can be seen as real-life evidence of the emergence of an autocratic leadership structure under high need for closure. It may not be too much of a stretch to propose that in real-world situations, characterized by considerable turmoil or uncertainty, such as war, revolution, or significant downturns in the economy, group members' need for closure may soar and a group culture will emerge that centers around an autocratic leadership.

### Motivated Closed Mindedness and the Tendency Toward Conservatism

In addition to a greater tendency toward authoritarianism and support of an autocratic leadership, a heightened need for closure, which induces an in-group bias and a reluctance to change the group norms, may foster a relatively closed, traditionalist society. Indeed, research examining political conservatism and motivated social cognition indicates that the need for closure and conservatism are positively related (Jost, Glaser, & Kruglanski, 2000; Jost, Kruglanski, & Simon, 1998; Kemmelmeier, 1997). That is, conservatism, defined as "the disposition and tendency to preserve what is established" or "opposition to change" (*Webster's New International Dictionary*, 1958, p. 568) may arise in situations in which the individuals experience a heightened epistemic, existential, and ideological need to resolve uncertainty, preserve what is familiar, and reject the unfamiliar. In a series of experiments, Jost and colleagues (1998) found that liberals were more likely to demonstrate tolerance and conservatives were more likely to demonstrate derogation (via personal evaluations) of an exchange student who espoused anti-American attitudes, and that this difference was significantly greater under high (vs. low) need for closure, manipulated by the presence (vs. absence) of environmental noise. Thus, increasing the need for cognitive closure appears to increase reliance upon chronically accessible ideological attitudes.

In real-world situations, cultural groups that are threatened by uncertainty or change may be more likely to cling to traditional or conservative worldviews. Thus, following the upheavals of World War II, American society in the 1950s epitomized conservatism. Similarly, following the social change and political turmoil of the 1960s and 1970s, conservative movements began to experience something of a renaissance. Within the United States, local and national politics have undergone a shift such that a more conservative agenda has entered mainstream politics. This ideological trend corresponds with renewed emphasis on traditional religious values in our country. Indeed, in the most recent political elections, religious faith has become a major focus and source of identity for the candidates. To the extent that moderate conservatism has become more in vogue in mainstream American politics, more extreme versions of it are cropping up among right-wing fringe groups with high levels of economic and social instability, and a consequent high need for closure. Indeed the "Militia Movement" and various "White Supremacist" groups place a strong emphasis on traditional religious and social values as well as racial and ethnic (i.e., outgroup) intolerance. Such groups are more likely to be found in areas of the country with greater economic instability or loss of jobs due to new immigrant populations, making these areas comfortable breeding grounds for a high need for closure and, consequently, for the development of right-wing cultural worldviews.

The need for closure can influence the level of conservatism or traditionalism of cultural groups in several ways. First, when members of a different cultural group come to live among a dominant or majority cultural group, they may subtly begin to influence or change the existing cultural norms, increasing uncertainty about "what is right" and putting the majority group members under a high need for closure. Thus, areas that have become home to increasing numbers of immigrants, minority racial groups, or members of minority religious groups are often plagued by right-wing violent activity. This can be seen in recent years in many (Western and Southern) European countries as waves of immigrants (from Eastern Europe, Africa, or Asia) have begun to make their homes in these formerly culturally homogenous lands.

Tendencies toward conservatism can also occur among members of an immigrant group whose confrontation with the new and often very different culture may foster considerable epistemic confusion and uncertainty (a kind of "culture shock"), in turn resulting in a heightened need for closure among the individuals concerned. As a response, the immigrants may shut themselves off in a cultural ghetto and resist assimilation to the general culture of their accepting homeland. This might depend, however, on the availability of a sufficiently numerous immigrant group to form such a cultural enclave. By contrast, isolated immigrants who lack access to their compatriots may instead work hard to learn the new cultural ways and means, and they may do so more intensely the higher their need for cognitive closure.

We have some preliminary data relevant to these ideas in which we treat the degree to which Croat immigrants to Italy demonstrate nostalgia for their old country as an inverse index of assimilation. Specifically, we find that the immigrants who arrive in Italy *in a group* long for their old country more if they are high versus low on need for closure. By contrast, Croat immigrants who arrive in Italy in relative isolation from their compatriots are less likely to long for the old country if they have a higher need for closure (A. Kosic, unpublished data, 1998).

## Motivated Closed Mindedness and the Promotion of Collectivism versus Individualism

What might a culture look like whose members are characterized by a high need for closure? It should be a collectivistic culture (Triandis, 1995) insofar as persons under high need for closure are typically consensus seekers, as noted earlier. Indeed, in a recent study, L. Nishi (unpublished data, 2000) obtained a positive and significant correlation between the need for closure and collectivism.

Research generally points to the collectivist cultural tendencies of Asian countries, whose citizens are more likely than those in individualistic societies to live with their larger extended families, show greater conformity to group norms, and have more conservative social beliefs and political ideologies (Hofstede, 1980; Triandis, 1994).

Some have suggested that the predominantly collectivist culture of certain Asian societies may have emerged, in part, from an existential insecurity, derived from ubiquitous uncertainties with regard to physical and economic survival (Broadbent, 1993). This uncertainty may contribute to a strong need for closure, as a defense against the gnawing uncertainty and the quest for reassurance.

The tendency toward collectivism observed in Japan, for example, could well have derived from such a need. Broadbent (1993) argued that "the snug embrace" of long-term group membership in Japanese society provides good collective insurance against hard times. Pushing one's own advancement at the costs of another group member runs against the grain. As such, the desire for cultural homogeneity contributes to a lower tolerance for diversity and individualism.

Tendencies toward collectivism and the accompanying reduced tolerance for deviance, although often discussed in terms of an individualistic United States versus a collectivist Asian context, have also been found within the United States itself. That is, although the United States is considered the prototypical individualist culture, Vandello and Cohen (1999) found important regional differences on the individualism–collectivism dimension. Specifically, they found stronger collectivist tendencies in the

Deep South compared to more individualistic tendencies in other parts of the United States. They explained this finding by arguing that certain historical factors and institutional practices, such as defeat in the Civil War, the institution of slavery, relative poverty, and the prominence of religion, have helped shape the South into a relatively collectivist region. These historical and cultural factors, particularly defeat in a war, poverty, and fundamentalist religion, could each be related to a heightened state of psychological uncertainty, and hence to a heightened need for closure. In addition to the Deep South, Vandello and Cohen (1999) found that Hawaii was the most collectivist state in the country, most likely because it is situated midway between Asia and North America, and its culture reflects strong Asian influences.

Overall, cultural groups that tend to be more collectivist are those that are somewhat isolated (as Hawaii is geographically and the Deep South is ideologically), suffer from economic hardship, war, or other social stressors, and have somewhat of a fundamentalist religious foundation. That is not surprising if one considers the development of collectivist cultures through the lens of need for closure theory. Conditions of economic or political hardship, for example, serve to increase the stress and uncertainty of individuals, heightening the need for closure and thus the tendency to cling to social shared realities that provide firm answers and reduce ambiguity. Individualism, by definition, engenders uncertainty and ambiguity to the extent that it stresses autonomy and independence of the self. Only under relatively secure environmental conditions can people have a low enough need for closure to venture out on their own into the ambiguous, uncertain, and often risky realm of individualism.

## Need for Closure and Economic Decision Making

One important and defining element of any culture is its economic structure. The United States, for example, is characterized in large part by its capitalist economy, whereas the economic structure of Communist China plays a significant role in defining Chinese cultural identity. The shape and form of a particular economic structure and its associated sociocultural ramifications depend on the decision-making strategies employed by members of a cultural group. Certain economic theoretical models and the consequences for economic development that they predict are similar in many ways to need for closure theory and the consequences for cultural development that it predicts.

According to classic economic theory, a person is always better off with more rather than fewer choices, and based on the choices available to them, people make rational economic decisions. This classical view of human economic behavior has been challenged in recent years by the burgeoning field of behavioral economics. Behavioral economics is inspired in large part by the decision-making theories of Tversky and Kahneman (1987). Behavioral economists argue, among other things, that contrary to rational decision-making processes, people do not always behave rationally and sometimes (a) prefer fewer rather than more choices, (b) have a bias toward the status quo, and (c) are risk averse. These tendencies are exacerbated under conditions of uncertainty or stress when the need for closure is heightened and reduced during less stressful periods.

Regardless of whether the cognitive processes one engages in occur within the realm of economics, politics, or social activities—each of which plays an important role in defining a cultural group—a heightened need for closure will lead a person to avoid uncertainty or ambiguity and, thus, prefer fewer (rather than more) choices and what is known or safe rather than what is not known or risky.

## CONCLUSION

This chapter delineated the various ways in which a need for cognitive closure—a basic human condition that arises from the need to have a firm social reality—contributes to the emergence of culture and to the perpetuation of particular cultural norms, beliefs, and behavioral patterns. Perhaps the main underlying force linking the need for closure to the development of culture is the drive to attain group consensus in order to reduce inconsistencies, ambiguities, and uncertainties in one's beliefs. Reaching general consensus contributes to a relatively homogenous cultural in-group, which serves to assure members of a permanent, or at least a relatively long-term, closure.

As a growing body of research on the need for cognitive closure demonstrates, such a need can have profound effects on individual internal cognitive processes, interpersonal communication within and between cultural groups, and larger cultural-level processes that contribute to the unique defining characteristics of particular cultural groups. The specific human phenomena brought about by a heightened need for closure are manifest in successively more encompassing levels of human functioning (intrapersonal, interpersonal, intracultural, and intercultural). These processes work in concert to promote not only the emergence of a culture, but the perpetuation of that culture and its unique norms and patterns.

As such, people's own need for certainty and stability, which might derive from stressful conditions, fatigue, or economic uncertainty, might increase their tendency to take on the beliefs of those around them. This tendency to allow oneself to be persuaded by others occurs not just with one individual but simultaneously within many individuals in a group. At the same time, in order to secure those beliefs and maintain the sense of closure that is so strongly desired, the group members, acting individually and together, take steps to ensure that potential dissenters within the group likewise adopt the larger group's beliefs and values. At this point in the development of the group consensus around emerging cultural norms, out-group derogation and in-group homogenization may take place. These group-wide efforts further affect the individual's sense of security and certainty and the ever-increasing desire to maintain that cherished sense of closure, perpetuating efforts toward consensus building yet further.

In a sense, there can be no culture, as this term is generally understood, without at least a modicum of closed mindedness. Culture represents a set of constraints upon what is believed, cherished, or valued. It represents an elimination of possibilities, via choice and commitment. A total open mindedness would render culture and tradition impossible. Rather, one would have a kind of anarchy in flux, affording little opportunity for orderly social life. But as with any good thing, culture-promoting closed mindedness is not without its trade-offs. As the research described here indicates, excessive closed mindedness may undermine societal effectiveness in a variety of respects. It may promote humdrum homogeneity, suppress creativity and innovation, foster an overidentification with one's in-group, and foster the derogation of alternative cultural groups. Moreover, overly closed-minded cultural groups may tend toward autocracy and may be inimical to democratic and egalitarian ways of self-governance. Such cultures may tend to prefer collectivism over individualism and experience difficulty communicating, negotiating with, or developing an appreciation for alternative cultural groups. Understanding the motivational underpinnings of such counterproductive patterns, with their antecedents, dynamics, and consequences, may help us to better achieve that ideal mix of closed and open mindedness that assures effective societal functioning even as it upholds tradition and preserves culture.

## REFERENCES


Allen, V. L., & Wilder, D. A. (1975). Categorization, belief similarity, and group discrimination. *Journal of Personality and Social Psychology, 32*, 971–977.

Asch, S. E. (1956). Studies of independence and conformity: A minority of one against a unanimous majority. *Psychological Monographs, 70* (Whole No. 416).

Berry, J. W., Poortinga, Y. H., Segall, M. H., & Dasen, P. R. (1992). *Cross-cultural psychology: Research and applications*. New York: Cambridge University Press.

Bond, M. H. (1988). Finding the universal dimensions of individual variation in multicultural studies of values: The Rokeach and Chinese value surveys. *Journal of Personality and Social Psychology, 55*, 1009–1015.

Broadbent, J. (1993, March). The "melting pot" versus the "pressure cooker": Cultural misunderstandings in the U.S.-Japan Trade Relations. *Law and Politics*, pp. 14–18.

Chiu, C. Y., Morris, M. W., Hong, Y. Y., & Menon, T. (2000). Motivated cultural cognition: The impact of implicit cultural theories on dispositional attribution varies as a function of need for closure. *Journal of Personality and Social Psychology, 78*(2), 247–259.

Clark, H. H. (1985). Language use and language users. In G. Lindzey & E. Aronson (Eds.), *Handbook of social psychology* (pp. 179–231). New York: Random House.

Clark, H. H., & Murphy, G. L. (1982). Audience design in meaning and reference. In J. F. Le Ny & W. Kintsch (Eds.), *Language and comprehension* (pp. 287–299). New York: North Holland.

de Dreu, C. K. W., Koole, S. L., & Oldersma, F. L. (1999). On the seizing and freezing of negotiator inferences: Need for cognitive closure moderates the use of heuristics in negotiation. *Personality and Social Psychology Bulletin, 25*(3), 348–362.

De Grada, E., Kruglanski, A. W., Mannetti, L., & Pierro, A. (1999). Motivated cognition and group interaction: Need for closure affects the contents and process of collective negotiations. *Journal of Experimental Social Psychology, 35*(4), 346–365.

Festinger, L. (1950). Informal social communication. *Psychological Review, 57*, 271–282.

Festinger, L. (1954). A theory of social comparison processes. *Human Relations, 7*, 117–140.

Heaton, A. W., & Kruglanski, A. W. (1991). Person perception by introverts and extroverts under time pressure: Effects of need for closure. *Personality and Social Psychology Bulletin, 17*, 161–165.

Hofstede, G. (1980). *Culture's consequence*. Beverly Hills, CA: Sage.

Hong, Y., Morris, M. W., Chiu, C., & Benet-Martinez, V. (2000). Multicultural minds: A dynamic constructivist approach to culture and cognition. *American Psychologist, 55*(7), 709–720.

Jost, J. T., Glaser, J., Kruglanski, A. W., & Sullaway, F. J. (in press). Political conservatism and motivated social cognition. *Psychological Bulletin.*

Jost, J. T., Kruglanski, A. W., & Simon, L. (1998). Effects of epistemic motivation on conservatism, intolerance and other system-justifying attitudes. In L. L. Thompson, D. M. Messick, & J. M. Levine (Eds.), *Shared cognition in organizations: The management of knowledge* (pp. 91–116). Mahwah, NJ: Lawrence Erlbaum Associates.

Kemmelmeier, M. (1997). Need for closure and political orientation among German university students. *Journal of Social Psychology, 137*(6), 787–789.

Korten, D. C. (1962). Situational determinants of leadership structure. *The Journal of Conflict Resolution, 6*, 222–235.

Krauss, R. M., & Fussell, S. R. (1996). Social psychological models of interpersonal communication. In E. T. Higgins, & A. W. Kruglanski (Eds.), *Social psychology: Handbook of basic principles* (pp. 655–701). New York, NY: Guilford Press.

Kruglanski, A. W. (1989). *Lay epistemics and human knowledge: Cognitive and motivational bases.* New York: Plenum.

Kruglanski, A. W. (1990). Lay epistemic theory in social cognitive psychology. *Psychological Inquiry, 1*, 181–197.

Kruglanski, A. W., Atash, M. N., DeGrada, E., Mannetti, L., Pierro, A., & Webster, D. M. (1997). Psychological theory testing versus psychometric nay saying: Need for closure scale and the Neuberg, et al. critique. *Journal of Personality and Social Psychology, 73*, 1005–1016.

Kruglanski, A. W., & Freund, T. (1983). The freezing and unfreezing of lay-inferences: Effects on impressional primacy, ethnic stereotyping, and numerical anchoring. *Journal of Experimental Social Psychology, 19*, 448–468.

Kruglanski, A. W., Shah, J. Y., Pierro, A., & Mannetti, L. (2002). When similarity breeds content: Need for closure and the allure of homogeneous and self-resembling groups. *Journal of Personality and Social Psychology, 83*(3), 648–662.

Kruglanski, A. W., & Webster, D. M. (1991). Group members' reactions to opinion deviates and conformists at varying degrees of proximity to decision deadline and of environmental noise. *Journal of Personality and Social Psychology, 61*, 212–225.

Kruglanski, A. W., & Webster, D. M. (1996). Motivated closing of the mind: "Seizing" and "freezing." *Psychological Review, 103*, 263–283.

Kruglanski, A. W., Webster, D. M., & Klem, A. (1993). Motivated resistance and openness to persuasion in the presence or absence of prior information. *Journal of Personality and Social Psychology, 65*, 861–876.

Latané, B. (1996). Dynamic social impact: The creation of culture by communication. *Journal of Communication, 46*, 13–25.

Lavine, H., & Latané, B. (1996). A cognitive-social theory of public opinion: Dynamic social impact and cognitive structure. *Journal of Communication, 46*, 48–56.

Mannetti, L., Pierro, A., Kruglanski, A. W., Taris, T., & Bezinovic, P. (2000). A cross cultural study of the need for cognitive closure scale: comparing its structure in Croatia, Italy, the USA and the Netherlands. *British Journal of Social Psychology, 47*, 719–731.

*Merriam-Webster's Collegiate Dictionary* (10th ed.). (1998). Springfield, MA: Merriam-Webster.

Miller, J. G. (1999). Cultural psychology: Implications for basic psychological theory. *Psychological Science, 10*(2), 85–91.

Neuberg, S. L., & Newsom, J. T. (1993). Personal need for structure: Individual differences in the desire for simple structure. *Journal of Personality and Social Psychology, 65*, 113–131.

Pierro, A., Mannetti, L., De Grada, E., Livi, S., & Kruglanski, A. W. (in press). Autocracy bias in informal groups under need for closure. *Personality and Social Psychology Bulletin.*

Richter, L., & Kruglanski, A. W. (1997). The accuracy of social perception and cognition: Situationally contingent and process-based. *Swiss Journal of Psychology, 56*, 62–81.

Richter, L., & Kruglanski, A. W. (1998). Seizing on the latest: Motivationally driven recency effects in impression formation. *Journal of Experimental Social Psychology, 34*, 313–329.

Richter, L., & Kruglanski, A. W. (1999). Motivated search for common ground: Need for closure effects on audience design in interpersonal communication. *Personality and Social Psychology Bulletin, 25*(9), 1101–1114.

Rosenbaum, L. L., & Rosenbaum, W. B. (1971). Morale and productivity consequences of group leadership style, stress, and type of task. *Journal of Applied Psychology, 55*, 343–348.

Rosenblatt, A., Greenberg, J., Solomon, S., Pyszczynski, T., & Lyon, D. (1989). Evidence of terror management theory: I. The effects of mortality salience on reactions to those who violate or uphold cultural values. *Journal of Personality and Social Psychology, 57*(4), 681–690.

Schachter, S. (1951). Deviation, rejection, and communication. *Journal of Abnormal and Social Psychology, 46*, 190–207.

Schaller, M., Boyd, C., Yohannes, J., & O'Brien, M. (1995). The prejudiced personality revisited: Personal need for structure and formation of erroneous group stereotypes. *Journal of Personality and Social Psychology, 68*, 544–555.

Shah, J. Y., Kruglanski, A. W., & Thompson, E. P. (1998). Membership has its (epistemic) rewards: Need for closure effects on in-group bias. *Journal of Personality and Social Psychology, 75*(2), 383–393.

Smith, P. B., & Bond, M. H. (1993). *Social psychology across cultures*. Boston: Allyn & Bacon.

Stephan, W. G., & Stephan, C. W. (1996). *Intergroup relations*. Boulder, CO: Westview Press.

Tajfel, H., Billig, M., Bundy, R. P., & Flament, C. (1971). Social categorization and intergroup behavior. *European Journal of Social Psychology, 1*, 149–178.

Tomasello, M. (2000). Culture and cognitive development. *Current Directions in Psychological Science, 9*(2), 37–40.

Triandis, H. C. (1994). *Culture and social behavior*. New York: McGraw Hill.

Triandis, H. C. (1995). *Individualism and collectivism*. Boulder, CO: Westview Press.

Tversky, A., & Kahneman, D. (1987). Rational choice and the framing of decisions. In R. M. Hogarth & M. W. Reder (Eds.), *Rational choice: The contrast between economics and psychology* (pp. 67–94). Chicago: University of Chicago Press.

Vandello, J. A., & Cohen, D. (1999). Patterns of individualism and collectivism across the United States. *Journal of Personality and Social Psychology, 77*, 279–292.

Webster, D. M. (1993). Motivated augmentation and reduction of the over-attribution bias. *Journal of Personality and Social Psychology, 65*, 261–271.

Webster, D. M., & Kruglanski, A. W. (1994). Individual differences in need for cognitive closure. *Journal of Personality and Social Psychology, 67*, 1049–1062.

Webster, D. M., & Kruglanski, A. W. (1998). Cognitive and social consequences of the need for cognitive closure. *European Review of Social Psychology, 8*, 133–174.

Webster, D. M., Richter, L., & Kruglanski, A. W. (1996). On leaping to conclusions when feeling tired: Mental fatigue effects on impressional primacy. *Journal of Experimental Social Psychology, 32*, 181–195.

*Webster's New International Dictionary* (2nd ed.). (1958). Springfield, MA: G&C Merriam.

# PART II

# HOW SPECIFIC CULTURAL NORMS ARISE

CHAPTER

# 6

# Biological Foundations of Moral Norms

Dennis Krebs
Maria Janicki
Simon Fraser University

All people acquire beliefs about how they should and should not behave. When such beliefs are adopted by most members of a culture, they constitute moral norms. How do moral norms originate and spread? Why do people preach them and behave in accordance with them? Why are some moral norms universal, and others relative to particular cultures? In this chapter we argue that to answer such questions, we must attend to the biological foundations of the mental mechanisms that give rise to moral norms and other aspects of culture.

## COMMON CONCEPTIONS OF BIOLOGICAL AND CULTURAL FOUNDATIONS OF MORALITY

If you ask laypeople where they get their morals, they will give you such answers as: "Morals are taught to us at a young age by our parents directly and by society indirectly." "Morals are passed on to us via overt direction (e.g., be kind to others) and less overt means, such as imitation." "People learn morals from social custom and conformity to group norms." If you ask laypeople what role inherited dispositions play in the acquisition of morality, they will probably answer, "little or none." Indeed, most laypeople believe that to become moral, people must be taught to resist the temptations of the flesh, to oppose their animal instincts, and to suppress or sublimate their natural urges.

Laypeople who harbor such "original sin" conceptions of human nature are in good company. Consider the conclusions reached by the following eminent evolutionary theorists:

> The behavioral dispositions that produce complex social interdependence and self-sacrificial altruism must ... be products of culturally evolved indoctrination that has had to counter self-serving genetic tendencies.... The commandments, the proverbs, the religious "law" [i.e., moral norms] represent social evolutionary products directed at inculcating tendencies that are in direct opposition to the "temptations" representing, for the most part, the dispositional tendencies produced by biological evolution. (Campbell, 1978, pp. 52–53)

> Be warned that if you wish, as I do, to build a society in which individuals cooperate generously and unselfishly toward a common good, you can expect little help from biological nature. Let us try to teach generosity and altruism, because we are born selfish. (Dawkins, 1989, p. 3)

### An Evaluation of Cultural Indoctrination–Social Learning Models of Moralization

It would be foolish to deny that cultural indoctrination and social learning play important roles in the acquisition of morality. We teach children to behave in accordance with the moral norms of their cultures, and children copy the moral behaviors of adults. However, in their traditional forms, cultural indoctrination and social learning models of moralization fail to explain (a) where the moral norms of cultures came from in the first place, or how they originated, (b) how people decide what norms to preach and what behaviors to sanction, (c) why people conform to some moral norms and deviate from others, and (d) why some norms are universal, whereas others are unique to particular cultures.

Implicit in original sin–cultural indoctrination models of moralization is the idea that biology and culture, or nature and nurture, constitute separate and independent sources of behavior, each opposing the other. We should know by now that such nature–nurture dichotomies are misguided. Cultural indoctrination and social learning are mediated by mechanisms in our brains, and our brains are evolved structures that are shaped by environmental experiences. To understand how the mechanisms that produced moral norms operate, we need to understand the adaptive functions such mechanisms performed in ancestral environments (Crawford, 2000).

## THE EVOLUTION OF MORALITY

Because moral norms pertain largely to the ways in which people should and should not treat one another, we would expect that when the mechanisms that give rise to moral norms are designed to solve adaptive problems, these problems will be social in nature. The biological reason why species acquire the adaptations necessary for sociality is that aggregating and living in groups foster their fitness (that is to say, chances of surviving, reproducing, and propagating their genes) better than living alone. Benefits of sociality may include enhanced defense against predators (including hostile members of one's own species), enhanced ability to acquire food and other resources (e.g., through group hunting and trading), and enhanced ability to mate. Significant among the potential costs of sociality are increased competition for resources. Humans are among the most social of all animals. A spate of evidence suggests that adaptations that enabled our hominid ancestors to foster their fitness in cooperative ways played a pivotal role in the evolution of the human species (e.g., Leakey & Lewin, 1977; Tooby & Devore, 1987).

Reaping the benefits of sociality and cooperation gives rise to an inevitable dilemma, which the philosopher John Rawls (1971) describes well in the opening pages of his book *Theory of Justice*:

> Although a society is a cooperative venture for mutual advantage, it is typically marked by a conflict as well as by an identity of interests. There is an identity of interests since social cooperation makes possible a better life for all than any would have if each were to live solely by his own efforts. There is a conflict of interests since persons are not indifferent as to how the greater benefits produced by their collaboration are distributed, for in order to pursue their ends, they each prefer a larger to a lesser share. (pp. 4)

Evolutionary theory leads us to expect members of groups to be evolved to try to induce other members of their groups to behave in ways that helped their hominid ancestors propagate their genes. One way of achieving this goal is for members of groups to reward others when others behave in ways that benefit them biologically, and to punish others when others behave in ways that reduce their chances of surviving and reproducing. Another way is for members of groups to persuade others to behave in ways that advance their (the persuaders') interests.

## The Adaptive Functions of Administering Sanctions and Making Moral Judgments

When theorists who advance cultural indoctrination models of morality assert that culture or teaching is the source of morality, they are defining culture primarily in terms of the moral judgments members of cultures preach and the moral sanctions they administer. Socializing agents teach children to conform to the moral norms of their culture by giving them moral instruction, by rewarding them when they are good, and by punishing them when they are bad. Adults induce members of their societies to conform to moral norms by indoctrinating them and by administering sanctions such as ostracism, fines, and incarceration. The difference between cultural indoctrination models and evolutionary models is that evolutionary models do not cast those who preach morality and administer sanctions as motivated to moralize recipients for the sake of morality. Evolutionary models view the moral judgments people preach to each other as outputs from evolved mechanisms designed to induce recipients to behave in ways that advanced the biological interests of senders in ancestral environments.

When people preach moral judgments to others, they are engaging in a form of communication. Biological analyses of communication in nonhuman species have revealed that most of the signals animals send to each other are manipulative, and many are deceptive (Dawkins, 1989; Mitchell & Thompson, 1986). Humans' large brains and resultant ability to plan, simulate events mentally, and take others' perspectives (referred to as "mind reading" by some psychologists) expand immensely their capacity to manipulate and to deceive others, as does their capacity for language. From a biological perspective, the function of moral judgments (and other aspects of culture) is to induce recipients to behave in ways that foster the interests of senders (cf. Cronk, 1995; Flinn, 1997).

There are two types of moral judgment, which philosophers have labeled *aretaic* and *deontic*. Aretaic moral judgments characterize people or acts as good or bad. We imagine that the precursor to the first moral judgment made in the human species was some paralingual signal communicating disapproval of a selfish or harmful act, or approval of an altruistic or cooperative act. Darwin (1871) believed that "love of praise and dread of blame" played key roles in the evolution of morality in the human species. From a biological perspective, aretaic moral judgments constitute social sanctions designed to control the behavior of those who are being judged.

Deontic moral judgments prescribe that people should or should not behave in particular ways. People usually buttress deontic moral judgments with reasons: "you should behave morally because. . . ." Many of the reasons people invoke to support moral norms involve explicit or implicit promises of reward or threats of punishment. Viewed biologically, such reasons constitute arguments designed to persuade recipients to behave in accordance with the prescriptions they are invoked to support.

### The Adaptive Functions of Conforming to Moral Norms and Copying the Normative Behaviors of Others

It is easy to understand why self-interested senders would preach moral norms and administer sanctions to those who uphold and violate them, but why would self-interested recipients conform to moral norms? Evolutionary theory leads us to expect an answer such as, because the mechanisms that mediate such conformity enhanced their fitness. The fitness-enhancing benefits of a mechanism containing a decision rule such as, "repeat behaviors that were followed by rewards (delivered by others) and stifle behaviors that were followed by punishment"—that is to say, a mechanism designed in terms of the principle of reinforcement—are obvious. A potentially more adaptive decision rule is, "anticipate the consequences of your acts and emit the acts with the greatest potential to advance your interests." Two important sources of information about potential consequences are (a) promises of reward and threats of punishment, and (b) perception of the consequences of acts performed by others. Social learning mechanisms such as vicarious learning, modeling, and conformity enable individuals to avoid the costs of trial and error learning. As Bandura (1986) stated, "Because people can learn approximately what to do through modeling before they perform any behavior, they are spared the costs and pain of faulty effort. The capacity to learn by observation enables people to expand their knowledge and skills on the basis of information exhibited and authored by others" (p. 47). (See Boyd and Richerson, 1995, for mathematical models comparing the fitness enhancing effects of individual learning and social learning.)

Evolutionary theorists have characterized social learning mechanisms as "a kind of special purpose adaptation constructed to selectively acquire information and behavior by observing other humans and inferring the mental states that give rise to their behavior" (Henrich & Boyd, 1998, p. 217). The question is, how is this adaptation designed? Some theorists believe that evolved mechanisms that mediate modeling and conformity are relatively undiscriminating. For example, Simon (1990) argued that a trait he calls *docility*, defined as the disposition to learn what others teach you and to believe what others want you to believe, evolved in the human species through the enormous fitness benefits it conferred on those who inherited it. Simon (1990) noted that the complexity of the world and the boundedness of human rationality prohibit people from independently evaluating every fact or suggestion they encounter. He suggested that people can be induced to behave altruistically because the costs of conforming to altruism-inducing words and deeds are outweighed by the "advantageous knowledge and skills acquired through docility" (p. 1667). Thus, according to Simon (1990), social learning-cultural indoctrination mechanisms are designed in ways that induce people quite indiscriminately to conform to the words, and to copy the deeds, of others.

Other evolutionary theorists believe social learning mechanisms are designed in significantly more discriminating ways than described by Simon (1990). For example, the biologists Flinn and Alexander (1982) suggested that evolved social learning mechanisms are guided by the following decision rules: "imitate those who appear successful" and "behave oppositely to those who don't"; "accept advice and instruction from those with an interest in one's success" and "view skeptically advice and instruction from those with conflicting interests with regard to the topic being instructed." Boyd and Richerson (1985) suggested that social learning mechanisms are affected by three "biases," which they have labeled indirect biases, direct biases, and frequency-dependent biases. Indirect biases are similar to the decision rules described by Flinn and Alexander. They induce people to copy the words and deeds of people who seem fit, are admired, respected, of high status, wise, and so on. Direct biases induce people to evaluate (consciously or unconsciously) the alternative beliefs or behaviors that are available, and to select those that they believe will best foster their fitness. The criteria used to evaluate alternative beliefs or behaviors may be genetically inherited, learned from one's own experience, or learned from others (Boyd & Richerson, 1985). Frequency-dependent biases induce people to copy the words and deeds that are most frequent in the population.

Empirical evidence supports the idea that social learning mechanisms are biased in the sorts of ways hypothesized by evolutionary theorists. Studies have found that the probability of modeling is affected by factors such as the similarity between the model and observer, the status of the model, the nurturance of the model, the extent to which the model controls resources, vicarious learning, and rewards and punishments (Burton & Kunce, 1995, pp. 151–152). Evolutionary theory supplies a framework for interpreting such piecemeal, empirically derived findings.

### Implications for the Evolution of Moral Norms

The idea that moral norms evolve through an interaction between the moral judgments, examples, and sanctions transmitted by senders who are evolved to advance their biological interests and the reactions of recipients who are evolved to advance their biological interests has several implications. First, people should attempt to invoke the moral norms with the greatest potential to benefit them, and there is evidence they do. Many investigators have found that people interpret moral norms in ways that foster their interests (Bandura, 1991; Batson et al., 1999; Krebs & Laird, 1998). As examples, Damon (1977) found that children faced with the task of distributing a resource such as an extra piece of pizza tended to invoke norms that favored their interests, and Leventhal and Anderson (1970) found that adults who contributed the most to tasks tended to invoke norms of equity that justified dividing resources in their favor.

Second, if people transmit moral norms to influence others, they should tailor the norms in ways that enhance their persuasive impact. As an example, we would expect senders to tailor moral norms to the cognitive sophistication and values of recipients, and the evidence suggests they do (e.g., see Carpendale & Krebs, 1992). Although we would expect senders to exhort recipients to perform more altruistic and self-sacrificial acts than recipients are inclined to perform, as original sin–cultural indoctrination models of morality imply, we would not expect exhortations such as "you should always sacrifice your interests for me" to have much persuasive impact. Inasmuch as the reactions of recipients determine whether transmitted judgments pay off for those who send them, recipients become agents of selection, in effect selecting the moral judgments that evolve. The inevitable result of the interaction between the vested interests of senders and the vested interests of receivers are moral norms that implicitly or explicitly preach: "We should foster our interests in ways that foster the interests of others, or at least do not harm them" and "we should behave in ways that foster our mutual interests." Do unto others as you would have them do unto you.

Third, we would not expect recipients to conform passively to the moral norms preached by others when the norms in question do not advance their interests. When people's interests differ, we would expect arguments and negotiations to occur, with each partner modifying his or her position in an attempt to find mutually beneficial common ground. This is exactly what we found in our research on moral conflicts experienced by couples in their everyday lives (Krebs et al., 2002). Note that philosophers such as Habermas (1984) believe that the best way to make truly moral decisions is through such negotiation and debate.

Finally, if moral norms are tools designed to solve the adaptive problems that arise when self-interested individuals seek to maximize their gains in social exchanges, we would expect the moral norms that people preach and practice to vary in accordance with the type of relationship they have with recipients and the accompanying confluences and conflicts of interest. We are not surprised by evidence that children adopt different norms in relations with adults than they do in relations with peers, as many developmental psychologists have found (see Krebs & Van Hesteren, 1994, for a review). We also are not surprised that social psychologists have found that adults tend to invoke more individualistically self-serving norms in relations with strangers than in relations with friends (Greenberg, 1978), that friends tend to invoke norms of equality (Austin, 1980), and that marital partners tend to invoke norms upholding mutual gratification of needs (Greenberg & Cohen, 1982). Clark, Mills, and Powell (1986) have distinguished between "exchange relationships," in which people invoke equity norms that enable them to balance their costs and benefits, and more intimate "communal relationships," in which people invoke more altruistic and needs-based norms. Social psychologists have attributed differences in the norms people invoke to variations in the "outcome interdependencies" (i.e., conflicts and confluences of interest) of the types of relationship in question. Like social psychological analyses, our analysis of the evolution of moral norms implies significantly more situational variation in the moral norms people invoke than expected in psychological theories such as those espoused by cognitive-developmental theorists, and the evidence supports this expectation (for reviews see Krebs & Denton, 1999; Krebs, Denton, Vermeulen, Carpendale, & Bush, 1991; Krebs, Denton, & Wark, 1997; Krebs, Vermeulen, Carpendale, & Denton, 1991).

Note that on our analysis there are no clear boundaries between biological and cultural determinants of moral norms. Biology (evolved mechanisms) shapes culture (moral norms). Culture originates in the evolved minds (biology) of people. Evolved mechanisms induce those who invent culture to transmit it to others. Evolved mechanisms in recipients determine whether they copy it and transmit it to others. Once generated, culture may shape evolved mechanisms. As examples, moral norms that constrain reproduction, prescribe ostracism, and uphold capital punishment may become agents of natural selection. Boyd and Richerson (1992) demonstrated that virtually any norm can evolve if members of groups punish those who fail to conform to it as well as those who fail to punish the nonconformists.

## HOW FIVE UNIVERSAL MORAL NORMS EVOLVED

If, as we have argued, humans are naturally inclined to conform to moral norms that enhanced the fitness of their hominid ancestors, it follows that, contrary to original sin models of human nature, we believe humans may be naturally inclined to behave in moral ways, and thus to be good by nature. Indeed, we believe such natural inclinations shaped several universal moral norms. It follows that we do not believe there is any necessary inconsistency between behaving morally and pursuing one's biological interests. That people are naturally inclined to foster their prospects of surviving, reproducing, and propagating their genes does not necessarily imply that they are born bad. Morality pertains to the *ways* in which people pursue these goals. On our analysis, it is moral to pursue one's biological interests in ways that are beneficial to others—that is to say, in mutually-beneficial ways—and immoral to pursue one's biological interests in ways that are destructive to others.

We turn now to a more detailed discussion of the evolution of behavioral dispositions that underlie five universal moral norms—norms that prescribe obedience to authority, reciprocity, care, social responsibility, and solidarity (Boehm, 2000; Brown, 1991; Colby & Kohlberg, 1987; Darwin, 1871; Gouldner, 1960; Snarey, 1985; Sober & Wilson, 1998; Wright, 1994). Each norm pertains to a different type of social relationship and is invoked for different reasons. Norms upholding obedience pertain to hierarchical relationships and are invoked to avoid punishment. Norms of reciprocity pertain to egalitarian exchange relations among peers and are invoked to foster gains in trade. Norms prescribing care and altruism pertain to communal, affectionate bonds among friends and relatives and are invoked to foster long-term fitness-enhancing relationships. Norms of social responsibility and solidarity pertain to relations between individuals and their groups and are invoked to uphold fitness-enhancing systems of cooperation. We next explain how upholding each of these norms could have helped our ancestors propagate their genes in mutually-beneficial ways.

For the sake of this discussion, assume the following: (a) Behaviors that conform to or are consistent with moral norms are the products of evolved decision-making rules, or genetically based behavioral strategies, (b) a variety of such strategies existed in ancestral populations, (c) these strategies competed against one another and against immoral strategies, and (d) each strategy produced replicas of itself in proportion to its competitive success. The genes that fostered winning strategies increased in frequency, and the genes that fostered losing strategies decreased in frequency until they went extinct. We explain how the strategies implicit in the five moral norms we consider could have won such evolutionary contests. In particular, we explain how they could have defeated the selfish strategies that original sin theorists believe reigned supreme.

It is important to note that it is the relative success of different strategies in particular populations that guides evolution. Although variants that win such evolutionary contests may be considered the best of those against which they have competed, they need not be the most optimal or the best imaginable. As we explain, moral behavioral strategies that would maximize benefits to every member of a group if adopted by all members of a group may nonetheless be defeated by more selfish strategies that enhance the relative fitness of particular members. Ironically, as selfish strategies increase in frequency, they may lower the absolute fitness of all members of a group. Note also that the adaptive consequences of specific acts—that is to say, their effects on biological fitness—are less important than the cumulative or net consequences of the strategy, disposition, or mechanism that gives rise to the acts over the lifetime of the actor. No strategy is successful all the time.

When people think of genetically based behavioral strategies, they tend to assume a higher degree of genetic determinism than we want to imply. Genes provide instructions for building proteins that create physical structures that house mental mechanisms. Genes do not control behavior directly; they are not puppet masters, pulling our strings. They influence behavior indirectly, by "programming" mental mechanisms with decision rules or strategies that on balance gave rise to behaviors that enhanced the biological fitness of those who inherited them. Such behaviors are not controlled by the genes themselves; they are mediated by an interaction between stimuli from the environment and the mental mechanisms built by genes.

It is important to acknowledge the important role the environment plays in the creation, design, and operation of evolved mechanisms. First, the environment supplies the raw materials for building mental structures. Second, inputs from the environment may supply triggers that turn mechanism-creating or mechanism-transforming genes on and off at various points during the life cycle of animals. Third, environmental stimuli may shape evolved mechanisms to respond to particular types of information and to ignore others. Fourth, environmental experiences early in life may calibrate or program the decision-making rules in psychological mechanisms, which may induce individuals who inherit the same genes but grown up in different environments to invoke different behavioral strategies. Finally, environmental stimuli active evolved mechanisms and supply information that guides the decisions they produce. For these and other reasons, Crawford and Anderson (1989) characterized evolutionary psychology as an "environmentalist discipline."

## Obedience Norms

Universal moral norms prescribing obedience to authority are reflected in exhortations to honor one's parents, supplicate oneself before gods, listen to one's elders, and obey the orders of one's leaders. We believe that dispositions to obey authority stem from evolved predispositions to defer to more powerful members of one's group.

In the conflicts of interest that inevitably occur between members of groups, the adaptiveness of the strategy one adopts will be contingent on one's relative power. Relatively powerless members of groups face a Hobson's choice: Either defer to those who are more dominant than they are, or get beaten up or killed by them. We would expect deferential strategies to evolve when they contributed more to an individual's biological fitness than more aggressive or blindly selfish strategies. When the prospects of future benefits for subordinates are sufficiently promising, deferring to more dominant members in the present will often be their most adaptive strategy. Deference enables subordinates to avoid the costs of fighting a losing battle, enabling them to make the best of a bad situation and to live to fight another day.

The social relations of many species are organized in dominance hierarchies or pecking orders. Members of groups determine in low-cost ways who is more powerful than whom, and accommodate to the resulting status. In such species, the costs of deference to more dominant members of groups may be compensated by the gains of dominating those who are lower in the pecking order. Deferential strategies have evolved in many nonhuman species (Alcock, 1998). With respect to moral norms, we would expect dominant members of groups to preach obedience norms to weaker members, and we would expect weaker members to accommodate behaviorally, believing it is right, and in their interest, to do so. See Boehm (2000), Krebs (1998, 2000b), and Sloman and Gilbert (2000) for more extended discussions of the adaptive value of deference.

***Ontogenetic Implications.*** In Piaget's (1932) pioneering research on moral development, he found that young children view morality primarily in terms of obedience to authority. Piaget labeled the moral orientation of young children "the morality of constraint." The cognitive-developmental psychologist Kohlberg (1984) also found that young children define morality in terms of "avoidance of punishment and the superior power of authorities" (p. 18). From our perspective, the reason why young children espouse and conform to norms prescribing obedience to authority is because young children are among the weakest and most vulnerable members of groups. Deference to adults is their most adaptive strategy.

Cognitive-developmental psychologists such as Piaget and Kohlberg also have found that as children grow older and interact more frequently with peers, they change their moral orientation from the morality of constraint to a more egalitarian "morality of cooperation" and "instrumental exchange" in which they uphold norms of reciprocity.

## Norms of Reciprocity

The adaptive potential in upholding norms of reciprocity is easy to see. As explained by Piaget (1932), reciprocity enables peers to resolve conflicts of interest in mutually beneficial ways, such as taking turns. Members of all social species inevitably need help from each other and want things others possess. Through gains in trade, individuals who adopt cooperative strategies that induce them to reciprocate resources and assistance may well do better than individuals who treat each other selfishly. This does not, however, guarantee the evolution of reciprocity. Although two reciprocating individuals may acquire more resources than two selfish individuals, a selfish individual interacting with a reciprocator may come out ahead by taking without giving in return. To evolve, cooperative strategies must contain antidotes to exploitation by selfish strategies (Cosmides, 1989).

One cooperative strategy that contains a built-in antidote to selfish exploitation is called tit for tat. It is based on the decision rule, "make a cooperative overture, then copy the response of your partner in subsequent interactions." In computer simulations of natural selection, Axelrod and Hamilton (1981) found that the tit-for-tat strategy could defeat more selfish strategies—that is to say, replicate at a faster rate—if it "invaded" populations in clusters (thus enabling the strategy to reap the benefits of interacting with itself). Tit for tat is a powerful strategy because it opens the door to a string of mutually beneficial exchanges with cooperative partners in its first move, but quickly cuts its losses against selfish partners on subsequent moves. Trivers (1971, 1985) and Dugatkin (1997) reviewed evidence that tit-for-tat strategies have evolved in nonhuman animals. There is a spate of evidence that norms of reciprocity have evolved in all human cultures (Gouldner, 1960; Wright, 1994).

***Ontogenetic Implications.*** Piaget (1932) attributed the change in children's moral orientation from obedience to cooperation to changes in their social relations—from relations with adults to peer relations. Kohlberg (1984) asserted that when children begin believing in norms of reciprocity, they stop believing in norms of obedience. From a biological perspective, we are not surprised that research has failed to support this assertion (see Krebs & Van Hesteren, 1994, for a review of relevant research). We would expect people to retain the beliefs and behavioral strategies they acquire early in life when such beliefs and strategies are biologically useful later in life. For this reason, we are not surprised to find adults preaching obedience to authority when they are in positions of power, and conforming to exhortations to obey authority when they are in subordinate positions, as they did in Milgram's (1974) classic experiments (Newitt & Krebs, in preparation). We also are not surprised that adults such as the Hatfields and McCoys and social groups such as the Protestants and Catholics in Ireland get into childish and self-defeating tit-for-tat type blood feuds. We would expect people to be naturally disposed to invoke and to conform to the moral norms with the greatest promise of fostering their fitness in the contexts in question. Thus, we would expect far more situational variation in moral norms espoused and practiced than cognitive-developmental theorists assume (see Krebs, Denton, Vermeulen, Carpendale, & Bush, 1991; Krebs et al., 1997; and Krebs, Vermeulen, Carpendale, & Denton, 1991, for elaborations of this expectation and evidence supporting it).

### Care-Based and Altruistic Moral Norms

***Caring for Friends.*** As children grow older, they begin to form enduring friendships. Tooby and Cosmides (1996) have pointed out that exchanges between friends are not usually based in the sorts of tit-for-tat decision rules invoked by young children and adults toward strangers. Friends do not expect to be paid back for each and every perk they bestow on each other. Cognitive-developmental theorists have found that, unlike young children who view morality in terms of reciprocal exchanges, teenagers and adults believe that people should help their friends and relatives when they are in need. We believe norms prescribing care and altruism toward friends and relatives are universal. In explaining how behavioral strategies upholding such norms could evolve, Tooby and Cosmides (1996) allude to a phenomenon called the bankers' paradox: Banks are least likely to lend you money when you need it the most. To resolve adaptive versions of the bankers' paradox, individuals invest in friends whom they expect to be there for them when they are in need. In this sense, upholding friendships is like buying an insurance policy. In a similar vein, Nesse (1999) and Frank (1988) have suggested that close relationships are based in emotional commitments rather than in tit-for-tat type strategies. Although commitments to friends may seem counter to selfish interests in the short term, Nesse (1999) argues that they pay off better than more selfish strategies in the end.

***Caring for Mates.*** People from all cultures also believe that mates are morally obliged to care for each other. Evolutionary theory has no difficulty explaining the selection of normative strategies that induce individuals to care for their mates. Inasmuch as members of the opposite sex are able to select their mates, they would be expected to select mates who are naturally inclined to care for them and their kin. Thus, strategies that induce individuals to care for their mates could evolve through sexual selection (see Krebs, 1998, for an elaboration of this process).

***Caring for Kin.*** In the final tally, mating counts little in evolution if the offspring from sexual unions fail to survive and to reproduce. No one is surprised by evidence from the animal kingdom of parents sacrificing their individual interests for the sake of their offspring, because such self-sacrificial behaviors help parents propagate their genes. In a classic paper, Hamilton (1964) pointed out that the biological value of parental investment can be extended to relatives other than offspring. The probability of individuals sharing genes varies in proportion to their degree of relatedness: 50% for parents and offspring; 50% for full siblings; 25% for cousins, and so on. Hamilton (1964) explained how a decision rule could evolve that induces individuals to help others when the coefficient of their relationship is greater than the cost to the helper of helping, divided by the benefits to the recipient ($r > c/b$). Given the genetic benefits of helping relatives, we would expect individuals to be biologically predisposed to discriminately help kin over non-kin, and for such dispositions to be reflected the moral norms of all cultures.

### Norms of Social Responsibility

Tit-for-tat forms of reciprocity pertain to direct, dyadic exchanges. It is easy to see that benefits to members of groups could be increased through the gains in trade made possible by more indirect forms of reciprocity. For example, if all members of a group helped those they were most qualified to help, or if they gave resources they needed the least to those who needed them the most, every single member of the group could come out ahead. To achieve such benefits, members of groups could take on tasks they were especially skilled at accomplishing, giving rise to divisions of labor in which people took on the roles they were best equipped to perform.

There are, however, two obstacles to the evolution of strategies that dispose individuals to fulfill their social responsibilities in ways that enable everyone in their group to maximize their gains through indirect reciprocity. First, it is more difficult to catch those who fail to fulfill their responsibilities than it is to catch those who cheat on more direct exchanges. Second, members of groups have less incentive to punish those who fail to fulfill their social responsibilities than they do to punish those who exploit them directly. To evolve, socially responsible strategies must contain mechanisms designed to catch and to punish cheaters (Axelrod, 1984; Boyd & Richerson, 1992; Cosmides, 1989). The evolutionary biologist Alexander (1987) hypothesized that systems of indirect reciprocity could evolve if members of groups (a) shared information about the selfish and altruistic behaviors of others through gossip and other means, (b) favored those who behaved altruistically, and (c) discriminated against those who behaved selfishly. In recent game theory research, Nowak and Sigmund (1998) supported Alexander's hypotheses. Nowak and Sigmund (1998) created a computer simulation of evolution in which behaving altruistically (that is to say, in socially responsible, cooperative ways) enhanced an individual's reputation or "image," and behaving selfishly degraded it. These investigators found that if socially responsible members of groups favored those with a good reputation, socially responsible strategies could evolve, become evolutionarily stable, and support systems of indirect reciprocity.

***The Problem of Appearance.*** We believe Nowak and Sigmund's (1998) model is limited in at least one important respect. When these game theorists set the parameters for their evolutionary contests, they programmed the images that observers formed of members of their groups to be valid. However, if being viewed as socially responsible and altruistic pays off, it would be in people's interest to fool others into believing they are more socially responsible and altruistic than they actually were. Instead of actually fulfilling their social obligations or actually sacrificing their needs for others, they could act like they were behaving in socially responsible and altruistic ways. If such impression-management strategies enabled people to reap the rewards of indirect reciprocity without paying the price, they could destroy the system of cooperation upon which they preyed. To evolve, all strategies must contain antidotes to strategies designed to exploit them.

A spate of evidence supports the idea that we humans inherit mechanisms designed to manage the impressions we make on those in positions to affect our welfare (Jones, 1990; Leary, 1995). We are all actors at heart, as Goffman (1958) so eloquently described in his classic, *The Presentation of Self in Everyday Life*. Fortunately, however, there are constraints on the evolution of impression-management strategies. First, it is difficult, or impossible, to act in socially responsible ways without behaving in socially responsible ways, in public, at least. Second, false impressions constitute adaptive problems for the recipients they are designed to manipulate. Inasmuch as being fooled is maladaptive, mechanisms designed to resist being fooled should evolve. Thus, we would expect a sort of arms race in which actors acquire mechanisms that induce them to present themselves as more moral than they really are, observers acquire mechanisms to detect such deceptions, and so on. See Alexander (1987), Cosmides and Tooby (1992), Krebs (1998, 2000a, 2000c), and Trivers (1985) for an elaboration of this process.

## Norms of Solidarity and Patriotism

All cultures contain moral norms that exhort individuals to sacrifice their immediate interests for the sake of their groups. One way in which dispositions that gave rise to such norms could have evolved is through the biological benefits of indirect reciprocity, as we have explained. In addition, such dispositions may have evolved through a controversial process called group selection. In *The Descent of Man*, Darwin (1871) considered this possibility, writing:

> A tribe including many members who, from possessing in a high degree the spirit of patriotism, fidelity, obedience, courage, and sympathy, were always ready to aid one another, and to sacrifice themselves for the common good, would be victorious over most other tribes; and this would be natural selection. At all times throughout the world tribes have supplanted other tribes; and as morality is one important element in their success, the standard of morality and the number of well-endowed men will thus everywhere tend to rise and increase. (p. 500)

The idea underlying group selection is that the benefits that altruistic individuals bestow on others who possess replicas of their "altruistic genes" may enable such strategies to evolve. In effect, the altruistic strategies help themselves by helping others who possess replicas of them. Note that the process of group selection is similar to the process of kin selection because both processes are based in the biological benefits individuals accrue when they help others who share the genes (that is to say, the strategies) disposing them to help. Because the strategy of helping all members of one's group is less discriminatory and less nepotistic than the strategy of helping one's kin, it more moral, but less likely to evolve.

The evolutionary obstacle to strategies that dispose individuals indiscriminately to help members of their group is, of course, that selfish members of the group (i.e., those who reap the benefits bestowed by the altruists without suffering the costs of behaving altruistically) fare better than the altruistic members. As put by Darwin (1871):

> It is extremely doubtful whether the offspring of the more sympathetic and benevolent parents, or of those who were the most faithful to their comrades, would be reared in greater numbers than the children of selfish and treacherous parents belonging to the same tribe . . . [i.e., within the group]. Therefore it hardly seems probable that the number of men gifted with such virtues . . . could be increased through natural selection. (p. 500)

Sober and Wilson (1998) have suggested that group-upholding strategies (thus norms) could evolve through group selection, but they acknowledge that such strategies could evolve only in special conditions, such as when the frequency of altruists varies across groups, altruistic groups fare better than selfish groups, and the altruistic and selfish groups eventually mix in the population. Could this have happened in the evolutionary history of our species through, perhaps, tribal wars? There is a spate of psychological evidence that humans quickly and deeply identify with groups to which they are even arbitrarily assigned, and favor the members of their in-groups over the members of out-groups (see Hornstein, 1978; Krebs & Denton, 1997; Tajfel, 1982; and Tajfel & Turner, 1985, for reviews of supporting research). Whether such dispositions and strategies evolved through group selection or though some other mechanism, such as the benefits of indirect reciprocity, remains to be determined.

## Reconceptualizing Kohlberg's Theory of Moral Development

Readers familiar with Kohlberg's (1984) theory of moral development may have noticed a parallel between the universal moral norms we been discussing and the types of behavior prescribed at each of Kohlberg's stages of moral development. This is no coincidence. We believe the moral judgments that define Kohlberg's stages of moral development uphold the evolved strategies we have been considering. In contrast to Kohlberg, however, we believe the reason why people of different ages tend to uphold different strategies is because they tend to face different kinds of adaptive problem.

### Implications and Qualifications

We have argued that the decision rules implicit in the behaviors upholding the five moral norms we have considered could well have constituted winning strategies in ancestral environments. As such, they could have evolved to become normative in the human species. We believe such norms have, in fact, evolved, and that they are culturally universal. If humans are naturally inclined to behave in moral ways, cultural norms prescribing moral behaviors would support, rather than oppose, evolved dispositions. From a biological perspective, beliefs such as "it is right to obey authority" and "people are morally obligated to help their friends" are functionally similar to beliefs such as it is right to foster your safety and security. People harbor moral beliefs because believing in the strategies or forms of conduct prescribed by such beliefs paid off better than believing in other strategies or forms of conduct. Viewed in this way, the pragmatic connotations of words such as "should" and "ought" make sense. When people say things like, "you should be loyal to your friends," they imply both that it is morally correct and that it will pay off in the end.

It is important to recognize that we are not saying that people are genetically programmed to emit the strategies implicit in moral norms as fixed action patterns. Moral strategies are based in decision rules that are contingent on executive mechanisms and a complex array of environmental cues. In effect, people decide which of the many strategies available to them will work best in the situations they encounter. As examples, we would expect decisions about deferring to and obeying authority to be contingent on estimates of the power of the authorities, the value of the resources in question, and the probability of reaping rewards and avoiding punishments. Decisions about upholding one's end of reciprocal exchanges should be guided by such factors as the relative costs of giving and receiving and the probability of future exchanges (Axelrod, 1984). Relationship-upholding strategies should be sensitive to factors such as the extent to which people anticipate needing help in the future, the number of alternative relationships available to them, the anticipated costs and benefits of cheating, and so on (Tooby & Cosmides, 1992).

## UNIVERSAL AND CULTURALLY RELATIVE MORAL NORMS

We have been focusing on universal moral norms that we believe have evolved in all cultures. Tooby and Cosmides (1992) labeled universal aspects of culture *metaculture*. They suggested that metaculture evolved through an interaction between the evolved mechanisms possessed by our hominid ancestors and the regularities in the social and physical environments of human societies that existed during the Pleistocene. We know, however, that cultures may differ significantly in the particular moral norms they adopt.

Tooby and Cosmides (1992) attributed some cross-cultural variations in norms to what they call *evoked culture*. Different norms evolve in different cultures because different environmental inputs impinge on the same evolved mental mechanisms of their members. Consider food sharing, for example. Anthropologists have found that moral norms upholding cooperative food sharing tend to evolve in hunter-gatherer societies in which the probability of success on a hunt is variable, but not in societies in which the probability of each individual obtaining food by gathering is more consistent (see Cosmides & Tooby, 1992). As another example, differences in cultural norms about which foods are edible may result from differences in the ecological conditions affecting food quality, variability, and availability. Henrich and Boyd (1998) suggested that mechanisms of conformist transmission (a frequency-dependent bias discussed earlier) may play an important role in maintaining cultural differences between groups.

## THE EVOLUTION OF NONADAPTIVE AND MALADAPTIVE MORAL NORMS

To this point, our analysis of the biological foundations of moral norms has been highly adaptationist. We have traveled a considerable distance on the back of the assumption that the psychological mechanisms that give rise to moral norms evolved because they fostered the fitness of our ancestors. It is now time to acknowledge that is also is possible for nonadaptive and maladaptive norms to evolve.

Let us first consider the radical position advanced by Dawkins (1989). Dawkins (1989) suggested that genes have built machines (i.e., brains) that have freed themselves from their creators, much the way computers, once programmed, may acquire the ability to think for themselves. In contrast to genes, the units of biological evolution, Dawkins termed the units of cultural evolution *memes*. Examples of memes are ideas, songs, stories, inventions, fashions, and norms. Dawkins suggested that memes compete against each other for space in people's minds. Some are selected, transmitted to other minds, increase in frequency, and evolve; others are rejected and go extinct. In contrast to biological evolution, which progresses at a glacially slow pace, cultural evolution may occur with great rapidity, as manifest in the growth of slang terms and changes in fashion. Dawkins believed that cultural evolution has become uncoupled from biological evolution; thus, it is a waste of time to search for the fitness-enhancing sources or effects of cultural memes.

Although Dawkins's point may be valid with respect to fads and fashions such as hula hoops, baseball caps worn backward, and culturally specific moral norms that bear little relation to the fitness of those who adopt them, we do not believe it pertains to the types of universal moral norm we have been considering. To quote Buss (1999):

> Because "information" emanating from other individuals in one's social group is limitless, a potentially infinite array of ideas compete for the limited attention span of humans. Evolved psychological mechanisms in the receivers must sift through this barrage of ideas, selecting only a small subset for psychological reconstruction. The subset that is selectively adopted and internally reconstructed in individuals depends on a foundation of evolved psychological mechanisms. (p. 406)

This is not, however, to deny that non-adaptive and maladaptive moral norms may evolve as by-products of the social learning mechanisms we have considered. For example, all three biases described by Boyd and Richerson (1985) could give rise to maladaptive norms. With respect to direct biases, people may misjudge the consequences of the choices available to them. Specific choices, such as whether or not to model the moral norms of a religious group, may have long-term negative consequences that are impossible to anticipate (Richerson & Boyd, 1989). With respect to indirect biases, people may copy behaviors of high-status models that evoke negative reactions from others. For example, teenagers living in conservative communities may suffer from copying the moral norms displayed or advocated by rap stars. Models also may manipulate observers into adopting norms that that advance the interests of the models. With respect to frequency-dependent biases, although evolved behaviors and beliefs are, by definition, common, maladaptive behaviors and beliefs such as those pertaining to drug taking could grow in popularity even though they ultimately decreased the fitness of those who modeled them.

And even if, as we have argued, the evolved social learning mechanisms and behavioral dispositions we have considered gave rise to adaptive moral norms in the environments in which they were selected, there is no guarantee that such mechanisms and dispositions will give rise to adaptive behaviors in current environments. As examples, mechanisms that disposed our hominid ancestors to imitate group members who were admired for their hunting skills, fighting ability, possession of resources, and popularity may, in modern environments, induce individuals to imitate the maladaptive behaviors of celebrities such as Mike Tyson. Mechanisms that disposed our ancestors to obey powerful authorities may be manipulated in modern environments by charismatic cult leaders. Mechanisms that disposed our ancestors to reciprocate, invest in friends, be faithful to their mates, and support their relatives may give rise to maladaptive behaviors in modern environments, where people are able to move to new locations, change groups frequently, and develop relationships over the Internet (see Janicki & Krebs, 1998, for a more extended discussion of evolutionary approaches to culture).

## SUMMARY AND CONCLUSION

To understand culture, one must understand the mechanisms that generate and refine it. In this chapter, we argue that the mental mechanisms that give rise to moral norms and other aspects of culture evolved because they helped our hominid ancestors reap the benefits of sociality. Children acquire moral norms through social learning and cultural indoctrination, but to understand such processes, we must understand the ways in which they were shaped by natural selection. The reason why people preach moral norms, administer sanctions, conform to moral norms, and copy normative behaviors is because such practices were biologically beneficial in ancestral environments. Our analysis of the evolution of moral norms implies (a) that people will attempt to induce others to invoke the moral norms that benefit them the most, (b) that people will tailor the moral norms they preach to others in ways that enhance their persuasive impact, (c) that recipients will be disposed to conform to the moral norms that best advance their biological interests, and (d) that people in different kinds of relationship will preach and practice different moral norms. Although we disagree with Dawkins's (1989) conclusion that it is a waste of time to search for the fitness-enhancing sources or effects of moral norms and other cultural memes, we acknowledge that nonadaptive and maladaptive moral norms may evolve as by-products of social learning mechanisms.

Moral norms differ cross-culturally because people from different cultures face different kinds of adaptive problem. Universal moral norms prescribing obedience to authority, reciprocity, care, altruism, social responsibility, solidarity, and patriotism evolved in all cultures because they helped our ancestors solve universal social problems. The reason why the moral norms people invoke vary across age, type of relationship, and social situation is because adaptive problems vary across age, relationships, and situations. Decisions about whether or not to behave in morally normative ways are contingent on a complex array of environmental cues.

We need to purge nature versus nurture conceptions of the relation between biology and culture from the social sciences forever. Culture originates in, is transmitted by, and is propagated through mental mechanisms that evolved through natural selection. Evolved mechanisms shape culture, which in turn may shape the evolved mechanisms that produce it. In contrast to the widely held idea that the function of moral norms is to constrain our animal instincts, we believe that moral norms stem from and reflect natural dispositions to behave in moral ways.

## REFERENCES


Alcock, J. (1998). *Animal behavior* (6th ed.). Sunderland, MA: Sinauer Associates.

Alexander, R. D. (1987). *The biology of moral systems*. New York: Aldine de Gruyter.

Austin, W. (1980). Friendship and fairness: Effects of type of relationship and task performance on choice of distribution rules. *Personality and Social Psychology Bulletin, 6*, 402–408.

Axelrod, R. (1984). *The evolution of cooperation*. New York: Basic Books.

Axelrod, R., & Hamilton, W. D. (1981). The evolution of cooperation. *Science, 211*, 1390–1396.

Bandura, A. (1986). *Social foundations of thought and action: A social cognitive theory*. Englewood Cliffs, NJ: Prentice-Hall.

Bandura, A. (1991). Social cognitive theory of moral thought and action. In W. M. Kurtines & J. L. Gewirtz (Eds.), *Handbook of moral behavior and development* (Vol. 1, pp. 54–104). Hillsdale, NJ: Lawrence Erlbaum Associates.

Batson, C. D., Thompson, E. R., Seuferling, G., Whitney, H., & Strongman, J. A. (1999). Moral hypocrisy: Appearing moral to oneself without being so. *Journal of Personality and Social Psychology, 77*, 525–537.

Boehm, C. (2000). Conflict and the evolution of social control. In L. D. Katz (Ed.), *Evolutionary origins of morality* (pp. 79–101). Exeter, UK: Imprint Academic.

Boyd, R., & Richerson, P. J. (1985). *Culture and the evolutionary process*. Chicago: University of Chicago Press.

Boyd, R., & Richerson, P. J. (1992). Punishment allows the evolution of cooperation (or anything else) in sizable groups. *Ethology and Sociobiology, 13*, 171–195.

Boyd, R., & Richerson, P. J. (1995). Why does culture increase human adaptability? *Ethology and Sociobiology, 16*, 125–144.

Brown, D. E. (1991). *Human universals*. New York: McGraw-Hill.

Burton, R. V., & Kunce, L. (1995). Behavioral models of moral development: A brief history and integration. In W. M. Kurtines & J. L. Gewirtz (Eds.), *Moral development: An introduction* (pp. 141–172). Boston: Allyn and Bacon.

Buss, D. (1999). *Evolutionary psychology: The new science of the mind*. Boston: Allyn and Bacon.

Campbell, D. (1978). On the genetics of altruism and the counterhedonic components in human nature. In L. Wispe (Ed.), *Altruism, sympathy, and helping: Psychological and sociological implications* (pp. 39–58). New York: Academic Press.

Carpendale, J., & Krebs, D. L. (1992). Situational variation in moral judgment: In a stage or on a stage? *Journal of Youth and Adolescence, 21*, 203–224.

Clark, M. S., Mills, J., & Powell, M. C. (1986). Keeping track of needs in communal and exchange relationships. *Journal of Personality and Social Psychology, 51*, 333–338.

Colby, A., & Kohlberg, L. (1987). *The measurement of moral judgment* (Vols. 1–2). Cambridge: Cambridge University Press.

Cosmides, L. (1989). The logic of social exchange: Has natural selection shaped how humans reason? Studies with the Wason selection task. *Cognition, 31*, 187–276.

Cosmides, L., & Tooby, J. (1992). Cognitive adaptations for social exchange. In J. Barkow, L. Cosmides, & J. Tooby (Eds.), *The adapted mind* (pp. 163–228). New York: Oxford University Press.

Crawford, C. B. (2000). Evolutionary psychology: Counting babies or studying information-processing mechanisms. In D. LeCroy & P. Moller (Eds.), Evolutionary perspectives on human reproductive behavior. *Annals of the New York Academy of Sciences, 907*, 21–38.

Crawford, C. B., & Anderson, J. L. (1989). Sociobiology: An environmentalist discipline? *American Psychologist, 44*, 1449–1459.

Cronk, L. (1995). Is there a role for culture in human behavioral ecology? *Ethology and Sociobiology, 16*, 181–205.

Damon, W. (1977). *The social world of the child.* San Francisco: Jossey-Bass.

Darwin, C. (1871). *The descent of man and selection in relation to sex* (2 Vols.). New York: Appleton.

Dawkins, R. (1989). *The selfish gene* (rev. ed.). Oxford: Oxford University Press.

Dugatkin, L. A. (1997). *Cooperation among animals: An evolutionary perspective.* New York: Oxford University Press.

Flinn, M. V. (1997). Culture and the evolution of social learning. *Evolution and Human Behavior, 18*, 23–67.

Flinn, M. V., & Alexander, R. D. (1982). Culture theory: The developing synthesis from biology. *Human Ecology, 10*, 383–400.

Frank, R. H. (1988). *Passions within reason: The strategic role of the emotions.* New York: W. W. Norton.

Goffman, E. (1959). *The presentation of self in everyday life.* New York: Anchor Books.

Gouldner, A. W. (1960). The norm of reciprocity: A preliminary statement. *American Sociological Review, 25*, 161–78.

Greenberg, J. (1978). Effects of reward value and retaliative power on allocation decisions: Justice, generosity, or greed? *Journal of Personality and Social Psychology, 36*, 367–379.

Greenberg, J., & Cohen, R. L. (1982). *Equity and Justice in social behavior.* New York: Academic Press.

Habermas, J. (1984). Interpretive social science vs. hermeneutics. In N. Haan, R. B. Bellah, P. Rabinow, & W. Sullivan (Eds.), *Social science as moral inquiry* (pp. 251–269). New York: Columbia University Press.

Hamilton, W. D. (1964). The evolution of social behavior. *Journal of Theoretical Biology, 7*, 1–52.

Henrich, J., & Boyd, R. (1998). The evolution of conformist transmission and the emergence of between-group differences. *Evolution and Human Behavior, 19*, 215–241.

Hornstein, H. (1978). Promotive tension and prosocial behavior: A Lewinian analysis. In L. Wispe (Ed.), *Altruism, sympathy, and helping: Psychological and sociological implications* (pp. 177–208). New York: Academic Press.

Janicki, M. G., & Krebs, D. L. (1998). Evolutionary approaches to culture. In C. Crawford & D. L. Krebs (Eds.), *Handbook of evolutionary psychology: Ideas, issues, and applications* (pp. 163–208). Mahwah, NJ: Lawrence Erlbaum Associates.

Jones, E. E. (1990). *Interpersonal perception.* New York: Freeman.

Kohlberg, L. (1984). *Essays in moral development Vol. 2 :The psychology of moral development.* New York: Harper & Row.

Krebs, D. L. (1998). The evolution of moral behavior. In C. Crawford & D. L. Krebs (Eds.), *Handbook of evolutionary psychology: Ideas, issues, and applications* (pp. 337–368). Hillsdale, NJ: Lawrence Erlbaum Associates.

Krebs, D. L. (2000a). The evolution of moral dispositions in the human species. In D. LeCroy & P. Moller (Eds.), *Evolutionary Perspectives on Human Reproductive Behavior. Annals of the New York Academy of Science, 907*, 1–17.

Krebs, D. L. (2000b). Evolutionary games and morality. In L. D. Katz (Ed.), *Evolutionary Origins of Morality: Cross-disciplinary approaches* (pp. 313–321). Exeter, UK: Imprint Academic.

Krebs, D. L. (2000c). As moral as we need to be. In L. D. Katz (Ed.), *Evolutionary Origins of Morality: Cross-disciplinary approaches* (pp. 139–143). Exeter, UK: Imprint Academic.

Krebs, D. L., & Denton, K. (1997). Social illusions and self-deception: The evolution of biases in person perception. In J. A. Simpson & D. T. Kenrick (Eds.), *Evolutionary social psychology* (pp. 21–47). Hillsdale, NJ: Lawrence Erlbaum Associates.

Krebs, D. L., & Denton, K. (1999). On the relations between moral judgment and moral behavior. In D. Garz, F. Oser, & W. Althof (Eds.), *The context of morality* (pp. 220–263). Frankfurt: M. Suhrlcamp.

Krebs, D. L., Denton, K., Vermeulen, S. C. Carpendale, J. I., & Bush, A. (1991). The structural flexibility of moral judgment. *Journal of Personality and Social Psychology, 61*, 1012–1023.

Krebs, D. L., Denton, K., & Wark, G. (1997). The forms and functions of real-life moral decision-making. *Journal of Moral Education, 20*, 131–145.

Krebs, D. L., Denton, K., Wark, G., Couch, R., Racine, T. P., & Krebs, D. L. (2002). Interpersonal moral conflicts between couples: Effects of type of dilemma, role, and partner's judgments on level of moral reasoning and probability of resolution. *Journal of Adult Development, 9*, 307–316.

Krebs, D. L., & Laird, P. (1998). Judging yourself as you judge others: Perspective-taking, moral development, and exculpation. *Journal of Adult Development, 5*, 1–12.

Krebs, D. L., & Van Hesteren, F. (1994). The development of altruism: Toward an integrative model. *Developmental Review, 14*, 103–158.

Krebs, D. L., Vermeulen, S. C., Carpendale, J. I., & Denton, K. (1991). Structural and situational influences on moral judgment: The interaction between stage and dilemma. In W. Kurtines & J. Gewirtz (Eds.), *Handbook of moral behavior and development: Theory, research, and applications* (pp. 139–169). Hillsdale, NJ: Lawrence Erlbaum Associates.

Leaky, R. E., & Lewin, R. (1977). *Origins*. New York: Dutton.

Leary, M. R. (1995). *Self-presentation: Impression management and interpersonal behavior*. Madison, WI: Brown & Benchmark.

Leventhal, G. S., & Anderson, D. (1970). Self-interest and the maintenance of equity. *Journal of Personality and Social Psychology, 15*, 57–62.

Milgram, S. (1974). *Obedience to authority*. New York: Harper.

Mitchell, R. W., & Thompson, N. S. (Eds.). (1986). *Deception: Perspectives on human and non-human deceit*. Albany: State University of New York Press.

Nesse, R. M. (1999). The evolution of commitment and the origins of religion. *Science and Spirit, 10*, 32–46.

Newitt, C., & Krebs, D. L. (in preparation). *The structural flexibility of real-life moral judgments*.

Nowak, M. A., & Sigmund, K. (1998). Evolution of indirect reciprocity by image scoring. *Nature, 393*, 573–577.

Piaget, J. (1932). *The moral judgment of the child*. London: Routledge & Kegan Paul.

Rawls, J. (1971). *A theory of justice*. Cambridge, MA: Harvard University Press.

Richerson, P. J., & Boyd, R. (1989). The role of evolved predispositions in cultural evolution. *Ethology & Sociobiology, 10*, 195–219.

Richerson, P. J., & Boyd, R. (1992). Cultural inheritance and evolutionary ecology. In E. A. Smith & B. Winterhalder (Eds.), *Evolutionary ecology and human behavior* (pp. 61–92). New York: Aldine de Gruyter.

Simon, H. (1990). A mechanism for social selection of successful altruism. *Science, 250*, 1665–1668.

Sloman, L., & Gilbert, P. (2000). *Subordination and defeat: An evolutionary approach to mood disorders and their therapy*. Mahwah, NJ: Lawrence Erlbaum Associates.

Snarey, J. (1985). Cross-cultural universality of social-moral development: A critical review of Kohlbergian research. *Psychological Bulletin, 97*, 202–232.

Sober, E., & Wilson, D. S. (1998). *Unto others: The evolution and psychology of unselfish behavior*. Cambridge, MA: Harvard University Press.

Tajfel, H. (1982). *Social identify and intergroup relations*. Cambridge, UK: Cambridge University Press.

Tajfel, H., & Turner, J. C. (1985). The social identity theory of intergroup behavior. In S. Worchel & W. G. Austin (Eds.), *Psychology of intergroup relations* (pp. 7–24). Chicago: Nelson-Hall.

Tooby, J., & Cosmides, L. (1992). The psychological foundations of culture. In J. Barkow, L. Cosmides, & J. Tooby (Eds.), *The adapted mind: Evolutionary psychology and the generation of culture* (pp. 19–136). New York: Oxford University Press.

Tooby, J., & Cosmides, L. (1996). Friendship and the banker's paradox: Other pathways to the evolution of adaptations for altruism. *Proceedings of the British Academy, 88*, 119–143.

Tooby, J., & Devore, I. (1987). The reconstruction of hominid behavioral evolution through strategic modeling. In W. G. Kinzey (Ed.), *The evolution of human behavior: Primate models* (pp. 183–237). Albany, NY: SUNY Press.

Trivers, R. L. (1971). The evolution of reciprocal altruism. *Quarterly Review of Biology, 46*, 35–57.

Trivers, R. L. (1985). *Social evolution.* Menlo Park: CA: Benjamin Cummings.

Wright, R. (1994). *The moral animal.* New York: Pantheon Books.

CHAPTER

# 7

# Cognitive and Emotional Processes in the Cultural Transmission of Natural and Nonnatural Beliefs

Ara Norenzayan
University of British Columbia

Scott Atran
Centre National de la Recherche Scientifique, Paris,
and
University of Michigan, Ann Arbor, Michigan

What makes an idea culturally successful, such as the widespread notion in many societies of ancestor spirits, a haiku, or the recipe for apple pie? To be sure, not all ideas are culturally successful. Some ideas are never represented in minds. Some are represented, but never communicated to others. Yet other ideas are successfully communicated to enough people that they become fashionable for a short time, but quickly fade away. But a small number of ideas are culturally successful: They permanently invade a group of minds. According to an *epidemiological approach* to explaining culture, then, "contagious" ideas and their material effects, such as texts, tools, buildings, and artwork, constitute what we call culture. According to this view, an idea is "cultural" to the extent that it is widespread in a group (Cavalli-Sforza & Feldman, 1981; Sperber, 1990, 1996; see also Campbell, 1974; Dawkins, 1982; Boyd & Richerson, 1985).

Many factors are important in determining the extent to which ideas achieve a cultural level of distribution. Some are ecological, including the rate of prior exposure to an idea in a population, physical as well as social facilitators and barriers to communication and imitation, and institutional structures that reinforce or suppress an idea. Others are psychological, including the ease with which an idea can be represented and remembered, the intrinsic interest that it evokes in people so that it is processed and rehearsed, and the motivation and facility to communicate the idea to others.

Of all the psychological factors, the mnemonic power of an idea is one of the most important. In fact, Sperber (1996) put forth memorability as a "law" of the epidemiology of representations, as a necessary (but of course not sufficient) condition for cultural success. The *memorability test* has two components:

1. Memorability places severe constraints on the cultural transmission of ideas. In oral traditions that characterize most of human cultures throughout history, an idea that is not memorable cannot be transmitted and cannot achieve cultural success.
2. Furthermore, even if two ideas pass a minimal test of memorability, a *more* memorable idea has a transmission advantage over a less memorable one (all else being equal). This advantage, even if small at the start, accumulates from generation to generation of transmission leading to massive differences in cultural success at the end.

The psychology of cognition in general, and memory in particular, is of great relevance to the anthropological study of how cultural belief systems emerge. This is true in two senses. First, memory plays a central role in how communicators of cultural materials transmit their messages. Historically, cultural innovators such as storytellers and religious leaders have been known to have remarkable mnemonic abilities in transmitting massive amounts of information to their audiences. More importantly, they have been adept at making their messages memorable to others. It is no coincidence that the minds of great cultural innovators of all time, such as Homer, were also the minds of great mnemonists and communicators as well. Second, memory is central to how the audience processes, recalls, and in turn transmits cultural materials to others. Ideas are not acquired and transmitted through a process by which culture "impinges" on a passive human mind. Rather, the minds of the receivers of cultural materials selectively represent, retain, transform, and transmit information. Thus the ordinary biases and transformations in human memory can constrain and sometimes even determine the content of cultural beliefs.

## NATURAL AND NONNATURAL BELIEFS

What sorts of beliefs are especially good at passing the test of memorability? One way to answer this question is by considering culturally successful beliefs actually known to us–the reverse of the analysis presented to far. These are beliefs that should be especially memorable, because they could not have achieved cultural success unless they passed the test of memorability. In examining what kinds of beliefs are widespread in societies around the world, one observation is inevitable: Most beliefs in all human societies known to anthropologists seem to be made of common sense notions about the world (Atran & Sperber, 1991; Geertz, 1975). Intuitive concepts such as "rock," "bird," and "person" form the bulk of the beliefs that people in different cultures entertain on a daily basis. These concepts, and the beliefs they support, are for the most part grounded in direct experience and observation, and are in principle accessible to every competent adult in a community. Moreover, these concepts and beliefs are part of common sense in that they are supported by intuitive "theories" about objects and events widely shared by everyone. Conversations, child rearing, subsistence, rituals, and even religion would be impossible without these intuitive concepts and theories.

Intuitive concepts are "intuitive," because built into them are implicit inferences about their properties. These intuitive inferences are rarely articulated explicitly. Rather, they are assumed, and make the concepts comprehensible and communicable. For example, the concept "bird" involves the implicit inferences that birds fly, that they grow and die, and that they drink when thirsty. These inferences are guided by intuitive *ontology* (Keil, 1989), or assumptions about the basic categories of existence, such as intentional beings, animals, inanimate objects, and events. Ontology is psychologically important, because it determines the appropriateness of inferences. For example, knowing that birds belong to the ontological category ANIMAL affords "automatic" inferences about biological properties, but not necessarily intentional agent properties. These inferences are possible because ontology is in turn governed by domain-specific "theories"—theories of mind, biology, and physics—that provide intuitive beliefs and explanations for the workings of each ontological category.

There are important cultural variations in many aspects of domain-specific theories: theory of mind (e.g., Choi, Nisbett, & Norenzayan, 1999; Lillard, 1998), biology (e.g., Medin & Atran, 1999), and physics (e.g., Peng & Nisbett, 1996; Lloyd, 1996). However, certain core elements of these theories appear so early, and are so widespread across human societies, that they may turn out to be psychological primitives that make cultural learning possible. For example, babies as young as 4 months already possess a "theory of physics," having a notion of what counts as a solid object, and assuming, for example, that an object cannot be in different places at the same time, or that a solid object cannot pass through another solid object (Baillargeon, 1998; Carey & Spelke, 1994; Leslie, 1982; Spelke, 1990). Similarly, preschoolers and adults in most cultures known to anthropologists have a "theory of biology" that dictates that species have biological "essences" and that superficial transformations performed on an animal do not alter its species-specific essence (Atran, 1990, 1998; Berlin, 1992; Berlin, Breedlove, & Raven, 1973; Gelman & Hirschfeld, 1998; Keil, 1994). Preschoolers and adults in many disparate cultures also have an elaborate "theory of mind," which entails, among other things, the attribution of beliefs and desires to people, and the appreciation that people may have false beliefs (Avis & Harris, 1991; Flavell, Zhang, Zou, Dong, & Qui, 1983; Gardner, Harris, Ohmoto, & Hamazaki, 1988; Leslie, 1994; Wellman, 1990).

These universal causal frameworks, or "intuitive theories," render different aspects of the world comprehensible, and provide a common set of assumptions that facilitate linguistic communication. A speaker who describes a pet bird does not need to enumerate all the assumed properties of birds. Listeners automatically infer that the bird is an animal, hence has biological properties, that it necessarily obeys the laws of physics, and that it does not necessarily share the properties of conscious beings. It is little surprise, then, that the beliefs supported by these theories are at the heart of everyday culture around the world.

Yet a second observation about widespread beliefs is that culturally important materials, such as myths, legends, folktales, and religious belief systems, invariably center on nonnatural concepts, such as supernatural agents and nonhuman animals with anthropomorphic properties. Unlike everyday natural concepts such as rock, bird, and person—which are consistent with domain-specific theories and are verifiable through experience—ghosts, fairies, talking frogs, and invisible mountains do not refer to observable entities accessible to everyone, violate ontological structures, and are inconsistent with theories of mind, biology, and physics that are at the base of these structures. Despite their incompatibility with intuitive ontologies, however, they are culturally ubiquitous. They consistently appear in every religious tradition, and in folk tales and myths that are instrumental in socializing children around the world.

This chapter has three goals. First, we review experimental evidence regarding the relative cultural success of natural and nonnatural beliefs in terms of their memorability. Second, we review the results of an experiment we conducted that examined not only the memorability of individual beliefs, but also whether there is an optimal combination of natural and nonnatural beliefs that maximizes cultural success of a set of beliefs as a whole. In the last part, we go beyond memory processes and consider the role of emotions that may guide the transmission of natural and nonnatural beliefs.

## COGNITIVE OPTIMALITY

It is necessary to bring together the two components of our discussion so far—the facts that memorability constrains and directs the cultural transmission of beliefs, and that many cultural belief systems consist of some mix of natural as well as nonnatural beliefs. Natural and nonnatural beliefs, and the way the two interact, may involve distinct patterns of memorability and transmission, and hence cultural success. This of course is not the argument that human memory is "designed" to produce certain kinds of natural and nonnatural beliefs. Rather, it is the opposite. Ideas that achieve cultural success must be those that happen to be the more successful at exploiting the peculiarities of the human memory system that evolved to solve problems having little to do with the propagation of culture. Thus there may be a cognitively optimal level of the naturalness of beliefs. One of the most elaborate accounts of how this is accomplished is that of the cognitive anthropologist Pascal Boyer (1994a).

According to Boyer (1992, 1994a, 1994b; see also Atran, 1990, 1996; Atran & Sperber, 1991; Sperber, 1975, 1996), religious and quasi-religious concepts (including those in folk tales and myths) are fundamentally similar to other, mundane, concepts in that they are grounded in theories of mind, biology, and physics. There is growing evidence that the same intuitive theories that guide much of thinking about mundane concepts also lie behind thinking about religious concepts. A telling example comes from a study by Barret and Keil (1996), in which the authors demonstrated that even religious people implicitly rely on their intuitive theory of intentional agents to reason about God, much as they would reason about human beings. For example, in recalling a story in which God saved the lives of people about to drown, participants made implicit inferences consistent with intentional agents—for example, that God cannot be in two places at the same time. This is despite the fact that they explicitly denied to the experimenter that they anthropomorphize God!

Despite this psychological commonality, religious concepts are different from mundane concepts in an important way: Religious concepts possess a small number of features that violate the ontological assumptions of the concept. Thus religious concepts are *minimally counterintuitive*: They are largely consistent with the ontological assumptions of the concept, whereas a few of their features are inconsistent with these same assumptions. An example of a minimally counterintuitive religious concept that is cross culturally widespread is that of a ghost (Boyer, 1992). A ghost satisfies most of the ontological assumptions of an intentional agent (it is conscious, has beliefs and desires, has biological needs, may die), yet it violates a few features of the physical ontology of intentional agents (which people everywhere intuitively expect to be embodied as animate beings): A ghost is invisible and can pass through solid objects.

According to Boyer, minimally counterintuitive concepts are cognitively optimal. The few counterintuitive features render the concept more salient and more interesting, whereas the implicitly represented intuitive features assure that the concept is comprehensible in terms of existing ontological structures. Concepts that have no ontology-violating features at all are not interesting. A man walking down a hill is not a particularly potent cultural idea. Concepts that have too many ontology-violating features are not easily comprehensible. A ghost that behaves according to the opposite of its beliefs, can be in multiple places at the same time, and has 100 lives is a very difficult ghost to comprehend, let alone remember and transmit. Religious concepts, if minimally counterintuitive, are more memorable, and hence enjoy a transmission advantage over mundane or highly counterintuitive concepts. This would help to account for the widespread nature of religious concepts, such as ghosts, animals that speak, and statues that cure diseases. It would also predict that religious and mythical traditions make significant and reliable use of minimally counterintuitive concepts.

Indeed this seems to be the case. For example, in a study of Ovid's *Metamorphoses*, Kelly and Keil (1985) showed that the ontological transformations experienced by the characters followed a distinct pattern: The number of transformations of one ontological category to other ontological categories decreased as the distance between the two categories increased. Thus, it was far more likely for a conscious being to be transformed into an animal (closer in ontological distance, resulting in few ontological violations), than for a conscious being to be transformed into an inanimate object (farther away in ontological distance, resulting in too many ontological violations). Transformations that occur across wide swaths of ontological distance are just too counterintuitive to have cultural value. The anthropological literature in general supports the claim that most concepts in religions and folktales in different cultures that violate ontological assumptions are of the minimally counterintuitive kind.

## MEMORABILITY OF MINIMALLY COUNTERINTUITIVE BELIEFS: EXPERIMENTAL EVIDENCE

One of the earliest accounts of the effects of memorability on the transmission of natural and nonnatural concepts was Bartlett's (1932) classic study of "the war of the ghosts." Bartlett examined the ways by which British university students remembered, and then transmitted a culturally unfamiliar story, in this case a Native American folktale. One of the interesting findings was that, over several generations of retelling the story, some culturally unfamiliar items or events were dropped from the retelling. Other unfamiliar items were distorted, being replaced by more familiar items. For example, a canoe (an unfamiliar item) was replaced by a rowboat (a familiar one). Bartlett reasoned that items inconsistent with the cultural schema of British students were harder to represent, harder to recall, and therefore were less likely to be transmitted than schema-consistent items (see also Kintsch & Greene, 1978, for evidence that culturally familiar information is better remembered).

Bartlett's other striking finding was that the very notion of the ghosts—so central to the story—was gradually eliminated from the retellings. If Boyer's hypothesis is correct—that a concept like "ghost" has a transmission advantage—this is a problematic finding. However, this finding may be explained by the idea that the effect of memory on cultural transmission also operates at the level of belief sets, such that the elimination of the ghost from the retellings contributed to the overall cultural survival of the story as a whole. We return to this issue later in the chapter.

Recent experiments have followed up on Bartlett's seminal study, directly testing the cognitive optimality of natural and nonnatural beliefs. The available evidence suggests that, under some conditions, minimally counterintuitive beliefs are indeed better recalled relative to intuitive beliefs, beliefs that are too counterintuitive, and beliefs that are bizarre but not counterintuitive.

In a series of experiments, Barret and Nyhof (2001) asked participants to remember and retell stories containing natural as well as nonnatural events or objects. In one experiment, participants read three of six different Native American folktales and then remembered as much of each as they could. A content analysis of what they remembered was revealing. Participants remembered 92% of minimally counterintuitive items, but only 71% of intuitive items.

In another experiment, Barret and Nyhof constructed a more tightly controlled narrative in which an intergalactic ambassador was visiting a museum on a planet where various objects, animals, and conscious beings indigenous to the planet were exhibited. Each item consisted of a description of an ontological category (living thing, physical object, intentional agent), plus a description of a feature. Participants were instructed to recall and retell as many of the items as possible. One-third of the items in each story were intuitive ("an object that is easy to see under normal lighting conditions"). One third were minimally counterintuitive with one ontological violation ("a single object that can be completely in more than one place at a time"). The final third were items that had one bizarre feature but did not violate any ontological assumptions ("an object that can be passed through openings in solid objects considerably smaller than it is"—for example, a compressible rubber ball).

After three generations of retelling the story, the proportion of items recalled in each category was measured. Results indicated that both counterintuitive and bizarre items were remembered in greater proportions than intuitive items. An examination of the memory distortions was also revealing. The most common distortions were bizarre items becoming counterintuitive (37.5%), whereas the least common distortions were from counterintuitive to bizarre (7.2%). Subsequent experiments demonstrated that the same recall advantage of minimally counterintuitive items over intuitive, as well as bizarre items emerges after a 3-month delay. This is crucial, because in most natural settings in which cultural narratives evolve, recall after a long delay plays a more important role than recall immediately following exposure to an idea. An idea that is memorable immediately, but decays over time could not be culturally successful. Overall then, the results of Barret and Nyhoff confirm the idea that minimally counterintuitive beliefs are better recalled than intuitive ones.

It is important to note that counterintuitiveness and bizarreness are orthogonal. Something can be counterintuitive but may not necessarily feel unfamiliar or evoke bizarre imagery (an invisible chair); or something can be bizarre without being counterintuitive (a giant gorilla in an opera house). The cognitive optimality hypothesis predicts that the transmission advantage of minimally counterintuitive beliefs over intuitive beliefs is a function of their minimal counterintuitiveness—not a function of bizarreness or unfamiliarity. In a study comparing recall of minimally counterintuitive and bizarre items, Barret and Nyhoff (2001) demonstrated that this is indeed the case. A salient but not counterintuitive object (e.g., a bright, pink newspaper flying in the wind) is remembered less well than a minimally counterintuitive object (e.g., a carrot that speaks). Furthermore, ratings of "familiarity," a measure of strangeness or bizarreness, do not predict recall as well as ratings of how "different" an item is from ordinary things, a measure of expectancy violation, or counterintuitiveness (Boyer & Ramble, 2001).

Thus, minimal violation of ontological assumptions and cultural familiarity are two distinct factors that contribute to recall. Although familiarity is a mechanism that is bounded by a particular culture, ontological violation is not. Intuitive ontology, supported by intuitive theories of mind, biology, and physics, appear to emerge at a very early age and are likely to have universal components. As a result, it is possible to expect that the recall advantage that minimally counterintuitive concepts enjoy may be cross culturally widespread. Boyer and Ramble (2001) tested this idea in three different cultures: Tibetan Buddhist monks in Nepal, West African participants recruited from a farmers' market in Gabon, and French university students. Unlike the secular environment in which French students live, Gabonese folk and Nepalese monks have greater exposure to supernatural concepts. Nevertheless, the same advantage for minimally counterintuitive concepts emerged for all three groups.

Another important finding that is consistent with the cognitive optimality hypothesis is that the effect of counterintuitiveness on recall is not linear. Too many ontological violations render a concept too counterintuitive to be memorable. Using stories similar to the "intergalactic ambassador," Boyer and Ramble (2001) demonstrated that concepts with too many violations were recalled less well than those that were minimally counterintuitive. They also observe, for example, that among many Catholics there is the belief in an artifact with cognitive properties (e.g., a statue of the Virgin that listens within proximity). Similarly, there is the belief that God can hear distant sounds. Yet the belief that a statue of the Virgin can hear distant sounds is uncommon. The anthropological literature also confirms that religious concepts with too many ontological violations are rather rare (Boyer, 1994a). Such concepts may be less memorable because of a poorer fit with ontological categories and intuitive theories. Another reason why such concepts are rare may be that its numerous violations "block" its inferential potential and undermine its usefulness as a concept.

To summarize, the available experimental evidence indicates that concepts that are minimally counterintuitive have a transmission advantage over concepts that are intuitive or those that are too counterintuitive. This advantage can be observed immediately after exposure, as well as after a 3-month delay, in cultures as diverse as the Midwestern United States, France, Gabon, and Nepal.

## COGNITIVE OPTIMALITY OF BELIEFS VERSUS BELIEF SETS

There is, however, a mismatch between this evidence and the apparent structure of culturally important narratives. If, as the evidence we reviewed suggests, minimally counterintuitive concepts are more successful than other concepts, they should dominate religions, folktales, and myths. The memory advantage they enjoy over intuitive and extremely counterintuitive concepts should be observed in naturally occurring culturally successful materials. However, even a casual perusal of culturally successful materials such as the Bible and some of the popular folktales in the Grimm Brothers' collection suggests that counterintuitive concepts and occurrences are in the minority. The Bible, for example, is a succession of mundane events—traveling by foot, fishing, eating, sleeping, preaching, funerals and weddings, rainstorms, drought—interspersed with a few counterintuitive occurrences, such as miracles and the appearance of supernatural agents such as God, angels, and ghosts.

In the Grimm Brothers' German folktales, the tale of Little Red Riding Hood—one of the most celebrated folk tales in Western culture—is mostly a series of mundane occurrences, seasoned with only two counterintuitive ones: the talking wolf, and the grandmother and little girl coming out of the wolf's belly alive. Similarly, Beauty and the Beast has only three violations—

the Beast as an animal with human properties, the magic mirror, and the transformation from beast to human. If minimally counterintuitive concepts are indeed more memorable than mundane concepts, one would expect that the proportion of minimally counterintuitive concepts would increase as a function of the cultural success of the folktale. The Bible and the popular Grimms' folktales would consist of nothing more than a succession of minimally counterintuitive concepts and events. But this is not the case.

One great advantage that common sense beliefs have over counterintuitive ones is that the former are supported by everyday experience and intuitive theories. Perhaps this accounts for why they are the majority of cultural beliefs, despite being at a transmission disadvantage relative to counterintuitive beliefs. This may explain why common sense beliefs are generally easy to think. But it fails to explain the prevalence of *specific* common sense beliefs. Somehow, the specific mundane events of Little Red Riding Hood—mother telling her to go and visit her grandmother, the walk in the forest, carrying a basket of strawberries, talking to a stranger, and so on—must be successfully remembered and transmitted if this tale is to survive the test of time.

The answer to this apparent puzzle may lie in examining the memorability of an entire set of beliefs as a single unit of transmission, rather than individual beliefs. The unit of cultural transmission is often, but not always, an individual idea. Under many conditions, a series of events or concepts is transmitted as a single unit of culture. Therefore, cognitive optimality might be at work not only at the level of individual beliefs, but at the level of belief structures as well. Boyer's theory does not address the cognitive optimality of belief structures. However, one can apply the same logic to this level.

Applying the principle of cognitive optimality to belief sets, we would expect that minimally counterintuitive belief sets—those that contain a small number of minimally counterintuitive beliefs—would be more memorable than all intuitive belief sets or belief sets with too many minimally counterintuitive beliefs. Interestingly, cognitive optimality at these two levels may come into conflict. What is good for a belief set may not be good for each individual belief that makes up the belief set. The most salient case of such conflict is when a belief set is made of mostly minimally counterintuitive beliefs. A folktale with many minimally counterintuitive concepts will be at a disadvantage if cognitive optimality is more important at the level of belief sets. Each minimally counterintuitive concept in this tale will be at an advantage if cognitive optimality is more important at the individual belief level.

As suggestive as the groundbreaking studies of Barret and Nyhof (2001) and Boyer and Ramble (2001) are, they leave unresolved a number of issues. First is the problem of incompatibility of this finding with existing cultural materials. Why do we not see minimally counterintuitive concepts take over most of the narrative structure of religions, folktales, and myths?

One possibility is that cognitive optimality may also operate at the level of belief sets, such that minimally counterintuitive belief sets enjoy a transmission advantage. This would lead to a state of affairs not unlike what we observe in real life: A successful belief system would be mostly intuitive, containing only a few minimally counterintuitive elements. This possibility has not been explored before. In earlier studies, an equal number of natural and nonnatural concepts were used in each story.

A second issue is that the materials used in these studies were constructed such that they may have encouraged participants to privilege the counterintuitive concepts over the intuitive ones. This could have happened in two ways. First, most studies used a "storytelling" format, in which participants were asked to memorize the story with the expectation of telling it to another person. The great advantage of using a storytelling format is that many instances of cultural transmission in real life occur in a storytelling context. Its drawback, however, is that it is not a clear test of the memorability criterion. Participants may have remembered any combination of intuitive and counterintuitive concepts, but reported more counterintuitive concepts because the latter would make a better story.

Other studies used a story that is about an intergalactic ambassador visiting a museum in another world. This may have encouraged attending to counterintuitives by suggesting to participants that the researcher is interested in extraordinary, science-fiction type events, rather than mundane occurrences. Although both storytelling and stories suggesting extraordinary events clearly have counterparts in natural settings (e.g., telling and retelling of folktales in a village), they are not the only form of cultural transmission, and may particularly favor transmitting counterintuitive ideas.

Finally, commonsense beliefs usually must be relevant to the listener to be successfully communicated and remembered (Sperber & Wilson, 1986). They must inform the listener of something that should be known or made salient, but was not before. The commonsense items in these experiments fail to meet such minimal criteria for relevance. For example, Barret and Nyhof (2001, p. 79) list as commonsense items "a being that can see or hear things that are not too far away," and "a species that will die if it does not get enough nourishment or if it is severely damaged." Indeed, such items fall so far below the ordinary expectation that items communicated should carry some new or salient information, that Barret and Nyhof report: "That common items were remembered so poorly relative to other items is particularly surprising given the reaction of some participants to these items.... In some instances of retelling these items, participants tried to make the common property sound exciting or unusual" (pp. 82–83). In other words, some subjects apparently tried to meet minimum conditions of relevance. For the most part, however, it appears that communication of common items failed these minimum standards.

## MEMORABILITY OF INTUITIVE AND MINIMALLY COUNTERINTUITIVE BELIEFS AND BELIEF SETS

"The war of the ghosts" (Bartlett, 1932) was one of the earliest accounts of the effects of memorability on the transmission of belief sets containing natural and nonnatural concepts. Bartlett found that the notion of the ghosts was gradually eliminated from the retellings. A possible explanation for this finding is that cultural transmission operates at the level of belief sets, such that the elimination of the ghost from the retellings contributed to the overall cultural survival of the story as a whole.

As Barret and Nyhof (2001) noted, however, Bartlett's finding is difficult to interpret. First, he did not directly compare the memorability of "ghosts" to control items. Second, the study was based on a single story, and idiosyncratic aspects of the story (such as its cultural unfamiliarity) may have contributed to the findings. More studies, with better experimental control and wider sets of information, are needed.

We conducted a study to examine the memorability of intuitive (INT) and minimally counterintuitive (MCI) beliefs and belief sets over a period of a week. Participants were 107 undergraduate students at a large American university in the Midwest. MCI beliefs were generated by transferring a property from its intuitive domain to a novel domain (e.g., thirsty door, closing cat). For each MCI belief, there was a corresponding INT belief (thirsty cat, closing door). Thus, each word—"cat," "door," "closing," and "thirsty"—were equally likely to appear in an INT item as in a MCI item. This resulted in a set of four statements that achieved a counterbalanced design, with each word in each statement serving as its own control. Recall was measured in two ways: planned free recall after a 3-minute delay, and a surprise free recall after a 1-week delay. This latter measure was the more important one, as it better reflects the role of recall in oral traditions.

This study differed from previous ones in a number of important ways. First, the cognitive optimality hypothesis was tested on two levels: at the level of individual beliefs, and at the level of structures of beliefs containing different proportions of INT and MCI beliefs. To examine recall at the level of structures of beliefs, participants were randomly assigned to one of four proportions of INT and MCI items on each list: All INT, Mostly INT, Equal, and Mostly MCI. Second, the INT and MCI items were matched, such that each word served as its own control (as can be seen in the earlier examples). This procedure ruled out any possible effects of the prior recall probabilities of the concepts in each belief.

Third, participants were told that they were in an experiment about memory, and were given a list of items to remember, without providing a story context. This served two purposes. First, this list-learning format was meant to provide as neutral a context as possible to measure recall, rather than participants' notions of what is interesting to report. Second, although stories are an important part of culturally successful materials, many of these stories often begin their life as a set of discrete images, events, and beliefs, not unlike lists of items, with little or no story structure (e.g., consider the sketchy nature of early Christian beliefs about the life events of Jesus of Nazareth, which cohered into a single chronological narrative centuries after the actual events). This format simulated the degraded informational context of nascent cultural materials.

Finally, unlike previous studies, basic-level concepts were used, such as door, cat, and infant. The basic level is where: (a) Many common features are listed for categories, (b) consistent motor programs are used for the interaction with or manipulation of category exemplars, (c) category members have similar enough shapes so that it is possible to recognize an average shape for objects of the category, and (d) the category name is the first name to come to mind in the presence of an object–for example, "table" versus "furniture" and "kitchen table," or "dog" versus "mammal" and "collie" (Rosch, Mervis, Grey, Johnson, & Boyes-Braem, 1976).

Two questions were addressed:

1. At the level of individual beliefs, which kinds of beliefs would enjoy better recall and lower memory degradation (measured as loss of information from immediate to delayed recall): minimally counterintuitive beliefs or their intuitive counterparts?
2. At the level of belief sets, what proportion of INT to MCI beliefs would maximize recall of the entire set?

It was expected, consistent with the cognitive optimality hypothesis, that the belief set with mostly INT beliefs combined with a few MCI beliefs would enjoy the highest rate of recall and lowest rate of memory degradation, followed by the belief set with equal proportions of INT and MCI beliefs. The set with All INT beliefs would be third, and the one with too many MCI beliefs would generate the lowest rate of recall and the highest rate of degradation.

A complex pattern of recall emerged for intuitive and minimally counterintuitive beliefs. First we consider the recall rates at the level of individual beliefs. Unlike the findings of Barret and Nyhof (2001), and Boyer and Ramble (2001), intuitive beliefs showed better recall rates than minimally counterintuitive beliefs. This was the case immediately, as well as after a 1-week delay. The only exception to this pattern was when counterintuitives made up the majority of beliefs, in which case there were no differences in recall rates. Because the two kinds of beliefs were matched, that is, each term in each belief was equally likely to occur in an intuitive and counterintuitive belief, we can conclude with relative confidence that it was the intuitiveness factor, not other unknown factors left to vary, that contributed to the recall advantage of the intuitives.

We have subsequently replicated this finding with a different set of ideas (Norenzayan & Atran, 2001a) where a sharper distinction was made between counterintuitive ideas and ideas that are intuitive but bizarre, and between degrees of counterintuitiveness. Participants received ideas that were (a) intuitive and ordinary, (b) intuitive but bizarre, (c) minimally counterintuitive, or (d) maximally counterintuitive. Results revealed a linear effect of intuitiveness on recall—immediately as well as a week later; intuitive ideas enjoyed the highest rate of recall, and maximally counterintuitive ideas received the lowest rate of recall. An analogous experiment is underway with Yucatec Maya participants who live in a traditional, semiliterate society in rural Mexico. This experiment will allow us to test the cross-cultural generality of these findings, as well as to examine possible cultural variation in the cognitive processes of cultural transmission.

How can we account for this pattern of results? Note that one important difference between our experiments and those of Barret and Nyhof (2001) and Boyer and Ramble (2001) is that in this study, participants were not led to expect nonnatural events (as in listening to a science fiction tale) and were not motivated to tell an interesting story. In such a context in which people expect that information will conform to a natural course of events, they are likely to attend to and remember beliefs that are consistent with ontological assumptions. This process would break down when the majority of the to-be-remembered beliefs are minimally counterintuitive. In such a situation, it is possible that people develop the expectation that the task is about recalling nonnatural events, or about reporting the "interesting stuff." As a result, intuitive beliefs would loose their privileged status and recall would be no different for intuitive and minimally counterintuitive beliefs. Under such conditions, it may even be possible to reverse the phenomenon, such that minimally counterintuitive beliefs are better recalled, as we saw earlier. This explanation has the virtue of accounting for both the findings of Barret and Nyhof and Boyer and Ramble, and the findings of the current study. But it remains a speculation waiting to be tested experimentally.

An intriguing finding that converges with the findings of Barret and Nyhof (2001) and Boyer and Ramble (2001) was that minimally counterintuitive beliefs were more cognitively resilient than intuitive ones, in that they degraded at a lower rate after immediate recall. This is despite the fact that overall, the former had a lower recall rate than the latter. Thus, minimally counterintuitive beliefs may have a potent survival advantage over intuitive beliefs: Once processed and recalled, they degrade less than intuitive ones. It is easy to see how this difference in cognitive resilience may be a significant factor in cultural survival. The disadvantage in recall (at least under the conditions set in this study) may be offset by resilience, so that over numerous generations of transmission, an idea that is less remembered, but also less degradable, can, in some situations, prevail over an idea that is initially remembered well but then eventually dies out because of a higher rate of degradation.

The picture that emerged at the level of belief sets confirmed that cognitive optimality at this level is at least as important as at the individual belief level. The effect of belief proportions on delayed recall followed an inverted U-shaped curve. The belief set that was mostly intuitive, combined with a few minimally counterintuitive ones had the highest rate of delayed recall and the lowest rate of memory degradation over time. This is the recipe for a successful cultural belief system, and it is the cognitive template that characterizes most popular folktales and religious narratives. The "equal proportions" belief set had moderate memorability. Critically, the belief set with a majority of minimally counterintuitive beliefs had the lowest rate of delayed recall and the highest level of memory degradation. Indeed, this is a cognitive template that is rarely encountered in existing culturally successful materials. We suggest that narratives with such a template may have been introduced by cultural innovators but failed to pass the test of memorability. As a result, they faded from culture. Thus, the way natural and nonnatural beliefs are combined is crucial to survival of a belief system.

Even though the concern of this chapter is not to elucidate memory processes per se, but to examine the role of memory in generating culturally stable materials, it is possible to offer some informed speculation about the cognitive processes that might render the majority intuitive belief set more memorable and resilient. One explanation is that minimally counterintuitive beliefs, because of their minimal incongruity with ontological assumptions, are surprising and interesting. Despite the fact that they themselves are not as memorable as intuitive beliefs, they may serve the purpose of drawing attention to the entire belief set in which they are embedded. They encourage paying more attention to the belief set as a whole, and thinking about it more often over time. The majority intuitive beliefs, supported by ontological assumptions and theories, then do the actual conceptual work by enhancing overall recall. Thus, a cognitive bootstrapping may be in operation between a minority of counterintuitives and a majority of intuitives. The former draw interest, and the latter ensure recall over time.

However, this process is highly dependent on the particular mix of beliefs. It works as long as minimally counterintuitive beliefs exist in small proportions. Once their proportion increases to very high levels, the belief set becomes too incongruent. It looses its capacity to arouse surprise and interest. In addition, because of the massive inconsistency with ontology, it also becomes harder to recall and transmit. If this reasoning is correct, then we can make the following prediction: Assuming that immediate recall is a rough measure of initial "interestingness," immediate recall (interestingness) of the counterintuitives should predict delayed recall of the intuitives, but not when the counterintuitives are in the majority. This was indeed the case. Immediate recall of the minimally counterintuitive beliefs was positively correlated with delayed recall of the intuitive beliefs in the "majority intuitive" condition, and in the "equal proportions" condition, but not in the "majority counterintuitives" condition.

## BEYOND COGNITION: THE ROLE OF EMOTIONS IN THE TRANSMISSION OF CULTURAL BELIEFS

So far in our discussion, we have been treating the transmission of beliefs in folk tales, myths, and religious systems as if the psychological processes that guide such transmission are the same for all culturally important materials. In fact, our discussion has been based on the proposal that folktales, religions, and other cultural beliefs are continuous on the cognitive dimension. That is, we have reviewed evidence that these cultural beliefs exploit the same cognitive operations based on intuitive ontologies and domain-specific theories of physics, biology, and mind.

This may indeed be the case, but we believe that a critical psychological difference still exists between religious and nonreligious cultural materials. Nonnatural religious beliefs seem to draw emotional commitment like no other beliefs. People feel deeply committed to them. In fact, the purely cognitive analysis of belief transmission that we have presented so far would lead us to conclude that ontological violations in the Road Runner or in Beauty and the Beast are indistinguishable from those in a religious narrative. But Moses receiving the word of God, the Immaculate Conception, and the Prophet Mohammad ascending to Heaven do not seem to have the same psychological status as Wile E. Coyote being suspended in air, the magic mirror in Beauty and the Beast, or a prophet holding an ordinary conversation with his people. Unlike nonnatural beliefs in folktales and cartoons, or natural occurrences in religious narratives, nonnatural religious beliefs evoke profound epistemological and emotional commitment, and coordinate group emotions to such an extent that people may even sacrifice their lives for these beliefs. How can we explain this phenomenon?

We propose that a possible explanation for the emotional grounding of nonnatural religious beliefs may lie in the way the human mind and human cultures have coevolved to resolve one of the most intractable problems that has been with us since we attained self-consciousness: awareness of mortality. As has been argued extensively elsewhere (Greenberg et al., 1990; Solomon, Greenberg, Schimel, Arndt, & Pyszczynski, this volume), many aspects of culture and commitment to group life seem to be organized to a large extent so that people are able to manage the debilitating consequences of the awareness and fear of death. Thus, experimentally inducing mortality salience leads to more positive evaluations of in-group members, more negative evaluation of out-group members, and a heightened sensitivity to threats to one's own cultural worldview (Greenberg et al., 1990). Awareness and fear of death may also be an emotional foundation of religion (Bloom, 1992; Feuerbach, 1843/1972; Freud, 1915/1957). The scholar of ancient religions Walter Burkert (1996, p. 31) thought so, when he wrote, "the utmost seriousness of religion is linked to the great overriding fear of death. The value of religion, manifest in the forms of religion's cultural transmission and in the insiders' confessions, is that it deals with the 'ultimate concern' and thus fits the biological landscape."

Consistent with this idea, recently we have found that inducing mortality salience directly affects religious commitment as well. Compared to control-group participants who were asked to reflect on their favorite foods, experimental group participants who were asked to reflect on their own death reported themselves to be more religious and were more likely to say that they believe in God (Norenzayan & Atran, 2001b).

We speculate that nonnatural beliefs, unlike those grounded in intuitive ontologies, offer a seeming causal resolution to the existential fear of death by evoking possible worlds of avoidance. Thus, nonnatural beliefs may be psychologically privileged under conditions where everyday common sense fails, as when people are faced with the reality of their and their family members' imminent mortality. Because the ordinary causal understanding of intuitive ontologies fails to deliver a resolution to this existential problem, people construct and accept a psychological realm that goes beyond the ordinary and appeals to the extraordinary. To reprieve cognition from constant attention to the factually unresolvable and attention-arresting anxieties of everyday life, there must be a countervailing emotional faith that people share in counterfactual and counterintuitive resolutions.

We propose the hypothesis that awareness of mortality—and perhaps other emotionally eruptive existential anxieties for which there appears to be no rational expectation of resolution, such as vulnerability (to injustice, pain, dominance), loneliness (abandonment, unrequited love), or catastrophe (disease, sudden loss)—should cause people to become cognitively susceptible to seek, encode, recall, and transmit information that goes beyond rational or intuitive understanding. This includes beliefs in supernatural entities that intervene to solve (the humanly insolvable) problems of humankind.

## CONCLUSION: ALTERNATIVE SCENARIOS OF CULTURAL TRANSMISSION

We have found that under ordinary conditions and over at least a 1-week period, natural beliefs enjoy a recall and hence transmission advantage over nonnatural beliefs that are minimally counterintuitive. This raises a question:

Why do narratives that have achieved a cultural level of distribution–tales, myths, religious beliefs–invariably contain nonnatural beliefs? Is there a psychological explanation for the success of this form of cultural beliefs?

One answer is provided in the data we described earlier. Nonnatural beliefs, as long as they come in small proportions, help people remember and presumably transmit the intuitive statements. A small proportion of nonnatural beliefs gives the story a memory advantage over stories with no nonnatural beliefs at all or with far too many nonnatural beliefs, just like moderately spiced-up dishes have a cultural advantage over bland or far too spicy dishes. Just as spices in and of themselves may have little nutritional value but help one consume nutritious food, nonnatural beliefs may have little psychological value but may help one remember and transmit beliefs that do have psychological value. This represents the first alternative scenario of cultural transmission: the *cognitive route*. Here, cultural innovators start with natural propositions, then spice up their narratives with nonnatural propositions making the narratives culturally attractive. Over multiple generations of trial and error, those belief systems that evolve this cognitive form enjoy a transmission advantage over others and eventually achieve cultural stability. This route may describe how folktales evolve in a culture. The typical cultural innovator of the cognitive route is the storyteller; its setting is around the campfire or the dinner table, and its ontological violations are for cognitive effect.

The second scenario of cultural transmission is the reverse of the first. This second possibility is that under some conditions, nonnatural beliefs (of the minimally counterintuitive kind) enjoy a transmission advantage–for example, when consumers of cultural materials have reason to expect that the cultural narratives will follow a nonnatural course (Barret & Nyhof, 2001; Boyer & Ramble, 2001). This may also happen if it turns out that even though nonnatural beliefs are less memorable in the absolute sense, they degrade at a slower rate, as hinted by the evidence we have. More importantly, in this second *emotional route* to cultural transmission, cultural innovators, faced with powerful existential anxieties of their group members, invoke nonnatural narratives that "transcend" common sense and offer seeming resolutions to these fears. Then the cultural innovators embed their nonnatural narratives within intuitive causal understandings, making the narratives comprehensible and communicable. Over multiple generations of trial and error, those belief systems that evolve this second cognitive form enjoy a transmission advantage over others and eventually achieve cultural stability. We speculate that this process may be a critical functional motivation for religious thought. The typical cultural innovator of the emotional route is the shaman and the prophet. Its setting is death as a result of disease, natural disasters, and war. Its ontological violations are for emotional effect.

Both routes–the cognitive and the emotional–may occur independently in the way all kinds of cultural beliefs emerge. Moreover, even though the outcome they produce may look cognitively similar in the way natural and nonnatural beliefs are combined, the origin, emergence, and underlying psychological processes that support these routes may be quite different.

## ACKNOWLEDGMENTS

We thank Brian Malley for his instrumental contribution to conducting the study reported in this chapter. Thanks also to Andrea Patalano and Jeffrey Sanchez-Burks for their helpful comments on an earlier draft.

## REFERENCES

Atran, S. (1990). *Cognitive foundations of natural history*. New York: Cambridge University Press.

Atran, S. (1996). Modes of thinking about living kinds: Science, symbolism, common sense. In D. Olson & N. Torrance (Eds.), *Modes of thought*. New York: Cambridge University Press.

Atran, S. (1998). Folkbiology and the anthropology of science: Cognitive universals and cultural particulars. *Behavioral and Brain Sciences, 21*, 547–609.

Atran, S., & Sperber, D. (1991). Learning without teaching: Its place in culture. In L. Tolchinsky-Landsmann (Ed.), *Culture, schooling and psychological development* (pp. 39–55). Norwood: Ablex.

Avis, J., & Harris, P. L. (1991). Belief-desire reasoning among Baka children. *Child Development, 62*, 460–467.

Baillargeon, R. (1998). Infants' understanding of the physical world. In M. Sabourin & F. Craik & M. Robert (Eds.), *Advances in Psychological Science* (Vol. 2, pp. 503–509). London: Psychology Press.

Barret, J. L., & Keil, F. (1996). Conceptualizing a non-natural entity: Anthropomorphism in God concepts. *Cognitive Psychology, 31*, 219–247.

Barret, J. L., & Nyhof, M. A. (2001). Spreading nonnatural concepts: The role of intuitive conceptual structures in memory and transmission of cultural materials. *Journal of Cognition and Culture, 1*(1), 69–100.

Bartlett, F. A. (1932). *Remembering: A study in experimental psychology*. Cambridge: Cambridge University Press.

Berlin, B. (1992). *Ethnobiological classification: Principles of categorization of plants and animals in traditional societies*. Princeton, NJ: Princeton University Press.

Berlin, B., Breedlove, D., & Raven, P. (1973). General principles of classification and nomenclature in folk biology. *American Anthropologist, 74*, 214–242.

Bloom, H. (1992). *The American religion*. New York: Simon and Schuster.

Boyd, R., & Richerson, P. J. (1985). *Culture and the evolutionary process*. Chicago: University of Chicago Press.

Boyer, P. (1992). Explaining religious ideas: Outline of a cognitive approach. *Numen, 39*, 27–57.

Boyer, P. (1994a). *The naturalness of religious ideas*. Berkeley: University of California Press.

Boyer, P. (1994b). Cognitive constraints on cultural representations: Natural ontologies and religious ideas. In L. A. Hirschfeld & S. A. Gelman (Eds.), *Mapping the Mind: Domain specificity in cognition and culture* (pp. 391–411). New York: Cambridge University Press.

Boyer, P., & Ramble, C. (2001). Cognitive templates for religious concepts: Cross-cultural evidence for recall of counter-intuitive representations. *Cognitive Science, 25*, 535–564.

Burkert, W. (1996). *Creation of the sacred: Tracks of biology in early religions*. Cambridge, MA: Harvard University Press.

Campbell, D. T. (1974). Evolutionary epistemology. In P. A. Schilpp (Ed.), *The philosophy of Kark Popper* (pp. 413–463). La Salle, IL: Open Court.

Carey, S., & Spelke, E. (1994). Domain-specific knowledge and conceptual change. In L. A. Hirschfeld & S. A. Gelman (Eds.), *Mapping the mind: Domain specificity in cognition and cognition* (pp. 169–200). Cambridge: Cambridge University Press.

Cavalli-Sforza, L. L., & Feldman, M. W. (1981). *Cultural transmission and evolution: A quantitative approach*. Princeton, NJ: Princeton University Press.

Choi, I., Nisbett, R. E., & Norenzayan, A. (1999). Causal attribution across cultures: Variation and universality. *Psychological Bulletin, 125*, 47–63.

Dawkins, R. (1982). *The extended phenotype*. Oxford: Oxford University Press.

Feuerbach, L. (1972). *The fiery book: Selected writings of Ludwig Feuerbach*. Garden City, NY: Anchor Books. (*Das Wesen des Christentums* originally written 1843)

Flavell, J. H., Zhang, X.-D., Zou, H., Dong, Q., & Qui, S. (1983). A comparison of the appearance-reality distinction in the People's Republic of China and the United States. *Cognitive Psychology, 15*, 459–466.

Freud, S. (1957). Thoughts for the time on war and death. In J. Strachey (Ed.), *The standard edition of the complete psychological works of Sigmund Freud* (Vol. 14). London: Hogarth Press. (Original work written 1915)

Gardner, D., Harris, P. L., Ohmoto, M., & Hamazaki, T. (1988). Japanese children's understanding of the distinction between real and apparent emotion. *International Journal of Behavioral Development, 11*, 203–218.

Geertz, C. (1975). On the nature of anthropological understanding. *American Scientist, 63*, 47–53.

Gelman, S. A., & Hirschfeld, L. A. (1998). How biological is essentialism? In D. L. Medin & S. Atran (Eds.), *Folkbiology* (pp. 403–446). Cambridge, MA: MIT Press.

Greenberg, J., Pyszczynski, T., Solomon, S., Rosenblatt, A., Veeder, M., Kirkland, S., & Lyon, D. (1990). Evidence for terror management theory II. *Journal of Personality and Social Psychology, 58*, 308–318.

Keil, F. (1989). *Concepts, kinds, and cognitive development*. Cambridge, MA: Bradford Books/MIT Press.

Keil, F. (1994). The birth and nurturance of concepts by domains: The origins of concepts of living things. In L. Hirschfeld & S. Gelman (Eds.), *Mapping the mind: Domain specificity in cognition and culture* (pp. 234–254). New York: Cambridge University Press.

Kelly, M. H., & Keil, F. (1985). The more things change . . . : Metamorphoses and conceptual structure. *Cognitive Science, 9*, 403–416.

Kintsch, W., & Greene, E. (1978). The role of culture-specific schemata in the comprehension and recall of stories. *Discourse Processes, 1*, 1–13.

Leslie, A. M. (1982). The perception of causality in infants. *Perception, 11*, 173–186.

Leslie, A. M. (1994). ToMM, ToBY, and agency: Core architecture and domain specificity. In L. A. Hirschfeld & S. A. Gelman (Eds.), *Mapping the mind: Domain specificity in cognition and culture* (pp. 119–148). Cambridge: Cambridge University Press.

Lillard, A. S. (1998). Ethnopsychologies: Cultural variations in theories of mind. *Psychological Bulletin, 1*, 3–32.

Lloyd, G. E. R. (1996). Science in antiquity: the Greek and Chinese cases and their relevance to problems of culture and cognition. In D. R. Olson & N. Torrance (Eds.), *Modes of thought: Explorations in culture and cognition* (pp. 15–33). Cambridge: Cambridge University Press.

Medin, D. L., & Atran, S. (Eds.). (1999). *Folkbiology*. Cambridge, MA: MIT Press.

Norenzayan, A., & Atran, S. (2001a). *The role of memory in the cultural transmission of natural and nonnatural beliefs*. Unpublished manuscript, University of British Columbia.

Norenzayan, A., & Atran, S. (2001b). [*The effect of mortality salience on religious commitment*]. Unpublished raw data.

Peng, K., & Nisbett, R. E. (1996). Cross-cultural similarities and differences in the understanding of physical causality. In G. Shield & M. Shale (Eds.), *Culture and science* (pp. 10–21). Frankfort, KY: Kentucky State University Press.

Rosch, E., Mervis, C., Grey, W., Johnson, D., & Boyes-Braem, P. (1976). Basic objects in natural categories. *Cognitive Psychology, 8*, 382–439.

Spelke, E. S. (1990). Principles of object perception. *Cognitive Science, 14*, 29–56.

Sperber, D. (1975). *Rethinking symbolism.* Cambridge: Cambridge University Press.

Sperber, D. (1990). The epidemiology of beliefs. In C. Fraser & G. Gaskell (Eds.), *The social psychological study of widespread beliefs* (pp. 25–44). Oxford: Clarendon Press.

Sperber, D. (1996). *Explaining culture: A naturalistic approach.* Cambridge, MA: Blackwell.

Sperber, D., & Wilson, D. (1986). *Relevance: Communication and cognition.* Cambridge, MA: Blackwell.

Wellman, H. M. (1990). *The child's theory of mind.* Cambridge, MA: MIT Press.

CHAPTER

# 8

# Self-Organizing Culture: How Norms Emerge in Small Groups

Holly Arrow
K. L. Burns
University of Oregon

> *[People] cannot help producing rules, customs, values and other sorts of norms whenever they come together in any situation that lasts for any considerable time.*
>
> –Sherif (1936, p. 3)

Thinking scientifically about culture and psychology is fraught with difficulties. It requires us to think about bidirectional influence between the macro level of large populations and the micro level of individual psychology. Culture clearly shapes human behavior, yet mapping out the process by which the cultural context affects the specific thoughts and actions of individuals is a daunting task. Individual thoughts and actions, of course, must influence culture in turn, for how else can we account for changes in culture over time, or the creation of culture in the first place? In large-scale modern societies, however, tracing the impact of individuals on culture is like tracing the impact of a small stream on the ocean, unless we focus on people who wield a degree of power that makes them quite atypical.

Scientists often tackle the sticky problem of bidirectional influence by picking one direction and leaving the other for a different group of scholars to study. A top-down approach investigates how culture affects individual behavior. A bottom-up approach stresses the impact of psychological mechanisms on the generation of culture. In a earlier draft of this chapter, we assigned these two approaches to various traditions (bolstered by quotes from prominent proponents), scolded them for emphasizing one type of influence over another, and then presented our integrated approach as a more appealing alternative. It was an attractive rhetorical device, and relatively easy to support with material by scholars who advanced their approach by denouncing others as misguided, reductionist, incoherent, and bound to outmoded traditions.

When we went back and read the original sources more carefully, however, attending to the context in which quotes used as ammunition were drawn, we had to abandon our cherished rhetorical device. Yes, some bodies of work pay little attention to how the architecture of the human mind might structure recurrent elements of culture. True, other bodies of work seem to emphasize the evolved architecture of the mind while giving less attention to how the sociocultural environment modulates behavior. However, a common theme was also apparent: a quest for integration identical to our own.

Berry, Poortinga, Segall, and Dasen (1992), who noted that cross-cultural psychologists are mainly interested in the flow of influence from population-level variables to individual outcomes, also acknowledged that "a full model must include feedback loops" (p. 11). Shweder (1990) asserted that cultural psychology is the study of how "psyche and culture, person and context ... dynamically, dialectically, and jointly make each other up" (p. 1). Tooby and Cosmides (1992), who highlight the psychological foundations of culture, also stressed that "both the genes and the developmentally relevant environment are the product of evolution ... the evolutionary process determines how the environment shapes the organism" (pp. 84–85). Explicit attempts to account for influences in both directions also include Boyd and Richerson's (1985) integration of social learning (cultural transmission) and individual learning from the environment, which can then diffuse through a population. Sperber's (1986) epidemiological notion of culture as a distribution of representations also interprets the content of transmitted culture as strongly constrained by human cognitive abilities and innate concepts.

The difficulty in translating the desire for integration into a coherent approach to studying culture and psychology is ample evidence that cultural psychology, cross-cultural psychology, psychological anthropology, and evolutionary psychology are all, in their own ways, trying to get purchase on a very difficult problem. In this chapter, we make our own attempt. We examine the interface between culture and individual psychology by focusing directly on the dynamic interplay between levels, and by looking at more levels than two. In particular, we view small groups as an excellent setting for observing the simultaneous, mutual influence of culture and psychological processes. Thus, paradoxically, we propose to make a hard problem easier not by subtracting levels and directional arrows, but by adding more.

Complexity science and dynamical systems theory can help us think about cultural dynamics in a way that explicitly handles cross-level mutual causality. We follow the lead of Caporael and Baron (1997), who apply complexity ideas to the problem of psychology and culture and differentiate the space between individual and population into dyads, small work groups, and larger bands. Focusing on small groups as complex dynamic systems helps us connect the multiple levels of individual, dyad, group, and population into a single framework.

To study the multilevel process of culture creation and change, we also need experimental paradigms that incorporate micro, meso, and macro levels. Although some psychologists have studied the emergence of cultural elements such as social norms experimentally, the menu of paradigms to choose from is brief and, in our view, inadequate to the task. Another project of this chapter is thus to describe an experimental paradigm we have developed to investigate the formation of small groups by individuals embedded in miniature societies. This multilevel paradigm can yield useful data on how cultural elements such as social norms both emerge from and shape individual cognition and collective behavior.

The chapter is organized as follows. First, we describe a variety of levels that constitute the interface between psychology and culture. We discuss the dynamics within and across levels using the frame of complexity science, an interdisciplinary set of concepts and methods for studying hierarchically organized systems (see Lewin, 1992, for a good introduction). Second, we give a selective overview of social experimental approaches to studying the emergence and transmission of norms, and describe a new experimental paradigm, an interactive card game called *social poker*. Third, we illustrate our conceptual and methodological approach with data gathered using this paradigm. We focus on how social norms governing group membership and the allocation of collective resources emerge and are stabilized, transmitted, and transformed.

## SELF-ORGANIZING CULTURE: A COMPLEXITY APPROACH

We are not the first to view the emergence of culture through the lens of complexity theory and nonlinear dynamics. Anthropologists (e.g., Culbert, 1988), organizational theorists (e.g., Harrison & Carroll, 1991), psychologists (e.g., Nowak & Vallacher, 1998), and political scientists (e.g., Axelrod, 1995) have considered the dynamics of cultural emergence and transmission in this light. Building on this foundation, we connect key features of complex systems to the dynamics of culture, with a focus on social norms. In small groups, social norms are collective expectations about how to behave that are enacted in the patterned behavior of members over time.

### Core Configurations of Human Social Life

Caporael and Baron (1997) hypothesize that there are four evolutionary core configurations in which people naturally associate, which are repeatedly assembled as the "natural environment" for the human mind. These are dyads, teams (work/family groups), bands, and macrobands. Modal size for the last three configurations is given as 5, 30, and 300 people.

Contemporary observations of naturally occurring groups in public places indicate that dyads are common, and few groups contain more than five or six people (see Moreland, Levine, & Wingert, 1996, for a review). The mode of 30 for a band corresponds to the size Jarvenpa (1993) gave for overwintering communities of 20–50 people in modern hunter-gatherer societies; Kelly (1995) reported an average size of 25 for nomadic bands. Researchers who study small groups in modern society also define 30 as the upper limit for how many people can plausibly function together as a small group (Hare, 1995). Much of the work in hunter-gatherer bands, however, is accomplished in small work groups. Allowing for a range of children, healthy adults, and the old and infirm or ill, Kelly estimates that a band of 25 would include seven to eight full-time foragers, on average—the size of a team. Size estimates for the "maximal" groupings of macrobands vary widely (see Kelly, 1995, pp. 209–211 for a discussion).

The core configurations each have modal tasks or functions. The dyad is the context in which infants learn microcoordination, and is also the unit for sexual reproduction. The work group is the unit for foraging or hunting, and is the context for the development of distributed cognition—the process of coordinating and integrating knowledge across people. Through interactions in small groups, children "master forming and internalizing norms and values" (Caporael & Baron, 1997, p. 331). The band is the focus of social identity for its members and the context for role specialization, higher level coordination, and the shared construction of reality. The macroband is a seasonal gathering for the exchange of resources and mate selection, and is the context for stabilizing and standardizing language.

### Multilevel Complex Systems

To give a reasonably complete description of a complex system, one should consider the flow of activity at three partially nested levels. Nonlinear *local dynamics* characterized by feedback loops give rise to emergent *global structure* at the next level up, which in turn constrains local events. The impact of *context variables* (also called control parameters) on the nature of global dynamics is the third level of analysis (Arrow, McGrath, & Berdahl, 2000). For the purposes of this chapter, individuals and the dyadic interactions among them comprise the local level, from which the small group emerges. Our small group, which corresponds to Caporeal and Baron's team, serves as the focal "global" level, the setting in which norms develop. The larger collective (neighborhood, business unit, classroom) in which the small group operates is the embedding context. In this section, we discuss how the levels from individual to band are involved in the emergence, transmission, and transformation of social norms.

The different levels of human social aggregates are not fully nested within one another like Russian dolls or proper sets. In groups the smallest units—members—are partially embedded individuals with a life that intersects with, but is not fully embedded within, any one group. As an example, an operating-room nurse in a group completing a coronary bypass operation may also be a father embedded in a family, a coach embedded in a soccer team, and a member of a hospital committee reviewing institutional policy. These groups are embedded in multiple larger collectives such as a neighborhood, a soccer league, and a hospital chain. The nurse will also have dyadic interactions with people (his patients, for example) who do not belong to any of the same groups that he does. Thus ideas and communication flow across multiple, overlapping, permeable group boundaries, which define the groups and partially contain their members.

## Individual Level: Psychological Mechanisms

At the individual level, psychological mechanisms relevant to the emergence of norms regulate human social behavior. In his overview of influence strategies, for example, Cialdini (1993) identified the principle of "social proof" as guide to human behavior. The principle is: When in doubt, copy the behavior of others who are similar to oneself in age and sex, particularly if they belong to one's "in-group" or have high social status. For humans to implement this principle reliably, they clearly need mechanisms that enable them to judge similarity to self in age and sex, assess social status, recognize membership in the same group, and imitate others. A similar principle, which we paraphrase as "imitate the most commonly observed behavior," underlies the conformist transmission of cultural behaviors proposed by Henrich and Boyd (1998).

Tooby and Cosmides (1992) proposed that a host of specialized cognitive and affective mechanisms have evolved to promote behavior that has proved adaptive for human social interaction. The four universal relational models (Fiske, 1991, 2000)—communal sharing, authority ranking, equality matching, and market pricing (described in more detail later) fit this profile, because the models provide information about the content of expected behavior. Integrating findings and concepts from several disciplines, Fiske proposed that all interpersonal interaction is structured by these species-wide models, which serve as a generative grammar for thinking about and coordinating relationships. We think of the models as core schemas–organized sets of associated concepts and rules (Taylor & Crocker, 1981) that coordinate the operation of more specialized cognitive modules for functions such as cheater detection, reading status cues, and generalized reciprocity, which are differentially appropriate for different social contexts and relationships. The context tunes the probability of selection for each model; acting in accordance with a model also shapes the immediate social environment. We describe in turn how social interaction is organized according to each relational model, and identify some psychological mechanisms that we believe are activated (or switched off) by these "cultural coordination devices" (Fiske, 2000).

In *communal sharing* relationships, people emphasize the common identity of group members and focus on what is good for the group as a whole. The preferred model of decision making is consensus, and people pool resources and draw on the pool without keeping track of individual contributions and withdrawals. Pooling and redistribution is commonly used for family food resources (Sahlins, 1996). Anyone defined as family is entitled to raid the refrigerator, regardless of whether they helped obtain the food. People who are not blood relatives have these privileges only if they have been classified as "family."

Some primary psychological mechanisms underlying this model are attachment to kin and, more generally, the fundamental human need for belonging (Baumeister & Leary, 1995), which motivates people to seek inclusion in groups. Other relevant mechanisms would be the ability to perceive group boundaries and the motivation to prevent outsiders from accessing group resources. Research on group perception (e.g., Perdue, Dovidio, Gurtman, & Tyler, 1990) and intergroup relations (e.g., Sherif, Harvey, White, Hood, & Sherif, 1961), plus abundant evidence in the natural world of friendship cliques, gang warfare, and cronyism, illustrates that people do indeed attend to group boundaries, showing generosity to those within the boundaries and hostility toward outsiders. When this model is activated, it should switch off unneeded mechanisms, such as the cheater detection module identified by Cosmides and Tooby (1992).

In *authority ranking* relationships, people structure their interactions according to status and position. A prototypical domain is the military, where personnel wear insignias of rank to signal status. One necessary mechanism for implementing this model is the ability to interpret status cues, a capacity that humans share with many nonhuman species that organize themselves into dominance hierarchies. Another is a propensity to obey those in higher status positions, demonstrated powerfully in the natural social world by soldiers, members of religious cults, and students in classrooms. In distributing resources, high-status members get more; low-status members get less. An authority ranking approach to distributing office space, for example, would give senior, higher level members more space and junior members less space, based on rank. However, rank also comes with obligations: Superiors are expected to provide for inferiors. Thus, when a group organized according to this model eats out, the highest-status person often picks up the bill. When this model is active, mechanisms governing reciprocal altruism (Trivers, 1971)—which are appropriate to the next model, equality matching—should be switched off.

In *equality matching* relationships, people reciprocate favors after some delay, and maintain a balance between giving and receiving. This model is commonly applied among people who consider themselves to be of equal status, such as friends, classmates, or colleagues. People in equality matching relationships often respond to favors by saying "I owe you one" or "I'll pay next time." Note the difference from authority ranking, in which an employee does not expect to reciprocate a meal by taking the boss out in turn. The psychological mechanisms necessary for reciprocal altruism are not specific to humans; this form of time-delayed exchange of favors has also been documented among chimpanzees and vampire bats (Cosmides & Tooby, 1992). According to Trivers (1971), the emotions of gratitude and sympathy help regulate this system, as does guilt when one has not reciprocated properly.

In *market pricing* relationships, people seek the best deal for themselves, and expect that others will do the same. This model, which commonly governs trade and other social exchanges among strangers or acquaintances, dictates that resources be divided based on the equity principle, with outcomes proportional to inputs. When eating out following this principle, people contribute based on what they ordered. When the exchange includes a time delay before the benefit is delivered, modules for assessing trustworthiness and cheating should be on alert. This relational model should trigger a single-minded focus on maximizing utility (Trivers, 1971), and should activate the "negative reciprocity" (Sahlins, 1996) of moral aggression if someone is caught cheating. Sympathy—the tendency to attend to the other's needs—should be switched off.

***Cultural Specification.*** Particular cultural implementations of these models (scripts, or specified sequences of actions) organize social exchange, distribution, contribution, decision-making, social influence, moral judgment, aggression, and conflict (Fiske, 1991). There is no practical limit, for example, to the types of objects or services that might be deemed appropriate or inappropriate to reciprocate the gift of a chicken or a color TV. Because scripts vary widely across time and place, they are, for the most part, particular elements of cultures, rather than psychological primitives, such as the principle of social proof, the relational models, and the mechanisms that (we believe) the "higher level" relational models switch on or off. Because different mechanisms specify different behaviors, the activation of a mechanism depends on a match with appropriate social cues. As Fiske (2000) and others (e.g., Caporeal & Baron, 1997; Tooby & Cosmides, 1992) have noted, psychological mechanisms and social cues and settings have evolved together and require one another. We turn next to the "core configurations" of social interaction which constitute the settings and provide the cues.

## Local Dynamics: Dyadic Interaction

The dyad is the setting for microcoordination of action and thought. Although this coordination is facilitated by shared models for interaction, it is initially based on a spontaneous coupling of action that does not require explicit, conscious effort to achieve. If two people (let's call them Anna and Francesco), are conversing, then what Anna says and does depends in part on what Francesco says and does, and vice versa. Francesco can see Anna's reactions while he is talking and can make immediate adjustments and corrections. The mutual, nonlinear nature of human face-to-face interaction, which includes "back-channel" feedback, makes coordination relatively easy to achieve. This skill at microcoordination develops in the primary dyad of mother and infant (see, e.g., Nwokah, Hsu, Dobrowolska, & Fogel, 1994). The dyadic relationship is thus the context in which the psychological mechanisms relevant to social interaction are first activated, and it is a context that these mechanisms help construct.

The coordination of thought and action among adults also requires and builds a shared understanding of the nature of the relationship. The different relational models specify different sets of responses, and the cultural context supplies a plethora of detail about how people might interact. In a new interaction, people's reading of cues and construction of the situation help direct their initial actions. The first person to act provides the initial move based on how the person has understood the relationship, and that person's action cues the other person's response. Even if two people (returning to Anna and Francesco) have different ideas about the appropriate model, Anna's initial action can trigger a train of interaction that unfolds in a smooth flow of coordinated behavior. Francesco's own actions in this exchange can alter his views about what is appropriate, leading to mid-course corrections to align belief and action (see Nowak & Vallacher, 1998, for a more detailed discussion of this kind of dynamic coupling).

## Global Level: Small Group

In small groups, coordination cues are provide by multiple actors, rather than a single partner. The behavior of each unit in a complex system is influenced directly by some of the other units, linking them together in a network of mutual influence. Principles such as "social proof" ensure that people will use the behavior of others as input to their own behavior. Out of this mutual influence, collective behavior becomes coordinated in a process called *entrainment* (Kelly, 1988). Because entrainment occurs naturally when dynamic components interact (whether they are grandfather clocks or heart cells or violin strings), simple coordination of behavior does not require explicit, conscious effort to achieve. Complex systems as different as chemical reactions (Prigogine & Stengers, 1984) and the flight of birds exhibit a common dynamic pattern: the emergence of order from nonlinear relationships among multiple interacting units (Casti, 1994).

In small groups, emerging group norms establish shared expectations that guide more complicated sequences of coordinated action than the relatively simple entrainment of gesture and turn taking in conversation. In their model of norm emergence, Bettenhausen and Murnighan (1985) proposed that people in a new group setting rely on their definition of the situation to retrieve an appropriate script. If we take the relational models as the basic forms for social interaction, the definition of the situation should activate one or more relational models, which narrows down the choice of appropriate scripts. What happens next depends on whether the models activated and the scripts retrieved are similar or different across group members.

When all members settle on the same relational model and retrieve similar scripts, interactions will be smooth and unproblematic, with no need for an explicit discussion of norms. If members retrieve different models and scripts, initial interactions will be frustrating and confusing (uncoordinated) and will trigger explicit discussion of how to proceed. If members retrieve similar scripts but have different models in mind, then initial interactions will either redefine the situation for dissenting members or lead to explicit discussion about what is appropriate. If members have the same model but different scripts, smooth initial coordination will break down as the scripts diverge. Group norms thus emerge from joint action and (in some cases) explicit discussion, a bottom-up process of local dynamics. Once created, however, the norm (a group-level structure) guides member activity at the local level in turn. In this way, process creates structure, which helps coordinate process.

This theory assumes that all members define the situation and retrieve scripts before interaction begins. However, people may also be uncertain, triggering the social proof mechanism of "imitate others." In a study of project groups, for example, Gersick (1988, p. 33) found that "lasting patterns can appear as early as the first few seconds of a group's life." Perhaps the same plan for action occurs to all members simultaneously. Given the variety of scripts possible even in narrowly defined situations, this seems unlikely. Instead, we believe new group members commonly rely on the actions of other members to help define the situation for them. They use these actions as cues to determine which relational model is being implemented. In a newly formed group, all members are new, and the uncertainty this entails makes them especially susceptible to mutual influence. Mutual influence in the collective search for a common frame of reference helps members converge on collective decisions and coordinate their actions.

As soon as a group acts collectively, it has established something new: a precedent. This precedent then shapes members' shared beliefs about appropriate behavior. All group members now have a shared script for "how we do this in this group." The next time the group needs to act, the process will be different, because of the precedent established by the first decision. The precedent coordinates collective cognition, as all members retrieve the same script: the one the group used before. Members may, of course, differ in their level of satisfaction or dissatisfaction with this script. The issue for the group when they face their next task or decision has changed: It is not "What shall we do?" but "Shall we proceed as before?"

Using the framework of dynamical systems thinking, we can identify the four relational models as potential *attractors* for social norms as the group sorts out how to behave. An attractor is an equilibrium state or cycle of states into which a system settles over time. From the initial state of confusion, the group will move toward one attractor. Which attractor the group settles on will depend on the relative preferences for the four models that each member holds (individual level) and the distribution of preferences among the members (group level). When all members have the same preference, the result is predictable. The group starts, essentially, within the "basin of attraction" for a single model. Just as water falling within a watershed will drain predictably to the same river, the activity of a complex system that starts out within the basin of an attractor will settle down on that attractor.

When members are uncertain (no clear preference) or differ in their preferences, they may collectively retrieve multiple models as possibilities. Because members are easily influenced in this initial stage of group formation, the first approach suggested or enacted can inspire a quick convergence on a single model. Which attractor they move toward, however, will depend on who acts or speaks first. Positive feedback can create substantial differences in outcomes based on very small initial differences in the system, a phenomenon known as sensitive dependence on initial conditions. In two groups of people with the same initial distribution of preferences, the social norm adopted by each group may differ based on who happened to express their preference first. Sensitive dependence effects are most likely when the system is unstable, and collective uncertainty among members creates instability. Divergence of initially similar systems can create distinctive group microcultures with different norms.

As a group works together over time, precedent quickly becomes "tradition"—which we define as any particular script the group has enacted twice. Newcomers conform to group norms by observing and copying regularities in the way other members behave, and in this process we see the classic top-down transmission of culture from a higher level (the group) to a lower level (individual). Dynamic instabilities at the local level of a complex system can also create spontaneous change even after the system appears to have "settled" into a persistent structure (Eidelson, 1997). This is bottom-up change. A newcomer may suggest an alternate approach, or may innocently ask why a group has chosen a particular procedure, such as dividing group resources by drawing straws. If existing members have no stronger reason than precedent for a particular norm, a simple request for information can lead to a reconsideration of how the group should behave. Thus what look like established norms at the group level can undergo sudden changes based on fluctuations at the local level of intra- and interpersonal dynamics.

### Embedding Context: The Band

A larger congregation of people might be a primary functional unit (such as the hunter-gatherer band) in which individuals repeatedly form smaller work groups of fluid membership. It might be a gathering of preexisting smaller groups. It might be a meeting of like-minded people that includes some work groups, some dyads, and some otherwise unconnected individuals. Or it might be an aggregation of strangers with no prior ties, such as students who sign up for the same class. The dynamics of norm emergence, differentiation, and diffusion in this larger grouping should differ depending on the preexisting structure of ties among the individuals involved.

Latané and colleagues have studied the self-organization of beliefs in collections of individuals connected by different geometries of communication links (Latané & L'Herrou, 1996). In their experiments, 24 people linked together on a computer network played a conformity game that simulates conformist transmission of beliefs. Players were rewarded for detecting the majority preference for red or blue, for example. Each person could send messages to four others in the network, and each received messages from four people (not necessarily the same four). Although people's initial beliefs were randomly distributed, the network quickly self-organized into coherent clusters of people with similar views. These clusters emerged as participants repeatedly adjusted their beliefs in response to messages from others.

In the "family" geometry, sets of four people were tightly linked to one another, with each member having one link outside the family. After several rounds of messages, the system "settled" into an attractor of homogeneous family groups, with most but not all of the family groups settling on the same collective belief (consolidation). In a continuous "ribbon" geometry, however, in which each person communicated with four adjacent neighbors, the group settled into distinct clusters with no consolidation.

Although Latané and L'Herrou's experiments demonstrate the self-organization of a larger population into coherent "groups" of people with similar beliefs, the "members" could not detect these groups. They are apparent only to an outsider (the experimenter, the reader) who can see the whole pattern. We believe that the diffusion and standardization of culture in a larger population, or the continued diversity of smaller groups within the larger unit, is also affected by what happens at the interface of perceived group boundaries. The social proof principle, for example, directs attention to in-group (not out-group) members as a model for behavior.

When people extend the idea of "us" to include the whole band, it should enhance the standardization of norms, as group members observe and copy the behavior of other groups. This diffusion from group to group helps creates a population-level standard (consolidation). When people tie their identity more closely to a smaller group, and view other small groups in the same embedding context as competitors or "other," that should strengthen intergroup differentiation (consistent with the predictions of optimal distinctiveness theory, see Brewer, 1991).

Diffusion of norms from the small group level up to the next level of band should be facilitated by overlapping membership in different small groups, whether simultaneous (people belong to multiple groups) or sequential (groups frequently dissolve and reform). The former creates a complex structure at a single point in time. The latter creates a complex structure distributed across time. An example is the fission–fusion pattern observed both in nonhuman primates (Janson, 1993) and in the fluid membership of temporary groups such as incident response teams (Goodman & Wilson, 2000). In fluid groups, socialization (transmission of culture to new members) can occur as members transfer what they have learned from group to group (diffusion at the global level), or when members access community resources such as shared data bases for guidance on how to proceed (influence from embedding context down to specific group).

When a larger band is the context in which small groups form, the dominant norms in the group's immediate embedding system will affect the likelihood of members accessing different models for behavior, and thus the likelihood of a group embracing equality matching norms, for example, as opposed to equity principles (market pricing). The bottom-up process of norm formation is also shaped by the top-down influence of the larger context on individuals. The arrows of influence go from embedding context to individual and back up to small group.

### Macrobands and Larger Aggregates

The only core configuration above the level of the band is the macroband of several hundred. In most contemporary societies, however, the levels of embedding context continue way beyond this level, up to and including aspects of global civilization made possible by developments such as the Internet. These larger embedding contexts play a role in transmitting cultural assumptions and norms to individuals, whether they are a corporation that employs thousands of people, a city of a million in which the person lives, or a nation with its own plethora of customs, symbols, and norms. Models and scripts that are common and valued in the most salient larger context–whether this is a corporation, a religious group, or society at large–should be more accessible and should feel more like the "right way" to behave.

### The Full Multilevel Framework

The multilevel framework is illustrated in Fig. 8.1. The macroband and band (a and b) are the embedding contexts (one proximal and one distal), the group is the main level of interest (c), and the dyad and individual (d and e) constitute the local level. The arrows represent influences within and across levels; the chevrons indicate changes over time at the same level.

At the local level, all individuals have an array of psychological mechanisms that guide social interaction. Depending on dominant norms in the larger embedding contexts and cues in the immediate social context of the dyad or small group, some of these will be activated (the light bulbs) and some will be "dormant" (the dark circles). Individuals can coordinate most quickly and easily in dyads, which facilitates interpersonal influence in larger settings.

When a group forms, members retrieve relational models and scripts for how to behave, look to the actions of others to help define the situation for them, or both. Individual action (by a member who has decided on a script) cues complementary actions by other members, and group patterns emerge. The emergent group pattern in the middle of the figure illustrates the authority ranking model. When a new member arrives in the group (right side of figure) either the norm is (f) transmitted and the newcomer conforms to the group pattern, or the norm is (g) transformed in response to the perturbation created by membership change. In the first case, group influence on the individual promotes socialization into existing patterns; in the second case, the influence of the newcomer on the group promotes

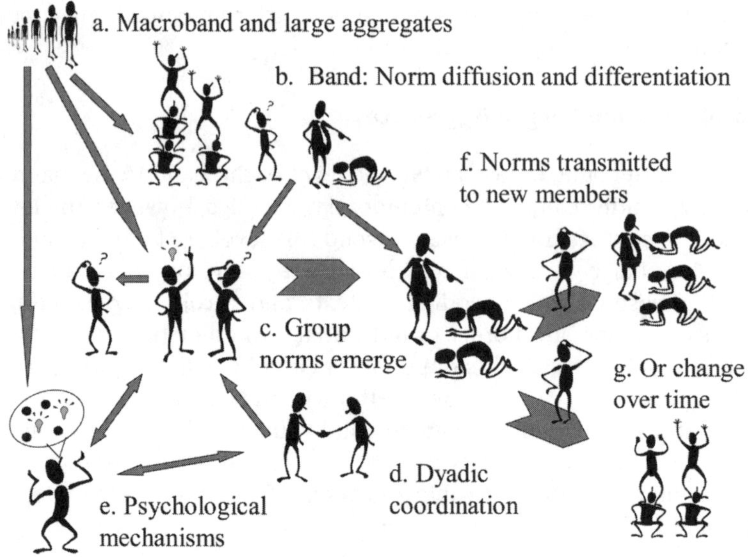


FIG. 8.1. A multilevel model of norm formation, transmission, transformation, and diffusion.

change. In both cases however, influence is bidirectional, part of a continuing negotiation between members and group (Moreland & Levine, 1988).

Emergent norms can diffuse across a wider population as groups, dyads, or individuals come together in larger gatherings, but some differentiation between subgroups, or divergent member behavior, should also persist (b). Although we have given little attention to the larger scale aggregations represented by (a) in the figure, we also presume bidirectional influence between "band"-sized groups and larger embedding contexts. In the next section, we describe a few experimental paradigms used to study norm formation processes, identify where they fall short for our purposes, and then introduce our own multilevel experimental paradigm, social poker.

## SOME EARLY STUDIES OF CULTURE IN LABORATORY GROUPS

The experimental study of culture in social psychology dates back to the 1930s, when Sherif studied the emergence of norms in ambiguous situations by placing people in darkened rooms and asking them how far a dot of light moved. In actuality, the light never moved: subjects were reporting their perceptions of illusory movement, the autokinetic effect (Sherif, 1936). If people made repeated solitary judgments, they established idiosyncratic personal distance standards, which varied between people. If they called out their judgments while sitting with others, they converged quickly on a common group norm, which persisted across trials but differed between groups. When a series of solitary trials was followed by group trials, individuals abandoned their personal standards to converge on a common group norm. When a series of group trials was followed by solitary trials, solitary judgments continued to follow the norm established in the group trials. This suggested that the group norm had been internalized: It was no longer dependent on the continued presence of other group members. The norm, an emergent group-level structure, continued to guide individual perceptions.

In the 1960s and 1970s, this paradigm was extended to investigate cultural transmission across generations of small groups, and broadened to include groups that were more explicitly interdependent. The focus in this next generation of work shifted from the emergence of culture to the stability of cultural elements as the membership of groups changed over time. Using Sherif's autokinetic task, Jacobs and Campbell (1961) investigated "the power of culture to perpetuate arbitrary beliefs" (p. 649). In their experiment, an extreme group norm was initially established with the help of one or more confederates, who gave estimates of light movement that substantially exceeded the distance naive individuals normally reported.

As charter group members were removed and replaced one by one with naive new members, the high-distance norm was transmitted to the new generations but became progressively less extreme. Eventually, as members continued to be replaced, the norm drifted downward to match the "natural" range of distance norms established by groups with no confederates. The researchers interpreted their results as demonstrating that cultural transmission of an arbitrary norm can survive the total replacement of all group members. However, their results also showed the eventual abandonment of an arbitrary norm that differed from individual observations. In effect, their experiment demonstrated both cultural persistence and some limits on persistence for the generational transmission of a *social reality norm* (McGrath, 1984, p. 201), which is a shared interpretation of reality.

A decade after the Jacobs and Campbell study, Weick and Gilfallan (1971) examined the cultural transmission of a *situational norm* (McGrath, 1984), which specifies rules for behavior in a specific class of situations. They chose a new task, the target game, that explicitly required groups of people to coordinate their actions to achieve a collective goal. They were interested in whether the persistence of a cultural practice (an assigned strategy for playing the target game) would differ based on whether an arbitrarily chosen strategy was more or less difficult to implement. Charter members of each group were instructed in a strategy (the assigned norm).

In the target game, the experimenter calls out a target number between 0 and 30, and the three members of a group must try to "hit" that target by independently (and privately) contributing a number between 0 and 10. The experimenter tallies and reports to group members the results of each trial; no direct communication among group members is allowed. The group is successful if the sum of the three contributions equals the target number. After a group completed 24 trials, one member was removed and replaced with a new person who had not been trained in a strategy. After the reconfigured group completed 24 trials, another member was replaced, and this procedure was repeated for 11 generations.

The difficulty of the assigned strategy made a difference in how long the assigned situational norm endured. The easy assigned strategy persisted unchanged. The "difficult" normative strategy, however, was abandoned by the fourth generation, and replaced (in most cases) by an easier emergent strategy. The stability of the situational norm thus depended on how well adapted it was to the demands placed on the group.

Together, the group experiments just described demonstrate the feasibility of investigating the formation and transmission of cultural elements such as beliefs and social practices in the microculture of small groups. They show that group norms (a) emerge among people with initially divergent views, (b) are internalized by group members, (c) differ across groups, and (d) are transmitted to new members across multiple generations of the group. They also demonstrate that problematic norms (e) change over time to either match the preferences of members more closely or match the structure of the environment more effectively.

The experimental studies just described did not allow group members to interact freely. When studying the emergence of a social reality norm, in which simply hearing the views of others can help shape one's own opinions about what is true, this is a reasonable constraint. The paradigms are also well suited for the study of what Opp (1982) called evolutionary norm formation, in which norms emerge implicitly, in an unplanned and unintended manner. According to Opp, norms can also form when institutions prescribe behaviors (institutional norm formation), or when people explicitly discuss appropriate behavior (voluntary norm formation). In the Weick and Gilfallan study, the normative strategy for playing the target game was imposed "top down" by the experimenters, an institutional process.

In contrast, voluntary and evolutionary norm formation are both bottom-up processes, one implicit, the other explicit. After the groups that were taught a difficult strategy for the target game abandoned it, a new, easier strategy emerged following the evolutionary route (Weick & Gillfallan, 1971, p. 188). The process depended on trial and error because group members were not allowed to communicate directly. Instead they had to feel their way toward a new strategy by acting, seeing the results, and making adjustments.

Our multilevel framework integrates the three routes of norm formation, and suggests how they might interact. Evolutionary norm formation is the emergence of global structure from interpersonal interaction. The arrow thus goes from lower level to higher level, and is similar to the process modeled by the conformity game developed by Latané and colleagues. Voluntary norms emerge from group discussion and negotiation, and subsequently guide member behavior. This involves the influence both of individuals on the group and the group on its members. Institutional norms are handed down from the embedding context (band or larger aggregate).

We view the three routes of norm formation as snapshots of a larger process. Coordinated behavior emerges from local interaction, which is itself shaped by context and constrained by individual-level mechanisms that supply content and guide social behavior. These patterns percolate upward to the embedding context through diffusion to other groups, and can then become standardized and subsequently imposed on other groups via the institutional route. At the member/group interface, norms that arose through any of these routes are transmitted to newcomers, who may (a) perceive group norms as "institutions" to be adopted, (b) discover what the group norms are through their own evolutionary process of trial and error, or (c) negotiate directly with the group about what their role should be (voluntary route).

In the next section, we describe a laboratory paradigm, called *social poker*, in which people organize themselves into groups, earn money, and then divide up the group's earnings. They accomplish these tasks by talking directly to one another. This restores an important feature of most natural groups, in which members reach joint understandings, coordinate actions, and make collective decisions by talking to one another, rather than responding independently to stimuli from an outsider. In social poker, multiple groups form out of a larger population, so the three levels of individual, group, and embedding context are all represented.

## SOCIAL POKER: A MULTILEVEL PARADIGM FOR SELF-ORGANIZED GROUP FORMATION

Social poker captures in a social card game the following characteristics of self-organized group formation:

1. The people who become members choose what groups to form or join—they are not assigned to groups by outsiders.
2. Groups have the power to regulate their own membership by deciding who to admit and who to exclude.

3. Members need to contribute to the group for it to be productive.
4. Group formation and pooling of resources and/or efforts allows members to access valued goods or benefits that the members could not produce on their own.
5. Multiple groups can form from a larger "society" of potential group members (Arrow, Bennett, Crosson, & Orbell, 1999).

The design is inspired by other interactive paradigms such as the bargaining game used by Bettenhausen and Murnighan (1985), but adds the extra level of a miniature "society" in which groups are embedded.

The game works as follows. After they are instructed in the rules of the game, eight people each receive three playing cards, plus an information sheet that tells them what cards every other player has. The objective of the game is to form a "social poker" hand of either four of a kind or three pairs, which are worth $10 or $7, respectively. No player has enough cards to form a hand alone, and thus people must form groups and pool their cards to form a hand. Once a group forms, members collectively decide how to distribute the earnings. Money can only be divided in whole dollar amounts (e.g., $1, 2, 3, etc.); divisions such as $3.33 are not allowed.

The size of the populations allows for multiple groups to form, and also for isolates—people who are not included in any group that forms. The distribution of cards is prearranged to ensure that a minimum of three players are needed to form a social poker hand. Groups larger than three are allowed, but groups can only turn in one card hand per round, and people can only be members of a single group each round. Groups earn money based entirely on the value of the hand they form. After each round, players turn in their cards, the groups disband, and players fill out individual questionnaires that ask (among other things) how their group decided on the division of money, how fair this process was, and how satisfied they were with the group decision, the division of the money, the behavior of other players, and the cards they received. The players then receive new cards and repeat the process. They are free to reassemble in the same group configuration as before or to form new groups. Players forming a group assemble at one of three round tables in the same large room. All interaction is videotaped.

In the next section, we focus on four sets of college students who participated in social poker experiments, and connect events in the groups they formed to different aspects of cultural dynamics. Equality matching is a strong default norm for college students who have the same status in the larger embedding context (introductory psychology classes). To ensure that more than one attractor (relational norm) would be activated, the card distribution made players unequal in the game. Although all players had cards that could be used to form hands in a variety of group arrangements, some players had critical cards for several possible $10 hands, whereas other players had cards that were only useful for a single $10 arrangement, or only for $7 hands. The choice of payoff amounts also made equal division difficult to achieve. Because of the "even dollar" rule, $7 was equally divisible only in groups of 7, which never formed, because groups could only turn in one hand. The $10 was equally divisible only in groups of 5 members.

To examine the relative stability of norms governing both the division of the population into groups and the division of money among group members, we "perturbed" the developing system by changing the distribution of power among members across rounds. When the structure of the distribution changes, the optimal solution for maximum wealth generation (two groups, each earning the maximum of $10) changes, so that different people are at high risk for being isolates, and groups that have settled on a stable membership will no longer be able to earn the same amount. Changing the power distribution allowed us to test the stability of membership and also to examine the stability of allocation norms when the relative power among players changed.

## CULTURAL DYNAMICS IN FOUR MINIATURE SOCIETIES

In this section, we summarize events in four different populations or miniature "societies" drawn from a larger study that included 31 populations. After each summary, we connect specific events to the dynamics discussed in our multilevel conceptual framework. The four populations were selected to provide a good mix of continuity and change, and because they include some interesting dynamics. They should not be taken as representative. The variety of developmental patterns across the four is, however, characteristic of how idiosyncratic the developmental paths were in these short-lived, artificial societies.

Participants were told that they would play "between 2 and 10 rounds," so that they would complete each round believing that continued interaction was likely. In reality all populations played 7 rounds of the game. The timing of the changes in power structure differed in some of the groups, and are noted at the start of each summary. All four societies started out excluding at least one member from their groups in round 1 or 2, but by round 3 all were partitioning into groups that included all eight people in the population. Early exclusion occurred in 75% of the 31 populations in the larger study, so this trend was typical but not universal.

Here are the cases, named based on some feature of their norms.

***Female Equality Society.*** Eight women—all Caucasian. Power structure changed in round 6. In this society, two 3-person groups formed in the first round, and two people were left out. From the second round on, the isolates were included in two 4-person groups, and the new group members were viewed immediately as full and equal members in both groups, even though they contributed no cards to the groups' social poker hands. Both groups adjusted their principles and procedures for allocating the money in round 2, switching from equality-based to equity-based or the other way around. (When groups allocated more money to the person who contributed two cards to a four-of-a-kind hand on the grounds that this person "deserved" more, we counted this as equity-based). By the third round both groups settled on a stable norm of equality matching for distributing earnings, although they used different procedures. One group divided their $10 by giving three members $2 and rotating the remaining $4 to different members each round. The other group compared the cumulative earnings of each member in every round, and divided the money so as to keep these earnings as even as possible.

When the power structure changed in round 6, the groups either had to rearrange their membership or accept a reduction in earnings from $10 to $7. To solve the problem, the entire population of eight gathered to discuss the best course of action, and to redistribute members among groups. In the last two rounds, both groups explicitly tried to "even out" cumulative earnings for each member, and came close to achieving this goal by the time the game ended.

This story illustrates the convergence of two groups on a single stable attractor (full inclusion, equality matching) after some initial fluctuations—in the first two rounds, both groups were the minimum size and tried out different allocation norms. It also illustrates the clear emergence of the whole society as a collective decision-making body when the population was perturbed by the change in power structure. The stability of equality matching is evident from what happened in these negotiations. The procedural norm of evening out earnings was adopted by both groups, an example of both diffusion between groups and the establishment of a higher level "institutional" societal norm that determined what each group should do. Equal allocation was reconceptualized from a within-group concept to a within-band concept, and was also made retroactive, so that inequality based on exclusion in early rounds was repaired through "restorative" payments. The boundaries of "we" were withdrawn to include the full society (the band).

***Culture Collision Society.*** Five women—4 Caucasians, 1 Asian; 3 men, all Caucasian. Power structure changed in round 3.

In this society, two isolates were left out in the first two rounds, but different people were excluded in round 1 and round 2. One group used a coin toss to allocate the "extra dollar." In the second round, they elaborated this procedure by having two coin tosses instead of one. The other group, which had only one member overlap between rounds 1 and 2, used an equity (market pricing) principle, giving more money to the person who contributed two cards to the hand. In the third round the power structure changed, and people rearranged themselves into two 4-person groups. This four/four configuration persisted for the rest of the game, although the composition of the groups varied.

The power rearrangement in round 3 brought together people who had used different principles (equity or equality) and different procedures for allocating their earnings in previous groups. One group continued with some variation of the coin toss for the rest of the game, with a departure in one round, when they gave $3 to contributors and $1 to the person with no useful cards. The other group fell into a muddle, with continuing confusion about how to divide the money and (after the round was complete) confusion about what principles and procedures had actually been used. Members gave conflicting reports on their questionnaires, with one person describing the allocation as "random." By the last two rounds, the confusion had abated somewhat, although the group still hadn't settled on a consistent procedure. In the last round this group employed a complicated combination of turn-taking, evening up totals across rounds, and the rock–paper–scissors game for people with equal totals. Although members were not consistent in describing this procedure they did all agree that it was "completely fair" (7 on a 7-point scale). The main difference between the muddled group and the continuing norm group seemed to be greater membership continuity in the critical round 3 in the more culturally stable group.

This case contrasts with the female equality pattern by showing clear norm differentiation between small groups. One instituted equality matching via the coin toss procedure; the other used the market pricing model of equity (earnings proportional to contributions). When the membership scrambled in response to the perturbation in power structure, two "mini-cultures" came into contact. In line with the Bettenhausen and Murnighan (1985) model, members of each new "multicultural" group retrieved different scripts based on different precedents. In one group, the coin toss and equality appeared to be stable attractors. These norms were transmitted to a new "generation" in the combined group. When the coin-toss procedure was dropped for one round (perhaps because the noncontributing player offered to take a smaller share), the group returned to the norm in the next round—more evidence of a strong, stable attractor. In the other group, the clash of ideas led to an almost total loss of coordination at the group level. Members were unable to predict or interpret the behavior of group members. The collapse of group structure made interpersonal dynamics confusing and unrewarding. When a process fails, we can see its function clearly.

The group level structure of shared norms simplifies and clarifies interaction, reducing the degrees of freedom in a way that facilitates smooth collective behavior.

***Group Charity Society.*** Three women–one Caucasian, one Japanese national, one Chinese-American; five men–four Caucasians, one Indian national. Power structure changed in round 5, then switched back and forth in rounds 6 and 7.

In this society, three-person groups formed in the first two rounds, earned $10, and gave extra money to the member who contributed the most cards to the hand. Starting in round 3 and continuing for the rest of the game, each group adopted one of the isolates and instituted the group charity norm. Each contributing group member received an equal amount ($3), and the remaining dollar was donated by the group to a noncontributing "charity case." Comments on questionnaires indicated that the core members did not consider the charity case a full member of the group. Indeed, even as the groups swapped isolates back and forth across rounds, the established group members reported on the questionnaires that their group membership "stayed the same." One called the noncontributor "groupless"; others explicitly referred to the $1 as "charity" based on people "feeling altruistic." This procedural norm survived several rearrangements of group membership in response to changes in the power structure, which transformed former core group members into charity cases. In the last two rounds, one of the groups gave the noncontributor the job of completing the paperwork for the group, transforming the meaning of her earnings via a "welfare to work" idea. In the other group, the money was divided as usual (3331), and then one of the contributors "swapped" his share with the charity case.

Members' private evaluations of their procedural norm were inconsistent. One person would rate the decision "completely fair" and also express dissatisfaction with the outcome, whereas another would express high satisfaction but say the decision "wasn't fair." Recipients of charity also seemed conflicted about the handout. In one of the few departures from the normative script, the charity case volunteered to take $0, but when her suggestion was implemented, she expressed unhappiness on the questionnaire. Core group members differed in whether they thought it was fair. In the next round they returned to their established procedure. Questionnaire responses throughout the game indicated ubiquitous internal struggles over how members wanted to behave, compared to "how they should behave." An individual would say one thing to fellow members of the group, then on the questionnaire report a different (often contradictory) preference. For example, the member who suggested giving the remaining $1 to a "charity case" then wrote on his questionnaire that he felt that person "should have gotten $0."

In this society, both groups shifted in tandem from a shared but unstable pattern of three-person groups and from the market pricing norm of equity to a new shared and more stable pattern. The synchronization of change in the two groups suggests mutual influence between them. We attribute it to the groups observing one another's actions: social proof in operation at the group level. From round 3 on, the groups did coordinate membership decisions, swapping the charity cases back and forth between them. Society-wide consolidation helped strengthen what continued to be a controversial norm. This norm combined elements of communal sharing at the group level (attend to group boundaries, and act differently toward nonmembers) and authority ranking at the society level of haves and have-nots, with the "upper class" donating a leftover dollar to the "lower class" (Fiske, 1991, p. 42).

The continued intrapersonal conflicts about how to behave (evident on the questionnaire responses) was never resolved. Had we focused only on this population's overt group behavior and not considered the continuing local dynamics, we would not have perceived the mismatch between the two levels of group behavior and individual preferences. The norm was apparently held in place by the power of precedent and the consolidation of a society-wide practice. This population also included citizens from two countries that score higher on "power distance" (a cultural syndrome that fits the authority ranking model) than the United States (Hofstede, 1980, p. 223), which may have decreased consensus about which relational models were most appropriate.

***Private Donor Society.*** Four men, four women, all Caucasian. Power structure changed in round 6. This society had a single isolate in the first round, then moved to total inclusion in round 2. As in the group charity society, people who lacked useful cards were viewed as outsiders and received a $1 "handout." In the private donor society, however, donations came explicitly from individuals, not groups. One group emphasized the individual nature of the donation by writing $3-3-4 on the group's earnings distribution sheet, and then crossing out the $4, writing in $3, and indicating that someone transferred their $1 to the "odd man out." One of these individual donors referred to the noncontributor as a "beggar" on the questionnaire and added, "I took pity [on him] and gave him one dollar." As in the group charity society, questionnaire responses indicated widespread dissatisfaction with the norm. In this society, however, the dissatisfaction led to a rejection of both inclusion and allocation norms.

In round 5, the society reconfigured into one 3-person group and one 5-person group. This shift preceded by one round the shift in power structure, so was clearly not caused by this external perturbation. Instead, two especially dissatisfied core players, one from each group, got together with one of the downtrodden. The former "odd man out" received $4, not based on having the most cards to contribute, but, as the members noted, "REGARDLESS of cards." The remaining five people formed a group, dropped all talk of "donation," and also moved toward equal status and equal allocations. In the next round, the membership shuffled again in response to the change in power structure. The revolutionaries split into different groups, and the norms diverged. The larger group divided the money equally, with all members giving this outcome the highest possible score for fairness. The smaller group shifted to an equity model, giving the person who contributed two cards more money. Members also rated the outcome high on fairness. Member satisfaction and desire to stay with the 3-person group was, however, lower than in the 5-person group, even though individual members of the smaller group earned more money.

This story provides an instructive contrast to the group charity society. Although both established two classes of people and gave noncontributors a dollar, the mixture of norms was actually different. The group charity society followed a mixed model with aspects of both communal sharing and authority ranking. The private donor society also followed a mixed model, but combined communal sharing (clear distinction between in-group and out-group) and market pricing (the extra dollar "belonged" to the person with more cards). The instability of this mixture may indicate incompatibility between these two norms, which are prototyically applied to family and to strangers, respectively.

The path by which the normative pattern of equal-sized groups and private donation was overthrown is also instructive. Although questionnaire data showed widespread dissatisfaction and internal conflict in both groups, these were private communications to the experimenters. In the private donor society, two individuals actually expressed their unhappiness to one another, found common ground, and acted to overturn the existing pattern. This shows the importance of the interpersonal level between individual and group. Coordinated dyadic action changed the structure at the group level. Uncoordinated private doubts failed to effect change.

After the established norm was overthrown, the new groups ended up on different attractors (equality matching and market pricing), which points up the unpredictability of change in these conditions. Closer inspection of the questionnaire data provided some insight into why the groups chose different norms when the two "revolutionaries" split up. Although they found common cause, the two were dissatisfied with the status quo for different reasons: one because it was unequal and therefore unfair, the other because the principle of equity was not being followed strictly, reducing his individual earnings. In essence, one of the actors was motivated by social justice (the desire to align action with the "correct" model indicated by the larger embedding context) and the other by the market pricing motivation to get a better deal for himself.

## The Layout of Attractors

The four cases illustrate that all four relational models—equality matching, market pricing, communal sharing, and authority ranking—guided allocation norms in at least some groups. Differences among the strength and stability of these norms as "attractors" for these miniature societies are evident. Equality matching is a broad, stable attractor. Market pricing is also important as an attractor, but less stable. Groups tend to transition from equity toward greater equality. A combined authority ranking/communal sharing model was unpopular but persisted. The groups stuck with this norm not because they were happy, but because dissatisfaction did not translate into coordinated action. The market pricing/communal sharing norm disappeared when a dissident dyad shook up the system. The new groups diverged toward either pure equity or pure equality, which suggests that the society was held for a while in the "in-between" mixed-model state because of the conflicting pulls of market pricing and equality matching attractors.

The path that each society traced from one allocation norm to another was also affected by emerging norms about how to handle the "redundant" people in the society. The choices were: exclude two people, exclude one person, or include everyone, in either equally or unequally sized groups. The societies described all showed a movement from less to more inclusion, and this trend was evident in the full data set as well. Pure equity dictated that these people should receive nothing, because they had no worthwhile cards to contribute. Yet with such a small population, the sense that these people were also part of the larger "group" of the eight-person society seemed to push toward inclusion, even when groups had adopted equity principles for their allocation of earnings. And once extra people were included, it was much harder to go backward and leave them out.

When we look closely at the local level of some groups that showed this pattern, it helps us identify a trajectory that leads to this trap. Moving from exclusion to inclusion can result from the suggestion of a single group member that "maybe we should include the others." The other group members may regret this decision, and the person who made the suggestion may also feel ambivalent later. Yet the group will (in many cases) not act on the views most members privately espouse. The contributing members of these groups felt conflicted between the pull of market pricing (which affirmed their right to get the best deal), and the pull of equality matching (which dictated a more equal division of money).

In the first few rounds, people drew their group boundaries narrowly, leaving out isolates. One way to regulate empathy for outsiders is to not pay attention to those in need, and according to market pricing principles, each person should act in their own self-interest. According to our framework, activation of the market pricing relational model will tend to "turn off" the empathy module. However, it was apparently hard to ignore the larger boundary containing the pool of eight members in a common setting, playing a game devised by the true "outsiders"—the experimenters. Sooner or later, someone would suggest including an extra member. Once someone has been invited in, however, that person can't be a nonmember again, only an ex-member. Engagement with these outsiders affirmed them as members of the larger population playing the game, and by taking an action at odds with market pricing, the group weakened that attractor.

Sahlins (1996) noted, "If friends make gifts, gifts make friends . . . the material flow underwrites or initiates social relations" (p. 26) echoing Trivers (1971): "Generosity from a non-friend is taken to be an overture to friendship" (p. 52). Inclusion reinforced expectations on both sides that the relationship was being reclassified as equality matching (the friendship norm), but the model was not fully implemented. The complex set of mechanisms that has evolved to make effective social action possible sometimes triggers incompatible emotions and expectations, preventing smooth coordination.

The compromise of minimal charity for lower class members, which was aligned neither with equality nor equity principles, did not resolve the intrapersonal conflict. Instead, the way out was to change the configuration of the problem, defining all members of the group as equal full members and developing a strong sense of group identity. The structure of inequality imposed by the experimenters made it difficult to implement the equality matching model. Some groups did, nonetheless, affirm and achieve equality among members. As one member of a strong equality matching group (not one of the four profiled) put it, "The process by which cards are received is not fair . . . but we [the group members] are making it fair."

## FULL CIRCLE: STUDYING CULTURE AS A MULTILEVEL PROCESS

What does the superstructure of complexity theory provide us, applied to the emergence and evolution of norms? What do the case studies tell us about the process of norm development? Together, they allow us to use the examination of local dynamics, at the level of intrapersonal and interpersonal process, to gain insight into how more global structures such as group norms emerge. Complexity theory also directs us to look at how the embedding context affects the strength and stability of attractors that shape local action.

What people will perceive as "fair," for example, depends on how they understand the situation, which will in turn be shaped by the larger context. Their interpretation of the situation highlights one or more relational models as appropriate, activating some of the psychological mechanisms that regulate social interaction. Norms in the embedding context of a U.S. university tend to favor market pricing and equality matching. If the experiment were run in a more collectivist society, or in institutional settings (such as the military) with different values, we would expect the strength and stability of attractors corresponding to the models to differ.

Another contribution of complexity theory is its emphasis on the dynamic processes that underlie the myriad diverse patterns of culture. The structure of the human brain provides a finite number of building blocks that make the generation of culture possible, and the existing cultural context provides extensive guidelines about which building blocks are appropriate in which domains (Fiske, 2000). Despite these constraints, however, the problem that we as humans face in deciding "how to behave" in a new setting is not fully resolved. The particulars of social norms for a particular group must be generated, negotiated, and confirmed by the people involved. In this setting, we can directly observe the interface of culture and individual in the dynamic flow of situated human action that creates, maintains, and transforms the "rules, customs, values and other sorts of norms" to which Sherif referred.

Culture, in all its diversity, performs everywhere the same function: It helps beings who have evolved to be fundamentally social coordinate their expectations, desires, and behaviors. The evolution of culture is typically viewed on a sweeping scale, both in the size of the collective involved and the time period considered. The initial creation of culture lies in the distant past of our species, and the forces of biological evolution that made it possible can only be inferred. Yet the emergence of recurrent coordinating structures is still happening all around us, in our everyday lives. We believe the dynamic self-organizing processes that continually generate culture can still be observed–and systematically studied–in the self-organizing microcultures of small groups.

## ACKNOWLEDGMENTS

We are grateful to Larry Sugiyama, Sara Hodges, and John Orbell for helpful comments on an earlier draft, and to Mark Schaller and Chris Crandall for their guidance in the revision process. This work was partially supported by a National Science Foundation grant (SES-9729320) to the first author and co-principal investigator John Orbell.

## REFERENCES

Arrow, H., Bennett, R. E., Crosson, S., & Orbell, J. (1999). *Social poker: A paradigm for studying the formation of self-organized groups* (Tech. Rep. 99-01). Eugene: Institute for Cognitive and Decision Sciences, University of Oregon.

Arrow, H., McGrath, J. E., & Berdahl, J. L. (2000). *Small groups as complex systems: Formation, coordination, development, and adaptation*. Newbury Park, CA: Sage.

Axelrod, R. (1995). *The convergence and stability of cultures: Local convergence and global polarization* (SFI Working Paper 95-03-028). Santa Fe, NM: Santa Fe Institute.

Baumeister, R. F., & Leary, M. R. (1995). The need to belong: Desire for interpersonal attachments as a fundamental human motivation. *Psychological Bulletin, 117*, 497–529.

Berry, J. W., Poortinga, Y. H., Segall, M. H., & Dasen, P. R. (1992). *Cross-cultural psychology: Research and applications*. Cambridge: Cambridge University Press.

Bettenhausen, K. L., & Murnighan, J. K. (1985). The emergence of norms in competitive decision-making groups. *Administrative Science Quarterly, 30*, 350–372.

Boyd, R., & Richerson, P. J. (1985). *Culture and the evolutionary process*. Chicago: University of Chicago Press.

Brewer, M. B. (1991). The social self: On being the same and different at the same time. *Personality and Social Psychology Bulletin, 17*(5), 475–482.

Caporael, L. R., & Baron, R. M. (1997). Groups as the mind's natural environment. In J. A. Simpson & D. T. Kenrick (Eds.), *Evolutionary social psychology* (pp. 317–344). Mahwah, NJ: Lawrence Erlbaum Associates.

Casti, J. L. (1994). *Complexification: Explaining a paradoxical world through the science of surprise*. New York: Harper Collins.

Cialdini, R. B. (1993). *Influence: The psychology of persuasion* (rev. ed.). New York: William Morrow.

Cosmides, L., & Tooby, J. (1992). Cognitive adaptations for social exchange. In J. H. Barkow, L. Cosmides, & J. Tooby, *The adapted mind* (pp. 163–228). New York: Oxford University Press.

Culbert, T. P. (1988). The collapse of classic Maya civilization. In N. Yoffee & G. L. Cowgill (Eds.), *The collapse of ancient states and civilizations* (pp. 69–101). Tucson: University of Arizona Press.

Eidelson, R. J. (1997). Complex adaptive systems in the behavioral and social sciences. *Review of General Psychology, 1*, 42–7.

Fiske, A. P. (1991). *Structures of social life: The four elementary forms of human relations*. New York: Free Press.

Fiske, A. P. (2000). Complementarity theory: Why human social capacities evolved to require cultural complements. *Personality and Social Psychology Review, 4*, 76–94.

Gersick, C. J. G. (1988). Time and transition in work teams: Toward a new model of group development. *Academy of Management Journal, 31*, 9–41.

Goodman, P. S., & Wilson, J. M. (2000). Substitutes for socialization and exocentric teams. *Research in Managing Groups and Teams, 3*, 53–77. Greenwich, CT: JAI Press.

Hare, A. P. (1995). Introduction. In A. P. Hare, H. H. Blumberg, M. F. Davies, & M. V. Kent. *Small group research: A handbook* (pp. 1–7). Norwood, NJ: Ablex.

Harrison, J. R., & Carroll, G. R. (1991). Keeping the faith: A model of cultural transmission in formal organizations. *Administrative Science Quarterly, 36*, 552–582.

Henrich, J., & Boyd, R. (1998). The evolution of conformist transmission and the emergence of between-group differences. *Evolution and Human Behavior, 19*, 215–241.

Hofstede, G. (1980). *Culture's consequences*. Beverly Hills, CA: Sage.

Jacobs, R. C., & Campbell, D. T. (1961). The perpetuation of an arbitrary tradition through several generations of a laboratory microculture. *Journal of Abnormal and Social Psychology, 62*(3), 649–658.

Janson, C. H. (1993). Primate group size, brains and communication: A New World perspective. *Behavioral and Brain Sciences, 16*, 711–712.

Jarvenpa, R. (1993). Hunter-gatherer sociospatial organization and group size. *Behavioral and Brain Sciences, 16*, 712.

Kelly, J. R. (1988). Entrainment in individual and group behavior. In J. E. McGrath (Ed.), *The social psychology of time: New perspectives* (pp. 89–110). Newbury Park, CA: Sage.

Kelly, R. L. (1995). *The foraging spectrum: Diversity in hunter-gatherer lifeways*. Washington: Smithsonian Institution Press.

Latané, B., & L'Herrou, T. L. (1996). Spatial clustering in the conformity game: Dynamic social impact in electronic groups. *Journal of Personality and Social Psychology, 70*, 1218–1230.

Lewin, R. (1992). *Complexity: Life at the edge of chaos*. New York: Macmillan.

McGrath, J. E. (1984). *Groups: Interaction and performance*. Englewood Cliffs, NJ: Prentice-Hall.

Moreland, R. L., & Levine, J. M. (1988). Group dynamics over time: Development and socialization in small groups. In J. E. McGrath (Ed.), *The social psychology of time: New perspectives* (pp. 151–181). Newbury Park, CA: Sage.

Moreland, R. L., Levine, J. M., & Wingert, M. L. (1996). Creating the ideal group: Composition effects at work. In E. Witte & J. H. Davis (Eds.), *Understanding group behavior: Small group processes and interpersonal relations* (Vol. 2, pp. 11–35). Mahwah, NJ: Lawrence Erlbaum Associates.

Nowak, A., & Vallacher, R. R. (1998). *Dynamical social psychology*. New York: Guildford Press.

Nwokah, E. E., Hsu, H.-C., Dobrowolska, O., & Fogel, A. (1994). The development of laughter in mother-infant communication: Timing parameters and temporal sequences. *Infant Behavior & Development, 17*(1), 23–35.

Opp, K.-D. (1982). The evolutionary emergence of norms. *British Journal of Social Psychology, 21*, 139–149.

Perdue, C., Dovidio, J., Gurtman, M., & Tyler, R. (1990). Us and them: Social categorization and the process of intergroup bias. *Journal of Psychology and Social Psychology, 59*, 475–486.

Prigogine I., & Stengers, I. (1984). *Order out of chaos*. New York: Bantam.

Sahlins, M. D. (1996). On the sociology of primitive exchange. In A. E. Komter (Ed.), *The gift: An interdisciplinary perspective* (pp. 26–38). Amsterdam: Amsterdam University Press.

Sherif, M. (1936). *The psychology of social norms*. New York: Harper & Brothers.

Sherif, M., Harvey, O. J., White, B. J., Hood, W. R., & Sherif, C. W. (1961). *Intergroup conflict and cooperation: The robber's cave experiment*. Norman, OK: Institute of Social Relations.

Shweder, R. (1990). Cultural psychology: What is it? In J. Stigler, R. Shweder, & G. Herdt (Eds.), *Cultural psychology* (pp. 1–43). Cambridge, UK: Cambridge University Press.

Sperber, D. (1986). Anthropology and psychology: Towards an epidemiology of representation. *Man (N.S.), 20*, 73–89.

Taylor, S. E., & Crocker, J. (1981). Schematic bases of social information processing. In E. T. Higgins, C. P. Herman, & M. P. Zanna (Eds.), *The Ontario symposium on personality and social psychology: Social cognition* (Vol. 1, 89–134). Hillsdale, NJ: Lawrence Erlbaum Associates.

Tooby, J., & Cosmides, L. (1992). The psychological foundations of culture. In J. H. Barkow, L. Cosmides, & J. Tooby, *The adapted mind* (pp. 19–77). New York: Oxford University Press.

Trivers, R. L. (1971). The evolution of reciprocal altruism. *Quarterly Review of Biology, 46*, 35–57.

Weick, K. E., & Gilfallan, D. P. (1971). Fate of arbitrary traditions in a laboratory microculture. *Journal of Personality and Social Psychology, 17*, 179–191.

CHAPTER

# 9

# Scientists and Science: How Individual Goals Shape Collective Norms

Christian S. Crandall
University of Kansas

Mark Schaller
University of British Columbia

When people talk about culture, they most often refer to the cultures attached to populations defined by geographic or ethnic boundaries. Some cultures, however, correspond to boundaries defined by shared interests, job descriptions, and professions, and the like. Frans de Waal (2001) suggests that culture exists when one community is distinguishable from another by unique behaviors; science is one such culture. Scientists speak a common language, and they share a common set of assumptions, values, and beliefs. Scientists thoughts and actions are guided by norms, customs, and rituals that are specific to scientific inquiry. Despite the many different subdisciplines that are called sciences, there is substantial agreement about what science is and what scientists do. So it's not surprising that the values and practices of the scientific culture have been as heavily studied as those of, say, the Kwakiutul or Kaw cultures. The same processes that govern the emergence and evolution of culture in other kinds of populations also govern the emergence and evolution of culture among scientists.

In this chapter, we focus on the cultural consequences of individuals' personal goals. We discuss some of the ways in which individual scientists' mundane and very human motives craft the collective values and practices that define the culture of science. Scientists may pay lip service to a set of abstract progressive values that appear to transcend the narrow concerns of individuals, but a careful examination of scientific culture reveals very clearly the fingerprints of scientists' psychological needs and practical self-interests. This analysis helps us to understand why science proceeds in the way it does, why it works as a means of inquiry, and also why it works imperfectly.

## SCIENTIFIC CULTURE

Cultures are defined by a variety of things that are relatively common across a particular population and that distinguish that population from other populations. These things include beliefs and behaviors, as well as the enduring artifacts that are produced as a result of those beliefs and behaviors.

The salient characteristics of scientific culture differ depending on how one studies it. Some of the different frames of inquiry that have been applied to the study of scientific culture are philosophy and history (Feyerabend, 1975; Hull, 1988; Kitcher, 1993, 2001; Kuhn, 1964), linguistics and rhetoric (Latour, 1987), sociology and anthropology (Merton, 1973), and epistemology and psychology (Fuller, 1997; Shadish & Fuller, 1994). Across these different styles of investigation, considerable attention has been paid to the abstract ethos and ideals that govern scientific behavior. Merton (1973) summarized four widely endorsed codes of scientific conduct that define the ethos of science: universalism (commitment to discovering universal truths, as opposed to, say, culturally specific facts), communism (commitment to sharing data and credit with colleagues), disinterestedness (detachment from any single ideology and a willingness to follow data wherever it leads), and skepticism (unwillingness to declare any perception or belief to be true until empirical support for it is substantial). Others (e.g., Lakatos, 1970; Laudan, 1977; Popper, 1972) have highlighted other fundamental facets of the scientific ethos, such as openness to new ideas and the encouragement of conceptual diversity. These ideals are endorsed vigorously by scientists. They help to demarcate the distinction between everyday intuition and the rigorous endeavor of scientific inquiry. They reflect well on the individual scientists, and are useful in sustaining a positive public image of science.

The culture of science is also defined by the more specific values that veteran scientists espouse and teach to their young. For instance, more than most other populations of intellectuals, scientists value objectivity. Research methods are judged to be better when those methods are more purely objective, and scientists themselves are judged to be acting more scientifically when their inferences and conclusions are perceived to be more objective. Scientists also place special values on particular characteristics of theories and other explanatory structures. Theories are judged to be more scientific—and therefore better—if they are more clearly testable by empirical observations. They also are judged better if they are more parsimonious.

The values that define scientific culture are revealed by the specific behavioral customs and practices of scientists. Consider, for example, the manner in which ethical transgressions are punished within the community of scientists. As some observers have noted, the specific linkages between crime and punishment are different within the culture of science than they are within the world at large (Hull, 1988). Scientists turn a relatively blind eye to matters of theft (e.g., the appropriation of one scientist's ideas by another without citation is typically treated as a trivial offense), but mete out unusually harsh punishments to peers who commit fraud (e.g., the falsification of empirical data).

In addition to these values and practices, the culture of science is also defined in part by an accumulation of artifacts. The artifacts that matter most in science are the published papers and articles—the archived literatures that define the accumulated cultural knowledge, beliefs, devices, and techniques in scientific disciplines. Of course, not all scientific theories and findings find their way into these cultural archives; many papers are rejected in the editorial review process and are never published. Publication itself does not guarantee a secure place in the cultural memory of a science; to contribute meaningfully to culturally shared scientific knowledge, a published paper must be attended to, remembered, and cited by other scientists in their own published articles and in texts. Some scientific theories catch on and remain prominent, whereas others, equally useful, may not (Campbell, 1974; Campbell & Overman, 1988). Some published articles become citation classics whereas others fade quickly into the cultural obsolescence of noncitation. Not all of this is based on the inherent merit of the paper. A complete understanding of scientific culture demands that we not only describe the processes through which scientific values and behavioral practices arise, but also describe the processes through which privately held scientific knowledge is transmitted and sustained within the public archives of a science.

It is easy to assume that the cultural values, practices, and artifacts that define scientific culture are simply products of the abstract ethos of science: Once scientists have acknowledged a set of ideals that defines their population, they might simply act accordingly. If this is so, then the values and practices of scientists—and the process through which scientific knowledge is accumulated and archived—should be consistent with those scientific ideals. This does not appear to be the case; many of the values and practices of scientists seem to be at odds with those abstract ideals.

A better explanation for the origins of scientific culture lies in the personal needs and goals that guide the behavior of individual scientists. In the pages that follow, we summarize systematically some of the ways in which the specific elements of human cognition, motivation, and material self-interest construct and sustain certain specific scientific values, and the specific behavioral norms within science that deviate from the abstract ethos of science. We also show how these individual goals, and the behaviors resulting from them, shape the transmission and accumulation of scientific knowledge, and thus govern (and sometimes inhibit) scientific progress.

## INDIVIDUAL NEEDS AND CULTURAL VALUES

The values that define any culture are, in large part, responsive to the needs of individuals within that culture. Legal prohibitions on acts such as murder, theft, and incest offer obvious examples of moral values that, in general, serve the needs of individuals living within populations defined by those ethics. It is no surprise to find considerable consistency between the values defining scientific culture and the individual needs of scientists.

Consider first one simple example. A fundamental value of science is veracity. As Merton (1942/1996, p. 268) wrote, "The institutional goal of science is the extension of certified knowledge." In fact, within many philosophies of science, the term *knowledge* itself implies veracity (Bechtel, 1988). Consequently, scientists use methods and engage in practices designed to avoid inaccurate conclusions, and are very devoted to the systematic elimination of inaccuracy from the scientific knowledge base. The value placed on veracity is certainly consistent with the abstract ethos of science, but that doesn't mean that the value has such a high-minded origin. The value is also consistent with the individual epistemic needs of scientists, who, like people everywhere, desire reliable means of predicting the world around them (Kruglanski, 1994). It is also consistent with scientists' professional self-interest. Scientists depend on their colleagues' results and conclusions to guide their own research; they must trust that these results and conclusions are accurate. Hull (1988, p. 311) noted, "If these results are mistaken, every one who uses them has their research set back." The high value that science places on veracity is an inevitable consequence of scientists' personal need to avoid this sort of professional misfortune.

The high value placed on parsimony is also very likely a product of the very human desire for epistemic and practical comfort. The logical basis for the value of parsimony has been questioned (Schaller, Rosell, & Asp, 1998; Sober, 1990). Indeed, it's usually the case that, compared to simpler models, more complex theoretical models provide richer and more accurate descriptions of phenomena; so the value placed on parsimony is often inconsistent with the broader ethos of science. The psychological basis for this scientific value is straightforward; human beings desire a certain epistemic efficiency. As part of this more general desire, we prefer simplicity to complexity (Kruglanski, 1989; Neuberg & Newsom, 1993). Scientists share this very human preference for simplicity (Kruglanski, 1994). Compared to complex scientific explanations, simpler explanations are easier to understand, to think about, and to communicate to others. At a purely psychological level, parsimony is seductive. This psychological appeal alone almost surely accounts for the scientific value placed on parsimony.

One good example of this phenomenon is in the area of attribution theory. There are a number of simple and straightforwardly elegant theories of attribution processes that have had a wide impact, have been heavily researched, and are widely discussed in textbooks (e.g., Jones & Davis, Kelley, Weiner). But the original theory that gave rise to this work (Heider, 1958) is substantially more complex, and it is a virtual certainty that human attribution processes are substantially more complex than the account given by the most popular, teachable theories (see Hilton, 1995).

Veracity and parsimony are just two examples. There are many other values espoused by scientists that are tacitly assumed or even explicitly defended as serving the ultimate goal of scientific progress. They might even serve that idealized goal. But if so, it's likely that this positive consequence is a happy by-product of values that emerged more directly to serve the psychological and material needs of scientists.

As in the example of parsimony, the best tests of this assertion are those cases in which scientific ideals are in some conflict with scientists' epistemic needs and material self-interests. There are plenty of such cases. The scientific ideal of objectivity clashes with scientists' desires for research results to conform to their personal predictions. The scientific ideal of openness can also have threatening consequences for individual scientists. Full public scrutiny of empirical results exposes scientists to the risk that their conclusions are exaggerated or in error. The idealization of novel ideas and conceptual diversity also sometimes clashes individual scientists' needs. New and different theories may be necessary for scientific progress, but because individual perceptions of veracity are guided by a sort of intuitive Bayesian reasoning, novel theories are less obviously true than older, more firmly established theories. Novel ideas thus threatens scientists' very human need for knowledge that is certifiably true and accurate.

What wins in these clashes between abstract scientific ideals and scientists' personal motives? Does the ethos of science trump the more human needs and goals of scientists, or do these individual needs and goals supersede the ideals that scientists aspire to uphold? In the sections that follow, we discuss evidence indicating that the individual needs and goals win. Despite the power of the scientific ethos, scientists' very human needs govern the emergence of institutionalized behavioral norms that define cultures of science, and that shape the accumulation of scientific knowledge.

## HOW INDIVIDUAL NEEDS AND GOALS CAN CREATE CULTURAL CONSERVATIVISM

Virtually every influential philosophy of science accords a central role to the introduction of novel ideas (e.g., Feyerabend, 1975; Kuhn, 1977; Lakatos, 1970; Laudan, 1977; Popper, 1972). Hull (1988, p. 254) summarized succinctly the necessity of innovation: "Without alternatives to be selected, scientific change cannot occur." For this reason, a central feature in the scientific ethos is the encouragement of new ideas, and Merton (1957, p. 645) observed, "originality can be said to be a major institutional goal of science, at times the paramount one."

Innovation and originality may be major institutional goals of science, but the immediate goals of individual scientists are often at odds with this abstract ethos. Human cognition proceeds naturally in a fairly conservative manner. Like most animals, human beings tend to be neophobic; we're wary of things that are new and different. This neophobia is witnessed perhaps most obviously in our avoidant reactions to unusual foods, strange peoples, and to unfamiliar situations. It extends also to new and different concepts and ideas.

This conservative cognitive tendency shows up in various guises. We maintain preexisting beliefs even in the face of new information that is inconsistent with those beliefs, and we devote considerable mental effort to do so. For instance, we search for and find ways to interpret new information in ways that are consistent with those prior beliefs (Kunda, 1990). Sometimes we selectively forget information that is inconsistent with those prior beliefs (Snyder & Uranowitz, 1978). This need is not something that we can easily turn off, even if we wanted to.

This fundamental aspect of human cognition has implications for the way in which scientists think and act. Scientists too feel a greater level of epistemic comfort when new information is consistent with pre-existing theoretical structures, and with their own personal expectations. At a broad level, the desire to confirm existing beliefs makes it hard for scientists' minds to conform to the positivist philosophy of science to which they typically endorse. Positivist philosophies of science trumpet the role of falsification, but human beings–including scientists–tend to be verificationists. We typically want to see plausible theories and hypotheses confirmed rather than disconfirmed. In many ways, this need for consistency and epistemic efficiency leads scientists' behavior to be inconsistent with scientific ideals. Scientists may idealize objectivity and disinterestedness, but abundant evidence reveals scientists to be anything but objective or disinterested in the ways in which they design experiments, analyze and report results, and interpret the results reported by others (Greenwald, Pratkanis, Leippe, & Baumgardner, 1986; Hull, 1988; Kruglanski, 1994; Mahoney, 1977; MacCoun, 1998). Scientific methods offer systematic means of minimizing the impact of prior theories and beliefs on research results, but these methods are still just tools in the hands of subjective scientists. It is inevitable that scientists—often without even realizing it—design studies and "'stage-manage" procedures in such a way as to compel research results to conform to their expectations (McGuire, 1973). If results are at all ambiguous, the ambiguity is typically resolved in favor of preexisting theories and personal expectations (Greenwald et al., 1986). This epistemic goal is amplified by material self-interest. Professional rewards such as publication and promotion are hard to come by when one's research results violate conventional wisdom (Garcia, 1981).

A neophobic response to new ideas is the result not only of a desire for cognitive consistency; it may result also from a quirk of intuitive reasoning that forges a psychological link between the conceptually distinct dimensions of novelty and veracity. Judgments made by human beings are guided by a sort of intuitive Bayesian logic (Gigerenzer & Murray, 1987): Our perception of the veracity of any proposition is influenced in part by the judged "prior probability" that the proposition is true. The conceptual novelty of a proposition serves as a heuristic indicating questionable veracity. Within any context in which there exists a powerful desire for accurate knowledge, the novelty of an idea may be held against it. This context exists very obviously within the scientific community. As we discussed earlier, scientists value veracity in part because they stand to suffer personally should they be misled by a false finding. Scientists seek to ensure that only certifiably accurate findings are published in the scientific literature.

> Too few reviewers of papers (for ecological journals, anyway) will advocate the acceptance of a paper they think is "wrong"; not many realize that, almost always, any innovative idea will be thought of as wrong by most of scientists. Not all wrong ideas are innovative, of course, but all truly innovative contributions must, on first reading, appear wrong. (Fretwell, 1975, p. 4)

Scientists must then reconcile this competition between an abstract ethos that encourages innovative ideas and conceptual risk-taking, and a personal psychology that makes them risk averse and wary of truly novel discoveries. It's clear that this conflict is resolved in favor of the personal motives and goals of scientists: A quick survey of the institutionalized norms and customs of scientists reveals that—in contrast to the pull of the abstract ethos—these norms tend to be conservative.

## Impact on Customary Practices of Analyzing and Reporting Research Results

Within the biological and social sciences, some of these conservative norms are apparent in the ritualistic use of statistical tools for analyzing and drawing inferences from data. There is a widespread norm within these sciences to adopt a threshold of $p = .05$ when making subjective decisions about whether the statistical null hypothesis offers a plausible alternative explanation for an ostensibly interesting empirical finding. In essence, these scientists say this: "Although the results are consistent with a novel conceptual hypothesis, I won't proclaim the interesting hypothesis to be supported unless the probability is less than 5% that any effect of at least this size could have emerged simply as a result of sampling error." The same decision-making scheme is routinely applied even to replication studies—a context in which the boring alternative explanation (mere sampling error) has already been essentially ruled out by prior results. Even when the conceptual hypothesis is explicitly directional (e.g., a correlation between two variables is predicted to be positive, not negative), the null-hypothesis-testing scheme is routinely applied in a nondirectional (i.e., "two-tailed") manner—an approach that further limits researchers' likelihood of claiming support for the hypothesis. There is no straightforwardly statistical reason for this practice—it borders on foolishness to decrease the probability of finding what one hypothesized, but it is nonetheless standard practice.

Of course, the harness of conservative statistical decision-making customs chafes a bit when scientists are testing hypotheses that they have strong expectations about. One resolution to this internal conflict can be seen in the culturally widespread use of a particular linguistic neologism: "marginally significant." Within the strict logical framework that governs scientists' subjective decisions about statistical significance, this term makes no sense (a finding is either statistically significant or not). Still, the term has entered the vocabulary of many scientists, largely because it serves researchers' goal of confirming an expected hypothesis under conditions in which the actual statistical results don't meet the standard $p = .05$ threshold.

This bit of inventive linguistic wiggle room notwithstanding, the explicitly prescribed normative decision rules reveal a culture-wide tolerance for errors of omission (failing to discover new and interesting phenomena) but not errors of commission (erroneously claiming to discover a phenomenon that does not actually exist). The ritualistic adherence to these cultural norms doesn't limit the total number of inference errors in any way. In fact, it almost certainly increases the number of inference errors and limits the accumulation of useful scientific knowledge (Schmidt, 1996). It merely limits the number of the one specific type of inference error that, for individual reasons, individual scientists worry the most about. The errors scientists prefer are biased in favor of promoting the status quo.

Another example of an institutionalized conservatism is apparent in the customary style of writing an empirical research paper. The custom is to present empirical work in such a way that it will appear empirically original and also conceptually derivative. In a sense, skeptical reviewers must be convinced that, while not mere replications of previous results, there still exists a high "prior probability" that the obtained results would, in fact, be obtained. Thus, the introductory sections of successful (i.e., published) articles often present readers with a rigorously linear argument as to exactly why the hypothesized results follow directly from existing knowledge. This style or introduction establishes the perception of a strong prior probability–which almost certainly enhances the likelihood that the results will be viewed as accurate and true, and thus worth publishing. It also leads some readers of published articles to erroneously perceive the results to be so inevitable as to be uninteresting (Schaller & Crandall, 1998; Wallach & Wallach, 1998).

The appeal of prior probabilities is sufficiently strong that written products sometimes misrepresent the extent to which their authors were aware of conceptual hypotheses prior to observation of the results (Kerr, 1998). Even if researchers themselves might not have anticipated their results, readers tend to be provided right away with an expectation that enhances the perceived prior probability of those results. Not every scientist believes that this practice is appropriate (e.g., Kerr, 1998), but others encourage this norm (e.g., Bem, 1987).

Practically speaking, it is wiser to follow this "reconstruction" strategy, and the vast majority of published articles do fit this model. If many laboratories are like ours, the process of data collection and analysis yields new insights about theory. The near complete absence of descriptions of such processes in articles, along with our experience of the commonness of discovering new insights after the data have been collected, suggests that many people are following this reconstructive strategy. This discrepancy suggests that people public follow the prevailing *public* norms, while privately they are pursuing their individual interest of cognitive efficiency, parsimony, and the self-interest of being published.

## Impact on Customary Practices of Reviewing Colleagues' Research

Given that scientists' professional outcomes depend greatly on their publication output, it's no surprise that they are often critical about the manuscript review process–often privately, and sometimes in print (e.g., Epstein, 1997; Wegner, 1992). Sometimes scientists lament the normative tendency for reviews to be overly harsh, critical, and nit-picking. This tendency may be due in part to the tacit assumption–supported by empirical evidence–that negative reviewers more than positive reviewers are perceived by others to be intelligent (Amabile, 1983). This culture of harsh criticism seems to occur in some scientific disciplines more than others, and psychological processes may account for these differences too. Job candidates are evaluated more harshly under conditions in which the number of opportunities is smaller (Ross & Ellard, 1988). The same sort of phenomenon very likely operates in the manuscript review process, so that negative reviewing occurs most often in the social sciences, such as psychology, in which journal page space is scarcer and rejection rates higher.

Higgins (1992) commented on one particular aspect of reviewer nit-picking within the psychological sciences, arguing that in psychologists are prevention oriented, emphasizing the avoidance of mistakes rather than the promotion of new ideas. Garcia's (1981) colorful account of the caviling reception of his work on classical conditioning highlights the influence of conceptual innovation on the review process. Like rats in the dumpster behind a smorgasbord restaurant, reviewers may exhibit neophobia to genuinely innovative findings, while timidly favoring orts from the familiar plate of established knowledge. Thus, in sharp contrast to the advice of some philosophers of science (e.g., Laudan, 1981) who argue that science benefits when innovative work is treated to a more lenient publication standard, in fact, truly innovative research seems to be held to an especially stringent standard instead.

These anecdotal observations are borne out by empirical data. One study bearing indirectly on this process was reported by Mahoney (1977). Acting in his role as editor of a psychology journal, Mahoney sent out a manuscript to reviewers whose preexisting beliefs and conceptual preferences were either supported or unsupported by the results reported in the manuscript. The reviewers' reviews were clearly predicted by these personal expectations. When results were consistent with reviewers' expectations, their responses were quite positive; when results were inconsistent with reviewers' expectations, their reviews were highly critical.

Crandall and Schaller (2002) conducted a more direct investigation into a potential antinovelty bias among reviewers. The participants in the study were all members of the Society of Experimental Social Psychology–active scientists and experienced reviewers. Participants were sent one of four vignettes summarizing a manuscript that they were to imagine they were reviewing "for a widely read, influential, and high-prestige journal in your field." In all vignettes, the manuscript was presented as meeting at least the basic criteria for publication in such a journal: "It is on a topic of some interest to you, and you think it might be of interest to at least some of your colleagues. The research reported in the manuscript tests hypotheses that have not previously been tested." The vignettes differed in their descriptions of the overall strength of the empirical results. Weak results were indicated by a description that the design "does not effectively rule out all possible alternative explanations," "some of the hypothesized effects did not materialize," and "the effect sizes seem relatively small (approximately $r = .20$), and many of the significance tests revealed only 'marginal' effects (e.g., $.05 < p\text{'s} < .12$)." Strong results were indicated by a description that "the research design is strong, and it seems to rule out all plausible alternative explanations," "the results almost completely support the hypotheses," and "the effect sizes seem relatively large (approximately $r = .40$), and almost all of the significance tests revealed 'highly significant' effects (e.g., $p\text{'s} < .01$)." The vignettes also differed in terms of the conceptual novelty of the underlying theoretical framework. Conceptually old results were indicated by the description, "The research is in a well-established area, where there is a relatively long history of prior work. The theory from which hypotheses are drawn is well-established and has been supported by much previous research." Conceptually novel results were indicated by the description, "The research is in a brand-new area, where there is little previous research. The theory from which hypotheses are drawn is novel, and has not been tested empirically."

Thus, participants were asked to pass judgment on a manuscript that was either empirically weak or strong, and was either conceptually derivative or innovative. How did these participants respond? Comparing across experimental conditions, there was an interactive effect of the two manipulations on participants own recommendations regarding publication. Under conditions in which the results were weak (and reviewers' reactions were generally quite unfavorable), there was a tendency to favor the conceptually novel manuscript over the conceptually derivative one. However, under conditions in which the results were strong (and reviewers' reactions were more favorable in general), there was clear antinovelty bias. The average likelihood of recommending an empirically strong and conceptually old manuscript for publication was almost 90%, but the likelihood of recommending an equally strong and conceptually innovative manuscript for publication was only about 80%.

How does this antinovelty bias in the peer-review process persist, given scientists' idealization of innovation and novelty? Part of the answer may be indicated in another result observed by Crandall and Schaller (2002). Participants were asked not only to indicate their own publication recommendations, but also to indicate what their typical peer's recommendation would be. Results indicated that participants' own recommendations were generally more positive than they thought their peers would be, and that this difference was especially strong in the conditions in which they evaluated conceptually novel manuscripts. Thus, even while demonstrating an antinovelty bias, scientists' perceive themselves to be greater advocates of novelty than their colleagues are.

## Implications on the Accumulation of Scientific Knowledge

The conservative normative practices that we've just described have an impact on scientists' inferences about their own research results, on the manner in which they write about their research results, and on their reviews of colleagues' research papers. Thus, these practices all influence the process through which privately held scientific knowledge becomes part of the scientific literature. Inevitably, there are consequences on the contents of this literature.

One consequence is on the characteristics of articles that are published. When scientists are risk-averse in their publication decisions, then they respond more favorably to articles that are more fully loaded with convincing empirical evidence. The literature in psychology shows a clear historical trend in this direction. The average article published in the most prestigious and influential psychology journals is much longer and contains more supportive evidence than the average article in the same journal just a quarter-century ago (Conway, 2001; Reis & Stiller, 1992). The positive consequence is that consumers are extraordinarily unlikely to be misled into thinking that a phenomenon exists when it really doesn't. Another consequence is that larger and larger amounts of practical resources (research time, journal space, etc.) are being devoted to the documentation of these phenomena. This constrains the sheer number of phenomena that can be discovered.

Another consequence is an institutionalized bias against the publication of truly novel, conceptually groundbreaking findings. This institutionalized bias may be weaker than the bias exhibited at the level of individual reviewers, or it may be even stronger; the magnitude is influenced by the nature of the decision-rules that govern the judgments of journal editors. In order to estimate the extent to which individual reviewer biases impact ultimate publication decisions, it is necessary to consider the consequences of the individual-level responses within a realistic publication decision scenario.

A typical scenario is something like this: An author submits a manuscript to a journal editor; the journal editor solicits reviews and recommendations from one or more expert referees, and reviews the manuscript him- or herself. Let us suppose that a manuscript submitted to a top psychological journal is evaluated by an average of three scientists. On the basis of these evaluations, the editor uses some decision rule in order to make a publication decision. Assuming that the manuscript in question meets certain minimal qualifications for conceptual coherence, scientific rigor, and presentation (and so will not be rejected out of hand), the likelihood that the manuscript will be accepted for publication is a compound probability that depends largely on two factors: (a) the likelihood that each individual reviewer recommends acceptance, and (b) the editor's decision rule.

A lenient rule might be "I'll publish the manuscript unless all of the reviewers recommend that additional supportive evidence be collected" (i.e., publish if at least one out of three reviewers recommend publication as is). A moderately strict rule might be "I'll publish the manuscript unless the majority of the reviewers recommend that additional supportive evidence be collected" (i.e., publish if at least two out of three recommend publication as is). A strict rule might be "I'll publish the manuscript unless at least one reviewer recommends that additional supportive evidence be collected" (i.e., publish only if all three reviewers recommend publication as is).

It turns out that individual reviewers' recommendations interact with editorial decision rules in determining the likelihood that a manuscript will be published. The tendency for individual reviewers to hold conceptually novel findings to higher standards has effectively no consequences under conditions in which editors use lenient decision rules. However, as editorial decision rules become increasingly strict, the impact of this individual-level tendency has an increasing impact on the actual likelihood of publication. Under strict decision-rule conditions, the individual-level bias against empirically strong but conceptually innovative work is magnified into an even stronger bias against the chances of innovative work finding its way into the scientific literature.

Within any scientific discipline, this bias is likely to be manifest primarily at the premier journals (which are presumably governed by stricter editorial decision rules). The bias against innovative work might not show up as much among manuscripts submitted to less visible outlets. Although there surely are publication outlets for conceptually new and unusual work, those outlets may not be effective in conveying that work to a wide scientific audience.

The archived cultural knowledge of different scientific disciplines may be differentially susceptible to this bias. Within scientific disciplines in which acceptance rates at even the best journals are fairly high (e.g., theoretical physics), the anti-innovation bias may not exist at all. However, within scientific disciplines in which acceptance rates are quite low (e.g., psychology), the individual-level anti-innovation bias may slow the rate at which new and unusual ideas become part of the cultural knowledge.

Given these sorts of institutionalized anti-innovation bias that can emerge within a science, it often takes a special individual effort to sneak innovative work into the public realm of scientific knowledge. One inspiring example is offered by the actions of Robert MacArthur, a theoretical biologist who made hugely inventive contributions to ecology and population biology from the 1950s to the 1970s. MacArthur deliberately bypassed the conservative review process at the usual journals and instead published much of his most innovative work in the *Proceedings of the National Academy of Sciences*—a publication that "once had the enlightened view that any idea that impressed one intelligent scientist . . . was worthy of publication" (Fretwell, 1975, p. 4). MacArthur also was instrumental in founding a monograph series and a journal (*Journal of Theoretical Population Biology*) to serve as outlets for the sort of conceptually innovative research that he championed.

## HOW INDIVIDUAL NEEDS AND GOALS SHAPE CULTURAL TRANSMISSION OF SCIENTIFIC KNOWLEDGE

Publication is one necessary step in the process whereby some bit of privately held scientific knowledge becomes part of the scientific culture, but it is hardly sufficient. In order for knowledge to become truly cultural, it must be noticed and learned by other scientists. As an indicator of impact on scientific cultural knowledge, publication of information is almost useless; far more indicative is the extent to which that information is cited by other scientists. If one uses citations in any scientific discipline as a standard of impact, it's clear that most published scientific work has little or no real impact on the cultural knowledge of that discipline (Cole & Cole, 1973; Menard, 1971). Within psychology, for instance, only 10% of those psychologists who publish are cited even once a year (Garvey, 1979). "In the face of figures such as these," wrote Hull (1988, p. 360), "it is difficult not to conclude that publishing a paper is roughly equivalent to throwing it away."

Ideally, of course, that small percent of a scientific literature that gets noticed represents the best work in the discipline. To some extent, this is surely true. On average, conceptually useful and empirically convincing work is almost certainly more likely to be cited than shoddy derivative work. But scientific "goodness" is clearly not the only thing that determines whether published scientific work becomes part of cultural knowledge or not. All sorts of "nonscientific" variables play roles as well, including such seeming trivial factors as punctuation used in titles (Whissel, 1999).

Psychological processes predicated on self-serving motives and goals also influence scientists' tendency to cite other scientists' work. Greenwald and Schuh (1995) found an ethnic bias in scientific citations: Authors with typically Jewish names showed a bias toward citing the work of others with Jewish names, whereas those with non-Jewish names showed a bias toward citing the work of others with non-Jewish names. This ethnic bias in scientific citation suggests that egocentric motives and goals that have diverse consequences in ordinary social life also have subtle influences on the accumulation of a body of culturally shared scientific knowledge.

Just as self-serving goals have an influence, so too epistemic goals may also influence which scientific products do and do not become part of cultural knowledge. Although scientists probably engage in complex multidimensional thinking more often than the typical layperson, scientists cannot escape the human desire for cognitive simplicity and efficiency. Consequently, published work that is more quickly apprehended and easily understood is likely to be better remembered. Perhaps even more important than ease of understanding is the ease of communicating the relevant scientific information. Interpersonal communication is essential to the emergence of culturally shared knowledge (Latané, 1996), so only knowledge that is easily transmitted from one individual to another is likely to become part of a cultural knowledge base (Dawkins, 1989; Schaller & Conway, 2001; Sperber, 1990). This is evident in the transmission of rumors, in which difficult-to-convey details often disappear, or are changed over the course of multiple instances of interpersonal communication. It is evident too in the persistence and change of stereotypic beliefs over time (Kashima, 2000; Schaller, Conway, & Tanchuk, in press). Might it also be the case in the transmission and persistence of published scientific knowledge?

Several different lines of empirical evidence suggest that it does. These lines of research reveal two distinct mechanisms through which individual epistemic motives can influence the cultural transmission of scientific knowledge. Each mechanism corresponds to a part of the broader evolutionary process that underlies culture change in general, and scientific progress in particular (Dawkins, 1989; Hull, 1988).

## Impact on Selective Remembering and Forgetting of Scientific Knowledge

One mechanism can be thought of as a sort of *selection* process. From the rich diversity of published scientific stories available to remember and tell to others, some will be selected for retransmission and recollection, whereas others will not. In general, simpler stories—simpler theories and less complicated empirical findings—are more easily recollected and retold, whereas more complicated ones are more likely to be collectively forgotten (see Norenzayan & Atran, chap. 7, this volume).

One recent study provides some empirical evidence for this sort of selection process (Schaller, Bordes, Conway, & Tanchuk, unpublished data, 2000). The subjects of this inquiry were the articles published in a particular volume of the *Journal of Personality and Social Psychology* (*JPSP*), in the year 1965. *JPSP* was a flagship journal in the field, and so can assume that each article had been judged by referees to have met high standards of scientific merit. Of course, the contents of some of these articles would be retransmitted (as measured by citation), and so would be collectively remembered; others would be essentially forgotten. The question of interest was: What characteristics of these articles predicted the extent to which their contents were retransmitted?

A variety of different features were measured, including some purely objective superficial features (e.g., the length of the article, whether there was a colon in the title or not, and so forth). Other variables were judged subjectively (e.g., the prestige of the lead author's institutional affiliation). Of particular interest were two subjectively rated variables. One was a rating of the ease of understanding the main point of the article, judged by reading just the abstract appearing at the beginning of the article. The second key variable was of the ease of communicating that main point to others, also judged by a reading of the abstract.

These variables were correlated with several different citation-based measures that served as indicators of the extent to which the contents of the article were culturally retransmitted. Two measures drew on the *Social Sciences Citation Index* (*SSCI*) and assessed the number of citations to each article a decade later and two decades later. Other measures estimated citations to each article later in social psychology and personality textbooks, and in introductory psychology textbooks.

Results revealed that in addition to the effects of several superficial features (the length of the article, the prestige of the first author's institution, and the presence of a colon in the title), there were effects also of the subjectively judged ease of understanding and ease of communicating the articles main point. Articles published in this volume of *JPSP* were more likely to be retransmitted and so to remain a part of collectively remembered cultural knowledge if their abstracts conveyed a scientific story that was more easily understood and more quickly conveyed to others.

Two other interesting patterns of results emerged. First, ease of communicating had generally stronger effects than ease of understanding. This suggests that information is lost from the collective mythology not merely as the result of individual-level consequences of epistemic goals (e.g., failure to understand the point of a complicated article), but also the interpersonal consequences of these goals (e.g., a decision to tell others a simpler rather than a more complicated story). Second, the effects became stronger as more time passed since publication. This implies that, as more opportunities arise for collective forgetting, the psychological processes that compel forgetting have a cumulative impact. This pattern is consistent with other research indicating that the "communicability" of knowledge has a greater impact on its cultural persistence as more time passes (Schaller et al., in press). This is still another example of the process by which the need for cognitive efficiency and the psychological delights of parsimony bias the scientific process. Because scientists have limited cognitive capacity, and a limited willingness to restructure what they know, easy and mentally congruent findings tend to persist. Difficult to read and difficult to understand ideas and articles do not persist—people don't read them, people don't understand them, and thus people don't use them.

## Impact on Mutation and Misremembering of Scientific Knowledge

The second mechanism is something of a mutation process. Not all scientific stories that are remembered and retold will be remembered or retold with perfect fidelity. Some will be remembered and retold accurately; others will be misremembered and altered in the process of retransmission.

There is plenty of evidence of this sort of mutation process at work in the sciences. Within psychology, for instance, there are many identified cases in which retransmitted summaries of previously published research contain errors (Berkowitz, 1971; Paul, 1987; Vicente & Brewer, 1993). Similar errors occur in the physical sciences as well (Vicente & Brewer, 1993). Some of these retransmission errors might be viewed as random or semi-random accidents that exert no systematic effects on the collective mythology of a scientific discipline. An occasional misattribution of a finding to the wrong team of researchers, for instance, probably does not substantially alter the cultural memory for that finding.

Other errors, however, may be responsive to systematic biases, and so may exert systematic effects on the discipline. Here the individual epistemic goals of scientists matter. The epistemic desire for simplicity is likely to exert a biasing effect when scientists' retransmit information about previous research findings that do not tell particularly simple stories. The upshot is that there is a tendency for theories and empirical findings to be mutated in such a way that, over time and with repeated retelling, the complexities and complicating pieces of information disappear.

One example is provided by a comprehensive case study reported by Ross (1999). This study focused on the tendency for psychologists to collectively misremember the results of a classic study by Hastorf and Cantril (1954).

Hastorf and Cantril (1954) showed Princeton and Dartmouth students a film of a recent football game between those two universities' teams, and asked these students to write down any rule infractions they saw. Results showed that Dartmouth students indicated roughly equal number of infractions against the two teams, but that Princeton students indicated more than twice as many infractions by the Dartmouth team than by the Princeton team. So, the reality of the scientific finding was somewhat complex: Princeton students showed a clear tendency to view their own team more favorably than the other team, but Dartmouth students did not show any clear evidence of this favoritism.

How were those results described when cited and summarized later in journal articles and in textbooks? Not surprisingly, Ross (1999) observed a large number of mutations. Some of these mutations reflected a sort of selective omission of complicating information: The results from the Princeton students were described, whereas the results from the Dartmouth students were largely ignored. An even greater number of mutations reflected a clear misremembering: Dartmouth students were described, erroneously, as showing the same pattern of favoritism toward their own team that the Princeton students showed. Thus, the complicated, asymmetric pattern of results was retransmitted in a way that erroneously presented it as symmetric and simple.

These results also revealed that these retransmission errors were more likely to occur in textbooks than in journal articles. Thus, it appears that the mutation process is sensitive to the interpersonal communication context. Under conditions in which scientists are addressing less cognitively sophisticated audiences, they are especially motivated to communicate complex information more simply.

The Hastorf and Cantril study is not the only study on memory biases to have fallen prey to the sorts of biases that it documents. Allport and Postman's classic study on rumor transmission has itself suffered distortions through retransmission (Treadway & McCloskey, 1987). The misremembering of classic studies isn't limited only to classic studies of misremembering. There are other examples of oversimplified cultural myth-making in the retelling of psychological findings (Bramel & Friend, 1981; Suedfeld & Coren, 1989).

These results compel a more general point: Even when complex scientific stories are not entirely forgotten, they may not be remembered with great fidelity either. Individuals misremember and retransmit scientific results as being simpler than they actually are. Thus the eventual cultural memory for these results is erroneously oversimplified. This certainly isn't consistent with any ideal of science, but it is consistent with the epistemic goals of individual scientists.

## PRIVATE NEEDS AND PUBLIC VALUES

Science is a culture, with its set of standards, mores, practices, languages, and dialects. Like other cultures, public mores and private behavior are often discrepant. Often this very dissonance provides the most illuminating view of cultural fault lines. What is publicly applauded as a main value may be more honored in the breech than in observance.

Merton (1973) provides the most commonly accepted public code; scientists value universalism, communism, disinterestedness, and skepticism. In this chapter, we've reviewed a portion of the studies that have shown that scientists may celebrate these four things, but they don't live up their values (with the probable exception of universalism). Rather than promoting communism, scientists actively seek primary credit for discoveries, and often play down contributions of others. Many scientists are reluctant to share data, and set up obstacles to this practice. Rather than promoting disinterestedness, scientists promote their own point of view, and they promote others' work and careers that advance preferred theories, methods, and ideologies. Finally, rather than promiscuous and constant skepticism, scientists seek confirmation of ideas, creating experiments that promote their preferred theories and group and self interests. Skepticism is used more like a weapon, applied more carefully to disliked and conflicting data and methods than to preferred and endorsed ones. Although Merton's (1973) account describes the public values of scientists, our actual behavior is not captured by his account. These discrepancies usually serve the individual needs of scientists, rather than the public goals of science itself.

The study of the culture of science differs from almost all other cultural accounts in two ways. First, the observer is usually an actual participant in the culture. In a few cases, philosophers and historians of science have a completely different outlook from their subjects, but the vast majority of students of science are scientists (full- or part-time) themselves. In these cases, the observer of science has a real stake in the outcome of her or his study; self-esteem, group esteem, public approval, peer approbation, access to funding, and the like will all be affected by the kinds of conclusions he or she draws.

Second, the student of science often compares actual behavior to a set of normative standards that lead to value judgments that would be inappropriate when studying Kwakiutl culture. This discrepancy between normative and descriptive conduct allows for some kinds of judgments not possible in other cultural studies. When people deviate from the public norms, they may be punished, ridiculed, or their articles may be rejected and their grant applications turned down. The open pursuit of self-interest is not highly valued.

We suggest that the discrepancy between private behavior and public value leads to a misunderstanding among scientists about how to behave, and what is appropriate and good for science. It is widely believed that disinterestedness is a positive value for progress in science (e.g., Merton, 1973). We disagree. In "The Organization of Cognitive Labor," Kitcher (1993) provided an analysis of self-interest (seeking fame, priority, power and research support) as a motive in science. He showed, convincingly, that self-interested motives can promote efficient organization, can promote diversity in the number of approaches and theories, and help avoid premature consensus. Self-interest is not merely a base motive—it's efficient and effective. We suggest that the real distortion in science is not being motivated by self-interest, but more important is the pretense that science and scientists are not self-interested.

A more serious problem than the pursuit of individual self-interest is the problem of bias. We suggest that communication biases, need for parsimony and closure, and preference for one's own way of viewing things can skew the science in ways that do not serve progress. Bias is often a hidden problem—reviewers can seek to sink articles that are problematic to their commitments (Mahoney, 1976), adjust their standards for funding grants, or promote weaker work that cites them and is consistent with their ideas. These processes are inevitable, we argue, but the harm is that their impact cannot be calibrated when they act in the dark. More can be known about bias when processes are open and public—when reviewers reveal their identity, when biases are clearly stated within articles, and so on.

## CONCLUSION

The limits of science are human limits, and it's unwise to think that we check our humanity at the laboratory cloakroom. We are limited in cognitive ability (some more than others), and we're limited in motivation to restructure our understanding. Scientific progress cannot be so fast that it outpaces the ability or motivation of scientists to understand and communicate knowledge.

We are limited by our values. Scientists have value commitments that can affect which areas we study, which we devalue, and which theories we will consider as a possibility (e.g., Einstein's famous "I do not believe that the Good Lord plays dice [with the universe]"). For example, social scientists are more often part of the "center/left consensus" than politically conservative (Tetlock, 1995), and this will affect the topics we study and the kinds of policy-relevant research we do (Redding, 2001).

Finally, we are limited in our altruism. We seek priority, fame, access to resources, good students, and approbation of our peers. We rarely seek obscurity, and scientific martyrdom is not often preferred. Although scientific programs and individual careers can go down in flames spectacularly, often with very good effect to science (e.g., the cold fusion controversy), this is rarely the career plan of the scientists involved.

### Envoi

Our study of science leads us to the following prescription: Scientists should open their arms to the reality of science—its humanity, its limits, and its strengths. If we allow into public discourse the private behavior that makes up the bulk of scientific endeavor, science will progress with more speed and less bias. We can eschew secrecy and embrace humanity, scientifically.

## REFERENCES


Allport, G. W., & Postman, L. (1947). *The psychology of rumor.* New York: Holt.

Amabile, T. M. (1983). Brilliant but cruel: Perceptions of negative evaluators. *Journal of Experimental Social Psychology, 19,* 146–156.

Bechtel, W. (1988). *Philosophy of science: An overview for cognitive science.* Hillsdale, NJ: Lawrence Erlbaum Associates.

Bem, D. J. (1987). Writing the empirical journal article. In M. P. Zanna & J. M. Darley (Eds.), *The compleat academic* (pp. 171–201). New York: Random House.

Berkowitz, L. (1971). Reporting an experiment: A case study in leveling, sharpening, and assimilation. *Journal of Experimental Social Psychology, 7,* 237–243.

Bramel, D., & Friend, R. (1982). Is industrial psychology none of Marxism's business? *American Psychologist, 37,* 860–862.

Campbell, D. T. (1974). Evolutionary epistemology. In P. A. Schilpp (Ed.), *The philosophy of Karl R. Popper* (pp. 413–462). LaSalle, IL: Open Court.

Campbell, D. T., & Overman, E. S. (1988). *Methodology and epistemology for social science: Selected papers.* Chicago: University of Chicago Press.

Cole, J. R., & Cole, S. (1973). *Social stratification in science.* Chicago: University of Chicago Press.

Conway, L. III (2001). Number and age of citations in social-personality psychology over the lifespan of the field: Older and wiser? *Dialogue, 16*(2), 14–15.

Crandall, C. S., & Schaller, M. (2002). How do scientists respond to truly innovative research? An empirical inquiry. *Dialogue, 17*(1).

Dawkins, R. (1989). *The selfish gene* (2nd ed.). New York: Oxford University Press.

de Waal, F. (2001). *The ape and the sushi master: Cultural reflections of a primatologist.* New York: Basic Books.

Epstein, S. (1997). This I have learned from over 40 years of personality research. *Journal of Personality, 65,* 3–32.

Feyerabend, P. (1975). *Against method.* London: New Left Books.

Fretwell, S. D. (1975). The impact of Robert MacArthur on ecology. *Annual Review of Ecology and Systematics, 6,* 1–13.

Fuller, S. (1997). *Science.* Minneapolis: University of Minnesota Press.

Garcia, J. (1981). Tilting at the paper mills of academe. *American Psychologist, 36,* 149–158.

Garvey, W. D. (1979). *Communication: The essence of science.* New York: Pergamon Press.

Gigerenzer, G., & Murray, D. J. (1987). *Cognition as intuitive statistics.* Hillsdale, NJ: Lawrence Erlbaum Associates.

Greenwald, A. G., Pratkanis, A. R., Leippe, M. R., & Baumgardner, M. H. (1986). Under what conditions does theory obstruct research progress? *Psychological Review, 93,* 216–229.

Greenwald, A. G., & Schuh, E. S. (1994). An ethnic bias in scientific citations. *European Journal of Social Psychology, 24,* 623–639.

Hastorf, A. H., & Cantril, H. (1954). They saw a game: A case study. *Journal of Abnormal and Social Psychology, 49,* 129–134.

Heider, F. (1958). *The psychology of interpersonal relations.* New York: Wiley.

Higgins, E. T. (1992). Increasingly complex but less interesting articles: Scientific progress or regulatory problem? *Personality and Social Psychology Bulletin, 18,* 489–492.

Hilton, D. J. (1995). The social context of reasoning: Conversational inference and rational judgment. *Psychological Bulletin, 118*, 248–271.

Hull, D. L. (1988). *Science as a process*. Chicago: University of Chicago Press.

Kashima, Y. (2000). Maintaining cultural stereotypes in the serial reproduction of narratives. *Personality and Social Psychology Bulletin, 26*, 594–604.

Kerr, N. (1998). HARKing: Hypothesizing after the results are known. *Personality and Social Psychology Review, 2*, 196–217.

Kitcher, P. (1993). The organization of cognitive labor. In *The advancement of science*. New York: Oxford University Press.

Kitcher, P. (2001). *Science, truth, and democracy*. New York: Oxford University Press.

Kruglanski, A. W. (1989). *Lay epistemics and human knowledge*. New York: Plenum.

Kruglanski, A. (1994). The social-cognitive bases of scientific knowledge. In W. R. Shadish & S. Fuller (Eds.), *The social psychology of science* (pp. 197–213). New York: Guilford.

Kuhn, T. S. (1964). *The structure of scientific revolutions*. Chicago: University of Chicago Press.

Kuhn, T. S. (1977).

Kunda, Z. (1990). The case for motivated reasoning. *Psychological Bulletin, 108*, 480–498.

Lakatos, I. (1970). Falsification and the methodology of scientific research programmes. In I. Lakatos & A. Musgrave (Eds.), *Criticism and the growth of knowledge* (pp. 91–196). Cambridge, UK: Cambridge University Press.

Latané, B. (1996). Dynamic social impact: The creation of culture by communication. *Journal of Communication, 46*(4), 13–25.

Latour, B. (1987). *Science in action*. Cambridge, MA: Harvard University Press.

Laudan, L. (1977). *Progress and its problems*. Cambridge, MA: Harvard University Press.

Laudan, L. (1981). *Science and hypothesis: Historical essays on scientific methodology*. Boston: Dordrecht.

MacCoun, R. J. (1998). Biases in the interpretation and the use of research results. *Annual Review of Psychology, 49*, 259–287.

Mahoney, M. J. (1976). *Scientist as subject*. Cambridge, MA: Ballinger.

Mahoney, M. J. (1977). Publication prejudices: An experimental study of confirmatory bias in the peer review process. *Cognitive Therapy and Research, 1*, 161–175.

McGuire, W. J. (1973). The yin and yang of progress in social psychology. *Journal of Personality and Social Psychology, 26*, 446–456.

Menard, H. W. (1971). *Science: Growth and change*. Cambridge, MA: Harvard University Press.

Merton, R. K. (1957). Priorities in scientific discovery: A chapter in the sociology of science. *American Sociological Review, 22*, 635–659.

Merton, R. K. (1973). Science and technology in a democratic order. *Journal of Legal and Political Sociology, 1*, 115–126.

Merton, R. K. (1996). Science and technology in a democratic order. In *On social structure and science*. Chicago: University of Chicago Press. (Original work published 1942)

Neuberg, S. L., & Newson, J. T. (1993). Personal need for structure: Individual differences in the desire for simpler structure. *Journal of Personality and Social Psychology, 65*, 113–131.

Paul, D. P. (1987). The nine lives of discredited data. *Sciences, 27*(3), 26–30.

Popper, K. R. (1972). *Objective knowledge; an evolutionary approach*. Oxford: Clarendon Press.

Redding, R. E. (2001). Sociopolitical diversity in psychology: The case for pluralism. *American Psychologist, 56*, 205–215.

Reis, H. T., & Stiller, J. (1992). Publication trends in JPSP: A three-decade review. *Personality and Social Psychology Bulletin, 18*, 465–472.

Ross, M. (1999). *Reconstructing data: Reporting and remembering research results*. Unpublished manuscript, University of Waterloo.

Ross, M., & Ellard, J. H. (1986). On winnowing: The impact of scarcity on allocators' evaluations of candidates for a resource. *Journal of Experimental Social Psychology, 22*, 374–388.

Schaller, M., & Crandall, C. S. (1998). On the purposes served by psychological research and its critics. *Theory and Psychology, 8*, 205–212.

Schaller, M., & Conway, L. C. (1999). Influence of impression-management goals on the emerging contents of group stereotypes: Support for a social-evolutionary process. *Personality and Social Psychology Bulletin, 25*, 819–833.

Schaller, M., Conway, L. G. III, & Tanchuk, T. L. (in press). Selective pressures on the once and future contents of ethnic stereotypes: Effects of the "communicability" of traits. *Journal of Personality and Social Psychology*.

Schaller, M., Rosell, M. C., & Asp, C. H. (1998). Parsimony and pluralism in the psychological study of intergroup processes. In C. Sedikides, J. Schopler, & C. Insko (Eds.), *Intergroup cognition and intergroup behavior* (pp. 3–25). Mahwah, NJ: Lawrence Erlbaum Associates.

Schmidt, F. L. (1996). Statistical significance testing and cumulative knowledge in psychology: Implications for training of researchers. *Psychological Methods, 1*, 115–129.

Shadish, W. R., & Fuller, S. (Eds.). (1994). *The social psychology of science*. New York: Guilford.

Snyder, M., & Uranowitz, S. W. (1978). Reconstructing the past: Some cognitive consequences of person perception. *Journal of Personality and Social Psychology, 36*, 941–950.

Sober, E. (1990). Teleological functionalism. In W. G. Lycan (Ed.), *Mind and cognition: A reader* (pp. 97–106). Cambridge, MA: Basil Blackwell.

Sperber, D. (1990). The epidemiology of beliefs. In C. Fraser & G. Gaskell (Eds.), *The social psychology of widespread beliefs* (pp. 25–44). Oxford: Clarendon.

Suedfeld, P., & Coren, S. (1989). Perceptual isolation, sensory deprivation, and REST: Moving introductory psychology texts out of the 1950s. *Canadian Psychology, 30*, 17–29.

Tetlock, P. E. (1995). Complex answers to a simple question: Is integrative complexity "politically correct?" In G. G. Brannigan & M. R. Merrens (Eds.), *The social psychologists: Research adventures* (pp. 265–278). New York: McGraw-Hill.

Treadway, M., & McCloskey, M. (1987). Cite unseen: Distortions of the Allport and Postman rumor study in the eyewitness testimony literature. *Law and Human Behavior, 11*, 19–25.

Vicente, K. J., & Brewer, W. F. (1993). Reconstructive remembering of the scientific literature. *Cognition, 46*, 101–128.

Wallach, M. A., & Wallach, L. (1998). When experiments serve little purpose: Misguided research in mainstream psychology. *Theory and Psychology, 8*, 183–194.

Wegner, D. M. (1992). The premature demise of the solo experiment. *Personality and Social Psychology Bulletin, 18*, 504–508.

Whissel, C. (1999). Linguistic complexity of abstracts and titles in highly cited journals. *Perceptual and Motor Skills, 88*, 76–86.

PART

# III

# HOW CULTURES PERSIST AND CHANGE OVER TIME

CHAPTER

# 10

# The Microgenesis of Culture: Serial Reproduction as an Experimental Simulation of Cultural Dynamics

Allison McIntyre
Anthony Lyons
La Trobe University

Anna Clark
Yoshihisa Kashima
University of Melbourne

Human mind is human to the extent that it enables and is enabled by culture. Despite some evidence for the existence of culturelike practices among primates, the complexity and significance of culture for *Homo sapiens* far exceed those of other species on Earth. At the core of culture is symbolic meaning. Evolutionary processes made it possible for human minds to use symbols to refer to what we regard as things and events in the world and to humans themselves. Human mind, however, is incomplete in and of itself; it presupposes input from culture. Whatever is the mind physically realized at this point in time is a result of the evolutionary, sociohistorical, and ontogenetic processes. Whatever will be a kind of mind humanity will have in the future also must be a result of the symbolic activities from this point onward. At the same time, the past symbolic activities have produced contemporary cultures around the world, and the current symbolic activities will produce cultures of the future. In this sense, the mutual constitution of culture and mind unfolds over time, never ceasing, extending from the past and continuing into the future. Cultural dynamics is no less than the totality of this symbolically mediated culture–mind interplay.

Culture is nonetheless an essentially contested concept in social science where multiple conceptions provide different perspectives on this critical influence on human mind. In the current intellectual landscape, culture is taken by different researchers as a system of meaning on the one hand and a process of meaning making on the other. Nevertheless, these conceptions merely reflect two sides of the same cultural dynamics, that is, the stability and change of culture. We argue that a central question of cultural dynamics should be how concrete individuals' micro activities in situ produce and reproduce, at least sometimes, an enduring, macro pattern of meanings that may be called a meaning system (Kashima, 2000a). Borrowing Duveen and Lloyd's (1990) term in the social representations research tradition, such processes may be called the *microgenesis* of culture.

The main objective here is to provide a metatheoretical, theoretical, and methodological approach that may facilitate a systematic inquiry into cultural dynamics. First of all, we focus our attention on a metatheoretical issue, namely, the *dynamics* of culture, or the stability and change of culture over time. This perspective emphasizes the formation, maintenance, and transformation of cultures over time generated by microlevel activities by concrete social agents. We then turn to theoretical questions about the microlevel cultural dynamics as cognitive and communicative activities. In particular, we describe communication processes as collaborative activities among social agents to construct mutual understandings. Bartlett's (1932) method of serial reproduction is then presented and examined as a methodological tool for examining the microgenesis of culture. Some empirical findings that illustrate cultural dynamics are discussed using stereotypes as prominent part of culture.

## A THEORETICAL PRELUDE: CONCEPTUALIZING CULTURE

The concept of culture has had a checkered history in the academic discipline of psychology. Despite psychology's interest in culture from its disciplinary beginning (e.g., Wundt's Völkerpsychologie; for an informed treatment of this disciplinary history, see Jahoda, 1992), an inquiry into relationships between culture and mind has been marginalized until recently. By the confluence of historical, sociopolitical, and academic trends, however, the question of how culture and mind constitute each other has become one of the central concerns of contemporary psychology (e.g., Kashima, 2000a, 2001). The label of cultural psychology is often used for this broad class of interest. Despite some polemics in the past stating that cultural psychology differs significantly from cross-cultural psychology, the time is ripe to abandon the doctrinaire attitude and divisive academic politics, and to marshal a broad front to advance the research on culture and psychology.

As Kashima (2000a) noted, there emerged a broad metatheoretical consensus in this area of inquiry. It is a physicalist approach to human mind (i.e., a mind is constituted by physical processes), which is a result of Darwinian evolution, historically constituted and ontogenetically enculturated. In this view, physical, phylogenetic, sociohistorical, and ontogenetic processes are all mutually constitutive of human psychology, and therefore temporally dynamic, that is, constrained and enabled by the past, and constraining and enabling possibilities for the future. In short, it is a psychology that takes both culture and time seriously. Against this background, however, two images of culture have emerged as contrasting approaches to inquiries into culture–mind relationships.

## Two Images of Culture

One image portrays culture as an enduring system of meaning. When Triandis (1972) defined subjective culture as "a cultural group's characteristic way of perceiving the man-made [sic] part of its environment" (p. 4), or when Geertz (1973) described culture as "a web of significance" and advocated the symbolic anthropological approach to culture taken as a public "text," culture was viewed as an enduring system of meaning. Culture in this view is a repository of symbols that are internalized by individuals and provide structure to their experience. Culture is seen as a given for a generation of individuals, and relatively stable within a historical period. The other image of culture is that of a process of meaning making. In this view, culture is a process of production and reproduction of meanings in particular actors' concrete activities in particular contexts in time and space. Psychologists influenced by Vygotsky's (1978) Russian sociohistorical tradition often belong in this camp (e.g., Cole, 1996; Rogoff, 1990; Lave & Wenger, 1991). The two images of culture recall the two types of linguistics de Saussure (1959) described, that is, a study of *langue* as a system of distinctions among linguistic signs, as opposed to a study of *parole*, speech or language use in concrete situations. Culture is a phenomenon associated with meaning one way or the other; language is a career of meaning par excellence. It is no accident that researchers of culture–mind relationships are caught in the analogous polarity.

Research on individualism and collectivism (Hofstede, 1980; e.g., Triandis, 1995, for a review) is a good example of work done from a systems perspective on culture (also see Nisbett, Peng, Choi, & Norenzayan, 2001). Individualism and collectivism are typically regarded as worldviews or clusters of values and beliefs that are centered around the individual as a distinctive, independent, and unique person (i.e., individualism) or a member of a group and of significant interpersonal relationships (i.e., collectivism). These worldviews are assumed to form relatively stable cultural syndromes, which permeate through a number of domains of social activities. In contrast, research illustrative of a meaning-making approach to culture would be research on schooling and intelligence (e.g., for a review, Rogoff & Chavajay, 1995). Typically, researchers found that abstract reasoning tasks are better performed by Westerners than by people in traditional societies with lower levels of industrialization. Within less industrialized societies, people with a longer period of formal schooling tend to perform reasoning tasks better. Instead of explaining this in terms of cognitive styles or intelligence, researchers adopting the meaning-making perspective explained this in terms of the similarity between the cognitive tasks taught at school and the abstract reasoning tasks in intelligence tests. Formal schooling provided the concrete contexts in which abstract reasoning tasks were taught and performed; those with greater experience in formal schooling should be able to perform similar tasks better in the context of intelligence testing.

It is important to recognize that these two images are not mutually exclusive, but are complementary views about culture. The difference lies in their time frame and context generality (for further explication, see Kashima, 2001). On the one hand, a meaning-system view takes a long term perspective, and treats culture *as if* it is stable over a period of time. In this perspective, what one seeks is an enduring aspect of meaning, that aspect of symbolic activities that appears to remain the same across contexts and over the historical period. On the other hand, a meaning-making view takes a short-term perspective, and captures culture in flux. Indeed, culture in this sense is constantly created and recreated as mental and behavioral patterns of symbolic activities. Short-term fluctuations and context specificity are integral to this view of culture.

Neither can claim a privileged insight into culture-mind relationships, and both are necessary for examining and theorizing about cultural phenomena of different time scales. On the one hand, it is necessary to adopt a meaning-system view of culture if one tries to compare two or more cultures at a particular period in human history, or two or more historical periods of one society. In this case, culture is treated as if it is an independent variable in a quasi-experimental design. If culture is treated as constantly in flux, there is no way of theoretically justifying cross-cultural comparisons. Cross-cultural psychology takes this approach by necessity. On the other hand, it is equally necessary to view culture as meaning-making activities if one tries to understand how children become full-fledged members of their society with their cultural competence to manage their relationships with the natural and social environment. If culture is treated as a static system, there is no way of explaining the continuity and discontinuity, the persistence and change of cultural practices from one generation to the next. Again, students of culturally sensitive developmental psychology find this perspective attractive for good reason.

What we espouse is an inquiry into cultural dynamics, that is, the stability and change of culture over time. On the one hand, the fact of cultural change is a challenge for a meaning-system view of culture. A culture clearly changes over time, but the meaning-system view does not have any internal mechanism to explain change. Cultural change must be explained in terms of factors external to cultural processes per se, such as technology. In contrast, both stability and change of culture are part and parcel of a meaning-making view. Yet it does not have a principled way of determining which meaning is to endure and which is to change. In principle, all meanings may be created on the spot. At worst, cultural change becomes a result of random fluctuation over time. And as Cole (1996) acknowledged, a meaning-making approach does not have a principled answer to Jahoda's (1980) criticism that it fails to explain the existence of what appears to be a context-general meaning system. What is needed is a sustained inquiry into the puzzle of how culture as a meaning system is generated, maintained, or transformed over time by concrete meaning-making activities of humans in concrete contexts in time and space.

## Interpersonal Communication and Cultural Dynamics

No doubt most human symbolic activities take place within individuals' minds, as well as between them through communication. Put differently, the engine of cultural dynamics is the cognitive *and* communicative processes of those who are engaged in symbolically mediated social interaction. It is mostly through interpersonal communication that people construct shared meanings, and come to believe that they have shared understandings of the world and themselves. At the beginning of a probe into the microgenesis of culture must lie an inquiry into the process of human communication. Some detailed analyses of communicative processes, and how culture may be implicated in them, are necessary in order to clarify the centrality of interpersonal communication in cultural dynamics.

***Coordination, Communication, and Common Ground.*** According to Clark (1985), communication has often been conceptualized as the transmission of information by the encoder and its interpretation by the decoder. The communicator encodes his or her mental representations into publicly available symbols. The symbols are then transmitted to the receiver, who then decodes them into his or her own mental representations. In this conception, most of the work for communication is done intrapersonally, within each person's mind. What occurs interpersonally is mere transmission of public symbols. However, this conduit metaphor of communication is problematic in two respects. First, theoretically, it tends to perpetuate an individualistic theory of meaning (Kashima, 2001). In this view, meaning is a mainly intrapsychic phenomenon, where the construction, transformation, and manipulation of mental representations in the mind constitute the construction of meaning. Second, empirically, it has been found wanting for detailed analyses of human communicative processes by early philosophical, sociological, and social psychological inquiries (e.g., Grice, 1975; Krauss & Weinheimer, 1966; Schegloff, Jefferson, & Sacks, 1977; Schegloff & Sacks, 1973). Although these researchers' specific contributions differ markedly, central to their understanding of human communication is the coordination of activities. That is, people collaborate to build on one another's perceived cognition and action, and jointly coordinate their activities so that they may eventually reach a mutual understanding about the topic of the communication. This dialogic view of communication (Krauss & Fussell, 1996) puts communication squarely in the realm of social psychology, that is, the interpersonal coordination of social activities.

More recently, in psychology, Clark and his colleagues have developed a framework called the collaboration model. The model describes how interactants (i.e., those who are engaged in symbolically mediated interaction with each other) collaborate in face-to-face interaction to reach a shared understanding (e.g., Clark & Brennan, 1991; Clark & Schaefer, 1989; Clark & Wilkes-Gibbs, 1986). In this model, communication is understood as consisting of the interactants' joint *contribution* to the *common ground* shared among them. In Clark's (1996) view, common ground is a form of mutual knowledge (e.g., Hardin & Higgins, 1996; Rommetveit, 1974) where the communicators believe or assume that they share the same knowledge. When strangers meet for the first time, they assume some common ground on the basis of group membership (e.g., same gender, same taste in clothing). As they begin to interact, they further build a common ground on the basis of the communication. When they meet again later, they may assume the existence of a common ground based on the past communication. The joint contribution to common ground occurs via *grounding*, the process by which both the content and process of communication are coordinated and a mutual understanding of what has been said is established. In short, the collaboration model regards interpersonal communication as a series of contributions jointly made by the interactants to the ever-accumulating common ground.

The building block of a grounding process is a contribution. It consists of the presentation of information by one speaker and the acceptance of this information by another speaker, thus jointly creating the state of both speakers' understanding, and of knowing that they share this understanding. Each contribution consists of a presentation phase (which begins with the first utterance/turn by a speaker) and an acceptance phase (which ends with both speakers giving evidence of mutual understanding). A simple contribution may consist of one presentation and one acceptance. For example:

Presentation (P): What time is it?
Acceptance (A): Six o'clock.

This simple P–A pair has grounded the fact that both people know that "we know it's six o'clock." Contributions, however, can be more complex, involving a number of presentations and acceptances and different forms of subcontributions within them (Clark & Schaefer, 1989). The following contribution, taken from our own research, is more complex. It illustrates these two phases, and shows the negotiation in the establishment of mutual understanding. This transcript is set out such that each line indicates a change in speaker.

| | | |
|---|---|---|
| Line 1 | P | Was that after he got caught? |
| Line 2 | A/P | After he got caught, yep, at the flower shop. |
| Line 3 | P/A | And this was on the way back to the police station, he crashed his car. Is that right? |
| Line 4 | A/P | No, it was . . . he left the scene. He fled the police. |
| Line 5 | P/A | Ohhhh . . . |
| Line 6 | A/P | [It was on the way to the dance party]* |
| Line 7 | P/A | [I thought that, fled]* |
| Line 8 | A/P | He fled |
| Line 9 | P/A | Yeah |
| Line 10 | A | Right, OK. |

* [ ] indicate overlapping speech

In this example, a clear, initial presentation begins a contribution (line 1), with its presentation spanning line 1 to line 3. In line 4, one of the contributors identifies the source of misunderstanding and begins the negotiation of the acceptance phase. At line 10, the contribution ends with both speakers indicating commitment to having achieved mutual understanding.

In order for a mutual knowledge to be established, communicators must seek and make use of the evidence provided by others of their understanding or misunderstanding of their partner's presentation or acceptance. Evidence in grounding can be positive, signaling understanding, or negative, signaling that one has not understood. For instance, positive evidence can be verbal or nonverbal behavior, taking the form of continued attention (e.g., eye contact), initiation of a relevant next turn (e.g., "So, what happened next?"), acknowledgments (e.g., "OK"), demonstration of the knowledge (e.g., paraphrasing). Negative evidence may be a statement (e.g., "I don't understand") or display of misunderstanding. In the absence of clear evidence, communicators may assume that some mutual understanding was attained (assumed grounding). Clark and colleagues suggest that communicators jointly work to a grounding criterion "sufficient for current purposes" (Clark & Brennan, 1991, p. 129) under the assumption of mutual responsibility typically guided by the principle of least collaborative effort. That is, communication partners will work together toward the joint goal of establishing mutual understanding for each contribution to the grounding criterion. They frame their utterances so as to achieve mutual understanding as quickly and as easily as possible, thus minimizing the collaborative effort required for grounding. A contribution is then added to the current common ground, which consists of the accumulated contributions so far during the interaction and what was assumed to be a common ground at the start of the interaction.

The current common ground is not just an endpoint of the communicative interaction so far, but also acts as a condition that both enables and constrains future communications. In particular, common ground is often reiterated and used for making sense of new information during communication (Horton & Keysar, 1996; Schober & Clark, 1989; Wilkes-Gibbs & Clark, 1992), and information consistent with common ground is more easily disambiguated and understood than that which is inconsistent (Keysar & Barr, in press). More generally, information that is consistent with the current common ground may be more efficiently grounded. This is because the listener would be less likely to question or misunderstand this information, which requires less explanation, is less ambiguous, and is more relevant (Grice, 1975; Higgins, 1992; Leudar & Browning, 1988; McCann, Higgins, & Fondacaro, 1991). Furthermore, whether it is Grice's maxims of quantity (to be brief), manner (to be coherent/understandable), or relevance (to make utterances relevant to the audience), communicators may have a better chance of satisfying Grice's maxims with information consistent with the common ground. Obviously, although information that is consistent, rather than inconsistent, with the current common ground may be more likely to be communicated at a given level of collaborative effort, a greater amount of collaborative effort may be expended to ground information inconsistent with the common ground. This way, the current common ground is never final. It continues to evolve as the interactants keep up their communicative interaction.

***Common Ground, Grounding, and Cultural Dynamics.*** A small group of individuals with the possibility of all its members interacting with each other face-to-face would produce its current common ground by virtue of their continual process of grounding joint contributions. Common ground of a small interacting group acts as something akin to culture for a large-scale human collective. Both the common ground of a small group and the culture of a large collective at one point in time provide symbolic resources that enable efficient future communication; they also constrain the future communication by making some other communication more difficult than before. They are both shared meanings that enable and constrain the construction of possible worlds in the future. However, there is a difference between the two. The common ground of a small group may evolve out of the direct grounding of all the members' joint contributions, but the culture of a large collective cannot. How then can a large collective, whose members cannot have direct interaction with each other at the same time, develop shared meanings? This is a central question of cultural dynamics, that is, how concrete activities in situ can form, maintain, and transform what appears to be an enduring system of meaning.

At present, there appear to be two major approaches to this question. One is to conceptualize cultural dynamics of a large collective as emerging out of small group interactions. For the sake of clarity, let us simplify the situation. Suppose that one man has a new idea. He may manage to add this idea to the common ground of a small group to which he belongs. Members of this group belong to other small groups as well, and then may manage to ground the idea to the common grounds of these other small groups. Through overlapping group memberships of various individuals, the idea that originated in one man may be gradually added to the common grounds of many overlapping small groups, eventually generating, maintaining, or transforming culture regarded as a meaning system.

Just such an approach was adopted by Garrod and Doherty (1994) in examining the emergence of a linguistic convention in an experimental setting. Participants in their experiments played a computer game in dyads. The game, developed by Garrod and Anderson (1987), required each player to move his or her position token from a place in a maze to a goal. However, in order for both players to reach their respective goals successfully, the players had to coordinate their tokens' movements to help each other out. In particular, they had to communicate to each other the locations of their tokens within the maze. In an earlier study, Garrod and Anderson (1987) had identified four major ways of referring to locations in a maze (e.g., using a coordinate system, for instance, "3rd column from left and 2nd row from the top"), and found that a dyad often established a convention for doing so. That is, typically a pair of players settled on using one of the four ways of referring to locations. Garrod and Doherty (1994) found that a linguistic convention for referring to locations emerged when a group of players switched their partners so that each person played with every other person in the group. However, a convention did not develop to the same extent when the same partners were playing with each other for the same number of games, or when one person played with different partners, who had not played with each other among themselves. Their results suggest that a group of people who did not interact with each other simultaneously nevertheless developed a common method of referring to locations in the maze, producing a group convention.

Nowak, Szamrej, and Latané's (1990) dynamic social impact theory can be considered to conceptualize the distribution of public opinions in a large collective as emerging from small group interactions. In their approach, as in typical cellular automata, simple processing units are arranged in a lattice structure where a unit is located at the crossing point of the lattice. The units take only two states (pro or anti), and influence each other with a certain rule of updating each unit as a function of the states of the surrounding units. In their model, each unit is understood to represent an individual, and the state of the unit is interpreted as either a pro or anti opinion. They observed that when the states of a large number of units are randomly set at the start, the collection of the units typically showed both polarization and clustering. That is, a majority opinion (i.e., the proportion of one state among the units is greater than 50%) tends to gain an even greater majority, but units with the minority opinion (i.e., the opposite state to the majority state) tend to cluster together. In their simulation, a unit and the other units that surround it acted as a "small group," which shared members with other "small groups" that were adjacent to each other in the lattice structure. According to Nowak and Vallacher (1998), this type of structuring of social distances among individuals is necessary for self-organization such as polarization and clustering to occur in their system, although other conditions (i.e., some units are less likely to change their states than others, the updating rule involves some nonlinearity) are also important.

The other approach is to regard cultural dynamics as resulting from the spread of ideas through a complex interpersonal (or communication) network. Again, for the sake of clarity, let us simplify the situation. When a woman has a novel idea, she may communicate it to another person with whom she often converses. This communication may establish a common ground between the first woman and her friend. This second person then may communicate the idea to a third person, and so on. As the idea is communicated to a greater number of people, the idea may spread further afield through the social network. In the long run, communicative activities through the social network may generate, maintain, or transform what may be characterized as culture as a system of meaning. This view is most apparent within the research tradition of social network analysis (see Emirbayer & Goodwin, 1994; Wasserman & Faust, 1994). In particular, White (1992) argued for the significance of social network as a structural basis of cultural narratives. More recently, researchers such as Friedkin and Johnsen (1990, 1999) and Robins, Pattison, and Elliott (2001) have examined the social influence process in a social network, which clearly bears on the emergence of cultural meanings in a large collective.

In summary, communication can be conceptualized as the continual process of establishing and renewing common ground among the interactants. That is, the interactants attempt to reach a mutual understanding of the topic to the extent that is necessary for the present purpose. This process consists of coordinated activities among the interactants where they build on each other's previous action. One interactant presents information, and another accepts it by providing various forms of evidence that the latter has understood what the former meant. Through iterative processes of presenting and accepting, a stream of information is grounded and added to their common ground. Thus, common ground is a continually evolving set of mutual knowledge among the interactants who communicate with each other directly face-to-face. As the interactants produce and reproduce their common ground, some of the information in the common ground may be further communicated to other individuals and groups by virtue of their memberships of other groups or through their networks of interpersonal relationships. These subsequent communicative activities may not only spread the information within a large collective, thus generating new shared meaning for the collective, but also may contribute to the dynamics involving the maintenance and transformation of the shared meaning system.

## SERIAL REPRODUCTION PARADIGM AS A METHOD FOR EXAMINING CULTURAL DYNAMICS

What is critical in considering the cultural dynamics of a large collective is a systematic examination of the type of information likely to be grounded and added to the common grounds in micro-interpersonal communication processes, and a consideration of cumulative effects of such microprocesses. Bartlett (1920, 1932) provided one vehicle for just that. In 1920, Bartlett reported for the first time that he had a number of people read and retell an Amerindian folktale of "the war of the ghosts." Not only did he have the same person reproduce the story multiple times (method of repeated reproduction), but also he had one person retell it to another, who in turn reproduced the story for still another person, and so on in a chain. This latter method of serial reproduction mimics the spread of information through an interpersonal network in theoretically important respects.

According to Kashima (2000c), the serial reproduction paradigm (SRP) captures at least two significant aspects of interpersonal communication in a large social network. First, in a social network, when some information is grounded between a pair, this information may spread to other people who are connected to the receiver. The originator of the information has control over neither the content of the communication nor the extent of information spread. Therefore, as the information traverses links among nodes of a social network, it is transformed over time. Second, the information thus spread through a network is detached from the original context of its production and transferred to other contexts of meaning making. The detachability and transferability of communicated information makes it especially susceptible to excessive objectification and reification.

Nevertheless, Bartlett's work has been viewed as a *cognitive psychological* contribution on memory processes in social psychology. After all, Bartlett explained most of his findings in terms of a schema, a cognitive structure that assists memory. In fact, he is probably best known as a theorist who introduced the schema concept to psychology. However, with Van Dijk (1990), we contend that Bartlett's *Remembering* (1932) should be regarded as a historical milestone in *social* psychology. Bartlett's use of serial reproduction "is the first contribution to the theory of discursively based reproduction of social cognitions" (Van Dijk, 1990, p.168). What we wish to do here is to recover Bartlett's SRP as a method for examining the microgenesis of culture, in which communication plays a central role.

## Past Research Using the Serial Reproduction Paradigm

The past research using the serial reproduction paradigm shows that as information is passed along serial reproduction chains, (a) the information tends to become conventionalized, (b) details tend to be lost, and (c) descriptions of people and groups tend to become abstract. Each of these findings are well illustrated by research conducted by Bartlett (1932), Allport and Postman (1948), and others more recently. We review their work in some detail and later show that they can be interpreted as results of communication processes, rather than memory processes, as often interpreted in the past.

***Conventionalization in SRP.*** Bartlett (1920, 1932) reported the first use of the method of serial reproduction in experimental psychology. According to Bartlett, conduct and experience are directly determined by social factors within a group and indirectly by beliefs, traditions, customs, sentiments and institutions characteristic of a group. Partly based on evidence from his ethnographic work, Bartlett (1932) proposed that when two groups or cultures come into contact, the process of *conventionalization* takes place. Conventionalization can be defined as the way a custom, technique, or institution changes, when it is adopted from one group or culture to another, until it reaches a new stable form. Aspects of the new custom are assimilated into already existing forms and peculiar elements are simplified. By using the method of serial reproduction, Bartlett introduced stimuli to his experimental social group, university students in most cases, to capture experimentally the process of conventionalization.

In his experiments, Bartlett used several types of material–folk stories, prose passages, newspaper articles, and pictorial material. In most cases, reproductions from 10 successive individuals were obtained. A number of findings were consistent across the stimulus types. The disappearance of material was common, with many details forgotten or abbreviated. The stimulus was rationalized with explanatory and connecting phrases included to produce a coherent reproduction. A bias to the concrete with the more concrete aspects preserved and arguments reduced to a statement of opinion was evident. Titles, names, and numbers were routinely lost along with peculiar or unusual features. For example, mystical and spiritual elements were lost from a folk story about a warrior fighting a war with ghosts. The "war of the ghosts" story became a straightforward war story. The findings exhibited a theme of conventionalization with stimuli transformed until reaching a stable and more conventional form.

Three papers based directly on Bartlett's (1932) work were published. Tresselt and Spragg (1941) used Bartlett's procedure and stimulus and were able to replicate his findings. In further experiments, Tresselt and Spragg introduced a mental set passage to participants before the stimulus "test" passage was read. It was found that the mental set influenced the direction of change of the stimulus test passage such that it changed to incorporate the focus of the mental set passage. It is clear that the context in which serial reproduction occurs can shape the transformations of the stimulus. Noting Bartlett's (1932) observation that the results of his serial reproduction experiments have parallels in social life, Ward (1949) found that coin designs illustrated both in the laboratory and in specimens from ancient artifacts exhibit conventionalization, thus extending his research.

Gauld and Stephenson (1967) conducted a series of experiments directly related to Bartlett's (1932) theory of remembering. It was their contention that Bartlett's participants were not concerned about whether they reproduced the stimulus detail for detail and so were not doing their best to remember accurately. Although Gauld and Stephenson did not obtain serial reproductions, the results obtained from single reproductions are relevant to Bartlett's work. Gauld and Stephenson emphasized to participants that accuracy was important and found that recall was far superior to that found by Bartlett. According to Gauld and Stephenson, where accuracy is not emphasized, participants are more concerned with producing a convincing, coherent story. This provides support for the idea that the serial reproduction task is not purely a memory task, that participants in addition to remembering material have other goals, for example, telling a convincing story, as argued by Edwards and Middleton (1987).

***Information Loss in SRP.*** Allport and Postman (1945, 1948) experimentally simulated the rumor transmission in a communication chain. The first participant in each rumor chain viewed a slide of pictorial material and was asked to give a description, and reproductions of the descriptions were passed along seven-person-long chains. In general, the reproductions grew shorter, more concise, and more easily grasped and told. Allport and Postman called the decline in detail *leveling*. The selective perception, retention, and reporting of a limited number of details from a larger context, called *sharpening*, was also present. Elements routinely sharpened were familiar objects, events of contemporary relevance and objects of prominence.

Allport and Postman (1948) also described the process of assimilation. They outlined a number of types of unemotional assimilation. Assimilation to a principal theme was where the message was made more coherent and well rounded, with inconsistencies ruled out. Assimilation to condensation was where several items or events were incorporated into one detail, effectively shortening the message. Assimilation to expectation was where the message was changed to portray objects or events as they usually are. A further type of unemotional assimilation was assimilation to linguistic habit where familiar phrases, jargon and verbal clichés were used. Allport and Postman reported that the message was changed in more highly motivated ways (highly motivated assimilation) to reflect the self-interest or special interests of the participants. In addition, the changes in the reproductions reflected the prejudices of the participants. In the original stimulus of one experiment a White man was holding a razor; however, in the final reproductions in more than half of the chains, a Black man was reported to be holding the razor. Allport and Postman argued that changes such as these, which reflect the view that Black men are more likely to carry a weapon than White men, were motivated by the prejudices held by the predominantly White participants. Although Allport and Postman explained their findings using different terms than those of Bartlett (1932), the results are compatible with Bartlett's findings. Reproductions grew shorter and more conventional with peculiarities omitted. Conventionalization is evident in Allport and Postman's findings. In the decade following Allport and Postman's (1948) rumor work, several papers reported research investigating how personal interest in the content influences the transmission of rumors (e.g., Higham, 1951; Zaidi, 1958).

It is interesting to note that the leveling, or information loss, found by Allport and Postman may be better explained as a consequence of communication rather than due to memory loss. Kurke, Weick, and Ravlin (1989) investigated organizational communication using the SRP. Bartlett's (1932) folk story "The War of the Ghosts" was used as the stimulus and the results were similar to Bartlett's (1932) showing that participants "condensed, highlighted and rationalised the story to enhance its apparent coherence and consistency" (Kurke et al., 1989, p.15). What was most intriguing in Kurke et al. (1989) was that information lost after being sent through a serial reproduction chain could be regained when the final reproduction was fed back through the same chain from the last person to the first person in the original chain. In other words, when participants did not transmit what they had received from their transmitters, it was not the case that they had forgotten the information they omitted. Rather, they remembered the information, but for some reason chose not to communicate it to their receivers.

***Abstraction in SRP.*** In some of the recent research in social psychology, research has typically identified a tendency for people to abstract information in SRP. According to Fiedler et al. (1989), Grice's (1975) maxims of communication encourage abstraction in person description in communication. The maxim of quantity encourages speakers to be as informative as necessary but as brief as possible. The maxim of manner also encourages as short a communication as possible. In the first study, they had participants to reproduce descriptions of four different social roles. The level of abstraction (operationalized using Semin and Fiedler's 1988 linguistic category model) was assessed at each position in the chain. The results showed that descriptions of social roles grew more abstract along the serial reproduction chain. In further studies, Fiedler et al. examined how the process of abstraction was reversed, and showed that descriptions became more concrete following a single reproduction when the communicator expected their descriptions to be challenged by their audience. Fiedler et al. pointed out that one important implication of this type of research concerns the issue of firsthand and secondhand information. Similar to Van Dijk (1987), they argued that knowledge about social groups is often gained from the media or everyday communication rather than personal experience. Therefore, "social stereotypes may in part be understood as a reflection of the normal communication rules imposed on the transformations of underlying second hand information" (Fiedler et al., 1989, p. 292; also see Maass, Salvi, Arcuri, & Semin, 1989).

Gilovich's (1987) findings on the effect of second hand information may be interpretable in line with this. Here, participants in two experiments viewed a video depicting behaviors of a target individual and were asked to describe on audiotape the target individual for second-generation participants. Strictly speaking, because the second-generation participants did not provide a reproduction of the stimulus, the experiment does not use the method of serial reproduction. However, participants (both first and second generation) provided trait ratings of the target and rated whether the causes of the behaviors were dispositional or situational. The results showed that the second-generation participants made more dispositional attributions than did the first-generation participants and that the impressions of the target formed by second-generation participants were more negative than were those of the first-generation participants. In a third experiment, Gilovich demonstrated that the impressions of a target were more polarized for participants who had gained the information secondhand, compared to participants who had direct experience of the target.

Gilovich argued that first-generation participants are exposed to more situational constraints than are second-generation participants. In their messages, first-generation participants, by conveying information about the actor, are conforming to the conversational norms of brevity and relevance and are being informative about the actor, the most interesting element in the environment. Thus, only the actor information was abstracted from the actor-in-situation information. Because the information received by second-generation participants focused on the actor rather than the situation, second-generation participants made more dispositional attributions and trait inferences than did first-generation participants.

## Serial Reproduction as Communication

In this section, we consolidate our argument that the serial reproduction paradigm should be considered as reflecting cultural dynamics involving both cognitive and communicative processes, rather than a reflection of memory processes per se. Although Bartlett's (1932) original research has been viewed as a study of remembering, we argue that the paradigm is best understood as showing how participants interpreted and reproduced information with the intent of communicating it to someone who shares their own culture. We show that the existing data are in line with this interpretation. In particular, the main findings of the past studies using the serial reproduction paradigm are interpreted in terms of the rules that are thought to govern communication (e.g. Grice, 1975; McCann & Higgins, 1992).

The review has shown that, as information is passed along serial reproduction chains, (a) details tend to be lost, (b) descriptions of roles and groups tend to become abstract, and (c) the information tends to become conventionalized. These findings can be explained by assuming that the experimental participants were following normative rules of communication, that is, Grice's maxims. First, a loss of detail, or leveling, was evident in the serial reproduction research. The relative brevity of the message following serial reproduction can quite clearly be predicted by Grice's (1975) maxim of manner, specifically the submaxim "be brief." Grice's maxim of quantity also encourages a shorter message whereby the communicator is obliged to make the contribution informative but not more informative than necessary, thus leaving out uninformative detail. Although some of the details may have been lost due to forgetting, the Kurke et al. (1989) study suggests that in many cases people strategically omitted some details although they could remember them.

Second, in the studies reviewed, there was a general tendency for serially reproduced descriptions to become more abstract. The rules of communication predict neither abstraction nor a bias to concrete language use.

In fact, there appears to be a trade-off between the maxim of quality and quantity. People following these maxims in some cases would produce an abstract communication, and in others a more concrete message, depending on task instructions and the participants' goals. The maxim of quality encourages speakers to be truthful and to say only that for which they have evidence. Concrete language helps to do this as it refers to specific verifiable behavioral episodes. In line with this, Fiedler et al. (1989) found that when being judged or challenged people produced more concrete language. On the other hand abstract communications are encouraged by the maxim of quantity. Abstract language allows more information to be conveyed in fewer words (Semin & Fiedler, 1988). Nevertheless, abstract categories do not refer to the specific behavioral events, but to traits and qualities of people. Therefore, they are more difficult to verify. Nevertheless, in the absence of explicit challenge or possibility of critical assessment, people in serial reproduction experiments would have anticipated that their reproductions would be received by others who share their culture (in fact mostly students from the same university). In these cases, the maxim of quantity may have had a high priority, resulting in a more abstract language use.

Finally, the process of conventionalization is pervasive in SRP, not only in Bartlett's original experiments, but also in Allport and Postman's rumor studies. Generally, peculiar features, odd occurrences, and supernatural elements were commonly omitted. This can be explained by two maxims: of manner and of relation. The maxim of manner, in particular the submaxims "avoid obscurity" and "avoid ambiguity," encourage a speaker to leave out peculiar characteristics that may be obscure or ambiguous to the audience. The maxim of relation encourages participants to omit any details that are irrelevant to communication. Just as peculiar details were omitted, those that were familiar were consistently retained. The use of familiar phrases and language is encouraged by the submaxims "avoid obscurity" and "avoid ambiguity." Serial reproduction research has demonstrated that by the final reproduction there was a conventional, coherent, concise message, with gaps filled and explanations given so that it represents things as they are expected to be.

Nevertheless, it is important to be reminded that what determines "ambiguity" and "obscurity" is the common ground between the communicator and the audience. To the extent that information is consistent or in some way "close enough" to (or within "the zone of proximal understanding" as Vygotsky, 1978, called it) what constitutes a common ground, it is more easily understood by the audience and it is likely that the communicator would regard it as less ambiguous and obscure. When the communicator and audience are not interacting with each other face to face, the only common ground that the communicator can reasonably assume the audience to have is their shared culture. Culture, then, becomes the least common denominator of participants in a serial reproduction chain.

In line with this reasoning, according to Bartlett (1932), features that were not part of the individuals' culture were often lost in the serial reproduction paradigm. This is discernible in serial reproduction experiments using information relevant to culturally shared stereotypes. As Kashima (2000b) suggested, stereotype inconsistent information may be seen to be more difficult to defend for the communicator (i.e., maxim of quality) and to understand for the audience (i.e., maxim of manner). Provided that culture is often taken for granted, and assumed to be part of the shared common ground of the communicator and audience, it is likely that information inconsistent with culturally shared expectations is lost in the serial reproduction paradigm. Gilovich's (1987) findings that person impressions became more polarized as they were communicated to others may also be interpreted in line with this. In English-speaking cultures, the individual person is often conceptualized as a decontextualized entity (e.g., Miller, 1984; see for a review, Kashima, 2001). For this reason, contextual information, which is largely irrelevant for the culturally shared conception of the person, may have been omitted as person information was communicated to others.

Most importantly, the preceding discussion suggests that the phenomenon of conventionalization can be interpreted as a process of cultural reproduction through communication. That is, individuals' concrete cognitive and communicative activities of obtaining information from others with the intent of communicating it to other people who share the same culture tend to reproduce information that is in general agreement with the very culture that they share. In this way, communicative processes backed up by the requisite cognitive capacity contribute to cultural dynamics.

## THE FORMATION AND MAINTENANCE OF STEREOTYPES AS CULTURAL DYNAMICS

Social stereotypes are part of culture. To the extent that stereotypes are shared within society, they constitute part of culture that people live by. Although emphasis on their shared nature varies from one theorist to another in the area of stereotypes (for a review, see Stangor & Lange, 1994), researchers of culture (e.g., Triandis, 1972) have regarded stereotypes as part of their object of investigation. More recently, Schaller and Conway (1999, 2001, in press) also made a case for examining stereotypes as cognitive and cultural processes. Systematic investigations of the formation, maintenance, and transformation of stereotypes, then, can shed light on cultural dynamics. In this section, we illustrate the cultural dynamics involving stereotypes as investigated within the serial reproduction paradigm.

## Stereotype Formation

Although most contemporary theories of stereotype formation have taken for granted that stereotypes are learned through direct intergroup contact, a number of researchers have recently suggested that significant portions of stereotypes may be formed and maintained by symbolically mediated interpersonal communication processes (e.g., Kashima, Woolcock, & Kashima, 2000; Schaller & Conway, 1999; Stangor, Sechrist, & Jost, 2001; Thompson, Judd, & Park, 2000). The method of serial reproduction is ideally suited to examine this process. Although few in number, studies of group impression formation that adopted SRP have shown that communicating group impressions from one person to another can produce stereotype-like group impressions, which are extreme and homogeneous.

Thompson et al. (2000) showed that group impressions formed on the basis of communicated information tend to be polarized and homogeneous. In one of their experiments, nine-person groups were formed, with a first generation of three receiving behavioral information about a group, but a second generation of three receiving the first three participants' written communications about the target group, and likewise a third generation receiving the second three's communications. One half of the second- and third-generation groups received no other information, whereas the remainder received the communications as well as the original behavioral information. Group impressions reported by the second and third generations of participants were more polarized and their perception of the prevalence of the group characteristics was greater than those of the first set of participants.

McIntyre (2000) examined the effect of audience on stereotype formation in SRP. Participants were given information about members of two (fictitious) university clubs. The stimuli contained behavioral descriptions of club members, including information that differentiated the clubs as well as nondifferentiating information. Participants received one of two sets of descriptions where, in one set, friendliness information differentiated the clubs and activity information was the nondifferentiating dimension, and vice versa in the other set. Participants were asked either to memorize the information and reproduce it as accurately as possible, or to reproduce the information in writing to communicate it to another participant. The communicative context was manipulated by providing participants with specific audiences to whom their reproductions would be directed. It was thought, due to impression management goals and the goal to be polite and relevant in communication (e.g., Schaller & Conway, 1999), that participants (whose membership was not specified) would describe their audience's in-group more positively than the audience's out-group. In line with this expectation, the characteristics that positively differentiated the audience's in-group from the out-group were reproduced more than the characteristics that positively differentiated the audience's out-group from the in-group, and the nondifferentiating information. Furthermore, the stereotypes formed became polarized across the positions in the serial reproduction chain when participants were instructed to communicate, but not when they were told to memorize. In other words, the identity of the audience exerted a directive effect on the transformation of the stereotypes formed when participants intended to communicate their impressions to their audiences.

### Stereotype Maintenance

Once formed, stereotypes may be maintained through interpersonal communication. In line with this, Haque and Sabir (1975) used SRP to investigate how stereotype relevant information is "socially remembered". According to them, in Pakistan during the 1965 Indo-Pakistan war, stereotypes of Indians as "cowardly, cruel, inefficient and lazy" (Haque & Sabir, 1975, p. 57) were common in the media and present in everyday communication. A passage about the Indian Army was used as the stimulus for the eight-person-long chain of participants, all students at the University of Sind in Pakistan. The final reproduction exhibited the stereotype that the Indian Army was lazy and unprofessional. Haque and Sabir concluded that in the serial reproduction of material, there is a process of selective filtering that highlights information that is meaningful to the individual and his or her culture displaying commonly shared stereotypical representations.

Kashima (2000b) also used the method of serial reproduction to examine how culturally shared stereotypes are maintained in a narrative. Participants reproduced a story containing male and female stereotype-consistent (SC) and stereotype-inconsistent (SI) information that was either plot relevant or background information in the story. They were told either to memorize or to tell a story in doing so. Results showed that there was an advantage of SI information over SC information for plot relevant information in the early positions of the serial reproduction chain. Despite this, by the end of the chains, SC information was favored over SI information in the reproductions. For background information, SC information was retained more than SI information throughout the reproductions. There was no clear effect of the instruction (memory vs. storytelling) condition. Results indicate that stereotypes ended up being maintained, possibly despite the individual story teller's intention to do otherwise. In line with Allport and Postman (1948), it was suggested that when narratives are transmitted through a chain of individuals the stereotype consistent information is retained because consensually shared stereotypes are the "least common denominator" (Kashima, 2000b).

Lyons and Kashima (2001, under review) examined the stereotype maintenance process when the SC and SI information about a central character were told and retold in writing with the intention to communicate or to memorize across chains of four individuals. Both stories were based on occupational stereotypes, one involving a professional football player and the other a politician. More consistent than inconsistent information was retained, rendering the stories increasingly more stereotypical over the serial reproduction chain. In terms of the story content, when compared across the chains, retold stories initially diverged but later converged around a certain set of content. In all, it would appear that collective communication had a normalizing effect on the stories. In both studies, this latter tendency was greater when participants were told to communicate the story than when they were told to remember it. In addition, in one of the experiments, the tendency to reproduce SC information more than stereotype inconsistent information was observed in the communication condition, but not in the memory condition, suggesting the significance of communicative intent in the stereotype maintenance in the serial reproduction paradigm.

Under what circumstances, then, does the stereotype maintenance process occur in SRP? In line with the theorizing about grounding and cultural dynamics, it was hypothesized that critical factors are whether the cultural stereotype is *actually consensually shared* by the communicators in serial reproduction chains, and whether it is *perceived to be consensually shared.* To examine this, Lyons and Kashima (in preparation) conducted experiments in which stereotypes were experimentally constructed by providing participants with stereotypelike descriptions of a novel group. As expected, when retelling a story about one member of the group in SRP, a bias toward retaining more SC information was present only when the participants *actually shared* the same impressions about the target group. When participants had different impressions about the group, no systematic tendency emerged. Against this backdrop, several factors were shown to produce the tendency for stereotype maintenance. First, when the participants were certain that the audience did not know the characteristics of the group, they tended to communicate more SC information than SI information. It was as if they tried to teach what they believed to be true about the group to those who had no knowledge of it. However, when they were certain that the audience shared the same impression of the group, no systematic bias emerged. It was only when the participants were less than certain about the audience's impressions of the group that an SC bias emerged. Second, when the participants were told that the wider community tended to share the same impressions about the group, an SC bias was present. However, when they believed that the wider community did not share the same impressions, the reverse of an SC bias was found—that is, they tended to produce more SI information than SC information.

These findings point to the possibility that cultural stereotypes may become self-perpetuating, at least in part, by virtue of them being consensually shared, and by influencing sequential communicators to transmit increasingly less inconsistent information. This may then contribute to maintaining the consensus by providing confirmation of existing stereotypes in the recipients of communication. However, perceptions of sharedness also play some role in the reproduction of cultural stereotypes. It is when group impressions are believed to be shared within a wider community that cultural stereotypes may self-perpetuate through interpersonal communication processes.

## Conversational Processes about Stereotypes in Serial Reproduction

Although written communications in the serial reproduction paradigm tend to reproduce information that is consistent with common ground and shared culture, evidence is scant about serial reproduction by conversation. To begin to address this issue, we explored how people would serially reproduce a story about Gary. The story is concerned with a young man who is a player of Australian rules football, a popular sport in the state of Victoria where the study was conducted. There is a clear stereotype of players of this masculine sport, and the story of Gary, who was arrested for drink driving, contained information that is consistent and inconsistent with the stereotype.

We focused on clearly stereotype relevant episodes for this analysis. Stereotype consistent episodes were:

- Gary and his mates drank several beers in the car.
- He decided to escape arrest.
- He swore at the policeman.

Stereotype inconsistent episodes were:

- Gary switched on some classical music in the car.
- He stopped to buy flowers at a roadside stand.
- He found himself crying.

Stereotypes, by definition, are categories shared by members of a society. Therefore, if one is communicating to someone else who shares one's culture, one could assume mutual knowledge of a cultural stereotype, or, to put it differently, one could assume that it already exists in the common ground. In terms of the grounding process, it could therefore be assumed that information consistent with a cultural stereotype would be easier to ground in conversation than information inconsistent with that stereotype, as it is essentially already shared, and assumed to be shared, by communicators from the same cultural background. Information inconsistent with the stereotype, however, may be harder to ground, resulting in a more elaborate or involved grounding process taking place. Inconsistent information is less likely to be shared, and more likely to be surprising and unexpected for the listener than consistent information, therefore requiring greater effort by both the speaker and listener to ensure a common ground is established.

Nevertheless, conversation affords greater flexibility than written communication. In the presence of immediate feedback and a possibility for repairing one's utterances in light of the feedback, conversations may make it possible or even probable for information inconsistent with shared culture to be grounded. The work of Ruscher and her colleagues (e.g., Ruscher & Hammer, 1994; Ruscher, Hammer, & Hammer, 1996) suggests that conversants can spend time talking about information that is inconsistent with their stereotype, for instance, when they are concerned about accuracy of their judgment about a target person. If this happens, it is important to explore how stereotype-inconsistent information may be grounded. The social cognitive literature on stereotype change suggests that a person who exhibits stereotype inconsistent behavior may be subtyped or individuated (Weber & Crocker, 1983; see Kashima et al., 2000, for a review). Similarly, a subtype of a stereotyped group may be generated in serial reproduction as well.

The first participant read the original story about Gary's experience and then had a conversation with the second participant, who then had a conversation with the third participant, and so on down the chain. The first participant in each dyad (i.e., who had read or heard the story already) played the role of the main information provider, and the second participant acted as the information seeker but knew that they would be the information provider in the next conversation. The participants simply had a conversation about Gary. Participants were left alone to have their conversations, which were videotaped and later transcribed. Subsequent to each conversation, the participants rated Gary on personality traits inconsistent with the footballer stereotype (intelligent, thoughtful, caring, sensitive). There were four 5-minute dyadic conversations in all.

The results showed an intriguing transformation of the image of Gary the footballer. They suggested that during the course of serial reproductions Gary was individuated or subtyped as a special kind of a footballer, who is quite different from typical footballers. First of all, the successive participants' impressions of Gary shifted from one of a stereotypical footballer to one of a not very stereotypical individual. Although the first participant regarded Gary as not intelligent, thoughtful, caring, or sensitive (all consistent with the footballer stereotype), Gary was seen to be increasingly intelligent, thoughtful, caring, and sensitive. By the fifth participant, Gary was regarded as a man who was quite inconsistent with the general stereotype of a footballer. There appears to have been some degree of individuation or subtyping.

This is reflected in the manner in which stereotype consistent and inconsistent information was talked about in conversation.

### *First Conversation.*

| | |
|---|---|
| Consistent: | *"Gary and his mates drank several beers in the car"* |
| P: | He's driving down the road with his mates and he's drunk. |
| A: | Mmmm Hmmm. |
| Inconsistent: | *"Gary switched on some classical music in the car"* |
| P: | So Gary likes classical music? |
| A/P: | Yeah, he likes classical music. |
| P/A: | Yeah, it sounds sort of- |
| A/P: | It's weird. |
| P/A: | Yeah, 'cos it doesn't seem to fit with the rest of his personality. |
| A: | Yeah. |

### *Last Conversation.*

| | |
|---|---|
| Consistent: | *"Gary and his mates drank several beers in the car"* |
| P: | He never usually drinks. Just out of the blue, he started drinking and got picked up for it. |
| A/P: | Maybe, did he know he was drinking? Maybe his drinks got spiked. |
| P/A: | I don't know. I wasn't there. I'm just assuming it was this bloke he was with, just influencing him in doing something he usually doesn't do. |
| A/P: | Yeah. |
| P/A: | A bit out of character. |
| A/P: | Interesting that. |
| A: | Yeah. |
| Inconsistent: | *"He stopped to buy flowers at a roadside stand"* |
| P: | And he was getting the flowers, and he got some flowers, and he was so frightened- |
| A: | [ Nods ] |

In the first conversation, it was immediately acceptable that Gary was drunk with his mates. By the fourth conversation, however, this was perceived as most unlike Gary. In the first conversation, the stereotype consistent information seemed expected, whereas the stereotype inconsistent information was more problematic and required a more complicated grounding. In the fourth conversation, however, it was the stereotype-consistent information that was problematic, and the stereotype-inconsistent information received the very simple acceptance of a nod, and grounding was achieved in just a simple exchange.

This qualitative shift of the image of Gary was reflected in the way stereotype-consistent and -inconsistent information was grounded. In accordance with Clark's analysis, a pair of utterances (or series of utterances) consisting of one speaker's presentation and the other speaker's acceptance was used as one unit of conversation called a contribution. The amount of the conversants' "discursive attention" jointly directed to stereotype relevant information was indexed by the total number of contributions made for each piece of stereotype consistent and inconsistent information. Four types of contributions were distinguished. The first criterion of classification was concerned with whether acceptance was given explicitly or implicitly. If acceptance was explicit (i.e., the accepter provided direct evidence that a mutual understanding was established), it may have been given immediately or after a delay. *Immediate grounding* occurred when a speaker gave evidence of understanding of a sentence or clause as soon as it was spoken, whereas *delayed grounding* occurred when the second speaker referred to information that had occurred prior to the last sentence spoken by the prior communicator. In these cases, when evidence indicated that the presentation had been understood and agreed to, it was called *positive* evidence. When evidence indicated that the presentation had been understood, but not agreed to and rather queried or challenged, it was called *negative* evidence. If acceptance was implicit (i.e., evidence that a mutual understanding was established was assumed or inferred in the absence of explicit indication), acceptance may have been assumed as no evidence to the contrary was available (*assumed grounding via no evidence*) or inferred as the accepter had made a new presentation that implied the establishment of a mutual understanding (*assumed grounding via new presentation*). Most contributions were either immediate grounding or assumed grounding via no evidence.

We also counted the number of times the conversants expressed their thoughts, feelings or opinions in their presentations or acceptances of the stereotype relevant information. We observed that during the course of a conversation of this type, people typically grounded narrative information without indicating their reactions to the event described in the narrative. Their utterances simply described the event without explicitly mentioning the narrator or the listener in the discourse. However, occasionally, the narrator's or listener's "self" emerged in the discourse as a person who is "surprised about" or "thoughtfully commenting on" a particular episode described in the discourse. We regarded this latter type of utterances as indicating the conversants' "positioning" of themselves relative to the stereotype-relevant information (e.g., Edwards, 1994) or as indicating the self-content relationship. In this study, we simply counted the number of times a conversant made utterances that indicated some self-content relationship without distinguishing different types of self-content relationships (e.g., surprise, comment, etc.).

Table 10.1 reports (a) the amount of "discursive attention," (b) the type of grounding, and (c) the number of mentions about self-content relationships received with each of the three most stereotype-consistent and three most stereotype-inconsistent information items. In particular, the ratio indicates the proportion of a given type of grounding for SC information. Stereotype-consistent and -inconsistent information appears to be grounded differently at the beginning and toward the end of the serial reproduction chain. At the beginning, stereotype-inconsistent information received a greater amount of discursive attention, more likely to receive immediate grounding and less likely to receive assumed grounding than stereotype consistent information. The conversants were more likely to use exclamations, evaluation, or speculations in relation to stereotype-inconsistent information, relative to stereotype-consistent information, as an acknowledgment of the inconsistency and unexpectedness. These finding are in line

TABLE 10.1
Ratings Made by the Participants and the Types of Grounding in the Conversations

| | *P1* | *P2* | *P3* | *P4* | *P5* |
|---|---|---|---|---|---|
| Intelligent | 1 | 4 | 5 | 6 | 7 |
| Thoughtful | 1 | 5 | 7 | 5 | 8 |
| Caring | 4 | 6 | 5 | 7 | 8 |
| Sensitive | 2 | 10 | 6 | 8 | 7 |

| | *C1* | *C2* | *C3* | *C4* |
|---|---|---|---|---|
| Contribution | .4 | .4 | .5 | .6 |
| Assumed Grounding | .9 | .5 | —[a] | .3 |
| Immediate Grounding | .3 | .5 | .6 | .7 |
| Self-Content Relation | .2 | .4 | .6 | .6 |

*Note.* P stands for participant; C stands for conversation. Ratings were done on a 10-point scale (1 = *strongly disagree*; 10 = *strongly agree*). Contribution, assumed grounding, immediate grounding, self-content relation = proportion of contribution, assumed grounding, immediate grounding, and self-content relationships for stereotype consistent information relative to the sum for both stereotype consistent and inconsistent information. The average values for the stereotype consistent and inconsistent information were summed for each conversation, and the value for stereotype consistent information was divided by the sum: .5 indicates that a given type of grounding took place equally frequently for both SC and SI; a number above .5 suggests that a given type of grounding was more frequent for SC than for SI information.

[a]No assumed grounding took place.

with our expectations that stereotype-inconsistent information would be harder to ground and would therefore require more elaborate negotiation in order to establish it as mutual knowledge. However, toward the end of the reproduction chain, all these differences were reversed. This reversal may be explained in terms of the individuation of Gary. As observed in the impression ratings of Gary, although the participants held the impression of "Gary the footballer" at the beginning of the chain, this changed to "Gary the person," thus removing the footballer stereotype from the central frame of reference for the later conversations. Furthermore, this new "Gary the person" was constructed in those terms that were inconsistent with the footballer stereotype.

So what do these results say about communication as a mechanism of cultural dynamics? In this serial reproduction chain, conversants have clearly been engaged in a process of meaning making in which they have negotiated Gary's characteristics so as to make sense of the narrated event. Gary, who was originally portrayed as a stereotypical drink driving footballer, became a sensitive, caring guy who was unlikely to have been deliberately drink-driving and must have been a victim of peer-group pressure! This illustrates both the maintenance of an existing stereotype and the creation of a new "subtype" in communication. At one level, in order to make sense of Gary, he was taken out of the footballer category, and the stereotype inconsistencies were reconciled by focusing on Gary the person. This "re-fencing" (Allport, 1954) of the footballer stereotype makes Gary an exception to it, and in many ways actually serves to maintain the stereotype (for a similar argument, see Weber & Crocker, 1983). At another level, however, we may have witnessed the emergence of a new subtype of footballers in this microgenesis of cultural discourse. Gary as a "sensitive, New Age" footballer is potentially a new meaning created in the experiment, and may be added to the shared culture as part of a meaning system. It is an open question whether this new meaning moves into the cultural discourse outside this particular experimental group, and is retained within the student body of the particular university where the study was conducted, or even in the larger collective of Australians as a whole.

## CONCLUDING COMMENTS

In this chapter, we argued that cultural dynamics is fundamentally cognitive *and* communicative processes. It is the cognition that presupposes communication, and the communication that is backed by cognition, which contributes to the maintenance and transformation of human culture. To recapitulate our argument, we first outlined two contrasting, but complementary images of culture as a meaning system and meaning making process. It is clear that concrete individuals' meaning-making activities in particular contexts would generate, maintain, and transform what may be regarded as a context-general meaning system. In our framework, communication processes by which communicators work toward establishing a mutual understanding, or grounding information to common ground, are central to this. There are at least two theoretical approaches to the microgenesis of culture. One conceptualizes a large collective as consisting of overlapping small groups, and the other regards it as a complex social network. We argued that the serial reproduction paradigm captures some of the more important aspects of interpersonal communications through a social network.

This view of the serial reproduction paradigm invites a reconsideration of the property of the method, which was after all popularized through Bartlett's book on memory. In all, from a theoretical, methodological, and empirical viewpoint, Bartlett's method of serial reproduction can be regarded as a way of experimentally simulating the microgenesis of culture. Theoretically, we are justified in considering the serial reproduction method as capturing some significant aspects of information communication through a social network. Methodologically, we have shown that it can be used not only as a method for transmitting written communications. Empirically, the interpretation of the serial reproduction paradigm as examining communication processes (more accurately, cognitive and communicative processes) seems justified. Although it clearly falls short of completely naturalistic observations of cultural dynamics, if it is conducted appropriately, it may be used as a method of "experimental ethnography" in which we seek to examine recurrent processes of meaning making.

Using SRP, we examined cultural dynamics involving stereotypes, which are a significant aspect of culture as shared meanings. The review of the studies showed both the formation and maintenance of stereotypes in SRP. First, serial reproductions tend to produce stereotypelike shared group representations. When group impressions are told and retold through serial reproduction chains, they become stereotypelike, in that group impressions are more polarized and more homogeneous. When group impressions are circulated within a group, regardless of the communicators' social identity, the audience's social identity is sufficient to produce a stereotype that is favorable to the audience's in-group and unfavorable to the audience's out-group. Second, serial reproductions tend to reproduce cultural stereotypes. When a story pertaining to a group is told and retold, to the extent that the group stereotype is shared and believed to be shared (with some uncertainty) among the group members, the story tends to retain stereotype-consistent information, thus supplying a steady flow of stereotype-confirming information through discourse.

Nevertheless, what is most intriguing about the microgenesis of culture is its possibility for a cultural change. If a culture as a meaning system is formed and maintained by microlevel meaning-making activities, an existing culture may be transformed by microlevel activities too. In our own small study, we were able to observe the emergence of a new subtype of the footballer stereotype. When Gary the footballer was transformed from a hard-drinking, macho man to a sensitive, New Age footballer, there emerged a possibility that this category may be used in a future conversation. Novel categories may be generated in conversations, and most would be forgotten. However, if some such categories survive as they traverse through the links of a complex social network, they may eventually be added to common ground of this social network, thus transforming an aspect of this culture. Although it is still unclear under what circumstances a culture tends to be maintained or to change, a systematic investigation of cultural dynamics requires greater attention in this period of cultural transformation.

## REFERENCES

Allport, G. W. (1954). *The nature of prejudice*. New York: Double Day.

Allport, G. W., & Postman, L. J. (1945). The basic psychology of rumor. *Transactions of the New York Academy of Sciences: Series 2, 8*, 61–81.

Allport, G. W., & Postman, L. (1948). *The psychology of rumor*. New York: Henry Holt.

Bartlett, F. C. (1920). Some experiments on the reproduction of folk stories. *Folklore, 31*, 30–47.

Bartlett, F. C. (1932). *Remembering: A study in experimental and social psychology*. Cambridge University Press: Cambridge.

Clark, H. (1985). Language use and language users. In G. Lindzey & E. Aronson (Eds.), *Handbook of social psychology* (Vol. 2, 3rd ed., pp. 179–231). New York: Random House.

Clark, H. H. (1996). Communities, commonalities, and communication. In J. J. Gumperz & S. C. Levinson (Eds.), *Rethinking linguistic relativity* (pp. 324–355). Cambridge, UK: Cambridge University Press.

Clark, H. H., & Brennan, S. E. (1991). Grounding in communication. In L. B. Resnick, J. M. Levine, & S. D. Teasly (Eds.), *Perspectives on socially shared cognition* (pp. 127–149). Washington, DC: American Psychological Association.

Clark, H. H., & Schaefer, E. F. (1989). Contributing to discourse. *Cognitive Science, 13*, 259–294.

Clark, H. H., & Wilks-Gibbs, D. (1986). Referring as a collaborative process. *Cognition, 22*, 1–39.

Cole, M. (1996). *Cultural psychology: A once and future discipline*. Cambridge, MA: Harvard University Press.

de Saussure, F. (1959). *Course in general linguistics* (W. Baskin, Trans.). New York: McGraw-Hill.

Duveen, G., & Lloyd, B. (1990). Introduction. In G. Duveen & B. Lloyd (Eds.), *Social representations and the development of knowledge* (pp. 1–10). Cambridge: Cambridge University Press.

Edwards, D. (1994). Script formulations: An analysis of event descriptions in conversation. *Journal of Language and Social Psychology, 13*, 211–247.

Edwards, D., & Middleton, D. (1987). Conversation and remembering: Bartlett revisited. *Applied Cognitive Psychology, 1*, 77–92.

Emirbayer, M., & Goodwin, J. (1994). Network analysis, culture, and the problem of agency. *American Journal of Sociology, 99*, 1411–1454.

Fiedler, K., Semin, G. R., & Bolten, S. (1989). Language use and the reification of social information: Top-down and bottom-up processing in person cognition. *European Journal of Social Psychology, 19*, 271–295.

Friedkin, N. E., & Johnsen, E. C. (1990). Social influence and opinions. *Journal of Mathematical Sociology, 15*, 193–205.

Friedkin, N. E., & Johnsen, E. C. (1999). Social influence networks and opinion change. *Advances in Group Processes, 16*, 1–29.

Garrod, S. C., & Anderson, A. (1987). Saying what you mean in dialogue: A study in conceptual and semantic coordination. *Cognition, 27*, 181–218.

Garrod, S. C., & Doherty, G. (1994). Conversation, coordination and convention: An empirical investigation of how groups establish linguistic conventions. *Cognition, 53*, 181–215.

Gauld, A., & Stephenson, G. M. (1967). Some experiments relating to Bartlett's theory of remembering. *British Journal of Psychology, 58*, 39–49.

Geertz, C. (1973). *The interpretation of cultures*. New York: Basic Books.

Gilovich, T. (1987). Secondhand information and social judgment. *Journal of Experimental Social Psychology, 23*, 59–74.

Grice, H. P. (1975). Logic and conversation. In P. Cole & J. L. Morgan (Eds.), *Syntax and semantics: Speech acts* (Vol. 3, pp. 41–58). New York: Academic Press.

Haque, A., & Sabir, M. (1975). The image of the Indian army and its effects on social remembering. *Pakistan Journal of Psychology, 8*, 55–61.

Harasty, A. S. (1997). The interpersonal nature of stereotypes: Differential discussion patterns about in-groups and out-groups. *Personality and Social Psychology Bulletin, 23*, 274–284.

Hardin, C. D., & Higgins, E. T. (1996). Shared reality: How social verification makes the subjective objective. In R. M. Sorrentino, E. T. Higgins, & R. M. Sorrentino (Eds.), *Handbook of motivation and cognition: Foundations of social behavior* (pp. 28–84). Chichester: Wiley.

Higgins, E. T. (1992). Achieving "shared reality" in the communication game: A social action that creates meaning. *Journal of Language and Social Psychology, 11*, 107–131.

Higham, T. M. (1951). The experimental study of the transmission of rumour. *British Journal of Psychology, 42*, 42–55.

Hofstede, G. (1980). *Culture's consequences*. Thousand Oaks, CA: Sage.

Horton, W. S., & Keysar, B. (1996). When do speakers take into account common ground? *Cognition, 1*, 21–37.

Jahoda, G. (1980). Theoretical and systematic approaches in cross-cultural psychology. In H. C. Triandis & W. W. Lambert (Eds.), *Handbook of cross-cultural psychology* (Vol. 1, pp. 69–141). Boston: Allyn & Bacon.

Jahoda, G. (1992). *Crossroads between culture and mind: Continuities and change in theories of human nature*. Cambridge, MA: Harvard University Press.

Kashima, Y. (2000a). Conceptions of person and culture for psychology. *Journal of Cross-Cultural Psychology, 31*, 14–32.

Kashima, Y. (2000b). Maintaining cultural stereotypes in the serial reproduction of narratives. *Personality and Social Psychology Bulletin, 26*, 594–604.

Kashima, Y. (2000c). Recovering Bartlett's social psychology of cultural dynamics. *European Journal of Social Psychology, 30*, 383–403.

Kashima, Y., Woolcock, J., & Kashima, E. (2000). Group impressions as dynamic configurations: The tensor product model of group impression formation and change. *Psychological Review, 107*, 914–942.

Kashima, Y. (2001). Culture and social cognition: Toward a social psychology of cultural dynamics. In D. Matsumoto (Ed.), *Handbook of culture and psychology* (pp. 325–360). New York: Oxford University Press.

Keysar, B., & Barr, D. J. (in press). Self anchoring in conversation: Why language users don't do what they "should". In T. Gilovich & D. Kahneman (Eds.), *The psychology of judgment: Heuristics and biases*. Cambridge University Press.

Krauss, R. M., & Fussell, S. R. (1996). Social psychological models of interpersonal communication. In E. T. Higgins & A. W. Kruglanski (Eds.), *Social psychology: Handbook of basic principles*. New York: Guilford Press.

Krauss, R. M., & Weinheimer, S. (1966). Concurrent feedback, confirmation and the encoding of referents in verbal communication. *Journal of Personality and Social Psychology, 4*, 343–346.

Kurke, L. B., Weick, K. E., & Ravlin, E. C. (1989). Can information loss be reversed? *Communication Research, 16*, 3–24.

Lave, J., & Wenger, E. (1991). *Situated learning: Legitimate peripheral participation*. Cambridge, UK: Cambridge University Press.

Leudar, I., & Browning, P. K. (1988). Meaning, maxims of communication and language games. *Language and Communication, 8*, 1–16.

Lyons, A., & Kashima, Y. (2001). The reproduction of culture: Communications tend to maintain cultural stereotypes. *Social Cognition, 19*, 372–394.

Lyons, A., & Kashima, Y. (under review).

Maass, A., Salvi, D., Arcuri, L., & Semin, G. (1989). Language use in intergroup contexts: The linguistic intergroup bias. *Journal of Personality and Social Psychology, 57*, 981–993.

Manis, M., Cornell, S. D., & Moore, J. C. (1974). Transmission of attitude-relevant information through a communication chain. *Journal of Personality and Social Psychology, 30*, 81–94.

McCann, C. D., & Higgins, E. T. (1992). Personal and contextual factors in "the communication game." In G. R. Semin & K. Fiedler (Eds.), *Language, interaction and social cognition* (pp. 144–172). London: Sage.

McCann, C. D., Higgins, E. T., & Fondacaro, R. A. (1991). Primacy and recency in communication and self-persuasion: How successive audiences and multiple encodings influence subsequent evaluative judgments. *Social Cognition, 9*, 47–66.

McIntyre, A. M. (2000). *Communication and stereotypes: Stereotype formation based on secondhand information*. Unpublished doctoral dissertation, La Trobe University, Melbourne, Australia.

Miller, J. G. (1984). Culture and the development of everyday social explanation. *Journal of Personality and Social Psychology, 46*, 961–978.

Nisbett, R. E., Peng, K., Choi, I., & Norenzayan, A. (2001). Culture and systems of thought: Holistic vs. analytic cognition. *Psychological Review, 108*, 291–310.

Nowak, A., Szamrej, J., & Latané, B. (1990). From private attitude to public opinion: A dynamic theory of social impact. *Psychological Review, 97*, 362–376.

Nowak, A., & Vallacher, R. R. (1998). *Dynamical social psychology*. New York: Guilford.

Robins, G., Pattison, P., & Elliott, P. (2001). Network models for social influence processes. *Psychometrika, 66*, 161–190.

Rogoff, B. (1990). *Apprenticeship in thinking*. Oxford, UK: Oxford University Press.

Rogoff, B., & Chavajay, P. (1995). What's become of research on the cultural basis of cognitive development. *American Psychologist, 50*, 859–877.

Rommetveit, R. (1974). *On message structure: A framework for the study of language and communication*. New York: Wiley.

Ruscher, J. B., & Hammer, E. D. (1994). Revising disrupted impressions through conversation. *Journal of Personality and Social Psychology, 66*, 530–541.

Ruscher, J., Hammer, E. Y., & Hammer, E. D. (1996). Forming shared impressions through conversation: An adaption of the continuum model. *Personality and Social Psychology Bulletin, 22*, 705–720.

Schaller, M., & Conway, L. G. (1999). Influence of impression management goals on the emerging contents of group stereotypes: Support for a social evolutionary process. *Personality and Social Psychology Bulletin, 25*, 819–833.

Schaller, M., & Conway, L. G., III (2001). From cognition to culture: The origins of stereotypes that really matter. In G. B. Moskowitz (Ed.), *Cognitive social psychology: On the tenure and future of social cognition* (pp. 163–176). Mahwah, NJ: Lawrence Erlbaum Associates.

Schaller, M., & Conway, L. G., III (in press). Unintended influence: Social-evolutionary processes in the construction and change of culturally-shared beliefs. In J. Forgas & K. Williams (Eds.), *Social influence: Direct and indirect processes*. Philadelphia: Psychology Press.

Schegloff, E. A., Jefferson, G., & Sacks, H. (1977). The preference for self-correction in the organization of repair in conversation. *Language, 53*, 361–382.

Schegloff, E. A., & Sacks, H. (1973). Opening up closings. *Semiotica, 8*, 289–327.

Schober, M. F., & Clark, H. H. (1989). Understanding by addressees and overhearers. *Cognitive Psychology, 21*, 211–232.

Semin, G. R., & Fiedler, K. (1988). The cognitive functions of linguistic categories in describing persons: Social cognition and language. *Journal of Personality and Social Psychology, 54*, 558–568.

Stangor, C., & Lange, J. (1994). Mental representations of social groups: Advances in conceptualizing stereotypes and stereotyping. *Advances in Experimental Social Psychology, 26*, 367–416.

Stangor, C., Sechrist, G. B., & Jost, J. T. (2001). Changing racial beliefs by providing consensus information. *Personality and Social Psychology Bulletin, 27*, 484–494.

Thompson, M. S., Judd, C. M., & Park, B. (2000). The consequences of communicating social stereotypes. *Journal of Experimental Social Psychology, 36*, 567–599.

Tresselt, M. E., & Spragg, S. D. S. (1941). Changes occurring in the serial reproduction of verbally perceived materials. *The Journal of Genetic Psychology, 58*, 255–264.

Triandis, H. C. (1972). *The analysis of subjective culture*. New York: Wiley.

Triandis, H. C. (1995). *Individualism and collectivism*. Boulder, CO: Westview.

Van Dijk, T. A. (1987). *Communicating racism: Ethnic prejudice in thought and talk*. Thousand Oaks, CA: Sage.

Van Dijk, T. A. (1990). Social cognition and discourse. In W. P. Robinson & H. Giles (Eds.), *Handbook of language and social psychology* (pp. 163–183). Chichester: Wiley.

Vygotsky, L. S. (1978). *Mind in society: The development of higher psychological processes*. Cambridge, MA: Harvard University Press.

Ward, T. H. G. (1949). An experiment on serial reproduction with special reference to the changes in the design of early coin types. *British Journal of Psychology, 39*, 142–147.

Wasserman, S., & Faust, K. (1994). *Social network analysis*. New York: Cambridge University Press.

Weber, R., & Crocker, J. (1983). Cognitive processes in the revision of stereotypic beliefs. *Journal of Personality and Social Psychology, 45*, 961–977.

White, H. C. (1992). *Identity and control*. Princeton, NJ: Princeton University Press.

Wigboldus, D. H. J., Semin, G. R., & Spears, R. (2000). How do we communicate stereotypes?: Linguistic bases and inferential consequences. *Journal of Personality and Social Psychology, 78*, 5–18.

Wilkes-Gibbs, D., & Clark, H. H. (1992). Coordinating beliefs in conversation. *Journal of Memory and Language, 31*, 183–194.

Zaidi, S. M. H. (1958). An experimental study of distortion in rumor. *Indian Journal of Social Work, 19*, 211–215.

CHAPTER

# 11

# Sustaining Cultural Beliefs in the Face of Their Violation: The Case of Gender Stereotypes

Deborah A. Prentice
Erica Carranza
Princeton University

One of the primary functions of culture is to solve the problem of what is male and what is female (Shweder, 1982). A culture's solution to this problem is enshrined in beliefs about the attributes that characterize men and women–so-called gender stereotypes. As a central feature of culture, gender stereotypes hold considerable intrinsic interest for students of cultural psychology. In addition, they provide a useful lens through which to examine broader questions about the psychological processes that underlie the perpetuation and revision of cultural beliefs.

In the case of gender stereotypes, their most striking feature in need of a psychological account is their stability. Despite substantial convergence in the activities, occupations, and social roles of men and women, even the most recent research suggests that traditional gender stereotypes persist (see, e.g., Eagly & Mladinic, 1993; Holt & Ellis, 1998; Spence & Buckner, 2000; although see Diekman & Eagly, 2000). For example, we conducted a study just last year that examined the current state of gender roles and stereotypes (Prentice & Carranza, 2002). Our results showed that current stereotypes, as reported by a group of college-age participants, are remarkably similar to traditional stereotypes. Their primary constituents–an emphasis on instrumentality and agency for men and on expressiveness, interpersonal sensitivity, and submissiveness for women–remain very strong today. What is most remarkable about this stability is that, with widespread changes in the roles and activities of men and women, people must witness behaviors that violate their gender stereotypes everyday. Why does this behavioral evidence for the invalidity of gender stereotypes not produce wholesale revision?

In this chapter, we resolve this question by describing several psychological processes that act to minimize the occurrence, or in some cases just the perceived occurrence, of gender stereotype violation. Specifically, we argue that people fail to revise their gender stereotypes because (a) they witness very few blatant violations of these stereotypes; (b) they fail to perceive as a violation most of the behavior they do witness; and (c) they devalue, and thereby marginalize, people whom they perceive to violate gender stereotypes. As a result, counterstereotypical behavior does not provide a strong impetus for stereotype change, a conclusion that applies to all stereotypes, but much more strongly to stereotypes based on gender. We begin by describing the properties of gender stereotypes that distinguish them from stereotypes of other social groups and make them especially resistant to disconfirmation.

## CONTENTS OF GENDER STEREOTYPES

Gender stereotypes, like other social norms, include both prescriptive and descriptive content (see Burgess & Borgida, 1999 for a review). Their prescriptive content is beliefs about attributes of the ideal man and woman—those attributes that men and women *should* demonstrate. Examples include the beliefs that men should be assertive and women should be sensitive to the needs of others. Their descriptive content is beliefs about attributes of the typical man and woman—those attributes that men and women *actually do* demonstrate. Examples include the beliefs that men are typically arrogant and women are typically moody.

The distinction between prescriptive and descriptive components has gained prominence in discussions of *gender* stereotyping because it highlights one of the unusual features of gender stereotypes: their highly prescriptive nature (see Fiske, 1998; Fiske et al., 1991; Fiske & Stevens, 1993; Glick & Fiske, 1999). All categorical stereotypes, including those based on gender, contain (presumably) descriptive information about category members. Stereotypes of African Americans, Asian Americans, Jews, Muslims, college athletes, science majors, and so on specify which attributes supposedly characterize members of these various groups. Most do not specify which attributes *should* characterize members of the groups. By contrast, gender stereotypes do. They include information both about attributes that are likely to characterize women and men and attributes that are supposed to characterize them. Women are not just likely to be warm and caring, for example; they are *supposed* to be warm and caring. Men are not just likely to be strong and ambitious; they are *supposed* to be strong and ambitious.

Gender stereotypes, unlike racial, ethnic, or other group stereotypes, provide images to live up to as well as images to live down.

What are those images? Numerous studies have documented the contents of gender stereotypes (for reviews, see Deaux & Kite, 1993; Fiske, 1998). Some of these studies have examined prescriptive stereotypes, by asking participants to rate the desirability for men and women of each of a set of attributes or activities (e.g., Auster & Ohm, 2000; Bem, 1974; Holt & Ellis, 1998). Others have examined descriptive stereotypes, by asking participants to rate the typical man and woman on each of a set of attributes (e.g., Spence & Buckner, 2000), the likelihood or probability that a man or woman possesses each of a set of attributes (e.g., Deaux & Lewis, 1984; Diekman & Eagly, 2000), or the percentage of men and women who possess each of a set of attributes (e.g., Cota, Reid, & Dion, 1991; Martin, 1987). In some cases, participants have indicated their own beliefs (e.g., Diekman & Eagly, 2000); in others, they have acted as spokespeople for society in general (e.g., Auster & Ohm, 2000). Virtually all of these studies have documented the persistence of traditional gender stereotypes, whereby women are expressive and emotional, and men are agentic and instrumental. Although there is considerable debate about the extremity of these stereotypes and the extent and rate of change over time (see, e.g., Auster & Ohm, 2000; Diekman & Eagly, 2000; Spence & Buckner, 2000; Twenge, 1997), there is general agreement on a considerable degree of stability.

Our own research on the contents of gender stereotypes illustrates this stability (Prentice & Carranza, 2002). We examined the prescriptive and descriptive contents of these stereotypes by asking participants to rate each of 100 attributes in terms of its desirability (in reference to American society) for a woman; desirability (in reference to American society) for a man; general desirability (in reference to American society); typicality for a woman; and typicality for a man. We used the desirability ratings to identify four types of attributes for each gender: gender-intensified prescriptions, gender-relaxed prescriptions, gender-intensified proscriptions, and gender-relaxed proscriptions. Gender-intensified and gender-relaxed prescriptions were both generally desirable. Gender-intensified prescriptions were attributes higher in desirability for the target gender than for the other gender and people in general—qualities to strive for. These replicated traditional prescriptive gender stereotypes. Women were supposed to be warm and kind, cooperative, sensitive to the needs of others, interested in children, excitable, polite, wholesome, friendly, cheerful, and patient, among other similar qualities. Men were supposed to be assertive, self-reliant, high in self-esteem, decisive, competitive, disciplined, willing to take risks, rational, high in leadership ability, athletic, and ambitious, among other similar qualities. Many of these attributes were gender-relaxed prescriptions for the other gender—that is, they were rated lower in desirability for that gender than for people in general. In addition, many other attributes were gender-relaxed prescriptions, especially for women. Thus, it was only moderately desirable that women be efficient, rational, intelligent, mature, worldly, principled, and concerned for the future, that they defend their beliefs, and that they have common sense. These are all very socially desirable attributes, highly valued in men and in people in general. They are valued also in women—just somewhat less so.

Gender-intensified and gender-relaxed proscriptions were both generally undesirable. Gender-intensified proscriptions were attributes lower in desirability for the target gender than for the other gender and people in general—qualities to avoid at all costs. For women, these included being sexually promiscuous, rebellious, cynical, arrogant, controlling, and stubborn. For men, they included being melodramatic, approval seeking, impressionable, shy, naive, superstitious, weak, yielding, moody, childlike, emotional, and gullible. Most of these attributes were gender-relaxed proscriptions for the other gender. Gender-relaxed proscriptions were rated as more desirable in the target gender than in general, and represent socially undesirable qualities that are more tolerated in men or in women by virtue of their gender.

We used typicality ratings to assess whether these four types of gendered attributes—gender-intensified prescriptions, gender-relaxed prescriptions, gender-intensified proscriptions, and gender-relaxed proscriptions—corresponded to perceived differences between women and men. In almost all cases, they did, though the exceptions were quite interesting. Both women and men fell short on a couple of prescribed attributes: Women were not perceived to be more playful, loyal, and flirtatious than men; and men were not perceived to be more clever, dependable, and disciplined than women. But by far the most exceptions to the correspondence between the desirable and the typical came for attributes that were gender-relaxed prescriptions for women. Even though being clever, disciplined, principled, efficient, mature, worldly, concerned about the future, intelligent, and filled with common sense were only moderately desirable qualities for women—significantly less desirable than for men or people in general—women were perceived to have these qualities at least as much as, and in some cases more than, men. Note that these deviations do not constitute violations of gender-intensified prescriptions. Although it may be less desirable for women to have these attributes, it is certainly not undesirable. Thus, women who are highly intelligent, clever, mature, and worldly are not violating what they are supposed to be; they are overachieving it. It is interesting that men were not perceived as overachieving their gender-relaxed prescriptions: Differences in the desirability of warmth, compassion, optimism, sensitivity, and so on were all mirrored by perceived differences in their typicality. We suspect that this asymmetry reflects an asymmetry in the extent to which women and men are taking on nontraditional roles (see Diekman & Eagly, 2000; also Prentice & Carranza, 2002, for further discussion). Virtually all of the attributes that were gender-intensified proscriptions for one gender or the other showed typicality differences, the only exception being child-like. Thus, on the whole, people perceive violations of gender-intensified prescriptions and gender-intensified proscriptions to be the exception to the rule.

These results reveal the multifaceted nature of normative gender beliefs. These beliefs include not only what researchers have referred to as prescriptive stereotypes: beliefs about the attributes that women and men should and should not have (gender-intensified prescriptions and proscriptions, which we refer to collectively as gender prescriptions throughout this chapter). They also include beliefs about the attributes that women and men can have and do not have to have. This latter set of attributes—the gender-relaxed prescriptions and proscriptions—do not qualify as gender prescriptions in the strictest sense, because they are not societally mandated nor socially enforced. They are, instead, domains in which societal standards are a bit lower, and perfection is not required.

It is interesting to speculate on why gender stereotypes include prescriptive content. Most recent accounts of the contents of gender stereotypes trace them to the social roles of men and women, whether they see these roles as biologically based (e.g., Sidanius & Pratto, 1999) or simply as social facts (e.g., Eagly & Steffen, 1984; Hoffman & Hurst, 1990; Jost & Banaji, 1994). The accounts differ in the psychological processes that lead from roles to stereotypes. Some argue that stereotypes are simply inferences drawn from the observation of role-constrained behavior (Eagly & Steffen, 1984). Others propose a motivated link, focusing on the role of stereotypes in explaining and defending the status quo (Hoffman & Hurst, 1990; Jost & Banaji, 1994; Sidanius & Pratto, 1999). The latter accounts trace the prescriptiveness of gender stereotypes to the investment people have in the existing social order. But they cannot explain why gender stereotypes are more strongly prescriptive than are stereotypes of other social groups. That is, why would the role relations of men and women be especially in need of psychological justification?

An answer to this question comes from Glick and Fiske's (1999) analysis of the "exploitative interdependence" that exists between men and women. They described the relationship of exploitative interdependence as one marked by the reliance of the dominant group on the subordinate group for some commodities, and an equal reliance of the subordinate group on the dominant group for others. In the case of men and women in American society, women depend on men for financial stability and participation in interpersonal relationships, whereas men depend on women for the same interpersonal prospects as well as family and household maintenance. Men and women, when they demonstrate many of the attributes associated with traditional roles (the role of the primary provider for men and the roles of wife and mother for women), act in cooperation with each other such that the needs of each group are met. Dominance in the interdependent relationship is determined by status; in the case of men and women, this position is held by men. Prescriptive stereotypes of both groups arise and are sustained because they preserve the status relationship. The greater the interdependence, the more investment both groups have in the status quo, and the more strongly prescriptive the resulting stereotypes.

According to Glick and Fiske (1999), the contents of the stereotypes likewise follow from the relationship between the groups. In relationships of exploitative interdependence, stereotypes categorize groups along two dimensions: competence and likability. The dominant group is held to high standards of competence, whereas the subordinate group is held to high standards of friendliness and likability. In contrast, in relationships of competition, stereotypes are more descriptive than prescriptive and more often include characteristics that are difficult to like or admire.

Comparisons of the societal stereotypes of African Americans and women illustrate the sensitivity of stereotypes to the relationship between groups (see Glick & Fiske, 1999). Fifty years ago, both African Americans and women were in relationships of exploitative interdependence with the dominant group (European American men), and both were stereotyped as not very competent but highly likable. As social changes shifted the relationship between European Americans and African Americans from one of interdependence to one of competition, the stereotype of African Americans became less prescriptive and more descriptive. Moreover, the descriptive attributes that now comprise this stereotype are highly unlikable—attributes such as hostile and criminal—whereas the prescriptive stereotype of old depicted a likable (albeit incompetent) group of individuals. In contrast, gender stereotypes have remained highly stable, despite structural changes within the government and the workplace, and despite increased opportunities for women in both occupational and educational domains.

In short, Glick and Fiske (1999) offered a compelling explanation of the contents of gender stereotypes that trace them to structural interdependence between women and men. This explanation can account for the persistence of gender stereotypes in the face of considerable structural changes in the social roles of men women, for despite these structural changes, the two groups remain interdependent and unequal in status. It can account for the prescriptive nature of these stereotypes, given the high investment that both groups have in the status quo. In addition, it is consistent with one final observation from our own studies (Prentice & Carranza, 2002). Perusal of the list of attributes we identified as gender-intensified prescriptions and gender-relaxed proscriptions for men and women suggests a negative relation between the two: Negative attributes that are relaxed proscriptions for one gender are offset by the gender-intensified prescriptions of the other. Relaxed proscriptions for men—being controlling, stubborn, arrogant, and sexually promiscuous—are offset by intensified prescriptions for women—being sensitive to the needs of others, yielding, polite, and loyal. Similarly, relaxed proscriptions for women—being melodramatic, superstitious, impressionable, and weak—are offset by intensified prescriptions for men—being consistent, rational, decisive, and strong in personality. We believe that this interdependence of content is unique to gender stereotypes and perhaps stereotypes of other groups in relationships of exploitative interdependence.

In summary, we have argued that gender stereotypes have a dual nature: They contain both descriptions of the attributes that (supposedly) characterize women and men, and prescriptions of the attributes that should characterize them. Although few stereotypes have this dual nature, many other kinds of cultural beliefs do. In particular, social norms often both describe a group's typical behaviors or attributes, and prescribe what those behaviors and attributes should be (see Cialdini, Reno, & Kallgren, 1990; Miller & Prentice, 1996). The research literature on social norms has much to say about the psychological processes involved in reactions to violations of norms that contain both descriptive and prescriptive content. We draw heavily on this literature in our analysis of the violation of gender stereotypes.

## STEREOTYPE VIOLATION

As we noted at the outset of this chapter, changes in social roles over the past few decades have created a disjunction between traditional gender stereotypes and the occupations and activities in which men and women are currently engaged. This is an unusual, although not completely novel, state of affairs. In the more typical case, roles and stereotypes support one another: Roles constrain behavior to be consistent with stereotypes, and stereotypes shape expectations to determine role assignments. Nevertheless, the tendency for cultural beliefs to lag behind social change—the so-called conservative lag—is quite familiar to social science researchers. For example, this dynamic characterized cultural norms regarding racial segregation in the wake of the civil rights movement (Fields & Schuman, 1976; O'Gorman, 1975; O'Gorman & Garry, 1976).

For traditional gender stereotypes to persist even as the social roles occupied by men and women change requires that people have some way of minimizing the occurrence and/or impact of stereotype violation. In fact they have several ways: They avoid violating gender prescriptions, underperceive violations they witness, and punish any violations they do perceive. We consider each of these processes in turn.

### Violations of Prescriptive Stereotypes Are Rare

First and foremost, people do not often violate gender stereotypic expectations, especially those imbued with prescriptive, as well as descriptive, significance. A fundamental lesson of the literature on social influence is that people conform to social norms and that they do so for two reasons. First, the descriptive component of norms—evidence of what other people do—provides useful information about what actions are likely to be appropriate and effective. Second, the prescriptive component of norms—evidence of what other people think is right and wrong—signals what actions are likely to be socially acceptable and unacceptable (see Cialdini & Trost, 1998; Turner, 1991). Gender stereotypes also have both of these properties and therefore elicit a high degree of conformity.

This is especially true for the prescriptive content of these stereotypes. Because social approval is a powerful incentive (and social disapproval an even more powerful disincentive), violations of gender prescriptions are exceedingly rare. In contrast, violations of stereotypic expectations that do not have prescriptive force are much more common, especially when the behaviors in question are prescribed by another social role. For example, women in traditionally male occupations often act in highly assertive, competitive, and decisive ways in line with their occupational role, thereby violating what is expected of women, but not what is prescribed. Gender prescriptions simply require that they avoid being perceived as aggressive, ruthless, and stubborn and that they remain compassionate, cheerful, and well groomed. Similarly, men in traditionally female occupations may act highly cooperative, warm, and sensitive to the needs of others, thereby violating what is expected of men, but again, not what is prescribed. As long as they avoid being perceived as yielding, emotional, and approval seeking and remain self-reliant, rational, and strong in personality, they will fall within the bounds of what is prescribed of men.

In short, when men and women take on nontraditional roles, they are likely to do so in ways that preserve their conformity to gender prescriptions. The research literature contains various empirical findings that support this claim, at least on the female side. For example, women smile more than men do, even when they are in a high-power, interviewer role (Deutsch, 1990). They are modest in their academic predictions, especially when interacting with a low-performing peer (Heatherington et al., 1993). And they behave communally, whether they are interacting with a superior or a subordinate (Moskowitz, Suh, & Desaulniers, 1994). Additional evidence that women adhere to feminine prescriptions, even when they occupy masculine roles, comes from research in the organizational domain. For example, Lauterbach and Weinter (1996) found that female and male middle managers use very different strategies when trying to influence their superiors. Women are more likely to act in the best interest of the organization, consider others' viewpoints, involve others in planning, and take account of interpersonal dynamics in their attempts to influence their superiors. Men are more likely to act in their own interest, disregard others' feelings, plan alone, and focus exclusively on the task at hand. Similarly, in a recent meta-analysis, Eagly and Johnson (1992) found that women in leadership roles tend to adopt a more democratic and less autocratic style than do men in similar roles. That is, women are more likely to allow and even to encourage subordinates to participate in decision making than are men. These various strands of research suggest that women tend to adhere to the prescriptions of their gender, even when they are in positions that require a very different set of qualities.

Thus, we maintain that gender prescriptions are rarely violated, even among occupants of nontraditional roles. Instead, stereotype violation most commonly involves attributes that are not prescribed—those that are considered optional or simply less prevalent in one gender than the other. This kind of stereotype violation may have resulted in some degree of change in descriptive aspects of the female stereotype (Diekman & Eagly, 2000; Prentice & Carranza, 2002); nevertheless, most traditional stereotypic expectations for women and men remain intact. This brings us to a second set of psychological processes that sustain gender stereotypes in the face of their violation.

## Descriptive Stereotype Violation Is Underperceived

People show a tendency to assimilate what they observe to their stereotypes (Olson, Roese, & Zanna, 1996). As a result, many violations of gender stereotypes—especially when they do not involve gender-intensified prescriptions or proscriptions—may go unnoticed. Although assimilation to the stereotype is strongest in the absence of additional, individuating information about the target, it can occur even in the presence of additional information (see Jussim, 1991; Kunda & Thagard, 1996; Madon et al., 1998).

Indirect evidence for the role of assimilation in the underperception of stereotype violation comes from a study by Jacobs and Eccles (1992). These investigators examined the impact of mothers' gender stereotypical beliefs on their perceptions of their children's abilities. They asked mothers to estimate the distribution of ability and the relative value of that ability across males and females in each of three domains: math ability (stereotypically male), sports ability (stereotypically male), and social ability (stereotypically female). In all three domains, mothers' stereotypes interacted with the sex of their child to predict perceptions of the children, even after accounting for the children's previous performance in the domain. In other words, mothers saw their own children's behavior as confirming their stereotypic expectations to a significantly greater extent than it in fact did. Moreover, these stereotype-tinged perceptions were a strong predictor of the beliefs children themselves held about their abilities.

More direct evidence that assimilation leads people to overlook violations of gender stereotypes, and thereby devalue women's performance on traditionally male tasks, comes from studies that have held constant the information provided about a target and simply varied whether it was a woman or a man. For example, numerous studies have revealed that a research paper attributed to a woman receives more negative evaluations than the identical paper attributed to a man (see Swim, Borgida, Maruyama, & Myers, 1989, for a meta-analysis). The same holds for resumés attributed to a woman or a man (see Olian, Schwab, & Haberfeld, 1988, for a meta-analysis). The fact that women are evaluated more negatively than men on these tasks must result from assimilation of their performance to stereotypic expectations, for there is no difference in the objective information provided about male and female targets in these studies.

Ironically, when violations of descriptive stereotypes are not overlooked, they often exert a disproportionate impact on perceptions and evaluations of the target. Whether that impact is positive or negative depends on the violation in question. For example, Jussim, Coleman, and Lerch (1987) found that black targets with an unexpected positive trait received higher ratings on measures of competence, hirability, and likability than did white applicants who demonstrated the same trait. Bettencourt, Dill, Greathouse, Charlton, and Mulholland (1997) confirmed that the direction of influence depends on the valence of the trait demonstrated. Stereotype violators who unexpectedly displayed a positive quality (e.g., eloquent football players) received more positive evaluations than their stereotypical counterparts, whereas stereotype violators who unexpectedly displayed a negative quality (e.g., inarticulate speech team members) received more negative evaluations. In the gender domain, these investigators also showed that gender-atypical targets (female sports writers and male fashion writers) received more positive evaluations than their stereotype-conforming counterparts (male sports writers and female fashion writers; see Bettencourt et al., 1997).

In our own research, we have examined the role of the assimilation process in producing positive effects of stereotype violation (Prentice & Carranza, 2001). Specifically, we reasoned that stereotype violators may get more credit for their positive but gender-atypical qualities because they are assumed also to have the positive stereotypical qualities associated with their gender. As an illustration of this logic, consider the Bettencourt et al. example of the male fashion writer. The prototypical fashion writer is a woman, who has all of a woman's positive and negative stereotypical qualities. She is aesthetic, creative, and, of course, impeccably groomed, but she is also materialistic, melodramatic, and perhaps a bit frivolous. In contrast, a male fashion writer must also be aesthetic, creative, and impeccably groomed, as his role requires. But as a man, he is likely to be more consistent, rational, and grounded than his female counterpart. In other words, because he is a fashion writer, he is assumed to have positive feminine qualities (and lack negative masculine qualities), and because he is a man, he is assumed to have positive masculine qualities (and lack negative feminine qualities). As a result, he should receive more positive evaluations than his stereotype-congruent female counterpart.

To test this claim, we asked participants to evaluate supposed applicants for admission to their university on the basis of personal essays. We wrote essays, each of which expressed either a positive masculine trait or a positive feminine trait. We then presented those essays as coming from either a male or a female applicant, and asked participants to indicate their perceptions and evaluations of the applicant. For example, one of our masculine essays depicted the applicant taking a leadership role:

> In the first semester of my junior year, I led my friends on a very risky venture.
>
> Early that year, a fellow student was implicated in a cheating scandal. I was sure that he was innocent. He was popular, but not a heavy partier. His academic record was impeccable. And he'd earned a high rank on our track team. He was, quite simply, a model student. The high school administration decided to have him expelled.
>
> He had gotten into some trouble with the administration before, for participating in a rather harmless prank. The administrators took it rather personally, but had little to go on other than rumors of his involvement. With evidence—as spurious as it was—that he could have been involved in the cheating scandal, they took the opportunity to nail him—an opportunity afforded mainly because our school had no established procedure for deciding serious disciplinary cases. They were thus free to punish him in whatever way they saw fit, and so chose to make an example of him even while lacking secure evidence that he was the culprit.
>
> Students' reactions ranged from confused to incensed. His teachers hadn't even been allowed to speak on his behalf. Within various circles of students were talks of an uprising; these students looked to me, then, for direction. I've always been a natural leader. I have a remarkable talent for motivating others towards a goal. People just find me inspiring—they trust my instincts, and respond to my conviction. And I have an innate ability to delegate tasks, give orders, and make final decisions in a way that makes them feel comfortable having me in charge. With a three-year tenure as student council president, I had already initiated my fair share of student movements—but this time we needed something really innovative. I came up with a plan.
>
> For two weeks after the initial scandal, I had a few of my better friends listen during school for well-stated opinions about the ruling, from students and

teachers alike. At the end of the second week, when I left for the day, I used a twig to prop open a rarely-used back door. At three a.m., when the janitors had surely left, we snuck out of our respective houses and met behind the school. I was armed with a stack of banners, and twenty rolls of masking tape. We spent two hours, working as swiftly as possible, adorning the lobby with quotes from disgruntled teachers and many of the more eloquent students, as well as pictures of our friend from the track team, National Honors Society, and Key Club, all blown up to nearly life-size. On the statue of Horace Mann, the father of education who stands, book open, in our main entryway, we hung a scroll with a message I had written in large black letters:

"We, the students of Horace Mann High, feel we have not been heard. While we do not ask that transgressions of academic integrity be ignored, we do ask that suspects be treated in accord with the spirit of our nation's laws. We wish for rulings of innocence until *proven* guilty, beyond a reasonable doubt. And we wish for fair trial in all investigations, with outlined procedures that do not deviate across cases." Our crowning touch was an anonymous call to the Town Gazette, which arrived promptly at eight that very morning.

With a little more pressing from parents and teachers—inspired by our handy-work—our request was granted. Our friend was re-admitted after a proper trial. The entire ordeal, from start to finish, had quite an impact on me. More than anything, it reinforced my self-confidence as a leader, able to effect change in the laws that govern my community using my ability to supervise a movement, my willingness to take risks, and my unique and innovative style.

Participants who read this essay agreed with us that the applicant who wrote it was masculine, whether male or female. But they perceived and evaluated the applicant differently depending on gender. The female leader was seen as more sensitive, cheerful, likable, cooperative, and warm and kind than the male leader, in line with traditional stereotypes. Similarly, the male leader was seen as higher in self-esteem, as well as more arrogant, competitive, self-righteous, controlling, domineering, stubborn, self-serving, ruthless, cynical, and insensitive, again in line with traditional stereotypes. Evaluations of the two applicants reflected this difference in the valence of the traits ascribed to them. Participants rated the female applicant as higher in social skills, were more interested in spending time with her, and endorsed her more highly for admission than they did her male counterpart.

To ensure that this positive effect of stereotype deviance was not unique to strong women, we wrote another version of this essay, in which we replaced the protagonist's masculine, leadership skills with more feminine, cooperative skills. In particular, the fourth paragraph of the essay read as follows:

Students' reactions ranged from confused to incensed. His teachers hadn't even been allowed to speak on his behalf. Within various circles of students were talks of an uprising, but nobody seemed prepared to make a move. I myself am not really the leader type—though I'm an active and intelligent person in general. I just prefer not to take on a role that involves delegating tasks, giving orders or making final decisions. And inspiring crowds to take action doesn't come naturally to me. But I am always happy to be part of the movement. I enjoy acting as part of the collective—lobbying, protesting or petitioning—doing whatever I can to advance the cause. I relish the frenzied excitement that accompanies working closely with others in order to achieve a common goal. Our student council president came up with a plan, and I quickly agreed to participate.

The essay concluded in a similar vein:

With a little more pressing from parents and teachers—inspired by our handywork—our request was granted. Our friend was re-admitted after a proper trial. The entire ordeal, from start to finish, had quite an impact on me. More than anything, it reinforced my view of myself as a citizen, able to help effect change in the laws that govern my community with my willingness to contribute my energy and resources in order to further the cause.

This time, participants agreed with us that the applicant was feminine, whether male or female, and again, they perceived and evaluated the applicant in line with traditional stereotypes. The male applicant was seen as more assertive and extroverted, with higher self-esteem and a stronger personality than his female counterpart. He was also seen as more stubborn, ruthless, and insensitive than the female, although he showed much less of these qualities than is typical for men. The female applicant was seen as more yielding and insecure than the male, and as especially low in self-righteousness and sense of humor. Evaluations of the two applicants again reflected the difference in the valence of the traits ascribed to them. Participants rated the male applicant as higher in social skills, were more interested in spending time with him, and endorsed him more highly for admission than they did his female counterpart.

These results illustrate that violations of stereotypes are often processed in a way that minimizes the perceived extent of the violation. Applicants were assimilated to gender stereotypes, even when they were recognized as manifesting qualities atypical for their gender. It is a misnomer to characterize these applicants as stereotype deviants because they were not, in fact, perceived as such. They were seen as androgynous—as manifesting the positive qualities of both genders—and were evaluated more positively as a result.

### Prescriptive Stereotype Violators Are Punished

In those rare cases in which a person is perceived to violate gender prescriptions, the likely outcome is some form of social punishment (Fiske & Stevens, 1993; Glick & Fiske, 1999; see also Burgess & Borgida, 1999; Rudman

& Glick, 1999). Thus, when women fail to be warm, friendly, and well groomed, or worse, show signs of being aggressive, forceful, and arrogant, they receive social censure. Similarly, when men fail to be self-reliant, decisive, and rational, or worse, manifest signs of being melodramatic, naive, and superstitious, they too are punished. As we have argued, overachieving relaxed prescriptions for one's gender or underachieving relaxed proscriptions for one's gender do not draw this kind of negative reaction. Only gender-intensified prescriptions and proscriptions are socially enforced (Prentice & Carranza, 2001).

Social punishment can take many forms. Consider, for example, the reactions of Stanley Schachter's (1951) participants in his classic study of reactions to deviance. Schachter asked groups of participants to read a short history of a juvenile delinquent, Johnny, and discuss appropriate means of handling his case. Most naive group members advocated a combination of compassion and discipline. Schachter instructed a confederate to act as a deviant by consistently advocating the harshest punishment possible, despite emerging group norms that prescribed a more judicious treatment. In the face of the deviant's behavior, naive participants reacted in three ways: First, they turned their attentions to the deviant and attempted to convince him of their logic. After failed attempts to bring the deviant back into the fold, they ostracized him. And, at the close of the meeting, on confidential ratings tasks, participants delegated menial tasks to the deviant for future possible meetings, and, should the group meet again with fewer members, voted him out.

Reactions to gender deviants can also involve explicit attempts to modify the offending behavior. For example, Boggiano and Barrett (1991) found that participants asked to choose strategies for coping with children who were struggling with an academic-type task prescribed differential treatment according to whether the child was handling the failure in a gender stereotypical or counterstereotypical manner. Participants prescribed supportive strategies (e.g., encouragement) more than coercive strategies for stereotype-congruent children, and coercive strategies (e.g., threat of punishment) more than supportive strategies for children who violated gender stereotypes. Similarly, Butler and Geis (1990) examined reactions to deviance among groups of participants engaged in a group judgment task. Each group included either a male or female confederate who, through the course of the discussion, took a leadership role. The researchers observed nonverbal affective responses to these leaders from behind a one-way mirror. The results showed that female leaders received more negative affective responses (e.g., head shakes and frowns) to their comments and suggestions than did their male counterparts.

In addition, gender deviants are punished by being evaluated negatively, especially on dimensions of popularity or social likability. For example,

Costrich, Feinstein, Kidder, Marecek, and Pascal (1975) found that competitive-aggressive women and passive-dependent men were rated lower in popularity and psychological adjustment than their stereotype-conforming counterparts. Similarly, Tepper, Brown, and Hunt (1993) found that men and women in an organizational setting were expected to maneuver in prescriptively stereotypical ways, with women using helpfulness and men using confident, "take-control" strategies. Violations of these expectations by either men or women led to lower performance ratings and lower access to mentoring opportunities. Rudman (1998; Rudman & Glick, 1999) documented what she called a backlash effect against agentic women, whereby women who self-promote enjoy enhanced ratings of competence but suffer decreases in ratings of social likability, from male and female perceivers alike. Rudman argues that the backlash effect provides an example of the punishment of prescriptive stereotype violators—that agentic women, because they violate prescriptions for feminine niceness, are perceived to be less likable. Of course, if they conform to these prescriptions, they are assimilated to the feminine stereotype and are thereby perceived to be less competent. Thus, women in traditionally male contexts are in a double bind: They are devalued whether they conform to or violate the female stereotype.

Real-world cases of reactions to working women provide evidence for all of these forms of punishment. Women who are perceived as violating feminine prescriptions receive more unfavorable evaluations in management reviews than do their male counterparts (Eagly et al., 1992; Nieva & Gutek, 1980; Ruble & Ruble, 1982). They are also less readily accepted in leadership positions (Eagly & Karau, 2001), less likely to receive promotions (Fiske et al., 1991), and more likely to be the targets of sexual harassment (Burgess & Borgida, 1999). Men who are perceived as violating masculine prescriptions almost certainly receive similar forms of social censure (Atkinson & Endsley, 1976; Coates & Person, 1985; Green, 1976; Fagot, 1977, 1985).

In our own research, we have examined the punishment of gender-stereotype deviants using our college application paradigm. We wrote essays very similar to those that produced positive effects of deviance, but this time included evidence that the applicant manifested some negative qualities. Specifically, these qualities were ones that were gender-relaxed proscriptions for the stereotypic gender and gender-intensified proscriptions for the deviant. Consider, for example, an essay in which the applicant behaved in a cooperative, team-oriented way in a group context, like the essay we described earlier, but this time also showed signs of weakness and uncertainty:

> I attend a small high school that, up until recently, did not have a student body government. But with a recent increase in enrollment, the school board

decided last year that it was time that one was established. Mr. Simmons, our government teacher, came up with a plan: We, in his class, were to form teams in which we would study governments—both foreign and domestic—and develop a proposal for the organization of the new student government, its platform, and its activities. We were then to support our proposal in a term paper using arguments based on our research. The school board would use the term papers to choose the three best proposals. These three teams would then present their proposal to the school, and follow it with a week-long political campaign. After the campaign, the school would vote, and the winning program would be implemented.

Within my team, Mr. Simmons assigned me the role of directing our strategies, assessing our progress, and choosing deadlines. At first I was a little upset. This was an important project, and I don't always feel comfortable delegating tasks, giving orders, or making final decisions. But as it turns out, we made most of the important decisions as a group. First, we each chose two chapters from our government textbook to read and outline. Then, after a month of hammering out our proposal, each of us wrote one section of our term paper. Our finished product must have been good, as our team's proposal was chosen as one of the top three. But then, of course, we had a whole new set of challenges to face—including the presentation we would be making in front of the whole school. To that end, we organized a Thursday night social hour where the team would gather at one of our houses each week to eat dinner, practice our presentation and assess its strengths and weaknesses. On my own time, I practiced even more. I'm not as good as some people are at speaking in front of large groups. My part of the presentation ran smoothly, though, and my teammates did exceptionally well. The next day we launched right into our campaign. For our campaign, we decided to use a multimedia approach. The two more artistic members of the team designed posters and buttons, we took turns making ourselves available each day to field questions, and we managed to put together a web site with information about our proposal. The campaign was an apparent success—our proposal was voted in by a large margin.

When I reflect upon last year's contest, I think about the time and effort that I put into leading our team. In the end, I guess I did a pretty good job, but I was also lucky to have an intelligent and hard working team. I never felt as if I was working alone, or against anyone. Our teacher loved our paper, and each of us put a lot of effort into both the presentation and the campaign. Overall, it was a very rewarding experience.

I learned a lot in that one semester. In particular, I learned a number of lessons about leadership that are, I believe, applicable to leadership positions of all kinds and will follow me throughout my academic career. A good leader must try to perform competently under pressure and in situations of all kinds. But really, it is the group as a whole that will determine whether or not a goal is achieved. At each stage of the project, I was depending on my teammates as much as they were depending on me. So even though I didn't always feel perfectly suited for the role, because my team worked so well together, I was able to rise to the occasion.

Participants were no longer favorably impressed with the male stereotype deviant. Those who read this essay from a male applicant saw him as highly yielding, shy, and insecure, as well as unusually lacking in maturity and sense of humor. In other words, he was seen as violating gender-intensified prescriptions and proscriptions for males and was punished accordingly: Participants rated him lower in social abilities, were less interested in spending time with him, and gave him a lower endorsement for admission than they did his female counterpart. These results are striking in conjunction with our earlier example of the positive reception that a cooperative and non-self-promoting male can receive. The key difference is that the male applicant who was rewarded for his feminine behavior did not appear to violate gender prescriptions, whereas the male applicant who was punished did. The former was androgynous, the latter deviant. There is a world of difference between the two.

## STEREOTYPE CHANGE

We began this chapter with a paradox: the persistence of gender stereotypes in the face of widespread social change. Having documented a number of psychological processes that sustain these stereotypes in the face of their violation, we now consider the implications of this analysis for stereotype change. The assessment of change in gender stereotypes has proven to be a complicated business, with some studies showing very little change in descriptive and prescriptive content (Harris, 1994; Spence & Buckner, 2000), and others suggesting a significant reduction in the extremity of these stereotypes (Auster & Ohm, 2000; Diekman & Eagly, 2000; Holt & Ellis, 1998). The most consistent evidence points to a reduction in stereotypic differences in masculine qualities as a result of increases in the desirability and typicality of these qualities for women (Auster & Ohm, 2000; Diekman & Eagly, 2000). Our own findings are consistent with this evidence, in that they show no differences in the typicality for men and women of a number of positive, traditionally masculine qualities (Prentice & Carranza, 2002). However, they also show that these qualities are still not quite as desirable for women as they are for men and for people in general. Thus, we believe that changes in social roles are having an impact on the descriptive content of the female gender stereotype: It is becoming more androgynous. However, gender-intensified prescriptions and proscriptions appear to remain largely insulated from the impact of social change.

The reasons for this insulation follow from the foregoing discussion. Of primary importance, people do not often violate gender prescriptions. In fact, on the contrary, they try very hard, consciously or unconsciously, to live up to them. Women try to be nice, and men try to be strong. Such is the nature of cultural prescriptions that they are internalized by a culture's members. This is not to say that people do not, at the same time, find them constraining. Nobody wants to have to be nice or strong all of the time. Moreover, fear of the social consequences that result if one shows signs of ill-temper or weakness is grounded in reality. As we documented, violations of these proscriptions receive various forms of social punishment. Thus, having to live up to cultural prescriptions can be a source of considerable discomfort and stress.

An additional source of stress of a very different sort may come from *not* having to live up to the other gender's intensified prescriptions. Consider the psychology of gender-relaxed prescriptions—those qualities that are generally desirable but somewhat less desirable for one's gender. It might seem that the freedom to demonstrate these qualities, combined with the low pressure to do so, would be liberating. In fact, we suspect that the opposite is true, especially when the optional attributes in question are required for success in a valued domain. For example, we conducted a second study of the contents of prescriptive and descriptive gender stereotypes, this time within a very masculine context (Prentice & Carranza, 2002). Specifically, we asked Princeton University students to rate each of a set of attributes in terms of its desirability and typicality for male and female Princeton undergraduates. Consistent with our view of the context as masculine, the results revealed almost perfect overlap between what was desirable for male undergraduates and what was generally desirable at Princeton. The two differed on only a handful of feminine attributes, some of them gender-relaxed prescriptions for men and others gender-intensified proscriptions. The results for the female stereotype replicated, more or less, the findings of our study of global stereotypes. In particular, they revealed a long list of gender-relaxed prescriptions for women. This list included being intelligent, rational, competent, overachieving, articulate, outspoken, confident, and goal oriented—in other words, all of the qualities most important for success at Princeton. These qualities are not as desirable for women at Princeton as they are for men or students in general. Women are free to manifest these qualities, of course, and do, at least as suggested by the typicality ratings. But the standards to which they are held are somewhat lower than the standards for men. This cannot be a positive experience for women at Princeton (Prentice & Carranza, 2002).

Even though violations of gender prescriptions are rare, our results and those of other investigators suggest that violations of the descriptive content of these stereotypes, and especially gender-relaxed attributes, are much more common. One might expect these violations—the ones most obviously produced by changes in social roles—to have spillover effects on gender prescriptions. There is no evidence that they do, unless the behavior itself spills over. For example, a woman who shows leadership ability—

an attribute that is atypical and a gender-relaxed prescription for women—is not seen as violating gender-intensified prescriptions or proscriptions, as long as she does not abandon her feminine attributes in the process. At the same time, she is no less accountable to gender-intensified prescriptions by virtue of her gender-atypical behavior (Rudman & Glick, 1999). Similarly, a man who shows interest in children is not seen as violating any ideals or oughts, so long as he does so in a masculine way. These stereotype violations may be overlooked or may reflect positively on the person who enacts them. Indeed, they may even have the potential to produce changes in the descriptive content of gender stereotypes. But they do not change what is prescribed for men and women.

In short, gender prescriptions are impervious to empirical disconfirmation. They are not empirical facts, based on behavioral evidence, but social ideals, rooted in the relationship of exploitative interdependence between women and men (Glick & Fiske, 1999). Thus, they direct behavior, rather than follow from it. The overlap between these prescriptions and the descriptive content of gender stereotypes results primarily from people's successful attempts to conform to what society requires of them. Because they have normative force, gender prescriptions limit the degree of change possible in descriptive stereotypes. They also limit the degree of change possible in social role assignments by making it difficult for men and women to abandon traditional roles and by restricting the ways in which they are allowed to perform the nontraditional roles they take on. In so doing, gender prescriptions function to preserve the existing social order, and perpetuate themselves in the process. They are a very powerful enemy of social change.

We have emphasized that the prescriptive nature of gender stereotypes distinguishes them from stereotypes of other social groups; we should note, in closing, that it does not distinguish them from other cultural beliefs and norms, many of which have prescriptive force. Our analysis of the psychological processes that sustain gender stereotypes thus applies to cultural prescriptions more broadly, whether those prescriptions concern the attributes men and women should manifest, the attitudes college students should hold (Prentice & Miller, 1993), the behaviors sorority members should engage in (Crandall, 1988), or the way Southern males should react to threat (Vandello & Cohen, chap. 12, this volume). These and other cultural prescriptions are held in place by a combination of internalization, assimilation, and social enforcement. The conditions under which they change, and the psychological processes implicated in that change, remain to be documented.

## REFERENCES

Atkinson, J., & Endsley, R. C. (1976). Influence of sex of child and parent on parental reactions to hypothetical parent-child situations. *Genetic Psychology Monographs, 94*(1), 131–147.

Auster, C. J., & Ohm, S. C. (2000). Masculinity and femininity in contemporary American society: A reevaluation using the Bem Sex-Role Inventory. *Sex Roles, 43*, 499–528.

Bem, S. L. (1974). The measurement of psychological androgyny. *Journal of Clinical and Consulting Psychology, 42*, 155–162.

Bettencourt, B. A., Dill, K. E., Greathouse, S. A., Charlton, K., & Mulholland, A. (1997). Evaluations of ingroup and outgroup members: The role of category-based expectancy violation. *Journal of Experimental Social Psychology, 33*, 224–275.

Boggiano, A. K., & Barrett, M. (1991). Strategies to motivate helpless and mastery oriented children: The effect of gender-based expectancies. *Sex Roles, 25*, 487–511.

Burgess, D., & Borgida, E. (1999). Who women are, who women should be: Descriptive and prescriptive gender stereotyping and sex discrimination. *Psychology, Public Policy, and Law, 5*, 665–692.

Butler, D., & Geis, F. (1990). Nonverbal affect responses to male and female leaders: Implications for leadership evaluations. *Journal of Personality and Social Psychology, 58*, 48–59.

Cialdini, R. B., Kallgren, C. A., & Reno, R. R. (1991). A focus theory of normative conduct: A theoretical refinement and reevaluation of the role of norms in human behavior. *Advances in Experimental Social Psychology, 58*, 1015–1026.

Cialdini, R. B., Reno, R. R., & Kallgren, C. A. (1990). A focus theory of normative conduct: Recycling the concept of norms to reduce littering in public places. *Journal of Personality and Social Psychology, 58*(6), 1015–1026.

Cialdini, R. B., & Trost, M. R. (1998). Social influence; Social norms, conformity, and compliance. In D. T. Gilbert, S. T. Fiske, & G. Lindzey (Eds.), *The handbook of social psychology* (4th ed., Vol. 2, pp. 151–192). New York: McGraw-Hill.

Coates, S., & Person, E. S. (1985). Extreme boyhood femininity: Isolated behavior or pervasive disorder? *Journal of the American Academy of Child Psychiatry, 24*(6), 702–709.

Costrich, N., Feinstein, J., Kidder, L., Marecek, J., & Pascal, L. (1975). When stereotypes hurt: Three studies of penalties for sex-role reversals. *Journal of Experimental Social Psychology, 11*, 520–530.

Cota, A. A., Reid, A., & Dion, K. L. (1991). Construct validity of a diagnostic ratio measure of gender stereotypes. *Sex Roles, 25*, 225–235.

Crandall, C. (1988). Social contagion and binge eating. *Journal of Personality and Social Psychology, 55*, 588–598.

Deaux, K., & Kite, M. (1993). Gender stereotypes. In F. L. Denmark & M. A. Paludi (Eds.), *Psychology of women: A handbook of issues and theories* (pp. 107–139). Westport, CT: Greenwood Press.

Deaux, K., & Lewis, L. L. (1984). Structure of gender stereotypes: Interrelationships among components and gender label. *Journal of Personality and Social Psychology, 46*, 991–1004.

Deutsch, F. M. (1990). Status, sex, and smiling: The effect of role on smiling in men and women. *Personality and Social Psychology Bulletin, 16*, 531–540.

Diekman, A. B., & Eagly, A. H. (2000). Stereotypes as dynamic constructs: Women and men of the past, present, and future. *Personality and Social Psychology Bulletin, 26*, 1171–1188.

Eagly, A. H., & Johnson, B. T. (1992). Gender and leadership style: A meta-analysis. *Psychological Bulletin, 108*, 233–256.

Eagly, A. H., & Karau, S. J. (2001). *Role congruity theory of prejudice toward female leaders*. Unpublished manuscript, Northwestern University.

Eagly, A. H., Makhijani, M. G., & Klonsky, B. G. (1992). Gender and the evaluation of leaders: A meta-analysis. *Psychological Bulletin, 111*(1), 3–22.

Eagly, A. H., & Mladnic, A. (1993). Are people prejudiced against women? Some answers from research on attitudes, gender stereotypes, and judgments of competence. In W. Stroebe & M. Hewstone (Eds.), *European Review of Social Psychology* (Vol. 5, pp. 1–35). New York: Wiley.

Eagly, A. H., & Steffen, V. J. (1984). Gender stereotypes stem from the distribution of men and women into social roles. *Journal of Personality and Social Psychology, 34*, 590–598.

Fagot, B. I. (1977). Consequences of moderate cross-gender behavior in preschool children. *Child Development, 48*(3), 902–907.

Fagot, B. I. (1985). Beyond the reinforcement principle: Another step toward understanding sex role development. *Developmental Psychology, 21*(6), 1097–1104.

Fields, J. M., & Schuman, H. (1976). Public beliefs and the beliefs of the public. *Public Opinion Quarterly, 40*, 427–448.

Fiske, S. T. (1998). Stereotyping, prejudice, and discrimination. In D. T. Gilbert, S. T. Fiske, & G. Lindzey (Eds.), *The handbook of social psychology* (4th ed., Vol. 2, pp. 357–411). New York: McGraw-Hill.

Fiske, S. T., Bersoff, D. N., Borgida, E., Deaux, K., & Heilman, M. (1991). Social science research on trial: Use of sex stereotyping research in Price Waterhouse v. Hopkins. *American Psychologist, 46*, 1049–1060.

Fiske, S. T., & Stevens, L. E. (1993). What's so special about sex? Gender stereotyping and discrimination. In S. Oskamp & M. Constanzo (Eds.), *Gender issues in contemporary society* (pp. 173–196). Newbury Park, CA: Sage.

Glick, P., & Fiske, S. T. (1999). Sexism and other "isms": Interdependence, status, and the ambivalent content of stereotypes. In W. B. Swann, J. H. Langlois, & L. A. Gilbert (Eds.), *Sexism and stereotypes in modern society* (pp. 193–221). Washington, DC: American Psychological Association.

Green, R. (1976). One-hundred ten feminine and masculine boys: Behavioral contrasts and demographic similarities. *Archives of Sexual Behavior, 5*(5), 425–446.

Harris, A. C. (1994). Ethnicity as a determinant of sex role identity: A replication study of item selection for the Bem Sex Role Inventory. *Sex Roles, 31*, 241–273.

Heatherington, L., Daubman, K. A., Bates, C., Ahn, A., Brown, H., & Preston, C. (1993). Two investigations of "female modesty" in achievement situations. *Sex Roles, 29*, 739–754.

Hoffman, C., & Hurst, N. (1990). Gender stereotypes: Perception or rationalization? *Journal of Personality and Social Psychology, 58*, 197–208.

Holt, C. L., & Ellis, J. B. (1998). Assessing the current validity of the Bem Sex-Role Inventory. *Sex Roles, 39*, 929–941.

Jacobs, J. E., & Eccles, J. S. (1992). The impact of mothers' gender-role stereotypic beliefs on mothers' and children's ability perceptions. *Journal of Personality and Social Psychology, 63*, 932–944.

Jost, J. T., & Banaji, M. R. (1994). The role of stereotyping in system-justification and the production of false consciousness. *British Journal of Social Psychology, 33*, 1–27.

Jussim, L. (1991). Social perception and social reality: A reflection-construction model. *Psychological Review, 98*, 54–73.

Jussim, L., Coleman, L., & Lerch, L. (1987). The nature of stereotypes: A comparison and integration of three theories. *Journal of Personality and Social Psychology, 52*, 536–546.

Kunda, Z., & Thagard, P. (1996). Forming impressions from stereotypes, traits, and behaviors: A parallel-constraint satisfaction theory. *Psychological Review, 103*, 284–308.

Lauterbach, K. E., & Weiner, B. J. (1996). Dynamics of upward influence: How male and female managers get their way. *Leadership Quarterly, 7*, 87–107.

Madon, S., Jussim, L., Keiper, S., Eccles, J., Smith, A., & Palumbo, P. (1998). The accuracy and power of sex, social class, and ethnic stereotypes: A naturalistic study in person perception. *Personality and Social Psychology Bulletin, 24*, 1307–1318.

Martin, C. L. (1987). A ratio measure of sex stereotyping. *Journal of Personality and Social Psychology, 52*, 489–499.

Miller, D. T., & Prentice, D. A. (1996). The construction of social norms and standards. In E. T. Higgins & A. W. Kruglanski (Eds.), *Social psychology: Handbook of basic principles* (pp. 799–829). New York: Guilford Press.

Moskowitz, D. S., Suh, E. J., & Desaulniers, J. (1994). Situational influences on gender differences in agency and communion. *Journal of Personality and Social Psychology, 66*, 753–761.

Nieva, V. F., & Gutek, B. (1980). Sex effects on evaluation. *Academy of Management Review, 5*, 267–276.

O'Gorman, H. J. (1975). Pluralistic ignorance and White estimates of White support for racial segregation. *Public Opinion Quarterly, 39*, 313–330.

O'Gorman, H. J., & Garry, S. L. (1976). Pluralistic ignorance—A replication and extension. *Public Opinion Quarterly, 40*, 449–458.

Olian, J. D., Schwab, D. P., & Haberfeld, Y. (1988). The impact of applicant gender compared to qualifications on hiring recommendations: A meta-analysis of experimental studies. *Organizational Behavior and Human Decision Processes, 41*, 108–195.

Olson, J. M., Roese, N. J., & Zanna, M. P. (1996). Expectancies. In E. T. Higgins & A. R. Kruglanski (Eds.), *Social psychology: Handbook of basic principles* (pp. 211–238). New York: Guilford.

Prentice, D. A., & Carranza, E. (2002). What women and men should be, shouldn't be, can be, and don't have to be: The contents of prescriptive gender stereotypes. *Psychology of Women Quarterly, 26*, 269–281.

Prentice, D. A., & Carranza, E. (2001). *What's good for the goose can be better for the gander: The rewards and punishments of stereotype violation.* Unpublished manuscript, Princeton University.

Prentice, D. A., & Miller, D. T. (1993). Pluralistic ignorance and alcohol use on campus: Some consequences of misperceiving the social norm. *Journal of Personality and Social Psychology, 64*, 243–256.

Ruble, D. N., & Ruble, T. L. (1982). Sex stereotypes. In A. G. Miller (Ed.), *In the eye of the beholder: Contemporary issues in stereotyping* (pp. 188–252). New York: Praeger.

Rudman, L. A. (1998). Self-promotion as a risk factor for women: The costs and benefits of counterstereotypical impression management. *Journal of Personality and Social Psychology, 74*, 629–645.

Rudman, L. A., & Glick, P. (1999). Implicit gender stereotypes and backlash toward agentic women: The hidden costs to women of a kinder, gentler image of managers. *Journal of Personality and Social Psychology, 77*, 1004–1010.

Schachter, S. (1951). Deviation, rejection, and communication. *Journal of Abnormal and Social Psychology, 46*, 190–207.

Shweder, R. A. (1982). Beyond self-constructed knowledge: The study of culture and morality. *Merrill-Palmer Quarterly, 28*, 41–69.

Sidanius, J., & Pratto, F. (1999). *Social dominance.* New York: Cambridge University Press.

Spence, J. T., & Buckner, C. E. (2000). Instrumental and expressive traits, trait stereotypes, and sexist attitudes: What do they signify? *Psychology of Women Quarterly, 24*, 44–62.

Swim, J. K., Borgida, E., Maruyama, G., & Myers, D. G. (1989). Joan McKay versus John McKay: Do gender stereotypes bias evaluations? *Psychological Bulletin, 105*, 409–429.

Tepper, B. J., Brown, S. J., & Hunt, M. D. (1993). Strength of subordinates' upward influence tactics and gender congruency effects. *Journal of Applied Social Psychology, 23*, 1903–1919.

Twenge, J. M. (1997). Attitudes toward women, 1970–1995: A meta-analysis. *Psychology of Women Quarterly, 21*, 35–51.

Turner, J. C. (1991). *Social influence.* Pacific Grove, CA: Brooks/Cole.

CHAPTER

# 12

# When Believing Is Seeing: Sustaining Norms of Violence in Cultures of Honor

Joseph A. Vandello
University of South Florida

Dov Cohen
University of Illinois

In general, many cultural norms develop because they are functional (that is, they help members of the culture adapt to their environment). However, norms may be perpetuated and sustained long after they cease to be useful and even when they may be maladaptive. Superstitions and norms involving contagion and magical thinking persist long after they are shown to be irrational and untrue (Rozin, Millman, & Nemeroff, 1986; Rozin & Nemeroff, 1999). Regions and groups remain loyal to political parties that no longer are aligned with their interests and values. Societies fail to govern effectively even after new institutions are put in place, because old patterns of distrust and hierarchy persist (Putnam, 1993). Groups that move to new land sometimes continue old ways of farming that are far from optimal in the new environment (Edgerton, 2000). Fertility customs that were adaptive in agricultural societies persist after societies have become urbanized and overcrowded (Triandis, 1994). Environmental norms and frontier attitudes outlast the frontier that gave rise to them. Old hatreds and prejudices survive even after contested resources have expanded, disappeared completely, or could be more profitably acquired through alliances formed against new outgroups. And so on.

Such situations reflect what Triandis (1994) refers to as "cultural lag." Cultural adaptations that may have been functional at some point persist even when the conditions that gave rise to them are gone. There are a number of explanations for why cultural lag occurs, including some that emphasize innate human cognitive shortcomings (Edgerton, 2000). But other explanations emphasize the more *social* processes that keep a culture strong, despite environmental or economic changes.

In this chapter, we attempt to describe some social psychological processes that might contribute to instances of cultural perpetuation and lag. We present a general hypothetical model describing one way that culture can develop and perpetuate social norms through a series of transition stages. We focus specifically on the latter stages in this model of cultural transition, describing psychological processes that may keep cultural traditions in place despite external forces that press for change. Much of the chapter focuses on our recent research on one such case of possible cultural lag in present-day America—the culture of honor among Whites in the U.S. South that has persisted despite great economic, demographic, and social changes in the region.

## ONE MODEL OF CULTURAL EVOLUTION AND PERPETUATION

The goal of this chapter is to consider how social psychological processes may be responsible for seemingly stubborn patterns of cultural persistence. These processes are part of a more general model of one possible trajectory of cultural evolution and persistence. We begin by briefly introducing a four-stage model for some hypothetical transition stages in cultural evolution. The majority of the chapter is devoted to considering the latter stages of the model, dealing with the persistence of outmoded or maladaptive cultural norms. We return to and elaborate on the model at the end the chapter; we introduce it here to frame the examples provided throughout. We should note from the onset that this model is speculative, stylized, and undoubtedly not applicable to many instances of cultural perpetuation or change. Nevertheless, we think it provides a helpful way to think about social processes behind at least some patterns of cultural perpetuation in the face of environmental change.

Figure 12.1 illustrates our hypothetical model of transitional stages of cultural evolution and persistence. The arrow going into the first box represents the idea that all cultures bring a history to their present circumstances that affects the new patterns that emerge. The first box, "the behavioral stage," represents a continuity with these old patterns and also a break from them in that people develop new behavioral adaptations as they respond to changes in their environments.

At the first stage, new behavior patterns emerge as adaptations to the environment. (The *environment* here refers to both the physical and social environment that makes a given pattern of behavior functional). For example, consider two groups that settle the same region. Because these groups

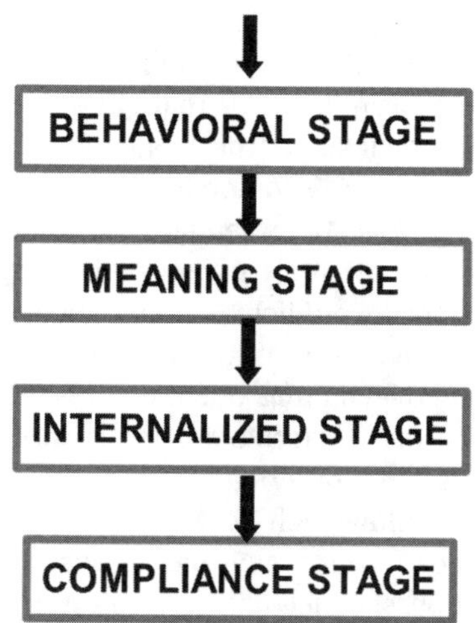


FIG. 12.1. One hypothetical model of transition stages in cultural evolution and persistence.

must compete for the same resources (land, water, grazing areas, fuel, food), conflict and hostilities might naturally arise between the groups. Indeed, classic theories of intergroup conflict such as Sherif's realistic group conflict theory (Sherif & Sherif, 1953) posit that such competition for valuable shared resources is the basis for intergroup hostilities. Zero-sum (win–lose) situations breed competitive behavior patterns.

At the second stage (the "meaning stage"), cultural norms develop in support of the functional behavior patterns. Through socialization processes, the patterns become culturally meaningful in addition to being adaptive at this stage, with self and social definitions incorporating these cultural norms. For example, children may be taught not to trust out-group members, and they may learn that the out-groups are fundamentally different than themselves, defining themselves against the out-group. Cultural norms, meanings, and identities support the new patterns of behavior that emerged originally.

At the third stage of the model (the "internalized stage"), behaviors may lose their adaptive value (perhaps because of ecological, economic, or demographic changes in the culture), but the norms continue to persist because they have become internalized into people's scripts and patterns of thought. As has been replayed countless times throughout history, continued ongoing intergroup hostilities may lose any adaptive benefit they once held—as evidenced in the high prices paid in terms of lives lost, valuable resources redirected to finance wars, and the psychological burdens of living in fear and hate. However, norms continue to be socialized and reinforced, becoming internalized scripts that are rarely consciously noted or questioned. At this stage, such cultural norms may become functionally autonomous from the original circumstances that gave rise to them.

In the fourth hypothetical stage (the "compliance stage"), internalization also eventually fades (Cohen & Vandello, 2001). Groups engaged in long-standing hostilities may cease to understand the value of continuing aggression, and individuals may privately question the persistence of intergroup hostilities (without actively publicly refuting them). They may have personal friendships with members of the outgroup, or they may have deep feelings of resentment over acting out their ingroup's prejudices. In this case, the norms are neither adaptive nor internalized, but they persist because either (a) people think others follow these norms or (b) people think others expect them to follow such norms.

The latter two stages in our rough model describe processes that may contribute to cultural persistence and lag. Cultural norms that at one time may have been adaptive continue long after they lose their adaptive value. We next present some evidence for such processes of cultural lag in the Southern U.S. culture of honor.

## THE CULTURE OF HONOR IN THE U.S. SOUTH

Throughout the history of the South, violence played a very visible role with the region's reputation for fighting, dueling, feuding, bushwhacking, lynching, and so on. Scholars began documenting an elevated rate of violence in the South early on. In one of the earliest studies, Redfield (1880) estimated that murder rates in the South in the 1870s were over 10 times those in the North. Sociologist H. C. Brearley (1932) found that homicide rates in Southern states were over two and a half times higher than the rest of the country during the early 1920s. This homicide difference between North and South was also documented during the middle part of the 20th century (Gastil, 1971; Hackney, 1969) and has continued into the later part. Richard Nisbett, Andy Reaves, and colleagues looked at homicide rates from 1976 to 1983 among non-Hispanic Whites (Nisbett, 1993; Nisbett & Cohen, 1996, chap. 2; Reaves, 1998) and found that rural Southern counties had homicide rates four times as large as rural midwestern counties.

In addition to regional homicide differences, greater violence in the South has taken other forms as well, including greater support for wars, more corporal punishment of children, and greater participation in violent pastimes and recreation (Baron & Straus, 1989; Cohen, 1998; Gorn, 1985). Laws and social policies in the South also tend to be more supportive of the use of violence for self-protection or for social control (cf. Cohen, 1996; Grantham, 1993, pp. 319–322). Even geographical locations and businesses in the South are more likely to have names with some connotations of violence (Kelly, 1999).

One theory proposed to account for greater southern violence that has received recent empirical support is that the South is home to a "culture of honor" (Nisbett & Cohen, 1996). According to this account, early historic, economic, and ecological conditions in the South made a vigilant, aggressive stance adaptive. Defending one's honor in this sense had to do with reputation, precedence, and self-preservation. The South, for much longer than the North, was a frontier region with a weak state. Law enforcement was often inadequate or nonexistent across much of the early South, and individuals and families had to fend for themselves. Honor norms developed as people needed to deter others threatening family, home, and property. Men had to be willing to use violence and let it be known that they were not to be trifled with even on small matters, or they could become vulnerable to theft or attack by others when stakes were much larger. Such cultures of honor often develop in places with weak state mechanisms to redress grievances (see, e.g., Peristiany, 1965; Schneider, 1971).

In addition to the frontier heritage of the South, settlers from the borderlands of Britain who pioneered much of the Southern backcountry brought with them a tradition of herding that became an important part of the economy of the early South (Fischer, 1989; McDonald & McWhiney, 1975). Herding cultures also often develop norms for honor and vigilance to protect their portable wealth from rivals. Herding economies the world over tend to be characterized by toughness, violence, and warfare, much more so than similar crop-farming cultures, where wealth is not as susceptible to theft and cooperation is required (Schneider, 1971).

A good deal of evidence has been found to support this culture of honor interpretation of southern violence (for reviews, see Cohen, Vandello, & Rantilla, 1998; Nisbett & Cohen, 1996). Archival analyses of homicides show that the South's greater incidence of murders is due largely to higher rates of argument-related and brawl-related homicides in the South (the types associated with honor issues), as opposed to felony-related homicides (e.g., those associated with robberies or burglaries; Nisbett, 1993; Nisbett, Polly, & Lang, 1995). In laboratory experiments using male students from the North and South, Southerners responded more aggressively in response to insults issued by an experimental confederate (Cohen, Nisbett, Bowdle, & Schwarz, 1996; Cohen, Vandello, Puente, & Rantilla, 1999). Survey data revealed regional differences in attitudes toward violence for personal honor or protection (Cohen & Nisbett, 1994). And evidence from field experiments showed that Southern employers and newspapers responded more sympathetically to individuals who committed honor-related violent acts (Cohen & Nisbett, 1997).

It is easy to see how the early herding and frontier conditions of the South could give rise to a culture of honor and violence. However, these conditions have largely disappeared or been supplanted (see also Vandello & Cohen, 1999). What is less clear is why honor traditions and accompanying high rates of violence still exist in the South. Our central argument is that sociopsychological forces can keep cultural norms about honor and violence in place long past the point of being functional for an individual. A number of forces are undoubtedly behind this perpetuation (see Cohen, 1998; Cohen, Vandello, & Rantilla, 1998; Cohen, Vandello, Puente, & Rantilla, 1999). Specifically, however, the main thesis of this chapter is that widespread pluralistic ignorance about cultural values is at least partly responsible for sustaining a culture of honor.

## PLURALISTIC IGNORANCE AND NORMS ABOUT VIOLENCE

In order to understand how cultural norms of honor are perpetuated, we may begin by emphasizing a couple of crucial features about aggression: First, male-on-male violence is generally *public* behavior with consequences for one's reputation; second, people do not always have access to others' private attitudes about aggression in the same way that they do to public behaviors. Because of these two points, it might be easy for an individual to assume people's private attitudes match their public behaviors regarding violence (see, for example, research on the fundamental attribution error; Ross, 1977). A man's fighting might be evidence of internal aggressive attitudes, but sometimes he may also fight simply because he thinks it is expected of him by others or is inevitable. Or, as John Reed (1972) put it when discussing Southern culture:

> Sometimes people are violent because they want to be and there is nothing to stop them. But sometimes people are violent, even when they don't want to be, because there will be penalties (disgrace is a very effective one) for not being violent. (p. 147)

This suggests one mechanism by which cultural norms supporting violence may be perpetuated in the South and elsewhere. That is, individuals may mistakenly believe that others value violence more than they do themselves, and they may publicly hide their disagreement with this perceived public norm out of embarrassment or fear of stigma. Thus, publicly many people appear to endorse a norm for violence more than they do in private. This mutual misperception about the beliefs and attitudes of members of the collective has been referred to as *pluralistic ignorance*

(Allport, 1924; Miller & McFarland, 1987, 1991; Miller & Prentice, 1994; Prentice & Miller, 1996).

Because instances of violence are quite salient, and because a reputation for toughness and strength is at least somewhat valued as a core component of masculinity (Gilmore, 1990), norms about violence might be particularly susceptible to such pluralistic ignorance. Unless people are willing to publicly speak out against violence and therefore expose their true attitudes, silence coupled with visible and salient instances of aggression can give the false impression that the culture condones, or at least excuses, such activity.

We have conducted some recent research that suggests that pluralistic ignorance might indeed be operating in the South, at least among a subpopulation of southern male college students. Of course, we are not arguing that pluralistic ignorance is the only mechanism perpetuating norms about honor and violence (Cohen et al., 1998). Honor norms are likely internalized to some extent; recent evidence suggests that honor cultures and nonhonor cultures do differ in their attitudes and values with respect to honor (see Cohen & Nisbett, 1994; Vandello & Cohen, in press). But pluralistic ignorance may play an important additional role that helps to perpetuate norms.

## Beliefs About the Self and Beliefs About Others

***Mistaken Beliefs About the Other.*** In an initial study by Cohen and colleagues (Cohen et al., 1996, Experiment 3), White male college students from the North and the South[1] were selected for a laboratory experiment. At one point in the study, the subjects were asked to take a questionnaire to a table at the end of a long narrow hall. As they walked down the hall, they were rudely bumped into and called an "asshole" by a confederate as he passed. A second confederate bystander looked on while this happened and later met the subjects. When subjects were asked to guess what this observer really thought of them, Southerners believed that their masculine reputation was diminished in the eyes of the onlooker who witnessed the insult. They thought that the person who saw the event would rate them as less masculine (manly, courageous, tough, and so on) than if they had not

[1]In our laboratory research, we have typically defined the South using the Census Bureau's classification (census divisions 5, 6, and 7: AL, AR, DE, FL, GA, KY, LA, MD, MS, NC, OK, SC, TN, TX, WV, VA). In addition, we consider Missouri and the southern part of Illinois as the South, because of their historical settlement patterns. Where the South actually begins and ends is a difficult question, but the definition employed here tends to agree with important distinctions made by demographers, political scientists, sociologists, anthropologists, and cultural geographers (see review in Cohen et al., 1999). Again, in this chapter, when referring to Southerners, we generally are referring only to non-Hispanic White Southerners, because regional differences in the culture of honor apply most directly to this group.

been insulted. This was not the case for insulted Northerners, who did not believe their reputation had been tarnished.

If observers really would think less of a man for not answering an insult, an aggressive response can be a rational behavior that may successfully reestablish lost status and help to avoid social stigma. However, if observers would *not* think less of them and are not particularly aggressive themselves, this might be evidence of a cultural norm being perpetuated at least in part by pluralistic ignorance. Public behavior and beliefs about others' expectations can then cyclically reinforce each other. If everyone believes others hold to an aggressive stance, the people in the culture may continually reinforce this belief by acting out culturally "appropriate" aggressive scripts. This in turn strengthens the belief that the public norm supports aggression, even as there may be little private support for it in fact.

In a second study (Vandello & Cohen, 1998), we showed Northern and Southern students videotapes of a person being insulted in a procedure similar to the Cohen et al. (1996) "asshole" study. In the videotapes, the insulted subject either responded aggressively or basically shrugged off the incident and kept walking. Although Southern subjects were much more likely to fear diminishment in the eyes of observers in the Cohen et al. (1996) experiment when they did not retaliate after an insult, observers (both Northern and Southern) who watched the videotapes actually preferred the less aggressive male. The diminishment in the eyes of the observers that insulted Southerners expected in Cohen et al. (1996) seemed to be more imagined than real, when actual observers were queried. Taken together, these two studies imply that Southerners envision their fellow students as holding to stronger honor norms that at least these data suggest they do.

***Perceived Self–Other Discrepancies.*** If pluralistic ignorance is operating among Southerners, one should also be able to find discrepancies between the degree to which Southerners themselves value violence and the degree to which they believe *others* value violence. To attempt to address this issue, we designed a short questionnaire and distributed it to White male college students on campuses in the North and South (Vandello & Cohen, 2002). The questionnaire asked men about their own attitudes regarding violence and their beliefs about other men on campus. We predicted that, in general, men would think that they themselves were less aggressive than their peers. But, importantly, we also predicted that this would be especially the case for Southerners.

Respondents were given short scenarios in which a male character was insulted in some way and then responded by punching his antagonist. For example, one scenario read: "Bill is in line at the movies, when a man cuts in front of him in line. When Bill says something to the man, the man says,

'Back off, creep.' Bill punches him." After each such scenario, respondents were asked to guess how likely it would be (0 to 100%) that they would have punched the person if they were in the same situation, and they were also asked to estimate the percentage of men on their campus that would have punched the person. We found that on average, subjects gave much lower estimates for themselves than for other men (a difference of over 16%). More interestingly, although Southern and Northern males did not differ in their self-reports of the likelihood that they would act aggressively, Southerners gave larger guesses for their peers. The self–other discrepancy was significantly larger for southerners than for northerners (19% and 13.5%, respectively).

## Enforcement and Perceived Enforcement of Norms

One possibility following from these studies is that mistaken beliefs may lead southerners to enforce aggressive norms on their peers, even when they do not in fact believe them. Even if they are reluctant to fight themselves, people who believe others value violence might publicly endorse and encourage violence among others. Fighting is risky business, but one may be able to achieve the desired effect of appearing tough or appearing to favor aggressive norms by enforcing these norms upon others, and at much less personal cost.

Enforcement of aggression by bystanders is sometimes in fact an important contributor to incidences of violence and homicide. Criminologist David Luckenbill (1977) suggested that whether or not a conflict will erupt into violence depends in part on the actions of the audience present. Bystanders can intervene to break up an escalating conflict, or they can encourage parties in dispute to act violently through taunts, encouragement, and "cheerleading." Witnesses to an event help resolve what Horowitz and Schwartz (1974, pp. 242–243) described as the "normative ambiguity" involved in deciding whether something is an affront calling for retaliation or not. Further, Martin Daly and Margo Wilson (1988) referred to violence that is derived from "escalated showing off contests" between men (p. 176). Implicit in this is the notion that the audience one is showing off for is approving of the action.

Enforcement of aggression by bystanders is also important in that it may be one major means by which women help to perpetuate norms of male honor, even if they do not participate in nearly as much violence themselves. Miller's (1990, 1993) studies of Saga Iceland are illustrative. Although Saga men are mythologized as some of the most feared, tough, and brutal fighters in history, they too might not have internalized these values to the extent that the public cultural norms prescribed. As Miller (1990) noted, it sometimes took the goading of womenfolk to shame men into fighting:

> The saga woman provoked her reluctant men to action by impugning their manhood. They were no better than women, they would better have been their father's daughters, they have the memories of pigs, or they are merely contemptible. (p. 212)

And even the Saga women themselves might have been doing this coaxing more because of public expectations than enthusiastic internalization of honor norms: "People expected a woman to play the role of the inciter and when she did not, there was a minor upset in the order of things that merited comment" (Miller, 1990, p. 213).

Following cultural norms of honor by fighting can be risky, and public enforcement by bystanders might represent one important means of giving actors the push they need to engage in action. Miller (1993) suggested that third-party enforcement of honor norms might represent one of "the elaborate cultural mechanisms and work needed for men to maintain the point of honor in the face of their own reluctance to expose themselves to risk" (p. 209).

## Do Southerners Enforce Norms of Aggression on Others?

We conducted a laboratory experiment to test whether Southerners would be particularly likely to goad others into violence in order to uphold norms of honor. In this study (Vandello & Cohen, 2002), we set up a situation to measure the extent to which subjects would encourage or discourage aggressive behavior in other people. The study was designed such that subjects (from the North and the South) would witness an ostensibly spontaneous threatening conflict unfold between two males.

Subjects were invited to a laboratory and asked to wait in a room until their experimenter arrived. Groups of four people entered the room and waited in chairs lined along a wall. Of the four participants, three were experimental accomplices and one was a naive subject. While they waited, one male accomplice announced that he had to use the rest room. As he got up to leave, he stepped on an eyeglass case that belonged to the person next to him (another male accomplice). Stepping on the glasses produced a loud crunching noise (simulated by dry rigatoni pasta positioned in the eyeglass case). The male "victim" opened his case and discovered that his glasses were broken and cracked. Rather than apologizing, the perpetrator acted rude and flippantly suggested that the victim should not have left his glasses on the floor. The two exchanged increasingly challenging words before the perpetrator left to use the restroom. With the victim left sitting in the room insulted and holding a pair of broken glasses, the issue was, what type of prodding or advice would naive subjects give him? For half the participants, the confederate probed the subject with either aggressive probes ("He was being an asshole, don't you think?" "I'm definitely going in there and kicking his ass"), and for the other half, he probed them with apologetic probes ("Do you think I should go in and apologize before this gets out of hand?" "I'm going to apologize before this gets out of hand.")

We recorded the confederate's interaction with the naive subjects, coding for whether the subjects seemed to be encouraging the victim to stand up for himself and use aggression or force. The procedure was effective in eliciting a wide range of responses. Perhaps not surprisingly, males were more encouraging of aggression than females. However, we found no evidence that Southern subjects were more encouraging of aggression than Northern subjects were. At least in this study, the hypothesis that Southern cultural norms of honor are perpetuated by direct enforcement was not supported.

## Perceived Enforcement of Norms

Even when there is not actual evidence of norm enforcement, however, there may be crucial differences in whether Southern and Northern Whites *perceive* norms to be enforced. This seems especially crucial when one considers the issue of ambiguous signaling. If others are silent while an event occurs, does it mean they are approving or disapproving of it? Do ambiguous comments or ambivalent actions communicate disapproval or a "sly wink" of encouragement? In the case of cultures with aggressive public norms, individuals may expect others to enforce such norms and thus may read ambiguous cues as encouraging aggression. Thus, the same behavior that is seen as neutral in one culture may be interpreted as goading on aggression in another culture. In this way, the public norms shape people's interpersonal perceptions.

In our "broken glasses" experiment, subjects' reactions to the conflict were videotaped, and in a follow-up study, we asked Northern and Southern subjects to watch tapes from these experimental sessions. In this follow-up, we showed participants a variety of subject reactions. In two of these tapes, the subjects seemed to be sending clear messages (on one tape, the subject told the confederate, "Don't go fight," and on the other, the subject told the confederate on three separate occasions to "kick [the other man's] ass."). Importantly, three of the other tapes had much more ambiguous or ambivalent signaling. On one tape, a subject told a confederate who asked if he should apologize, "No, probably not" and then said "up to you" when the confederate said he would apologize. On another tape, the subject responded "Yeah, probably" when the confederate asked whether he had "pissed [the other man] off," but then when asked if he should go apologize, the subject told the confederate, "he could have been a little more apologetic himself." On a third tape, the subject gave little response except to nod after the confederate's probes.

We asked Northern and Southern subjects to watch these videotapes and rate the extent to which they believed that the stimulus targets were encouraging a violent or peaceful resolution to the conflict. As predicted, Southerners perceived significantly more enforcement of aggression than Northerners did, particularly when the subjects gave more ambiguous or ambivalent signals. As they watched the very same videotapes, Southern subjects perceived more enforcement of aggression on every tape, with the North–South difference being especially large for the more ambiguous tapes.

Thus, not only are Southerners particularly likely to believe other men are more aggressive than themselves, but also there is some evidence that they actually perceive that aggressive norms are enforced more so than do Northerners who watch the same interactions unfold. Just as Southerners expected the "generalized other" to stigmatize their passive reaction in the Cohen et al. (1996) study and just as they expected other men to be more violent than themselves when asked about various scenarios, Southerners also projected onto the "generalized other" signals that this other was encouraging aggression and enforcing violent norms.

In a study of teenage male delinquents, Jussim and Osgood (1989) distinguished between the *subjective* influence of others (influence based on one's *perceptions* of significant others) and *objective* influence (influence based on significant others' actual attitudes and values). They found that objective influence mattered little, whereas subjective influence was quite predictive. Mapping this on to the regional differences found earlier, we can see the importance of Southerners' subjective experience of the "generalized other" from their peer group. Pluralistic ignorance could lead to Southerners following aggressive norms that they think others hold to, even when few of their peers are deeply committed to such norms in fact.

Of course, all pluralistic ignorance claims are necessarily tenuous if one does not have an appropriate sample to determine what the "true" sentiment in a population is. However, in the North–South studies just described, the sample giving the signals (in the broken glasses study) and the sample reading those signals (in the videotape study) were drawn from the same population. Although Northerners and Southerners did not differ in the signals they sent, they did differ in the signals they read. In the absence of a "gold standard," an alternative interpretation is that it is the Northerners who were not seeing the true aggressiveness of our participants. However, although this may be true, the general convergence of evidence suggests the reverse–that people overestimate the aggressiveness of their peers and that Southerners are particularly prone to do so.

## NORMS, EXPECTATIONS, AND VIOLENCE

Given that Southerners think that violence in at least some circumstances is normative, this can lead to violent behavior in a number of ways. First, to the extent that Southerners believe that others disapprove of passivity and thus regard honor-related violence as a perceived *prescriptive* norm, they should be more likely to engage in violence to gain social approval–or at least to avoid disapproval. (Anderson [1994, p. 82] noted that respect is an entity often "hard-won but easily lost.") And second, to the extent that Southerners believe others will act aggressively and regard honor-related violence as a *descriptive* norm, Southerners should be more likely to engage in aggression themselves as an act of "self-defense."

### Perceived Prescriptive Norms

One possibility is that men might behave aggressively in public in order not to lose status in front of others (see Cialdini, Kallgren, & Reno, 1991, on injunctive norms, and McAdams, 1997, summarizing an esteem theory of norms). This would be consistent with an impression management account of aggression (Felson, 1978, 1982). According to this view, retaliatory aggression may often be an attempt to reinstate a favorable situational identity when one has been attacked or challenged. This may partially help explain why insulted individuals are more likely to aggress when an audience is present, especially males in front of males (Borden, 1975; Felson, 1982; Luckenbill, 1977).

A suggestive study by Richard Felson and his colleagues (Felson, Liska, South, & McNulty, 1994) demonstrated how aggression and violence might be driven more by group norms than by internalized individual values promoting violence. Using questionnaire data from boys from 87 different high schools, they found that the school culture played a large role in predicting boys' violent actions. Even after controlling for a boy's own values, the values of his schoolmates (i.e., the group norm) predicted his aggressive behavior. Earlier, Short and Strodtbeck (1965) studied delinquent youths in gangs and found discrepancies there between public norms and the youths' private attitudes. Working-class delinquent youths endorsed middle-class values in private but not in front of their peers. The delinquency and violence of these males may partially reflect their misconceptions about the values of their peers. Thus, much of the aggressive bravado enacted by delinquent youths might be misguided attempts to impress others who are mistakenly believed to value such behavior.

## Descriptive Norms, Expectations, and Defense

In terms of perceiving violence as a descriptive norm, the belief that others hold to violent norms can also lead to violence because it changes one's beliefs about what other people's actions mean and how likely violence is to ensue. Given that both parties know insults will be answered with violence, in some honor cultures, hostile attributions will be made for violations. In these cultures, the threshold for judging what is a threatening situation that must be answered with hostility may be lowered (cf. Cohen, 2001; Cohen & Vandello, 2001; Cohen et al., 1999). In writing about such thresholds in the inner city, for example, Anderson (1994) noted that "many of the forms that dissing [disrespecting] can take seem petty to middle-class people (maintaining eye contact for too long, for example), but to those invested in the street code, these actions become serious indications of the other person's intentions. Consequently, such people become very sensitive to advances and slights, which could well serve as warnings of imminent physical confrontation" (p. 82; see also Horowitz & Schwartz, 1974, pp. 240–241).

Dodge, Crick, and colleagues have described how aggressive youths often hold attribution biases, such that they interpret others' actions as aggressive and hostile (Crick & Dodge, 1994; Dodge, 1985; Dodge, Bates, & Pettit, 1990; Dodge & Coie, 1987; Dodge & Crick, 1990; Dodge & Schwartz, 1997). We suggest that in some cultures of honor these tendencies are more prevalent because in some social environments these potentially offensive actions *are* reliable cues to future aggression. But here, too, the issue is one of self-reinforcing cycles of action. Believing that action X by person A is a cue to A's hostile intentions, person B will react with hostility, and A will probably counter that hostility with aggression of his own. Thus, action X will seem to be a reliable cue that A will act in a hostile way, but this may be only because it has become so through B's expectations. Action X may or may not have been a reliable cue to A's original intentions; but because of a self-fulfilling prophecy, it can seem to be a reliable cue to his ultimate actions.

The belief that others are ready to use violence can lead to a self-fulfilling prophecy either (a) when one is trying to decode the ambiguous actions of others (was it an indication of hostility or an honest mistake?) or (b) when it is plain that a bona fide conflict has arisen. In terms of the latter case, once the conflict is out on the table, two parties may race to the first blow as a matter of self-defense. Southern historian Grady McWhiney (1988), for example, recounted how a cycle of deadly violence perpetuated itself among those in the Old South who had ready access to guns:

> As one observer of the South noted, enemies would meet, exchange insults, and one would shoot the other down, professing that he had acted in self-defense because he believed the victim was armed. When such a story was told in court, "in a community where it is not a strange thing for men to carry about their person deadly weapons, [each member of the jury] feels that he would have done the same thing under similar circumstances so that in condemning him they would but condemn themselves." Consequently, they free the slayer, "and a hundred others, our sons and half grown lads amongst them, resolve in their hearts, that since every man may go armed and everyone is therefore justifiable in slaying his enemy, they will do likewise." (p. 163; quotations from J. A. Lyon, in *Columbus* [Mississippi] *Eagle*, June 1, 1855)

In terms of the present-day inner city, Anderson (1994) also noted that inner-city youths who do not subscribe to the "code of the streets" (code of honor) still must follow it as a defensive strategy. Anderson argued that the vast majority of inner-city residents have not internalized the "code of the streets." Yet in many situations, it is necessary for them to play by its rules merely because others, making similar calculations, also find it necessary to play by the code. As Anderson wrote, "Knowledge of the code is largely defensive; it is literally necessary for operating in public. Therefore, even though families with a decency orientation are usually opposed to the values of the code, they often reluctantly encourage their children's familiarity with it to enable them to negotiate the inner city environment" (p. 82). Individuals may follow the code merely because they expect others to do the same; as Axelrod and Hamilton (1981) and Putnam (1993) showed, such environments in which people distrust their neighbors and thus act uncooperatively or aggressively can be remarkably stable and persistent over time (see also Axelrod, 1984, on the potential stability of both uncooperative social strategies and reciprocity).

## CULTURAL RESISTANCE AND CULTURAL CHANGE

It might seem that an outdated social norm that no longer has adaptive value is a fragile and unstable thing that should be easy to overturn. But as the examples at the beginning of the chapter make clear, outdated cultural norms and practices can have surprisingly long lives. In the case of long-standing historical honor norms, how have these norms had such staying power? As described earlier, situations in which people expect that insults will lead to violence can result in situations where insults (or in some cases, things that only potentially look like insults) really do lead to violence. For a cultural norm to change, not only do individual values need to change, but often there needs to be a shared public recognition of this change.

Despite surprising cultural inertia in the South, there is reason for hope. Cultural norms are also susceptible to unpredictable and rapid shifts, and groups of cooperating actors can band together to form subcultures that can gradually or rapidly expand. The example of ending the long-standing practice of footbinding young girls in China provides an illustration of a norm that was rapidly changed. The thousand-year-old practice of footbinding died in just over a generation in some regions of China after a number of families got together to form anti-footbinding societies and pledged not to let their sons marry women whose feet had been bound (Mackie, 1996; Rosen, 1997, p. 178). This was an effective strategy perhaps because it gave people opposed to the practice an opportunity to find each other and form interacting networks with the opposite norm. (For another modeling of how small numbers of cooperating individuals can band together, find reciprocating partners, and dramatically expand their presence in a population, see also Axelrod's [1984] *Evolution of Cooperation*, pp. 63–69.) Relatedly, the anti-footbinding societies were perhaps also effective because they broke down a more widespread pluralistic ignorance regarding how people privately felt about the practice of binding women's feet.

In the laboratory, social psychologists have demonstrated how much power a small minority can have in challenging a norm. Asch's (1955) classic conformity studies demonstrated how conformity effects could be wiped out by breaking the perceived consensus of the group. When even a single dissenter was present among an otherwise unanimous (but incorrect and privately wary) majority, subjects' conformity was greatly diminished. Extrapolating a bit, the same processes might be involved in creating cultural change. A public cultural norm might be presumed to reflect consensus, even as private dissent festers below the surface. However, even a small minority can be enough to disrupt this perceived consensus and allow people to break ranks and eventually overturn the public norm.

Given that attitudes endorsing culture of honor values are not as strongly internalized among some southerners as they might first appear, one key to changing these public norms would be to signal that a perceived consensus is illusory. Of course, there are reasons one might not want to change these norms, and these are discussed more fully in Cohen et al. (1998) and Cohen et al. (1999). But if there were to be purposeful actions to alter the norms, there are several potential approaches at various levels of intervention.

At a broad level, laws and social policies may serve to shape cultural norms. Recently, legal scholars have begun a movement to explore how laws might be used to shape cultural meanings and customs (Kahan, 1998; Lessig, 1995, 1998). Laws are typically seen as influencing behavior directly, through their power to create compliance, but laws can influence behavior indirectly and nonlegally as well, by influencing social norms. For instance,

McAdams (1997, 2000) talked about an *expressive* function of laws. That is, laws symbolize societal values and express a culture's standards. By making policy that expresses a culture's condemnation of violence, law can be used to overturn norms perpetuated through pluralistic ignorance. In other words, laws can shape values; further, to the extent that there are public–private discrepancies in people's attitudes, laws can also publicize a societal consensus that might otherwise have remained hidden in people's private beliefs.

Cooter (1997) provided a colorful example of the way expressive laws or formal enforcement of standards can also catalyze informal, private enforcement. He gave the example of "pooper scooper" laws requiring owners to clean up after their dogs. Given the social awkwardness of taking someone to task for not cleaning up after their pet, pluralistic ignorance might develop regarding general attitudes toward tolerance for messy public spaces. However, formal "pooper scooper" laws can make it easier for people to enforce informal norms regarding the same behavior. "No smoking" laws may work similarly: It is easier and much less awkward to remind someone of the law or simply point to a "No Smoking" sign than it is to deliver a stern moral lecture on the evils of secondhand smoke or the (literal) tragedy of the commons that will result from promiscuous pooping. By giving people a channel or an easy, legitimate way to correct norm violators, expressive laws can increase the private enforcement of norms. Thus, expressive law can both clarify and publicize a social consensus and make it easier for people to enforce the norms against those who would violate these consensual standards.

At a more micro level, intervention programs aimed at exposing pluralistic ignorance may prove effective in changing cultural norms. Indeed, there is some evidence that this can be a very effective tactic. Schroeder and Prentice (1998) were able to effectively reduce alcohol use among college students by implementing a program to expose pluralistic ignorance. Students participated in peer-oriented discussion groups in which data were presented that showed students' misperceptions about drinking attitudes on campus. These students later reported less drinking than a control group who had gone through a more standard individual-oriented program. Perhaps a similar approach could be used to change cultural norms regarding violence among strong honor subcultures. Such an approach is more micro in scope than attempting to create laws and social policies to shape broad cultural norms, but perhaps such modest changes would be enough to create momentum among cultural members and expose unpopular or outdated cultural norms on a larger scale (see, e.g., Schelling, 1978; see also Gladwell, 1996). As discussed in this volume, recent modeling research by Latané and colleagues (Huguet & Latané, 1996; Latané, 1997, 2000; Schaller & Latané, 1996) also demonstrated how changes in local norms can rapidly spread through dynamic social impact processes to create larger clusters of social representations.

## CONCLUSIONS

One popular explanation in sociology for cultural differences in violence has been the *subculture of violence* thesis (Wolfgang & Ferracuti, 1967). This theory proposes that cultures affect individual behavior by shaping the values (for instance, courage, honor, toughness) of the members of the subculture. These values, in turn, lead to differences in the acceptability of violence. However, the research we reported in this chapter suggests that culture might also have a very large part of its influence on violence not through shaping individuals' values, but through establishing shared public norms.

The processes contributing to cultural persistence discussed in this chapter are part of a more general model for some hypothetical transition stages in cultural evolution (see Fig. 12.1). At the first stage ("the behavioral stage"), behavioral patterns arise as functional adaptations to the environment. That is, the patterns are adaptive (even if not optimally adaptive) for individuals. At this stage, they are not necessarily internalized, and they are not necessarily normative. Various ecological, economic, and historical circumstances provide a reasonable explanation for why a rational behavior pattern of vigilance and violence in response to threats or challenges may have developed in the South. The region was originally a frontier area with a large herding economy (McWhiney, 1988). There was little law enforcement, and the South remained a frontier region relatively late into its development. Being able to defend oneself, one's possessions, and one's family had obvious survival value that did not necessarily need to be buffered by an elaborate cultural ideology or system of meanings.

At the second stage (the "meaning stage"), cultural norms spring up to support the functional behavior patterns. At this stage, the patterns become more than simply adaptive; they also become culturally meaningful. Norms about honor, toughness, and masculinity become embedded into appropriate gender roles, scripts, expectations, and cultural definitions of personhood. Children are socialized to incorporate the cultural values and behaviors associated with the shared norm. In his book, *Manhood in the Making*, David Gilmore (1990) discussed this stage of the cultural process when he talked about what it takes to be a man:

> To be a man, most of all, they must accept the fact that they are expendable. This acceptance of expendability constitutes the basis of the manly pose everywhere it is encountered; *yet simple acquiescence will not do. To be socially*

> *meaningful, the decision for manhood must be characterized by enthusiasm combined with stoic resolve or perhaps "grace." It must show a public demonstration of positive choice, of jubilation even in pain, for it represents a moral commitment to defend the society and its core values against all odds.* (pp. 223–224, emphasis added)

Thus, at this stage, the norms can become deeply incorporated into self and social definitions.

At the third hypothetical stage (the "internalized stage"), behaviors may lose their adaptive value (perhaps because of ecological, economic, or demographic changes in the culture), but the norms continue to persist because they have become internalized into people's scripts and patterns of thought. In the case of honor norms, they are part of what it means "to be a man." Honor norms continue to be socialized into children, reinforced by strong communities, enshrined in social policy, and buffered by religion (Cohen, 1998; Cohen et al., 1998; Ellison, 1991; Ellison & Sherkat, 1993). Such cultural transmission can involve *explicit* instruction and *implicit* as well (Cohen, 1997). John Reed (1981) described the means by which norms about violence are learned:

> Like the words to "Blessed Assurance," the technique of the yo-yo or the conviction that okra is edible, [honor norms are] absorbed pretty much without reflection, in childhood. Southerners learn, as they grow up, that some disputes are supposed to be settled privately, violently sometimes, without calling in "the authorities." . . . If you were called out for some offense, you fought. I guess you could have appealed to the teacher, but that just—wasn't done. And that phrase speaks volumes. (p. 13)

Edgerton (2000) has described the way cognitive limitations and habits of cognitive miserliness can keep cultural patterns in place. (See also Chiu, Morris, Hong, & Menon, 2000, on how the need for closure promotes reliance on the most salient and prominent cultural theories.) Cultural patterns become internalized scripts and habits that are rarely consciously noted; if noted, rarely questioned; and if questioned, rarely energetically refuted (Cohen, 1997; Triandis, 1994). In Lessig's (1998) terms, such norms may sometimes be both primarily backgrounded and uncontested. At this stage, both explicit and implicit norms, scripts, and cultural practices may have become internalized and be functionally autonomous from the original circumstances that gave rise to them. The various social mechanisms that then explicitly and implicitly perpetuate a culture at this point may be particularly ripe for analysis by psychologists (Cohen et al., 1999).

In the fourth hypothetical stage (the "compliance stage"), the internalization can also eventually fade (Cohen & Vandello, 2001). In this case, the norms are not necessarily adaptive, nor are they internalized, but they persist because either (a) people think others follow these norms or (b) people think others expect them to follow such norms. The norms may or may not be foregrounded in people's private psyches, but they remain relatively uncontested in the public domain (Lessig, 1998). People's continued compliance and their beliefs that others expect it of them reinforce each other in ways we have described in this chapter. Such processes may keep outdated cultural norms in place for generations in a type of cultural lag or conservative lag (Miller & Prentice, 1994; Triandis, 1994; see also Cohen, 1998, 2001, for more discussion of cultural change).

This single model of cultural persistence and evolution is clearly stylized and often inaccurate or inapplicable. The boundaries between transition stages are often, of necessity, blurry. Many cases will be found where norms disappear rapidly after they are no longer functional (thus bypassing stages 3 and 4). Cases will be found where the processes of internalization did not take hold. Importantly, in many instances, the "behavioral" and "meaning" stages will have emerged together. And certainly it is true that the preexisting meanings of a culture will shape what becomes an acceptable behavioral solution (Kluckhohn, 1965, pp. 42–70; see also Cohen, 2001, on the intracultural niche in which cultural traits emerge). Nevertheless, this stylized, hypothetical model might prove useful in thinking about some of the issues discussed with respect to adaptive explanations, public and private attitudes, functional autonomy, and the multiple equilibria that arise from social interdependence (Cohen, 2001; Cohen & Vandello, 2001). It might be one useful model among the multiple models needed for developing what Sperber (1985, 1990) has called an "epidemiology of beliefs" or "epidemiology of representations."

In terms of the phenomena described in this chapter on violence, these hypothetical transition stages of cultural persistence and evolution may help to explain why although conditions have changed considerably in the South, vestiges of a culture of honor tradition remain. Returning to the studies reviewed here, for at least some populations of the region, the collective public norm persists despite changes in the attitudes of the individual members of the culture. In Miller and Prentice's (1994) terms, the "collective norm" may continue to favor honor-related values, even though the "aggregate norm" does not. This is not to say that Southerners have not internalized culture of honor norms to some extent. Indeed, survey evidence indicates that there are some consistent regional differences when considering honor-related issues (Cohen & Nisbett, 1994). However, public Southern honor norms and public behavior may tend to show far stronger regional differences than more private attitudes do.

We have focused our analysis on the specific case of violence, particularly violence in the U.S. South. However, many of the processes described in this chapter are also applicable to other issues involving cultural perpetuation. We suspect that some of the most important questions in our rapidly changing world will relate to the issues of how persistent various cultural patterns will be and how these various patterns maintain themselves (or change) in the face of changing circumstances. To explore these questions, much attention is needed to the social processes that occur as individuals and cultures "make each other up" (Kitayama & Markus, 1999; Shweder, 1990). We expect that psychologists will have a lot to contribute to this interdisciplinary discussion.

## REFERENCES

Allport, F. H. (1924). *Social psychology*. Boston: Houghton Mifflin.

Anderson, E. (1994). The code of the streets. *Atlantic Monthly, 5*, 81–94.

Asch, S. E. (1955). Opinions and social pressure. *Scientific American, 193*, 31–55.

Axelrod, R. (1984). *The evolution of cooperation*. New York: Basic Books.

Axelrod, R., & Hamilton, W. D. (1981). The evolution of cooperation. *Science, 211*, 1390–1396.

Baron, L., & Straus, M. A. (1989). *Four theories of rape in American society: A state-level analysis*. New Haven, CT: Yale University Press.

Borden, R. J. (1975). Witnessed aggression: Influence of an observer's sex and values on aggressive responding. *Journal of Personality and Social Psychology, 31*, 567–573.

Brearley, H. C. (1932). *Homicide in the United States*. Chapel Hill, NC: University of North Carolina Press.

Chiu, C., Morris, M., Hong, Y., & Menon, T. (2000). Motivated cultural cognition: The impact of implicit cultural theories on dispositional attribution varies as a function of need for closure. *Journal of Personality and Social Psychology, 78*, 247–259.

Cialdini, R. B., Kallgren, C. A., & Reno, R. R. (1991). A focus theory of normative conduct: A theoretical refinement and reevaluation of the role of norms in human behavior. In L. Berkowitz (Ed.), *Advances in experimental social psychology* (pp. 201–234). New York: Academic Press.

Cohen, D. (1996). Law, social policy, and violence: The impact of regional cultures. *Journal of Personality and Social Psychology, 70*, 961–978.

Cohen, D. (1997). Ifs and thens in cultural psychology. In R. S. Wyer (Ed.), *Advances in social cognition* (Vol. 10, pp. 121–131). Mahwah, NJ: Lawrence Erlbaum Associates.

Cohen, D. (1998). Culture, social organization, and patterns of violence. *Journal of Personality and Social Psychology, 75*, 408–419.

Cohen, D. (2001). Cultural variation: Considerations and implications. *Psychological Bulletin, 127*, 451–471.

Cohen, D., & Nisbett, R. E. (1994). Self-protection and the culture of honor: Explaining Southern violence. *Personality and Social Psychology Bulletin, 20*, 551–567.

Cohen, D., & Nisbett, R. E. (1997). Field experiments examining the culture of honor: The role of institutions in perpetuating norms about violence. *Personality and Social Psychology Bulletin, 23*, 1188–1199.

Cohen, D., Nisbett, R. E., Bowdle, B. F., & Schwarz, N. (1996). Insult, aggression, and the southern culture of honor: An "experimental ethnography." *Journal of Personality and Social Psychology, 70*, 945–960.

Cohen, D., & Vandello, J. A. (2001). Honor and "faking" honorability. In R. Nesse (Ed.), *Evolution and the capacity for commitment*. New York: Russell Sage.

Cohen, D., Vandello, J., Puente, S., & Rantilla, A. (1999). "When you call me that, Smile!" How norms for politeness, interaction styles, and aggression work together in southern culture. *Social Psychology Quarterly, 62*, 257–275.

Cohen, D., Vandello, J. A., & Rantilla, A. K. (1998). The sacred and the social: Honor and violence in cultural context. In P. Gilbert & B. Andrews (Eds.), *Shame: Interpersonal behavior, psychopathology, and culture* (pp. 261–282). Cambridge: Oxford University Press.

Cooter, R. D. (1997). *Normative failure theory of law*. Unpublished manuscript: University of California at Berkeley.

Crick, N. R., & Dodge, K. A. (1994). A review and reformulation of social information-processing mechanisms in children's social adjustment. *Psychological Bulletin, 115*, 74–101.

Daly, M., & Wilson, M. (1988). *Homicide*. Hawthorne, NY: Aldine.

Dodge, K. A. (1985). Attributional bias in aggressive children. In P. C. Kendall (Ed.), *Advances in cognitive and behavioral research and therapy* (Vol. 4, pp. 73–110). New York: Academic Press.

Dodge, K. A., Bates, J. E., & Pettit, G. S. (1990). Mechanisms in the cycle of violence. *Science, 250*, 1678–1683.

Dodge, K. A., & Coie, J. D. (1987). Social information-processing factors in reactive and proactive aggression in children's playgroups. *Journal of Personality and Social Psychology, 53*, 1146–1158.

Dodge, K. A., & Crick, N. R. (1990). Social information processing bases of aggressive behavior in children. *Personality and Social Psychology Bulletin, 16*, 8–22.

Dodge, K. A., & Schwartz, D. (1997). Social information-processing mechanisms in aggressive behavior. In D. Stoff, J. Breiling, & J. Masur (Eds.), *Handbook of antisocial behavior* (pp. 171–180). New York: Wiley.

Edgerton, R. (2000). Traditional beliefs and practices: Are some better than others? In. L. Harrison & S. Huntington (Eds.), *Culture matters* (pp. 126–140). New York: Basic Books.

Ellison, C. G. (1991). An eye for an eye? A note on the southern subculture of violence thesis. *Social Forces, 69*, 1223–1239.

Ellison, C. G., & Sherkat, D. E. (1993). Conservative protestantism and support for corporal punishment. *American Sociological Review, 58*, 131–144.

Felson, R. B. (1978). Aggression as impression management. *Social Psychology, 41*, 205–213.

Felson, R. B. (1982). Impression management and the escalation of aggression and violence. *Social Psychology Quarterly, 45*, 245–254.

Felson, R. B., Liska, A. E., South, S. J., & McNulty, T. L. (1994). The subculture of violence and delinquency: Individual vs. school context effects. *Social Forces, 73*, 155–173.

Fischer, D. H. (1989). *Albion's seed*. New York: Oxford University Press.

Gastil, R. D. (1971). Homicide and a regional culture of violence. *American Sociological Review, 36*, 412–427.

Gilmore, D. D. (1990). *Manhood in the making*. New Haven, CT: Yale University Press.

Gladwell, M. (1996, June 3). The tipping point. *The New Yorker*, pp. 32–38.

Gorn, E. J. (1985). "Gouge and bite, pull hair and scratch": The social significance of fighting in the Southern backcountry. *American Historical Review, 90*, 18–43.

Grantham, D. W. (1993). *The South in modern America*. New York: Harper Collins.

Hackney, S. (1969). Southern violence. *American Historical Review, 74*, 906–925.

Horowitz, R., & Schwartz, G. (1974). Honor, normative ambiguity, and gang violence. *American Sociological Review, 39*, 238–251.

Huguet, P., & Latané, B. (1996). Social representations as dynamic social impact. *Journal of Communication, 46*, 57–63.

Jussim, L., & Osgood, D. W. (1989). Influence and similarity among friends: An integrative model applied to incarcerated adolescents. *Social Psychology Quarterly, 52*, 98–112.

Kahan, D. M. (1998). Social meaning and the economic analysis of crime. *Journal of Legal Studies, 27*, 609–622.

Kelly, M. H. (1999). Regional naming patterns and the culture of honor. *Names, 47*, 3–20.

Kitayama, S., & Markus, H. (1999). The yin and yang of the Japanese self. In D. Cervone & Y. Shoda (Eds.), *The coherence of personality* (pp. 242–302). New York: Guilford.

Kluckhohn, C. (1965). *Mirror for man*. New York: McGraw-Hill.

Latané, B. (1997). Dynamic social impact: The societal consequences of human interaction. In C. McGarty & S. A. Haslam (Eds.), *The message of social psychology: Perspectives on mind in society* (pp. 200–220). Malden, MA: Blackwell.

Latané, B. (2000). Pressures for uniformity and the evolution of cultural norms: Modeling dynamic social impact. In D. R. Ilgen & C. L. Hulin (Eds.), *Computational modeling of behavior in organizations: The third scientific discipline* (pp. 189–220). Washington, DC: APA.

Lessig, L. (1995). The regulation of social meaning. *University of Chicago Law Review, 62*, 943–1045.

Lessig, L. (1998). The new Chicago school. *Journal of Legal Studies, 27*, 661–692.

Luckenbill, D. F. (1977). Criminal homicide as a situated transaction. *Social Problems, 25*, 176–186.

Mackie, G. (1996). Ending footbinding and infibulation: A conventional account. *American Sociological Review, 61*, 999–1017.

McAdams, R. H. (1997). The origin, development, and regulation of norms. *Michigan Law Review, 96*, 338–433.

McAdams, R. H. (2000). *An attitudinal theory of law's expressive function*. Unpublished manuscript, University of Illinois at Urbana-Champaign.

McDonald, F., & McWhiney, G. (1975). The antebellum Southern herdsman. *Journal of Southern History, 41*, 147–166.

McWhiney, G. (1988). *Cracker culture*. Tuscaloosa: University of Alabama Press.

Miller, D. T., & McFarland, C. (1987). Pluralistic ignorance: When similarity is interpreted as dissimilarity. *Journal of Personality and Social Psychology, 53*, 298–305.

Miller, D. T., & McFarland, C. (1991). When social comparison goes awry: The case of pluralistic ignorance. In J. Suls & T. Wills (Eds.), *Social comparison: Contemporary theory and research* (pp. 287–331). Hillsdale, NJ: Lawrence Erlbaum Associates.

Miller, D. T., & Prentice, D. A. (1994). Collective errors and errors about the collective. *Personality and Social Psychology Bulletin, 20*, 541–550.

Miller, W. (1990). *Bloodtaking and peacemaking: Feud, law, and society in Saga Iceland*. Chicago: University of Chicago Press.

Miller, W. (1993). *Humiliation*. Ithaca, NY: Cornell University Press.

Nisbett, R. E. (1993). Violence and U.S. regional culture. *American Psychologist, 48*, 441–449.

Nisbett, R. E., & Cohen, D. (1996). *Culture of honor*. Boulder, CO: Westview Press.

Nisbett, R. E., Polly, G., & Lang, S. (1995). Homicide and U.S. regional culture. In B. R. Ruback & N. A. Weiner (Eds.), *Interpersonal violent behaviors*. New York: Springer.

Peristiany, J. G. (Ed.). (1965). *Honour and shame: The values of Mediterranean society*. London: Weidenfeld and Nicolson.

Prentice, D. A., & Miller, D. T. (1996). Pluralistic ignorance and the perpetuation of social norms by unwitting actors. In L. Berkowitz (Ed.), *Advances in experimental social psychology, Vol. 28* (pp. 161–209). New York: Academic Press.

Putnam, R. (1993). *Making democracy work*. Princeton, NJ: Princeton University Press.

Reaves, A. (1998). *The cultural ecology of rural white homicide in the southern United States*. Unpublished manuscript, University of Alabama.

Redfield, H. V. (1880). *Homicide, North and South*. Philadelphia: Lippincott.

Reed, J. S. (1972). *The enduring South: Subcultural persistence in mass society*. Lexington, MA: Lexington Books.

Reed, J. S. (1981). Below the Smith and Wesson line: Reflections on southern violence. In M. Black & J. S. Reed (Eds.), *Perspectives on the American South: An annual review of society, politics, and culture*. New York: Cordon & Breach Science Publications.

Rosen, J. (1997, October 20). The social police. *The New Yorker*, pp. 170–181.

Ross, L. (1977). The intuitive psychologist and his shortcomings: Distortions in the attribution process. In L. Berkowitz (Ed.), *Advances in experimental social psychology* (Vol. 10, pp. 173–219). New York: Academic Press.

Rozin, P., Millman, L., & Nemeroff, C. (1986). Operation of the laws of sympathetic magic in disgust and other domains. *Journal of Personality and Social Psychology, 50,* 703–712.

Rozin, P., & Nemeroff, C. (1999). Magic and superstition. In R. A. Wilson & F. C. Keil (Eds.), *The MIT encyclopedia of the cognitive sciences* (pp. 503–505). Cambridge, MA: MIT Press.

Schaller, M., & Latané, B. (1996). Dynamic social impact and the evolution of social representations: A natural history of stereotypes. *Journal of Communication, 46,* 64–77.

Schelling, T. C. (1978). *Micromotives and macrobehavior.* New York: Norton.

Schneider, J. (1971). Of vigilance and virgins. *Ethnology, 9,* 1–24.

Schroeder, C. M., & Prentice, D. A. (1998). Exposing pluralistic ignorance to reduce alcohol use among college students. *Journal of Applied Social Psychology, 28,* 2150–2180.

Sherif, M., & Sherif, C. W. (1953). *Groups in harmony and tension.* New York: Harper.

Short, J. F., & Strodtbeck, F. L. (1965). *Group process and gang delinquency.* Chicago: University of Chicago Press.

Shweder, R. (1990). Cultural psychology: What is it? In J. Stigler, R. Shweder, & G. Herdt (Eds.), *Cultural psychology* (pp. 1–43). Cambridge: Cambridge.

Triandis, H. C. (1994). *Culture and social behavior.* New York: McGraw-Hill.

Vandello, J. A., & Cohen, D. (1998, May). *The perpetuation of southern cultural norms of violence: A case of pluralistic ignorance?* Poster presented at the annual meeting of the Midwestern Psychological Association, Chicago.

Vandello, J. A., & Cohen, D. (1999). Patterns of individualism and collectivism in the United States. *Journal of Personality and Social Psychology, 77,* 279–292.

Vandello, J. A., & Cohen, D. (2002). *Pluralistic ignorance and the perpetuation of southern norms about male aggression.* Manuscript submitted for publication, University of South Florida.

Vandello, J. A., & Cohen, D. (in press). Male honor and female fidelity: Implicit cultural scripts that perpetuate domestic violence. *Journal of Personality and Social Psychology.*

Wolfgang, M. E., & Ferracuti, F. (1967). *The subculture of violence.* London: Tavistock.

CHAPTER

# 13

# Move the Body, Change the Self: Acculturative Effects on the Self-Concept

Steven J. Heine
Darrin R. Lehman
University of British Columbia

The ever-growing body of research on acculturation is in agreement on at least one issue: Moving to a new culture involves psychological adjustment. This adjustment occurs over a wide variety of domains, including acquiring a new language, learning new interpersonal and social behaviors, becoming accustomed to new values, adapting to a new diet, and becoming a member of a minority group (e.g., Berry & Kim, 1988; Church, 1982; Dornic, 1985; Feldman, Mont-Reynaud, & Rosenthal, 1992; Furnham & Bochner, 1986; La-Fromboise, Coleman, & Gerton, 1993; Pasquali, 1985; Schwarzer, Bowler, & Rauch, 1985). More pertinent to self-researchers, however, is research on the adjustment of the *self-concept* in the acculturation process.

## METHODOLOGICAL APPROACHES FOR THE STUDY OF CULTURE AND PSYCHOLOGY

Cultural psychology maintains that culture and self are mutually constituted (e.g., Markus, Mullally, & Kitayama, 1997; Shweder, 1990). That is, individuals seize meanings and resources from their culture in the construction of their selves, and likewise, the collective sharing of meaning and resources among individuals shapes the cultural environment. Despite the straightforwardness of this theoretical view, empirical evidence for the cultural foundation of the self-concept is not immediately obvious, nor is its assessment a simple task. For example, it is extraordinarily difficult for a cultural insider to observe the cultural foundation of the self-concept without another culture with which to make comparisons. Culture is largely invisible to members of it, because what is unique to the culture cannot be distinguished from what people understand to be human nature (Heine, Lehman, Peng, & Greenholtz, 2002).

There have been two primary methodological approaches to studying cultural influences on the self-concept. A typical approach utilized by *cultural* psychologists is to explore a single culture outside of their own, thus providing researchers with a more objective vantage point. The culture under study is contrasted with that of the researcher's own either implicitly, by focusing on those cultural aspects that appear novel, or explicitly with cross-cultural data. Any differences that are identified between the two cultures serve to illuminate the role of culture by inviting a cultural psychological explanation to account for them (Greenfield, 1997; Miller, 1999). Because cultural psychologists are interested in the exploration of cultural artifacts in the self-concept, it is incumbent on them to have a detailed knowledge of the culture under study. This approach assumes that only through a rich understanding of the culture will a rich understanding of the self-concept be achieved. Thus, a common strategy for cultural psychologists is to focus their research on a single culture, perhaps living there, learning the language, reading much about the culture, and collaborating with members of that culture (Greenfield, 1997).

However, the cultural psychological approach is not without its limitations. Any differences that are identified between two cultures on a particular psychological process might tell us something about how one culture appears relative to the other, but they do not tell us much about that culture relative to the rest of the world. Frequently it seems that much of cultural psychology is conducted from the perspective of North Americans (at least those north of the Mason–Dixon line). Any cultural differences that are found in comparison to North Americans are typically interpreted as telling us something about how culture has shaped the "other" group. However, the peculiar cultural phenomenon in need of explanation may instead be the North American case (e.g., Lipset, 1996). That is, in many respects the more unusual finding, for example, is not that much of the world is collectivistic but that Westerners are individualistic (Geertz, 1974/1983; Markus & Kitayama, 1991); not that Southerners participate in a "culture of honor" but that Northerners lack concern with honor (Nisbett & Cohen, 1996; Vandello & Cohen, chap. 12, this volume); not that Indians focus on beneficence obligations but that Americans focus on justice obligations (Miller & Bersoff, 1992); not that Japanese are self-critical but that Canadians and Americans are self-enhancing (Heine, Lehman, Markus, & Kitayama, 1999); or not that East Asians reason holistically but that Americans reason analytically (Nisbett, Peng, Choi, & Norenzayan, 2001). Binary comparisons render explanations relative to the comparison culture (usually North American); however, if our goal is to investigate human nature, absolute assessments of cultural phenomena (or at least assessments relative to the world as a whole) would seem to be of greater utility.

Likewise, if a psychological process under study is compared across cultures that are hypothesized to differ in terms of a dimension such as individualism/collectivism and a cultural difference is found, we cannot say with confidence whether individualism fosters the psychological process, or whether collectivism inhibits the process, or both. Moreover, cultures are of course far too complex to be reduced meaningfully to any single dimension. Any cultural differences that are identified may be due to other dimensions of culture on which the two groups differ that are concealed by a reliance on two-culture comparisons.

Examining a multitude of cultures at once, the prototypical strategy of *cross-cultural* psychology (e.g., Diener & Diener, 1995; Hofstede, 1980; Schwartz & Bilsky, 1990) is an approach that mitigates some of these difficulties. Large-scale multinational comparisons allow us to see how each culture compares not just to a single cultural target, but to the larger matrix of other cultures in the study. This approach strives to map out the world in terms of a number of cultural dimensions. However, this method also has its shortcomings. First, as no individual is particularly knowledgeable about *all* cultures under study, cross-cultural psychologists face the problem of having limited knowledge about their objects of study. This approach does not allow one to explore how culture shapes the psychological process, as the researchers do not have access to information regarding the makeup of those cultures beyond their psychometric measures. Moreover, as there are serious validity concerns with cross-cultural comparisons of many kinds of psychometric measures (e.g., Heine et al., 2001; Heine et al., 2002; Peng, Nisbett, & Wong, 1997), accepting the data from large multinational comparisons at face value would seem to require a leap of faith. Both of the conventional approaches to studying culture and psychology thus have their strengths and weaknesses.

A third possible approach for investigating the role of culture on the self is to examine the acculturating individual. In many cases of migration, individuals' culturally constructed selves are at odds with the cultural meaning system of the new culture to which they have moved. The study of acculturation makes it possible to identify changes in the self-concept that individuals experience when encountering a new culture. Investigations of the acculturating individual allow researchers to assess the effects of a measured degree of exposure to a particular cultural environment on individuals' self-concepts. This approach has been rarely employed in the past (e.g., Cross, 1992; Minoura, 1992), but it can provide us with a perspective on cultural influences different from those provided from cultural or cross-cultural psychological approaches. We utilized this approach in the studies described next.

## CULTURE AND HUMAN NATURE

Cultural psychology recognizes that the development of the individual is bound up within the process of socialization, that is, the process of the individual orienting him or herself within a system of meaning (Shweder et al., 1998). Humans have the longest period of socialization of any species, which reflects our great dependency on acquiring cultural sources of meaning. Geertz (1973) argued that humans are born into an "information gap"—that is, there is a pronounced discrepancy between the amount of instinctual information that is hard-wired into us at birth and the amount of information that we need to survive. Survival depends on the individual's ability to successfully learn the language, technology, and customs of his or her surrounding cultural environment. Thus, humans must come into the world prepared to attend to and seize cultural meanings from around them. In fact, humans are unique in their tendencies to imitate and mimic novel behaviors of social models (Boyd & Silk, 1997; Tomasello, 2001). Humans appear to be biologically programmed to seize, make use of, and depend on cultural meanings.

Indeed, culture itself may have played an integral role in the evolution of our meaning-seizing capacities. Geertz (1973) maintained that the evolution of culture did not follow human evolution, as has traditionally been assumed, but that the two evolved simultaneously. Our abilities to make use of cultural information, such as our ability to learn technologies to procure food, to communicate our needs to our caretakers, to make ourselves attractive to potential mates, and to marshal political support for our causes were likely selected throughout our evolution. That is, the development of culture did not begin after we passed some magical threshold to modern *Homo sapiens*, but was a selective force itself in the evolution of our capacities to make use of cultural meanings. In this way, culture was "ingredient" to our evolution, not just a product of it (Geertz, 1973, p. 47). Importantly, it was not the ability to make use of *specific* forms of cultural information that was selected throughout our evolution, but *general* forms of it. For example, the ability to master antelope hunting in the African savanna would only be an evolutionary cost as soon as our ancestors expanded into new environments that contained no antelopes. Rather, the ability to seize meaning from whatever cultural environment that we were born into would maximize our likelihood of survival. Our common evolutionary heritage has provided us with a universal mind, although it emerges in one of manifold mentalities through our participation in particular cultural worlds (Shweder et al., 1998). As Geertz (1973) famously asserted, "we all begin with the natural equipment to live a thousand kinds of life but end in the end having lived only one" (p. 45).

According to this view, our nature is ultimately that of a cultural being. It is difficult to conceive of a "cultureless" human, as the process of becoming human is contingent on the orientation of oneself within, and the seizing of meanings from, a particular cultural environment—any cultural environment. An individual that was somehow raised in isolation from a culture thus would lack some of the very characteristics that we often consider integral to "human nature."[1] The process of normal human development can thus be seen to hinge on being socialized into a *particular* cultural meaning system. The question that this chapter concerns itself with is, what happens to individuals who are socialized into more than one cultural meaning system?

## A SENSITIVE PERIOD FOR ACQUIRING A CULTURAL MEANING SYSTEM

To the extent that humans evolved as cultural beings, we should see evidence for our brains being preprogrammed to learn a cultural meaning system. One such source of evidence would be an indication that there is a sensitive period for being enculturated. Typically, behavioral skills do not worsen with age; rather they increase. In contrast, some developmental domains have a sensitive period in which the ability to learn reaches a peak (typically early in life) and quickly drops off. The existence of a sensitive period suggests that the acquisition of skills occurs by virtue of a set of innate constraints that are present during the sensitive period but weaken with maturation (Newport, 1991). Computer modeling has revealed that to the extent that the degree of mastery of certain skills confers a survival advantage throughout the individual's lifespan, a sensitive acquisition period should be evident (Hurford, 1991).

---

[1]Perhaps the closest example of relatively "culture-free" humans can be observed in autistic children, who are less able to interact with their environment in a way that enables the internalization of cultural meanings. Indeed, in many ways the thoughts and behavior of autistic children do appear to be somewhat free of cultural influences (Tomasello, Kruger, & Ratner, 1993) and also somewhat different from the thoughts and behavior we typically associate with normal human functioning. Similarly, extreme cases of cultural deprivation such as that inflicted on "Genie" by her abusing father (she was isolated in an attic until the age of 13), also seem to impair thoughts and behavior relative to those raised to participate in a culture (Curtiss, 1977). We must remember, though, that each of these culturally-deprived cases makes poor controls to compare with fully "cultured" individuals as there are many confounding variables.

There is considerable evidence that there is a sensitive period for the acquisition of language (e.g., Hurford, 1991; Lenneberg, 1967; Newport, 1991; but see Singleton, 1989 for a contrary view). Early in life (before puberty), humans have a superior capacity for acquiring and mastering languages (both first and second languages, although adults may initially outstrip children when they begin to learn a second language; Johnson & Newport, 1989), but this capacity declines with maturation (Lenneberg, 1967; Newport, 1991). That we learn a language in a particular stage of development, and do not simply acquire one at any point in our lives, is evidence that our capacity for learning language is, as Chomsky (1982) put it, "highly useful and very valuable for the perpetuation of the species and so on, a capacity that has obvious selectional value" (pp. 18–19). We have a biological predisposition to learn a language in this sensitive period.

Learning a language is a necessary aspect of being socialized in a particular culture. Edward Sapir stated "Language is a great force of socialization, probably the greatest that exists" (Mandelbaum, 1951, p. 15). In this respect, we should expect that language acquisition parallels cultural acquisition, and to the extent that our ability to seize cultural meanings was a selective force, a sensitive period for cultural learning should also be evident.

The measurement of the acquisition of culture, however, is much less straightforward than the measurement of the acquisition of language. Cultures do not have as tangible and measurable a grammar, accent, morphology, or vocabulary. Despite these methodological challenges, Minoura (1992) launched a large-scale investigation of a sensitive period for learning culture. She developed an elaborate coding system which assessed the cultural acquisition of cognitive, behavioral, and emotional domains of culture. Minoura interviewed Japanese-born children who had moved to the United States at various different ages. Her results suggest that people appear to be internalizing cultural meaning systems from birth; however, after 9 years of age some permanence in the retention of learned cultural meanings emerges. That is, those participants who moved to the United States before the age of 9 reported becoming largely "Americanized," and felt relatively distant from their Japanese heritage. Those who moved to the United States between the ages of 9 and 15 still retained some Japanese cultural sensibilities but also felt reasonably comfortable with American ways. Those who moved to the United States after the age of 15, however, were never able to fully embrace American culture, particularly with respect to their emotional experience. They continued to see the world through Japanese cultural lenses. Just as older second-language learners often maintain an indelible accent from their mother tongue, older second-culture learners often preserve an echo of the emotional repertoire of their mother culture.

The developmental sequence of culture-learning identified by Minoura nicely coincides with that found in second language acquisition (Johnson &

Newport, 1989). Moreover, the variable that correlated most strongly with American cultural mastery in Minoura's study was English language ability. Cultural meaning system acquisition and language acquisition may be inextricably intertwined as they both involve efforts to extract meaning from the social environment. Thus far, Minoura's study is the only one to provide empirical data regarding a sensitive period for the acquisition of culture, and although any single study is limited in the extent of its explanatory power, the parallels of her findings with those from studies of language acquisition are compelling.

## LIVING IN TWO CULTURAL WORLDS

Most cross-cultural studies have contrasted people from two or more distinct cultures, but some of this research has also included samples of biculturals that are intermediate to the two cultures under study. For example, Asian Americans comprise a group that have exposure to both mainstream European American culture and their family's traditional Asian culture. It follows that such individuals should evince ways of thinking intermediate to that of European American and Asian samples. In general, studies that have investigated these three cultural groups, on a wide variety of measures relevant to the self, have found evidence consistent with this pattern (e.g., Heine et al., 2001; Heine & Lehman, 1997a, 1999; Iyengar, Lepper, & Ross, 1999; Kitayama, Markus, Matsumoto, & Norasakkunkit, 1997; Norenzayan, Choi, & Nisbett, 2002). These results are consistent with the notion that Asian-Americans come to embrace a view of self in between that of European-Americans and Asians.

However, it is not necessarily the case that the self-concept of acculturating groups is the product of some kind of blending of the two self-concepts from their host and home cultures. Another possibility is that acculturating individuals have access to two cultural meaning systems, and they oscillate between the two of them (e.g., Anderson, 1999; DuBois, 1903/1989; LaFromboise et al., 1993). The intermediate results obtained in past research with Asian Americans might thus reflect that at the time of the studies some Asian-Americans were operating in "European American mode," whereas others were operating in "Asian mode." Indeed, a number of researchers have argued that culture is akin to a meta-schema, and that we can have potential access to multiple meta-schemas at once (Hong, Morris, Chiu, & Benet-Martinez, 2000; Lee, Aaker, & Gardner, 2000; Trafimow, Triandis, & Goto, 1991). Research consistently reveals that those cultural schemas that are currently activated guide thoughts and behavior. For example, when primed with thoughts associated with interdependence, individuals from various cultural backgrounds are more likely to make situational attributions (Hong et al., 2000), opt for risky investment decisions (Mandel, 2000), adopt a prevention focus (Lee et al., 2000), or place more emphasis on attending to social norms (Ybarra & Trafimow, 1998). In this regard, moving to a new cultural context involves the socialization of a new cultural meaning system that exists parallel to the system of the individual's original culture. The notion that there is a sensitive period for cultural acquisition suggests that the chronic accessibility of a cultural meta-schema is more likely if it is acquired before puberty.

## ACCULTURATION OF SELF-ESTEEM

Self-esteem is the most researched construct related to the self-concept; over 18,000 studies investigating it have been published over the past 35 years (this is a rate of more than 1 publication per day!). Since many of these studies were conducted across cultures we have an empirical base with which to evaluate cultural influences on self-esteem. To the extent that we can identify a clear pattern of cultural differences on self-esteem, we can explore acculturative changes of self-esteem when individuals from one culture migrate to a culture that sustains different levels of self-esteem.

Much research suggests that values associated with individualism and independence are associated with higher self-esteem (e.g., Heine, in press). A cultural orientation that views individuals as the basic social unit will also tend to encourage people to believe in their own integrity qua individuals. In North America, for example, where individualism is prized, the culture urges individuals to view themselves as independently functioning agents (e.g., Bellah, Madsen, Sullivan, Swindler, & Tipton, 1985; Sampson, 1977). People who embrace an independent view of self tend to have a sense of identity that is anchored in its internal attributes and is viewed as the source of action and the center of control (Markus & Kitayama, 1991). Maintaining this autonomous sense of agency and identity is fostered by identifying and affirming these inner attributes (Heine, in press). A habitual positive self-view confirms for the individual that they possess the requisite characteristics to fulfill cultural tasks associated with independence, self-sufficiency, and autonomy (Heine et al., 1999).

It follows then that the more autonomous and self-sufficient individuals perceive themselves, the more positively they should feel. Evidence for these relations are found in correlational studies of self-esteem and independent views of self: Regardless of the culture within which the study is conducted, people who have a more independent view of self also report higher self-esteem (correlations range from .33 to .52 within cultures; Heine et al., 1999; Singelis, Bond, Lai, & Sharkey, 1999; comparable correlations have been identified between independence and self-enhancement; Heine &

Renshaw, 2002). There is thus a considerable degree of overlap between the concepts of independence and positive self-views.

A Confucian framework of interdependence, which is at the core of the self in many East Asian cultures, including Japan (e.g., Heine, 2001; Markus & Kitayama, 1991; Su et al., 1999), provides an alternative conception of self. This view of self brings with it cultural goals that conflict with desires to be self-sufficient and autonomous. Individuals are connected to each other via relationships and with respect to the roles that are inherent in those relationships. These various relationships constitute a coherent hierarchy within which the individual has a place defined by a clear set of obligations and duties towards other members of their groups. Inadequate performance of the duties associated with one's roles indicates that the individual is not doing his or her part in contributing to the group's success and is thus not fulfilling important cultural obligations associated with interdependence. Individuals' commitments to in-group members render them obligated to live up to the standards associated with their roles—standards that are importantly not determined by the individuals themselves but consensually by others in the hierarchy, and to a certain extent by society as a whole (Heine et al., 2001; Kitayama et al., 1997). Individuals thus must be sensitive to ways that they might fall short of these standards, thereby failing to live up to the obligations that they have, and communicating to others that one is not doing their part towards the group's success. They must be vigilant to any shortcomings indicating where they need to make greater efforts to better fulfill their roles. This orientation, in contrast to self-enhancement, is termed self-criticism (Heine et al., 1999).

This reasoning suggests that interdependence is not associated with enhanced positive self-views, and may even be linked with more self-critical views. Correlational studies conducted with a variety of measures of interdependence and positive self-views reveal that, regardless of the culture in which the study was conducted, individuals higher in interdependence do not have higher self-esteem or show evidence of greater self-enhancement ($r$ values range from –.01 to –.44 within cultures; Heine et al., 1999; Heine & Renshaw, 2002; Kiuchi, 1996; Singelis et al., 1999; Yamaguchi, 1994). Interdependence is orthogonal, or even antagonistic, to positive self-views, within North American and East Asian cultures.

This difference in the relations between independence and interdependence and self-esteem *within* cultures, suggests that there should be corresponding differences in self-esteem *between* cultures that differ in terms of their independence and interdependence. Much evidence from a variety of disciplines has suggested that values associated with independence are most closely associated with North Americans (Bellah et al., 1985; Lipset, 1996; Markus & Kitayama, 1991; Sampson, 1977; Triandis, 1989) whereas those associated with interdependence are more strongly embraced by

East Asians, particularly Japanese (Bachnik & Quinn, 1994; Hamaguchi, 1985; Lebra, 1976; Markus & Kitayama, 1991; Triandis, 1989; but note the lack of supportive psychometric evidence on trait measures for this cultural difference, Matsumoto, 1999, and Takano & Osaka, 1999; and explanations for this lack of support, Heine et al., 2002, and Peng et al., 1997). Thus, evidence of high self-esteem should be less evident in East Asian cultures such as Japan than it is in North America.

## EVIDENCE OF CULTURAL DIFFERENCES IN SELF-ESTEEM BETWEEN JAPANESE AND NORTH AMERICANS

Empirical research on positive self-views can be roughly divided into three categories: possessing, enhancing, and maintaining positive self-views. A review of the evidence in each domain among North American and Japanese samples reveals pronounced cultural differences.

### Possessing a Positive Self-View

In a review of the Western self-esteem literature, Baumeister, Tice, and Hutton (1989) observed that, without exception, the mean and/or median self-esteem scores were higher than the conceptual midpoints of the scales, regardless of the measures used. Thus, the distributions of self-esteem scores are heavily skewed such that the vast majority of North Americans report having high self-esteem. The characteristic self-evaluation for those living in a culture characterized by independence and individualism, namely North America, is unambiguously positive. North Americans who do not tend to endorse items about their value as an individual (i.e., who score below the theoretical midpoint on self-esteem inventories) are relatively rare (less than 7% of one large European Canadian sample; Heine et al., 1999).

Such positive views of self are not as common among Japanese. Kashiwagi (1986) suggested that a "negative evaluation of the self, or strong awareness of weaker aspects of self, is sometimes pointed to as one of the general characteristics of self-concept among the Japanese" (p. 180). This self-critical orientation is reflected in their self-esteem scores. Japanese consistently have exhibited lower self-esteem scores than North Americans (e.g., Bond & Cheung, 1983; Yeh, 1995; similar cultural differences have also been noted for subjective well-being, Diener & Diener, 1995), and in contrast to the heavily skewed distributions found in North American studies of self-esteem, Japanese' mean self-esteem scores are roughly normally distributed around the theoretical midpoint of the scale (Heine et al., 1999).

Self-critical views among Japanese are also evident in measures of actual–ideal self-discrepancies. These discrepancies indicate feelings of dissatisfaction with one's current self, a proxy for self-criticism. Japanese exhibited larger actual–ideal and actual–ought self-discrepancies than North Americans (Heine & Lehman, 1999; Meijer, Heine, & Yamagami, 1999), and, importantly, these self-critical views appear to be associated with fewer negative consequences, such as depression, for Japanese compared with North Americans (Heine & Lehman, 1999).

### Enhancing the Positivity of One's Self-View

The importance of a positive self-view in North American culture is further documented in research on self-enhancing biases. Reviews of this literature (e.g., Greenwald, 1980; Miller & Ross, 1975; Taylor & Brown, 1988) indicate that North Americans' self-perceptions tend to be systematically biased toward an overly positive view of the self.

There is much less evidence for self-enhancement among Japanese than North Americans. Cross-cultural studies reveal that the better-than-average effect (Heine & Lehman, 1997a; Markus & Kitayama, 1991), self-peer biases (Heine & Renshaw, 2002), unrealistic optimism (Heine & Lehman, 1995), and self-serving attributional biases (e.g., Kitayama, Takagi, & Matsumoto, 1995) are less pronounced among Japanese compared with North Americans. Everyday situations in Japan are seen more in terms of opportunities for self-criticism, in contrast to the clear self-enhancing opportunities perceived by North Americans (Kitayama et al., 1997). The literature indicates that self-enhancement is not as strong a motivation among Japanese.

### Maintaining a Positive Self-View

Further testimony to the importance of positive self-views in Western culture is found in the ever-growing body of research on self-evaluation maintenance. This literature documents the variety of compensatory self-protective responses that are elicited when people encounter threats to their self-esteem. Such strategies include: self-evaluation maintenance (e.g., Tesser, 1988), self-affirmation and dissonance reduction (e.g., Steele, 1988), compensatory self-enhancement (e.g., Baumeister & Jones, 1978), downward social comparison (e.g., Wills, 1981), motivated reasoning (e.g., Kunda, 1990), and self-handicapping (e.g., Tice, 1991). That such a wide variety of self-esteem maintenance tactics exists highlights the importance of maintaining a positive self-evaluation, at least within North American culture.

In contrast, few clear demonstrations of any of the aforementioned self-esteem maintenance strategies have been found with East Asian samples (e.g., Cross, Liao, & Josephs, 1992). A cross-cultural laboratory study with

Canadians and Japanese failed to find evidence for dissonance reduction or self-affirmation among Japanese in contrast to the pronounced effects among Canadians (Heine & Lehman, 1997b). Japanese have been found to demonstrate a *reverse* compensatory self-enhancement effect, in which they respond to negative self-relevant feedback by decreasing their self-evaluations in other unrelated domains (Heine, Kitayama, & Lehman, 2001). A recent cross-cultural exploration of motivated reasoning biases found that Americans were more inclined to believe ostensible scientific arguments that cell phone use leads to hearing loss if they didn't use a cell phone regularly, whereas Japanese agreement was unaffected by their own cell phone use (Heine, 2002).

Other research provides striking evidence of self-critical tendencies among Japanese. For example, Japanese are more likely to attend to and recall negative than positive information, whereas Americans demonstrate the opposite tendency (Meijer et al., 1999). Canadians tend to be more easily convinced of their successes than their failures, whereas Japanese are quicker to conclude that they have failed than succeeded (Heine, Takata, & Lehman, 2000). Moreover, this vigilance for information indicating weaknesses appears to serve an important function for Japanese: It highlights where they need to direct efforts for self-improvement. A series of cross-cultural laboratory studies on intrinsic motivation revealed that Japanese persisted longer when they discovered a shortcoming in their performance, whereas North Americans persisted longer when they discovered a strength (Heine et al., 2001). Self-criticism in Japan thus appears to serve a similar purpose to self-enhancement in North America: it enables people to perform at their best.

Much convergent evidence thus indicates that tendencies to possess, enhance, and maintain positive self-views are less evident among Japanese than among North Americans. These differences are also evident for those aspects of their selves that Japanese view as most important to them (Heine et al., 2001; Heine & Lehman, 1999; Heine & Renshaw, 2002; but see Ito, 1999, for evidence of the opposite pattern among Japanese), and in studies conducted with hidden or behavioral measures (see Heine et al., 1999, for a review), and thus cannot be interpreted as solely due to cultural differences in self-presentation norms. Motivations to maintain a positive self-view, as it is typically operationalized in the literature, are less evident among Japanese compared with North Americans (although Japanese surely have other important self-relevant motivations, such as a desire to maintain face; Heine et al., 1999).

To the extent that habitual positive evaluations of the self (i.e., self-esteem) are fostered by cultural experiences that emphasize the independence and autonomy of the individual, time spent in a Western cultural environment should be associated with exposure to a dialogue that stresses the value of possessing positive self-views. That is, with exposure to the cultural values, scripts, practices, customs, and institutions that are hypothesized to encourage self-enhancement (see Heine et al., 1999, for a review) it would seem that individuals would respond to these cultural meanings and become sensitive to detecting positive features within themselves. In short, exposure to Western culture should be associated with positive self-views.

The process of acculturation provides us with a unique window through which to investigate such effects of culture. When an individual moves to a new culture, he or she will likely undergo some kind of "psychological acculturation" (Graves, 1967), learning how to interact within his or her new cultural environment. With increasing time spent in the host culture, it is likely that the host culture's influence on the individual's self-concept and ways of thinking will also increase. Experiences in a new cultural environment may thus lead individuals to adopt ways of viewing themselves that are normative within the host cultural environment. One way of investigating the relation between self-esteem and Western cultural values is to analyze acculturating individuals' self-esteem scores at various points in the acculturation process.

## STUDY 1

### Method and Results

We sought to investigate whether there are differences in self-esteem among individuals who differ in their exposure to Western culture. We included the Rosenberg Self-Esteem Scale (Rosenberg, 1965) in a large number of questionnaire studies that were conducted with students from universities in Vancouver, Canada, and in a variety of cities in Japan. We created a large file that included participants' self-esteem responses and some demographic variables (a total of over 5,000 participants). The participants came from the University of British Columbia and Simon Fraser University in Canada, and from Aichi Gakuin, Doshisha University, Kansai Gaikokugo University, Kyoto University, Nagasaki University, Nara University, Ritsumeikan University, and Toyama University in Japan. Japanese participants completed the scale in Japanese and Canadian participants completed the scale in English. The original Rosenberg Scale was translated into Japanese, back-translated into English, and any discrepancies between the two versions were discussed among three translators.

As a large proportion of university students in the two Canadian universities are of Asian descent, from a variety of different countries with the most common ethnic heritage being Chinese (self-criticism is also evident among Chinese; e.g., Yik, Bond, & Paulhus, 1998), and as a significant number of the Japanese students had spent time in a Western country, we were able to analyze the data with respect to how much time participants had been exposed to Western culture.[2] A continuum of increasing exposure to Western culture was created by classifying participants into the following groups:

1. Japanese who had never been outside of Japan ($n$ = 1657).
2. Japanese who had spent some time in a Western country ($n$ = 577).
3. Recent Asian immigrants to Canada ($n$ = 244).
4. Long-term Asian immigrants to Canada ($n$ = 289).
5. Second-generation Asian Canadians ($n$ = 431).
6. Third-generation Asian Canadians ($n$ = 38).
7. European Canadians ($n$ = 1466).

A total of 388 participants from a variety of ethnic backgrounds did not fit any of these categories and were not included in the analyses.

We conducted a culture by sex analysis of variance (ANOVA) on self-esteem for the entire sample. A pronounced difference for culture emerged, $F(6, 4690) = 244.86$, $p < .001$, which is depicted in Fig. 13.1. Replicating past research, European Canadians scored higher on self-esteem than did Japanese (they scored higher on 9 of the 10 items; the item "I certainly feel useless at times" showed no cultural difference). The other cultural groups formed a remarkably monotonically increasing pattern between these two extremes. Self-esteem rose among people of Asian descent with exposure to Western culture to the point that third-generation Asian Canadians had self-esteem scores that approximated those of European Canadians. The more exposure individuals had to cultural situations, scripts, and institutions associated with higher self-esteem, the more positively they viewed themselves. The small size of the third-generation Asian Canadian sample warrants caution in interpreting the results, but if we assume it is reliable, this suggests that three generations is enough for people of Asian descent to fully acculturate to Canadian culture in terms of their self-esteem.[3]

---

[2]We reported the results of a similar analysis in Heine et al. (1999); however, we have since collected more data than is included in the present analyses.

[3]Surprisingly, there was no main effect for sex despite the massive size of this sample, $F(1, 4690) = 1.83$, *ns*. However, the results are qualified by a small culture by sex interaction, $F(6, 4690) = 4.24$, $p < .001$. Males exhibited nominally higher self-esteem scores than females in the "Been Abroad Japanese," "Long-Term Asian Canadian," "Second-Generation Asian Canadian," and "European Canadian" samples, but females had nominally higher self-esteem scores than males in the "Never Been Abroad Japanese," "Recent Asian Canadians," and "Third-Generation Asian Canadian" samples. We are at a loss for making sense of this pattern of sex differences.

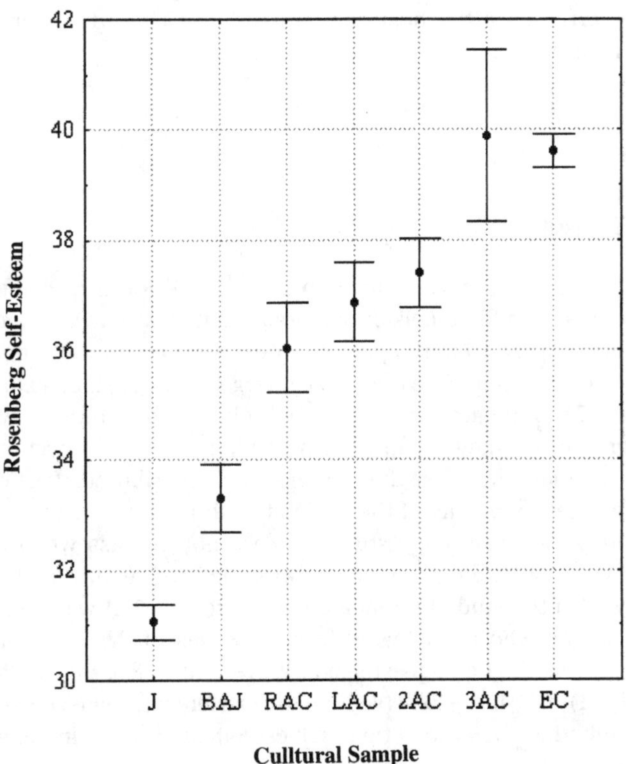


J – Japanese who have never been abroad
BAJ – "Been Abroad Japanese" (i.e., they have spent time in a Western country).
RAC – "Recent Asian-Canadians" (i.e., they have moved to Canada within the past 7 years)
LAC – "Long-Term Asian-Canadians" (i.e., they have moved to Canada more than 7 years ago)
2AC – Second-generation Asian-Canadians
3AC – Third-generation Asian-Canadians
EC – European-Canadians

FIG. 13.1. Cross-sectional comparisons of self-esteem.

Cross-sectional studies such as this have some interpretative limitations. For example, there may be cohort effects distinguishing the different cultural groups in terms of a number of demographic variables, such as their reasons for migrating to Canada, their past education history, or their performance at school, which may relate to their self-esteem scores. We felt it was imperative to replicate this basic finding employing a controlled longitudinal design in order to avoid these interpretive ambiguities. Three separate longitudinal studies were conducted in which individuals' self-esteem was measured at two points in time: (a) before leaving one's home culture (or just after arriving in the host culture) and (b) 7 months after having lived in the host culture.

## STUDY 2A

### Method and Results

Two days after arriving in Vancouver to begin an 8-month exchange program, 84 students from Ritsumeikan University (out of 99 who were enrolled in the program) agreed to participate in a questionnaire study. One of the measures in the questionnaire was Rosenberg's (1965) Self-Esteem Scale. Approximately 7 months later, in one of their classes, the students were invited to attend an evening lecture during which a second questionnaire, which also included the Rosenberg Scale, was distributed. Participants completed Japanese versions of the scale at both points in time.

Unfortunately, because many students were not in class when the announcement was made, only 35 students attended the lecture and participated in Wave 2 of the study.[4] A repeated-measures ANOVA was conducted on the 35 students who participated in both waves of the questionnaire. Participants showed higher self-esteem at Wave 2, $M = 38.5$, than at Wave 1, $M = 36.7$; $F(1, 33) = 4.04$, $p = .052$ (see Fig. 13.2). Hence, Japanese exchange students exhibited an *increase* in their self-esteem after living in Canada for 7 months.

## STUDY 2B

A potential confound of Study 2a is that acculturation experiences per se might have led to the self-esteem increases of the Japanese sample. Perhaps anyone who moves to a new cultural environment, regardless of their cultural background or destination, experiences increases in self-esteem due to their expanding horizons and feelings of competence associated with being able to survive in a foreign environment. To the extent that it is

[4]The considerable attrition of this sample necessitates caution in interpreting the results. In an effort to determine the impact of the sample's attrition on the results, we conducted an analysis of variance (ANOVA) comparing the self-esteem scores at Wave 1 of those who only completed the questionnaire at Wave 1 and those who completed them for both waves. The two groups did not differ in their self-esteem at Wave 1, $F < 1$, suggesting that participation in the second lecture is not related to the student's initial level of self-esteem. Moreover, it is difficult to conceive how those who came to the lecture should differ from those who did not in the extent of their self-esteem change. This suggests that the attrition of the sample did not unduly influence our measurement of self-esteem change across waves 1 and 2.

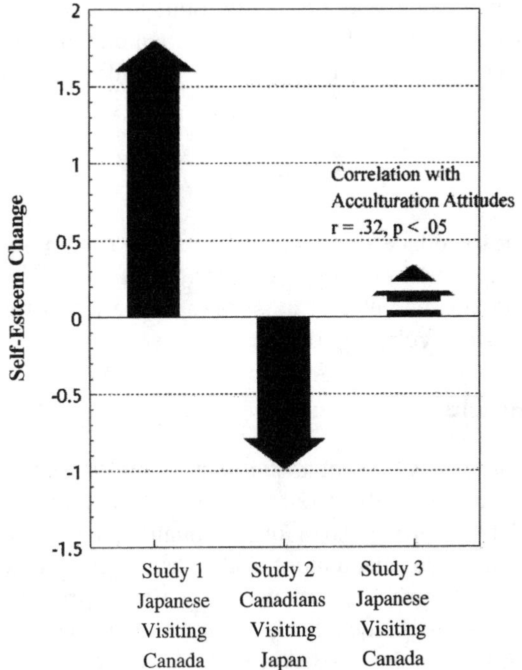


FIG. 13.2. Longitudinal comparisons of self-esteem.

experiences in North American culture that are associated with self-enhancement (or experiences in Japanese culture that are associated with self-criticism; Heine et al., 1999; Kitayama et al., 1997), and not acculturation experiences per se, we should expect to see self-esteem *decreases* among North Americans moving to Japan. Study 2b investigated this possibility.

## Method and Results

Shortly before leaving Canada, 73 Canadian English teachers who were heading to Japan to participate in the Japan Exchange and Teaching (JET) program completed a questionnaire packet including Rosenberg's Self-Esteem Scale. Seven months later the teachers were mailed a second questionnaire that also included the Rosenberg Scale. Sixty-nine of the teachers completed the second wave of the study. A repeated-measures ANOVA reveals that the teachers' self-esteem was lower at Wave 2, $M = 42.16$, than at Wave 1, $M = 43.15$; $F(1, 67) = 4.93$, $p < .03$. Canadian English teachers thus displayed a *decrease* in their self-esteem after living in Japan for 7 months. Acculturation experiences per se are not associated with increasing levels of self-esteem. Canadians who were removed from a cultural environment that bolsters self-esteem and placed in an environment characterized by various practices associated with self-criticism (e.g., Heine et al., 1999; Lewis, 1995) appeared to become more self-critical after 7 months.

## STUDY 2C

Study 2c sought to replicate the self-esteem increase among Japanese students in Study 2a, and to explore whether acculturation attitudes moderated the relation between mere exposure to Western culture and the internalization of Western cultural norms.

### Method and Results

One month prior to leaving Japan, 82 Ritsumeikan University students (out of 93 who were enrolled in the program) who were heading to Vancouver as exchange students were given a questionnaire packet including Rosenberg's Self-Esteem Scale. Seven months after arriving in Canada, 74 students completed a second questionnaire as part of a class project, which also included Rosenberg's Self-Esteem Scale as well as John Berry and colleagues' Acculturation Attitudes Scale (Berry, Kim, Power, Young, & Bujaki, 1989), which was modified specifically for Japanese exchange students coming to Canada (Davis, 1995). This scale assesses the positivity of students' attitudes towards Canada and Japan, and this scale was included to investigate whether individual differences in attitudes towards Canada relate to self-esteem change.

A repeated measures ANOVA revealed that students' self-esteem scores were nominally, although not significantly, higher at Wave 2 ($M = 34.5$) than at Wave 1 ($M = 34.2$; $F < 1$). Hence, we failed to replicate the significant increase in self-esteem among Japanese exchange students living in Canada that was demonstrated in Study 1.

An overall composite of subjects' acculturation attitudes was formed by summing all the items expressing positive attitudes towards Canada (Assimilation and Integration subscales) and subtracting the items expressing negative attitudes towards Canada (Separation and Marginal subscales). This total value reflects how positive students' attitudes were towards Canadian culture, and is a proxy for how much students made efforts to "become Canadian" while on the exchange program. This total acculturation score was then correlated with participants' *self-esteem change* scores. This analysis revealed a positive relation between how positive participants' attitudes were toward Canadian lifestyles and how much their self-esteem increased, $r = .32$, $p < .01$. That is, the more participants were open to Canadian culture (and theoretically the more they were influenced by Canadian cultural values), the more their self-esteem increased during their stay in Canada. This provides another source of evidence to suggest that the self-concepts of those who were participating in Canadian culture were influenced by the cultural environment.

## GENERAL DISCUSSION

The investigation of the ways in which culture affects the self-concept is fraught with methodological obstacles. For example, there are no appropriate control groups of "cultureless" humans with which to compare the different varieties of "cultured" ones, there are no direct measures of cultural grammars, and people cannot be randomly assigned to different cultural environments. One quasi-experimental approach, however, which rarely has been pursued, investigates changes in the self-concept that occur during sojourns to new cultures.

We investigated acculturative effects on an evaluative component of the self-concept: global self-esteem. Much research has maintained that self-esteem, as it has traditionally been operationalized within Western psychology, is a construct that is enhanced by participation in North American culture (e.g., Heine, in press; Heine et al., 1999; Kitayama et al., 1997; Markus & Kitayama, 1991). The results of the present studies provide further evidence that self-esteem is intimately related with Western cultural values. Study 1 revealed a clear relation between self-esteem and exposure to North American culture in a large-scale cross-sectional study. Study 2a demonstrated that time spent in Canada led to an increase in self-esteem for Japanese students, whereas Study 2b revealed that time spent in Japan led to a decrease in self-esteem for Canadians. Exposure to new cultural environments seems to have been associated with movement in sojourners' self-esteem towards levels that are normative of their host cultures. Study 2c failed to replicate the significant self-esteem increase found in Study 2a, but demonstrated that those Japanese most receptive to Canadian cultural values displayed a greater increase in self-esteem than those who resisted the host culture. This relation is also consistent with the notion that greater exposure to Western culture leads to higher self-esteem. Taken together, these four studies are suggestive of a significant Western cultural component in the construct of self-esteem. One interpretation of these results, consistent with past research with biculturals (e.g., Hong et al., 2000), is that the longer one is in a culture the more likely it is that the metaschema of thoughts and feelings that is activated in them is associated with the host culture.

Cultural differences in self-esteem between Japanese and North Americans appear to yield some of the largest effect sizes between cultures of any of the aspects of the self-concept investigated thus far (the effect size in

Study 1 between the European Canadians and Japanese who had never been abroad was 1.35), and there is much theoretical reasoning consistent with these cultural differences (e.g., Heine, in press; Heine et al., 2001; Heine et al., 1999; Kitayama et al., 1997; Markus & Kitayama, 1991). In these respects, self-esteem is an especially useful tool for identifying acculturative effects on the self-concept. However, self-esteem is likely also confounded by experiences of success and failure that are part and parcel of the acculturation experience, and thus the self-esteem assessments obtained here are unlikely to be pure measures of acculturation. Future research investigating other aspects of the self-concept known to be influenced by culture, such as tendencies to make situational attributions (Hong et al., 2000), perceptions of agency (Morling, Kitayama, & Miyamoto, in press), self-improving motivations (Heine et al., 2001) or feelings of independence (Singelis, 1994) could move the field forward.

In the present studies we compared mean scores on subjective Likert scale attitude measures across cultural groups. Such comparisons can potentially be undermined by reference-group effects (Heine et al., 2002). That is, people evaluate themselves by implicitly comparing themselves to those around them. What makes this problematic for cross-cultural comparisons is that people from different cultures are comparing themselves to different referents (Biernat & Manis, 1994; Heine et al., 2002; Heine et al., 2001; Peng et al., 1997). However, that we found evidence for Japanese self-esteem *increasing* when surrounded by higher self-esteem Canadians, and for Canadian self-esteem *decreasing* when surrounded by lower self-esteem Japanese is not consistent with the notion that the findings are due to the different reference groups of the samples.

Much past research on acculturation has assumed that the lower self-esteem scores among sojourners and immigrants reflects the psychological distress inherent in difficulties in the acculturation experience (e.g., Furnham & Bochner, 1986; Taft, 1977). Although it is possible that negative experiences associated with "culture shock" lead to lower self-esteem, the present findings suggest that this is not the best explanation to account for the relatively low self-esteem of immigrating Asians. Japanese have the lowest self-esteem scores *before* they have left their country, and the self-esteem scores of Asian immigrants in North America are only low relative to those of European-descent North Americans or second- and third-generation Asian-descent North Americans. In comparison to their compatriots in their home cultures, the self-esteem scores of Asian sojourners and immigrants are relatively high.

That we observed changes in self-esteem in sojourns as brief as 7 months provides testimony to the influences culture has on the self-concept. Moreover, that these differences were found with young adults suggests that people continue to seek cultural meaning systems even after they have been socialized in a different culture. To the extent that there is a sensitive period for acquiring a cultural meaning system before puberty (e.g., Minoura, 1992), we assume that the changes in self-esteem observed in the present studies would have been larger had we conducted the study with prepubescent children. The clearest evidence of acculturative effects on the self-concept should be observable among children, whose more plastic minds are still adjusting to the cultural meanings with which they interact.

## MOVE THE BODY, CHANGE THE CULTURE?

The acculturating individual provides one perspective by which to view the mutual constitution of self and culture. When individuals participate in a novel cultural environment, their self-concept appears to change accordingly. The self is shaped by cultural experiences.

However, cultural influences on the self-concept represent only one side of the relations between self and culture hypothesized by cultural psychologists (e.g., Markus & Kitayama, 1991; Shweder, 1990). Cultures arise from the interaction of the individual selves that make them up. As new individuals move into a culture, changing the composition of the culture's membership, it follows that the culture should change as well. Cultures are shaped by individual selves. How are cultures affected by the incorporation of new members from different cultural backgrounds?

The impact of immigrating selves on a culture would appear to hinge on the model of cultural integration that is dominant. It seems that there are at least two models by which cultures incorporate new members. One potential model is sometimes referred to as a "melting pot" (e.g., Sidanius, Feschbach, Levin, & Pratto, 1997). New cultural members assimilate themselves to fit into a single, dominant cultural framework, regardless of the individuals' original cultural backgrounds. The incongruities of the individual's heritage culture and the host culture are resolved by the individuals "melting" away the cultural idiosyncracies from their heritage culture. In this model, it would appear that the host culture does little to accommodate the new selves. The adjustment largely occurs in the immigrants' selves, whereas the dominant culture would continue to persist, largely unchanged.

That aspects of cultures often are relatively stable, despite the great influx of new members, provides support for the notion that sometimes acculturating individuals are assimilating into, rather than changing, the cultures. For example, Vandello and Cohen (chap. 12, this volume) provide compelling evidence that a culture of honor persists in the Southern United States, despite the fact that the original basis of this aspect of the culture (a herding-based economy) is no longer dominant. It appears that people who migrate to the U.S. South, whether they are from other states or other countries, are socialized to believe that defending one's honor is an important way to earn others' respect. Even if every individual member of the culture is ultimately replaced by subsequent individuals who join the culture either by birth or migration, each of the new individuals must adjust to the prevailing cultural worldview and adopt thoughts and behaviors that are associated with perceived greater rewards in that worldview. Such cultural persistence would seem to be more prevalent in cultures in which a clear dominant model is identifiable, tangible, and desirable to the acculturating individuals.

A second way by which cultures integrate new members can be described as an "ethnic pluralism" model, which is sometimes referred to as a "salad bowl" (e.g., Sidanius et al., 1997). This model refers to the coexistence of a number of ethnic subgroups within a society, each preserving their own distinctive cultural heritages. Although acculturating individuals tend to learn the ways of the host culture, they do not shed their cultural backgrounds. In such a model, a dominant cultural framework would appear to be somewhat weak and intangible; the culture consists of the collective sum of the individual subcultural elements.

For individuals acculturating into an ethnically pluralistic culture characterized, in contrast to those acculturating into a melting pot, the impact of the migration would appear to be considerably greater on the culture. To the extent that a dominant cultural model is not as tangible or stable in pluralistic societies, there would appear to be less pressure for individuals to assimilate. Rather, the host culture itself must change to accommodate these new individuals. Ethnically pluralistic societies would appear to have less persistence of cultural ways, as the influx of people with different cultural backgrounds would change the perception of what thoughts and behaviors are normative, or are associated with benefits and costs.

In the concrete example of self-esteem change among acculturating individuals, it would seem that self-esteem change should be more pronounced to the extent that a melting pot model is in operation. Low self-esteem individuals moving to a culture characterized by higher self-esteem, for example, would tend to learn a culturally-congruent form of self, and their self-esteem would subsequently increase to that of the cultural norm, leaving the cultures' perceived norm for largely intact. In contrast, low self-esteem individuals acculturating into an ethnically pluralistic society would likely assimilate less, as their self-concept is not divergent from their subculture's dominant view of self. Ethnically pluralistic societies should be more likely to preserve the self-concept of immigrating individuals, and the overarching culture would adjust in response to the change in the proportions of the various subcultures.

## CONCLUSION

In this age of globalization, a growing number of bodies are moving back and forth across cultural boundaries. Such migrations are likely to leave their tracks both on the selves of the individuals that are acculturating, and on the cultures that are exchanging the selves. Individual selves need to assimilate to new cultural environments, and cultures need to accommodate the new selves. The effects of this self-concept assimilation and cultural accommodation are only beginning to be examined. A number of questions have appeared in the literature, but thus far scant research has explored them. Is there a sensitive period for the acquisition of a cultural meaning system (e.g., Minoura, 1992) as there appears to be with language acquisition (e.g., Newport, 1991)? Do multicultural individuals consistently maintain multiple selves (e.g., Hong et al., 2000), or is there an inevitable blending at some point? Do all aspects of the self-concept assimilate in the same ways that we observed in the acculturation of self-esteem? Questions regarding how cultures accommodate new members and new ideas are legion, and this volume sets the stage for much future work.

Finding the culture in the self is a pursuit compromised by many methodological challenges. Conventional cross-cultural and cultural psychological methodologies each have their own strengths and weaknesses, and we suggest that research on acculturative effects on the self-concept provides another tool with which to identify the cultural components of human nature. To the extent that evidence from these different approaches converges, the cultural foundation of the self will come into fuller view.

## REFERENCES

Anderson, E. (1999). *Code of the street: Decency, violence, and the moral life of the inner city.* New York: Norton.

Bachnik, J. M., & Quinn, C. J. Jr. (1994). *Situated meaning: Inside and outside in Japanese self, society, and language.* Princeton, NJ: Princeton University Press.

Baumeister, R. F., & Jones, E. E. (1978). When self-presentation is constrained by the target's knowledge: Consistency and compensation. *Journal of Personality and Social Psychology, 36,* 608–618.

Baumeister, R. F., Tice, D. M., & Hutton, D. G. (1989). Self-presentational motivations and personality differences in self-esteem. *Journal of Personality, 57,* 547–579.

Bellah, R. N., Madsen, R., Sullivan, W. M., Swindler, A., & Tipton, S. M. (1985). *Habits of the heart: Individualism and commitment in American life.* Berkeley: University of California Press.

Berry, J. W., & Kim, U. (1988). Acculturation and mental health. In P. R. Dasen, J. W. Berry, and N. Sartorius (Eds.), *Health and cross-cultural psychology: Toward applications* (pp. 207–236). Newbury Park, CA: Sage.

Berry, J. W., Kim, U., Power, S., Young, M., & Bujaki, M. (1989). Acculturation attitudes in plural societies. *Applied Psychology: An International Review, 38,* 185–206.

Biernat, M., & Manis, M. (1994). Shifting standards and stereotype-based judgments. *Journal of Personality and Social Psychology, 66*, 5–20.

Bond, M. H., & Cheung, T. (1983). College students spontaneous self-concept. *Journal of Cross-Cultural Psychology, 14*, 153–171.

Boyd, R., & Silk, J. B. (1997). *How humans evolved.* New York: Norton.

Chomsky, N. A. (1982). *The generative enterprise: A discussion with Riny Huybregts and Henk van Riemsdijk.* Dordrecht: Foris.

Church, A. T. (1982). Sojourner adjustment. *Psychological Bulletin, 91*, 540–572.

Cross, S. E. (1992, June). *Cultural adaptation and self: Construal of self, stress, and coping.* Paper presented at the Conference on Emotion and Culture, Eugene, OR.

Cross, S. E., Liao, M., & Josephs, R. (1992, August). *A cross-cultural test of the self-evaluation maintenance model.* Paper presented at the annual convention of the American Psychological Association, Washington, DC.

Curtiss, S. (1977). *Genie: A psycholinguistic study of a modern-day "wild-child."* New York: Academic Press.

Davis, C. G. (1995). *Analyses of the Acculturation Attitudes Scale adapted for Japanese exchange students in Canada.* Unpublished manuscript, St. Francis Xavier University, Antigonish, NS.

Diener, E., & Diener, M. (1995). Cross-cultural correlates of life satisfaction and self-esteem. *Journal of Personality and Social Psychology, 68*, 653–663.

Dornic, S. (1985). Immigrants' language and stress. In L. H. Ekstrand (Ed.), *Ethnic minorities and immigrants in a cross-cultural perspective* (pp. 149–157). Lisse, the Netherlands: Swets & Zeitlinger.

DuBois, W. E. B. (1989). *The souls of Black folk.* New York: Penguin. (Original work published 1903)

Feldman, S. S., Mont-Reynaud, R., & Rosenthal, D. A. (1992). When East moves West: The acculturation of values of Chinese adolescents in the U.S. and Australia. *Journal of Research on Adolescence, 2*, 147–173.

Furnham, A., & Bochner, S. (1986). *Culture shock.* London: Methren.

Geertz, C. (1973). *The interpretation of cultures.* New York: Basic Books.

Geertz, C. (1983). "From the native's point of view": On the nature of anthropological understanding. In *Local knowledge: Further essays in interpretative anthropology* (pp. 55–70). New York: Basic Books. (Original work published 1974)

Graves, T. D. (1967). Psychological acculturation in a tri-ethnic community. *Southwestern Journal of Anthropology, 23*, 337–350.

Greenfield, P. M. (1997). Culture as process: Empirical methods for cultural psychology. In J. W. Berry, Y. H. Poortinga, & J. Pandey (Eds.), *Handbook of Cross-Cultural Psychology* (Vol. 1, pp. 301–346). Boston: Allyn & Bacon.

Greenwald, A. G. (1980). The totalitarian ego: Fabrication and revision of personal history. *American Psychologist, 35*, 603–618.

Hamaguchi, E. (1985). A contextual model of the Japanese: Toward a methodological innovation in Japan studies. *Journal of Japanese Studies, 11*, 289–321.

Heine, S. J. (2001). Self as cultural product: An examination of East Asian and North American selves. *Journal of Personality, 69*, 881–906.

Heine, S. J. (2002). *Cultural differences in motivated reasoning biases.* Unpublished data, University of British Columbia.

Heine, S. J. (in press). An exploration of cultural variation in self-enhancing and self-improving motivations. *Nebraska Symposium of Motivation.*

Heine, S. J., Kitayama, S., & Lehman, D. R. (2001). Cultural differences in self-evaluation: Japanese readily accept negative self-relevant information. *Journal of Cross-Cultural Psychology, 32*, 434–443.

Heine, S. J., Kitayama, S., Lehman, D. R., Takata, T., Ide, E., Leung, C., & Matsumoto, H. (2001). Divergent consequences of success and failure in Japan and North America: An investigation of self-improving motivations and malleable selves. *Journal of Personality and Social Psychology, 81*, 599–615.

Heine, S. J., & Lehman, D. R. (1995). Cultural variation in unrealistic optimism: Does the West feel more invulnerable than the East? *Journal of Personality and Social Psychology, 68*, 595–607.

Heine, S. J., & Lehman, D. R. (1997a). The cultural construction of self-enhancement: An examination of group-serving biases. *Journal of Personality and Social Psychology, 72*, 1268–1283.

Heine, S. J., & Lehman, D. R. (1997b). Culture, dissonance, and self-affirmation. *Personality and Social Psychology Bulletin, 23*, 389–400.

Heine, S. J., & Lehman, D. R. (1999). Culture, self-discrepancies, and self-satisfaction. *Personality and Social Psychology Bulletin, 25*, 915–925.

Heine, S. J., Lehman, D. R., Markus, H. R., & Kitayama, S. (1999). Is there a universal need for positive self-regard? *Psychological Review, 106*, 766–794.

Heine, S. J., Lehman, D. R., Peng, K., & Greenholtz, J. (2002). What's wrong with cross-cultural comparisons of subjective Likert scales? The reference-group effect. *Journal of Personality and Social Psychology, 82*, 903–918.

Heine, S. J., & Renshaw, K. (2002). Interjudge agreement, self-enhancement, and liking: Cross-cultural divergences. *Personality and Social Psychology Bulletin, 28*, 442–451.

Heine, S. J., Takata, T., & Lehman, D. R. (2000). Beyond self-presentation: Evidence for self-criticism among Japanese. *Personality and Social Psychology Bulletin, 26*, 71–78.

Hofstede, G. (1980). *Culture's consequences: International differences in work-related values.* Beverly Hills, CA: Sage.

Hong, Y., Morris, M. W., Chiu, C., & Benet-Martinez, V. (2000). Multicultural minds: A dynamic constructivist approach to culture and cognition. *American Psychologist, 55*, 705–720.

Hurford, J. R. (1991). The evolution of the critical period for language acquisition. *Cognition, 40*, 159–201.

Ito, T. (1999). Self-enhancement tendency and other evaluations: An examination of "better-than-average effect" [in Japanese]. *Japanese Journal of Psychology, 70*, 367–374.

Iyengar, S. S., Lepper, M. R., & Ross, L. (1999). Independence from whom? Interdependence with whom? Cultural perspectives on ingroups versus outgroups. In D. Miller & D. Prentice (Eds.), *Cultural divides: Understanding and overcoming group conflict* (pp. 273–301). New York: Sage.

Johnson, J., & Newport, E. L. (1989). Critical period effects in second language learning: The influence of maturational state on the acquisition of English as a second language. *Cognitive Psychology, 21*, 60–99.

Kashiwagi, K. (1986). Personality development of adolescents. In H. Stevenson, H. Azuma, & K. Hakuta (Eds.), *Child development and education in Japan* (pp. 167–185). New York: Freeman.

Kitayama, S., Markus, H. R., Matsumoto, H., & Norasakkunkit, V. (1997). Individual and collective processes in the construction of the self: Self-enhancement in the United States and self-criticism in Japan. *Journal of Personality and Social Psychology, 72*, 1245–1267.

Kitayama, S., Takagi, H., & Matsumoto, H. (1995). Causal attribution of success and failure: Cultural psychology of the Japanese self. *Japanese Psychological Review, 38*, 247–280. (In Japanese).

Kiuchi, A. (1996). Independent and interdependent construals of the self: Cultural influences and relations to personality traits [in Japanese]. *Japanese Journal of Psychology, 67*, 308–313.

Kunda, Z. (1990). The case for motivated reasoning. *Psychological Bulletin, 108*, 480–498.

LaFromboise, T., Coleman, H. L. K., & Gerton, J. (1993). Psychological impact of biculturalism: Evidence and theory. *Psychological Bulletin, 114*, 395–412.

Lebra, T. S. (1976). *Japanese patterns of behavior.* Honolulu: University of Hawaii Press.

Lee, A. Y., Aaker, J. L., & Gardner, W. L. (2000). The pleasures and pains of distinct self-construals: The role of interdependence in regulatory focus. *Journal of Personality and Social Psychology, 78*, 1122–1134.

Lenneberg, E. H. (1967). *Biological foundations of language.* New York: Wiley.

Lewis, C. C. (1995). *Educating hearts and minds.* New York: Cambridge University Press.

Lipset, S. M. (1996). *American exceptionalism: A double-edged sword.* New York: W. W. Norton & Company.

Mandel, N. (2000). *Priming, shifting selves, and decision making: The role of personal meaning systems in consumer choice.* Unpublished doctoral dissertation, University of Pennsylvania.

Mandelbaum, D. G. (1951). *Selected writings of Edward Sapir in language, culture, and personality.* Berkeley: University of California Press.

Markus, H. R., & Kitayama, S. (1991). Culture and the self: Implications for cognition, emotion, and motivation. *Psychological Review, 98*, 224–253.

Markus, H. R., Mullally, P., & Kitayama, S. (1997). Selfways: Diversity in modes of cultural participation. In U. Neisser & D. Jopling (Eds.), *The conceptual self in context: Culture, experience, self-understanding* (pp. 13–61). Cambridge: Cambridge University Press.

Matsumoto, D. (1999). Culture and self: An empirical assessment of Markus and Kitayama's theory of independent and interdependent self-construal. *Asian Journal of Social Psychology, 2*, 289–310.

Meijer, Z., Heine, S. J., & Yamagami, M. (1999, August). *Remember those good old days? Culture, self-discrepancies, and biographical memory.* Symposium presentation at the 3rd Conference of the Asian Association of Social Psychology, Taipei, Taiwan.

Miller, D. T., & Ross, M. (1975). Self-serving biases in the attribution of causality: Fact or fiction? *Psychological Bulletin, 82*, 213–225.

Miller, J. G. (1999). Cultural psychology: Implications for basic psychological theory. *Psychological Science, 10*, 85–91.

Miller, J. G., & Bersoff, D. M. (1992). Culture and moral judgment: How are conflicts between justice and interpersonal responsibilities resolved? *Journal of Personality and Social Psychology, 62*, 541–554.

Minoura, Y. (1992). A sensitive period for the incorporation of a cultural meaning system: A study of Japanese children growing up in the United States. *Ethos, 20*, 304–339.

Morling, B., Kitayama, S., & Miyamoto, Y. (2002). Cultural practices emphasize influence in the U.S. and adjustment in Japan. *Personality and Social Psychology Bulletin, 28*, 311–323.

Newport, E. L. (1991). Contrasting concepts of the critical period for language. In S. Carey & R. Gelman, (Eds.), *The epigenesis of mind: Essays on biology and cognition. The Jean Piaget Symposium series* (pp. 111–130). Hillsdale, NJ: Lawrence Erlbaum Associates.

Nisbett, R. E., & Cohen, D. (1996). *Culture of honor: The psychology of violence in the south.* Boulder, CO: Westview Press.

Nisbett, R. E., Peng, K., Choi, I., & Norenzayan, A. (2001). Culture and systems of thought: Holistic vs. analytic cognition. *Psychological Review, 108*, 291–310.

Norenzayan, A., Choi, I., & Nisbett, R. E. (2002). Eastern and Western folk psychology and the prediction of behavior. *Personality and Social Psychology Bulletin, 28*, 109–120.

Pasquali, E. A. (1985). The impact of acculturation on the eating habits of elderly immigrants: A Cuban example. *Journal of Nutrition for the Elderly, 5*, 27–36.

Peng, K., Nisbett, R. E., & Wong, N. Y. C. (1997). Validity problems comparing values across cultures and possible solutions. *Psychological Methods, 2*, 329–344.

Rosenberg, M. (1965). *Society and the adolescent self-image.* Princeton, NJ: Princeton University Press.

Sampson, E. E. (1977). Psychology and the American Ideal. *Journal of Personality and Social Psychology, 35*, 767–782.

Schwartz, S. H., & Bilsky, W. (1990). Toward a theory of the universal content and structure of values: Extensions and cross-cultural replications. *Journal of Personality and Social Psychology, 58*, 878–891.

Schwarzer, R., Bowler, R., & Rauch, S. (1985). Psychological indicators of acculturation: Self-esteem, racial tension and inter-ethnic contact. In L. Ekstrand (Ed.), *Ethnic minorities and immigrants in a cross-cultural perspective* (pp. 211–229). Lisse, the Netherlands: Swets & Zeitlinger.

Shweder, R. A. (1990). Cultural psychology: What is it? In J. W. Stigler, R. A. Shweder, & G. Herdt (Eds.), *Cultural psychology: Essays on comparative human development* (pp. 1–43). Cambridge: Cambridge University Press.

Shweder, R. A., Goodnow, J., Hatano, G., LeVine, R. A., Markus, H., & Miller, P. (1998). The cultural psychology of development: One mind, many mentalities. In W. Damon & R. M. Lerner (Eds.), *Handbook of child psychology* (Vol. 1, pp. 865–937). New York: John Wiley and Sons.

Sidanius, J., Feshbach, S., Levin, S., & Pratto, F. (1997). The interface between ethnic and national attachment: Ethnic pluralism or ethnic dominance. *Public Opinion Quarterly, 61*, 102–133.

Singelis, T. M. (1994). The measurement of independent and interdependent self-construals. *Personality and Social Psychology Bulletin, 20*, 580–591.

Singelis, T. M., Bond, M. H., Lai, S. Y., & Sharkey, W. F. (1999). Unpackaging culture's influence on self-esteem and embarrassability: The role of self-construals. *Journal of Cross-Cultural Psychology, 30*, 315–331.

Singleton, D. (1989). *Language acquisition: The age factor.* Clevedon, UK: Multilingual Matters.

Steele, C. M. (1988). The psychology of self-affirmation: Sustaining the integrity of the self. In L. Berkowitz (Ed.), *Advances in experimental social psychology* (Vol. 21, pp. 261–302). San Diego, CA: Academic Press.

Su, S. K., Chiu, C.-Y., Hong, Y.-Y., Leung, K., Peng, K., & Morris, M. W. (1999). Self organization and social organization: American and Chinese constructions. In T. R. Tyler, R. Kramer, & O. John (Eds.), *The psychology of the social self* (pp. 193–222). Mahwah, NJ: Lawrence Erlbaum Associates.

Taft, R. (1977). Coping with unfamiliar cultures. In N. Warren (Ed.), *Studies in cross-cultural psychology* (Vol. 1, pp. 121–153). San Diego, CA: Academic Press.

Takano, Y., & Osaka, E. (1999). An unsupported common view: Comparing Japan and the U.S. on individualism/collectivism. *Asian Journal of Social Psychology, 2*, 311–341.

Taylor, S. E., & Brown, J. D. (1988). Illusion and well-being: A social psychological perspective on mental health. *Psychological Bulletin, 103*, 193–210.

Tesser, A. (1988). Toward a self-evaluation maintenance model of social behavior. In L. Berkowitz (Ed.), *Advances in experimental social psychology* (Vol. 21, pp. 181–227). San Diego, CA: Academic Press.

Tice, D. M. (1991). Esteem protection or enhancement? Self-handicapping motives and attributions differ by trait self-esteem. *Journal of Personality and Social Psychology, 60*, 711–725.

Tomasello, M. (2001). Cultural transmission: A view from chimpanzees and human infants. *Journal of Cross-Cultural Psychology, 32*, 135–146.

Tomasello, M., Kruger, A. C., & Ratner, H. H. (1993). Cultural learning. *Behavioral and Brain Sciences, 16*, 495–552.

Trafimow, D., Triandis, H. C., & Goto, S. G. (1991). Some tests of the distinction between the private self and the collective self. *Journal of Personality and Social Psychology, 60*, 649–655.

Triandis, H. C. (1989). Cross-cultural studies of individualism and collectivism. *Nebraska Symposium of Motivation, 37*, 41–133.

Wills, T. A. (1981). Downward comparison principles in social psychology. *Psychological Bulletin, 90*, 245–271.

Yamaguchi, S. (1994). Collectivism among the Japanese: A perspective from the self. In U. Kim, H. C. Triandis, C. Kagitcibasi, S.-C. Choi, & G. Yoon (Eds.), *Individualism and collectivism: Theory, method, and applications* (pp. 175–188). Thousand Oaks, CA: Sage.

Ybarra, O., & Trafimow, D. (1998). How priming the private self or collective self affects the relative weights of attitudes and subjective norms. *Personality and Social Psychology Bulletin, 24*, 362–370.

Yeh, C. (1995). *The clinical grounding of self and morality in Japan and the U.S.* Unpublished doctoral dissertation, Stanford University, Stanford, CA.

Yik, M. S. M., Bond, M. H., & Paulhus, D. L. (1998). Do Chinese self-enhance or self-efface? It's a matter of domain. *Personality and Social Psychology Bulletin, 24*, 399–406.

# EPILOGUE

CHAPTER

# 14

# Toward a Conception of Culture Suitable for a Social Psychology of Culture

Glenn Adams
University of Kansas

Hazel Rose Markus
Stanford University

The chapters in this volume mark an important shift in the study of culture and psychology. Instead of psychological phenomena investigated in different "cultures," psychologists are increasingly taking the phenomenon of *culture*, itself, as a suitable topic focus of study. With this change in focus comes an obligation to devote greater theoretical attention to the concept of culture than has been typical in social psychology. After the excellent beginning provided by contributions to this volume, it may be helpful to pause and reconsider what we think culture is before embarking too far on a project to articulate its psychological foundations. We take this as our task for the conclusion chapter.

## CULTURE: WHAT IS IT?

Psychologists have often been reluctant to define culture explicitly (Jahoda, 1984; Segall, 1984). On one hand, this reluctance reflects the difficulty of the exercise. As the editors of this volume note in their introduction chapter, *culture* gets used in many different ways by many different people, and it is probably impossible to find a definition upon which most people would agree.

On the other hand, the reluctance to define culture reflects a perspective that this book is trying to transcend. Studies in social psychology usually do not consider culture directly, as a psychological phenomenon in its own right, but only indirectly, as a source of group-based variation in other psychological phenomena. In other words, the focus of most research is not necessarily culture, but instead the extent to which more standard psychological phenomena—like perception, cognition, emotion, motivation, self, attribution, conformity, or dissonance—vary "across cultures." Given this focus, it is not really necessary to define culture (Segall, 1984). Instead, "culture" is simply shorthand for a grouping variable of secondary interest.

When theoretical interest shifts from cultural variation to culture per se, questions of definition rise to the fore. It may be unnecessary to develop a conception of culture that has universal approval (Schaller, Conway, & Crandall, chap. 1, this volume); however, it is important to recognize that "what's in a name" or definition has important implications for theory and research (Shweder, 1990; Veroff & Goldberger, 1995). With this in mind, we turn the discussion to the concept of culture. The purpose of this discussion is not to propose the "definitive" or ultimate definition (although we do suggest a definition that we think is useful). Instead, our purpose is to trace the implications of two, broad conceptions.

## THE "CULTURE DEBATE" IN CULTURAL ANTHROPOLOGY

It is somewhat ironic that, at a time when there has been renewed interest in culture within the field of psychology, there has been increasing doubt about the usefulness of the concept in cultural anthropology, a field in which culture is a defining concept (Appadurai, 1996; Hannerz, 1992; Meyer & Geschiere, 1999). Space does not permit an extended discussion of this "crisis" (see instead Shweder, 2001), but a key theme concerns the issue of cultural dynamics.

### Subjectivity

One way the issue of cultural dynamics arises is in the question of subjectivity. Classic ethnographic accounts tend to portray culture as a totalizing system that exerts deterministic influence on more-or-less passive recipients. In contrast, recent analyses have emphasized that people do not absorb cultural elements in a direct, faxlike manner or respond to cultural dictates in automatic, robotlike fashion (Comaroff & Comaroff, 1993; Holland, Lachicotte, Skinner, & Cain, 1998; Strauss, 1992). Instead, people often demonstrate subjectivity by selectively appropriating cultural elements and actively resisting cultural dictates. Accordingly, recent ethnographic analyses have devoted greater attention to individual subjectivity (and even personal agency) than one might imagine, given disciplinary stereotypes that define anthropology as the study of collectives and psychology as the study of individuals.

### Reification

Another way the issue of cultural dynamics arises is the problem of reification: turning dynamic, flowing patterns into static, fixed "cultures" (Hannerz, 1992; Hermans & Kempen, 1998). One form the reification of culture takes is the *construction of the other* (Said, 1978). This phrase refers to the tendency for scientific description to present the object of observation as a homogenous out-group, defined less by its objectively observable features than by perceived differences from the observer's ingroup. A second form the reification of culture takes is the *invention of tradition* (Hobsbawm & Ranger, 1983). This phrase typically refers to the tendency for political players to claim legitimacy by associating themselves with a carefully constructed (which is *not* the same as *false*) past. However, one can extend the idea to refer to the tendency of scientific description to turn historically contingent patterns into timeless, "traditional" customs. A third form the reification of culture takes is the *fixing of identity* (Meyer & Geschiere, 1999): the closure or solidifying of identity boundaries and associated ways of being that were previously more permeable and flowing (Appiah, 1992; Appadurai, 1996).

### Culture in the Context of "Globalization"

The need for a less reifying conception of culture has become particularly clear in the context of globalization (Hannerz, 1992; Hermans & Kempen, 1998). As Meyer and Geschiere (1999) noted in the introduction to their volume *Globalization and Identity*, the phenomenon of globalization has served to highlight both the fluid nature of cultural influence and the need for a conception of culture that can capture this fluidity. In particular, it requires that scientists discard what we refer to as an *entity* conception of culture:

> the classic view—propagated by anthropology, but internalized by social scientists in general *and* by the people concerned—of the world as a conglomerate of separate and internally homogenous cultures, each with its own essence, so that intercultural contacts are understood in terms of loss of authenticity. (Meyer & Geschiere, 1999, p. 4)

## CONTRASTING CONCEPTIONS OF CULTURE IN SOCIAL PSYCHOLOGY

How is this debate about culture relevant for the discussion of psychological foundations? First, scholars note a similar tendency toward the reification of culture in the discipline of psychology: "People turn names into things and endow nations, societies, and cultures with the qualities of internally homogenous and externally distinctive objects" (Hermans & Kempen, 1998; p. 1113; cf. Adams & Markus, 2001; Hong, Morris, Chiu, & Benet-Martinez, 2000). A discussion of psychological foundations would do well to recognize and avoid this problematic conception of culture from the outset.

Second, and more important, this debate suggests a place for psychology in the study of culture. Part of the "emerging consensus" (Kashima, 2000) in the psychological study of culture is that cultural and psychological are linked in a dialectical, mutually constituting relationship: in other words, that culture and psyche "make each other up" (Shweder, 1990, p.24). Previous research has emphasized one side of this dialectic, the importance of "cultural" for the study of "psychological." Although this research has served as a necessary corrective to the historical neglect of cultural grounding in the discipline of psychology (Segall, Lonner, & Berry, 1998), an exclusive emphasis on this side of the mutual constitution dialectic affords an "oversocialized" (Wrong, 1961) conception of cultural influence as a static, monolithic force. It tends to understate the multiple, flowing nature of cultural influence, and it neglects the role of individual agency in actively appropriating cultural patterns and reproducing cultural realities (Adams & Markus, 2001; Hermans & Kempen, 1998; Kashima, 2000).

In contrast, the "flip side" of the mutual constitution dialectic emphasizes that cultural worlds are not miraculously conceived apart from human activity nor completely prescribed by structural forces apart from human interpretation (cf. Ross & Nisbett, 1991). Instead, these worlds are themselves psychological products: produced, re-produced and sometimes changed in the course of everyday activity (Berger & Luckmann, 1966; Cole, 1996; Rogoff, 1992). Herein lies the potential contribution of social psychology to the study of culture: to provide an account of this dynamic, constructive agency that, although itself culturally grounded, reveals the role of the psychological subject in reproducing cultural worlds (more on this point later).

## Culture as Group Entity: The Prevailing Conception

The *Merriam-Webster OnLine* dictionary (2002) offers six definitions of culture. The first definition—"cultivation, tillage"—makes explicit the etymological roots that *culture* shares with words like *cultivate* or *agriculture*. Subsequent definitions build upon these etymological roots and imply a conception of *culture* that resonates with the concerns of developmental psychology. On one hand, these roots refer to the *process* of nurturing an organism. On the other hand, they refer to the dynamic, flowing *medium* that allows an organism to flourish (as in "bacteria culture"). It is not surprise, then, that conceptions of culture as dynamic process or flowing medium are relatively common among developmental psychologists (Cole, 1996; Greenfield, 1997; Rogoff, 1992; Tomasello, 1999).

In contrast, social psychologists are more likely cite definitions of *culture* like definition 5b of the *Merriam-Webster OnLine* dictionary (2002): "the customary beliefs, social forms, and material traits of a racial, religious, or social group" (Lau, Chiu, & Lee, 2001; Richter & Kruglanski, chap. 5, this volume). There are two noteworthy features of this definition. First, it implies a conception of culture as a relatively "fixed" system of "customary beliefs, social forms and material traits." Second, it associates this system with a readily identifiable, "racial, religious, or social group."

The relative popularity of this definition is a reflection of the underlying, *entity* conception of culture that prevails in social psychology. This conception of culture is evident in phrases like "members of culture X" and in the practice of using *culture* synonymously with *society*, *nation*, or *ethnicity*. It is evident in methodological practice, especially the sort of "cross-cultural" research where investigators operationalize culture as membership in national or ethnic groups and then treat these groups as discrete categories in a factorial design (Betancourt & Lopez, 1993; Greenfield, 1997; Hermans & Kempen, 1998; Phinney, 1996). Finally, an entity conception of culture is implicit in notions like *multicultural*—membership in two or more entitylike groups—that, somewhat ironically, are often used to discuss shortcomings of an entity conception of culture (e.g., Hermans & Kempen, 1998; Hong et al., 2000).

Although it is beyond the scope of this chapter to consider why an entity conception of culture is prominent among social psychologists, a couple of possibilities stand out. One possibility is the historical importance of the *group* concept in social psychology. Another possibility is the emphasis on experimental methodology and resulting use of categorical, independent variables. Whatever the case, this entity conception of culture has several undesirable consequences.

***Stereotyping.*** One undesirable consequence of an entity conception of culture is to promote a stereotype-prone account of cultural difference (Matsumoto, 1999; Takano & Osaka, 1999). Just as an implicit, "entity" theory leads perceivers to interpret social events with reference to categorical stereotypes (Levy, Plaks, Hong, Chiu, & Dweck, 2001), so may an entity conception of culture promote interpretation of cultural difference in terms of categorical types. In other words, an entity conception of culture turns descriptions of loosely bounded, continuous patterns into properties of tightly bounded, discrete groups. It turns statements like "an interdependent construction of self is more prominent in East Asian settings than North American settings" into statements like "an interdependent construction of self is more prominent in the East Asian group than the North American group."

***Homogenizing.*** Closely related to the problem of stereotyping is that of homogenizing. Just as an implicit, "entity" theory leads perceivers to exaggerate within-group similarity and between-group difference (Levy et al., 2001), so may an entity conception of culture promote an experience of "cultures" as "internally homogenous, externally distinctive objects" (Hermans & Kempen, 1998, p. 1113). In other words, it turns statements like "an interdependent construction of self is more prominent in East Asian settings than North American settings" into statements like "an interdependent construction of self is true of East Asians and not of North Americans." Not only are descriptions of modal patterns interpreted as properties of categorical groups; in addition, these properties are taken to apply to all members of the group—past, present, and future.

***Essentializing.*** A third consequence of an entity conception of culture is to promote *essentialism*. Just as perceiving a collection of people as a group entity promotes the sense that the collection of people share some group-related essence (Yzerbyt, Corneille, & Estrada, 2001), so may an entity conception of culture promote the sense that people in a setting share some cultural essence. Thus, not only are descriptions of modal patterns interpreted as properties of a homogenous category; in addition, these properties are treated as if they were inherent in the group—either in the members or in the category—rather than the product of circumstances associated with the group (Holland et al., 1998). In other words, an entity conception turns external patterns (e.g., "an interdependent construction of self is prominent in East Asian settings") into internal dispositions (e.g., "East Asian people are inherently interdependent").

***Reifying.*** A fourth consequence of an entity conception of culture is to promote *reification*. As noted above, an entity conception turns diffuse communities of people who share cultural patterns into solid group entities who share cultural essence. The point here is not about the source of cultural tendencies (shared patterns versus shared essence), but instead the ontological status of the collectivities with which these tendencies are associated. By associating loosely bounded patterns with discrete, categorical groups, an entity conception of culture contributes to the reality of these groups, gives them a more solid ontological status than they would otherwise have. That is, it turns statements like "an interdependent construction of self is a prominent pattern in East Asian settings" into statements like "an interdependent construction of self is a defining feature of East Asian culture."

To summarize, an entity conception of culture has several negative consequences. It takes dynamic, flowing patterns and freezes them into fixed traditions or inherent properties of rigid, homogenous "groups." More important for present purposes, though, is that an entity conception of culture obscures the role of psychology in the study of culture. On one hand, it treats cultural tendencies as ascribed, essential features rather than dynamic appropriations. On the other hand, it treats cultural-group categories as natural or inevitable rather than collective, psychological products.

## Culture as Patterns

In contrast to this stereotype- and reification-prone conception of culture as group entity, we borrow from a classic definition and advocate a conception of culture as *patterns*:

> Culture consists of explicit and implicit *patterns* of historically derived and selected ideas and their embodiment in institutions, practices, and artifacts; cultural patterns may, on one hand, be considered as products of action, and on the other as conditioning elements of further action. (based on Kroeber & Kluckhohn, 1952, p. 357)

This definition makes clear that culture resides, not in group membership, but instead in the patterned worlds that are sometimes—although not always—associated with group membership. Besides this location of culture in patterns, there are several other features of this definition that are worthy of elaboration.

***Explicit and Implicit.*** The first noteworthy feature of this definition is that culture consists of both explicit and implicit patterns. Discussions of culture in social psychology have typically referred to patterns—like value orientations, ideologies, and norms—that are more or less consciously considered and explicitly associated with a readily identified, "cultural" entity. However, cultural influence does not just happen through explicit patterns. Nor are all cultural patterns associated with an explicit, reified entity. Instead, culture is also mediated by implicit, unrecognized patterns that are embedded in the structure of everyday life and need not coincide with explicit, cultural-group boundaries (Morris, Menon, & Ames, 2001).

***Historically Derived and Selected.*** A second noteworthy feature of above definition is that cultural patterns are "historically derived and selected." The "derived" portion of this phrase emphasizes that cultural patterns are an accumulated product from a history of human activity. This gives cultural influence a slightly different flavor than it has in contemporary social psychology. Given the prevailing conception of culture as group entity, social influence becomes cultural by taking on *collective* dimension: extending beyond interpersonal or small-group interactions to the whole of a nation or society. In the conception of culture proposed by the preceding definition, social influence becomes cultural by taking on a *temporal* dimension: extending beyond interpersonal interaction to the worlds inherited by subsequent actors.

The "selected" portion of this phrase suggests the extent to which culture is an evolutionary process. In this way, it resonates with evolutionary approaches to culture. (However, the present perspective requires greater appreciation than most evolutionary approaches concede for the extent to which the emergence of culture constituted a selective pressure on the emergence of psyche; see later discussion.) Just as environmental forces exert selective pressure on the genetic stuff that persists across generations of organisms, so too may environmental forces exert selective pressure on the cultural stuff that persists across generations of cultural activity. There are certainly cases where cultural patterns "lag" and cease to be adaptive in the face of changing environmental circumstances (Prentice & Carranza, chap. 11, this volume; Vandello & Cohen, chap. 12, this volume). In general, though, patterns that persist into the present are likely to have conferred some adaptive advantage and represent some measure of time-tested wisdom about local realities.

As contributors to this volume note, environmental forces are not the only source of selective pressure on cultural patterns; in addition, psychological forces also serve as a source of selective pressure. Everyday action creates a multitude of potentially cultural patterns. Features of human psychology—particularly, memory processes (Norenzayan & Atran, chap. 7, this volume), communication processes (Lau, Lee, & Chiu, chap. 4, this volume; McIntyre, Lyons, Clark, & Kashima, chap. 10, this volume) and even self-interest (Crandall & Schaller, chap. 9, this volume)—play an important role in determining which patterns "catch" and become cultural: that is, appropriated by others, reproduced, and thereby perpetuated (Sperber, 1984).

***Mental and Material.*** A third noteworthy feature of this definition is that cultural patterns consist of both mental and material elements. Cultural patterns are more than just sets of ideas. Instead, they include the manifestations of these ideas in structures, institutions, practices, and artifacts (cf. Moscovici, 1984; Sperber, 1984). By explicitly linking mental and material aspects of cultural patterns, the above definition provides a conceptual tool that helps bridge across a number of problematic dualisms: the debate about whether culture is primarily material or ideational (Kashima, 2000; Rohner, 1984); the debate about whether the study of culture should concern itself with behaviors or meanings (Shweder, 2001); and the distinction between culture and structure (see later discussion).

The field of social psychology has been deeply influenced by Triandis's (1972) emphasis on *subjective* aspects of culture—attitudes, beliefs, norms, and especially values—rather than material manifestations of culture. The benefit of this emphasis has been to render the topic of culture amenable to psychological study. Culture is not limited to "man-made features of the environment" (Herskovits, 1948, p. 17), but resides in the kind of stuff that is of interest to psychologists.

However, an exclusive focus on "subjective" aspects of culture has also promoted what Bruner (1990) referred to as an "overlay" conception of cultural influence. It tends to limit cultural influence to value orientations, response norms, and superficial ideologies that color interpretation of a more basic, precultural reality. Rather than something that happens "after" or "on top of" basic experience, the present definition emphasizes that culture resides in the everyday worlds that condition basic experience in the first place. Cultural influence is not limited to values, beliefs, or ideas *about* reality, but includes differences in reality itself. From this perspective, there is no such thing as a general, acultural world; instead, people inhabit worlds that come culturally patterned.

This is a point that is worth repeating, so we will do so with examples from our own research. Given an exclusive emphasis on "subjective culture", there is a tendency to interpret cultural patterns like independent and interdependent construals of self (Markus & Kitayama, 1991) as differences in subjective *beliefs*. Instead these concepts refer to different *constructions*: beliefs built into the physical patterns of everyday life. The independent constructions of self and relationship that are prominent in mainstream American settings are not merely beliefs about separation. Instead, they are linked to a reality of separation that is built into structures of everyday life like dating practices, residence in apartment units, and individual ownership. Similarly, the more relational or interdependent constructions of self and relationship that are prominent cultural patterns in many West African settings are not merely beliefs about connection. Instead, they are linked to a reality of connection that is built into structures of everyday life like arranged marriage, residence in lineage compounds, and the practice of eating meals from a communal bowl.

***Mutual Constitution of Culture and Psyche.*** Finally, this definition explicitly links cultural patterns and psychological activity in a dialectical relationship of mutual constitution. "Products of action" at one moment, cultural patterns constitute the stimulus world that serves as a "conditioning element of further action" in the next.

Kashima (2000) aptly noted that scholars who discuss the mutual constitution process typically have more to say about the cultural grounding side of the dialectic ("culture shapes psyche") than the dynamic construction side ("psyche shapes culture"). Earlier, we suggested one source of this lopsided emphasis. Given the historical neglect of culture in the field of social psychology, the primary task of the "first wave" of research has been to highlight the cultural grounding of psychological functioning. Here we suggest another source of this lopsided emphasis. Discussion of the "flip side" of the mutual constitution dialectic–the dynamic construction of cultural realities–has been hindered by an overly reified conception of culture.

Given a conception of culture as group entity, discussion of the process by which "psyche creates culture" requires an unlikely account of how an aggregation of individual, psychological activity generates a macrolevel system. The present approach to culture makes this task a more reasonable undertaking via two means. First, a conception of culture as flowing patterns changes the nature of the explanatory task. Rather than creation of cultural entities, one must explain the reproduction, maintenance, and modification of cultural patterns. The phenomenon under consideration becomes the redirection of cultural flow rather than outright creation of that flow.

Second, a conception of culture as patterns locates the unit of culture at a "micro" level of analysis. From this perspective, research like that described in this volume (e.g., chapters in this volume by Arrow & Burns, Harton & Bourgeois, Lau et al., and McIntyre et al.) already qualifies as an account of the dynamic construction of cultural reality. Although an interesting topic for research, it is not necessary to extend such accounts from microlevel patterns to macrolevel "cultures" before one can refer to the process as "cultural."

## Contrasting Implications

Some aspects of the preceding discussion may appear to suggest that the distinction between entity and patterns approaches to culture is primarily a difference in degree rather than a difference in kind. Perhaps cultural patterns and cultural groups are both forms of cultural entities, but differ in level (micro vs. macro), degree of boundedness (diffuse and flowing vs. contained or fixed), or perceived entitativity (low vs. high). If so, it may be possible to reconcile the two conceptions. That is, if one relaxes the unit of culture to include not only high-entitativity groups (e.g., citizens of a particular nation), but also low-entitativity sets (e.g., people who have attended college), then perhaps an entity conception of culture can accommodate the patterns conception.

Such a move to extend the concept of culture from bounded, fixed, macrolevel groups to diffuse, flowing, microlevel patterns is certainly consistent with the spirit of this chapter. However, the difference between a conception of culture as patterns and the more typical conception of culture as group is more than a difference in perceived entitativity. In addition, these two conceptions also differ in their conception of cultural involvement. A conception of culture as group implies a framing of cultural involvement as membership; that is, the influence of culture happens by being a member of the associated cultural group. In contrast, a conception of culture as patterns emphasizes that one need not be a member of some cultural group (e.g., "mainstream Americans") to engage and be shaped by cultural patterns (e.g., those associated with mainstream American settings).

This is partly a statement about perceived entitativity and the extent to which cultural engagement is conscious and explicit. For example, one need not consider oneself a member of a group of city dwellers to be shaped by patterns that arise as a byproduct of being a city-dweller. One can be shaped by this "group" experience, even if one did not think about the experience in group membership terms.

More important, though, this statement entails a recognition that one can be shaped by cultural patterns associated with entities in which one has never been, is not now, nor ever will be a member. For example, consider the cultural force of Protestantism. Although an entity conception of culture would seem to limit Protestantism's influence to members of a Protestant group, the more pervasive and enduring source of Protestantism's power is as a cultural pattern. It is an often implicit, unrecognized part of the institutions, practices, and artifacts that constitute everyday reality in widely scattered cultural settings. For example, the legacy of Protestantism persists in contemporary, mainstream American settings in the idea that success is the result of self-discipline and hard work, in the relationship of control feelings and internal attributions to happiness and well-being, or in the relationship of self-control ideology to the association of *fat* with *immoral* (Crandall, 1994; Ji, Peng, & Nisbett, 2000; Kluegel & Smith, 1986; Lachman & Weaver, 1998). Regardless of personal identity, people in mainstream American settings necessarily encounter this cultural legacy in the course of everyday activity. People in these settings can fervently embrace cultural patterns associated with other religious affiliations (e.g., Judaism, Catholicism, etc.), but they must simultaneously engage—often unwittingly—the Protestantism-informed patterns that dominate everyday reality in mainstream American settings. A person need not be a member of a Protestant group, or even be aware of Protestants as a reference group, to engage and be shaped by Protestant cultural patterns.

Thus, the present approach marks a shift in the conceptual location of culture from collections of people to the worlds they inhabit. It does not limit psychologically relevant aspects of culture to values, norms, and other forms of group doctrine, but recognizes that cultural influence is also embodied in and mediated by local worlds (Ratner, 1996). The cultural shaping of behavior need not involve explicit indoctrination, but often occurs as an unintended byproduct of engagement with these worlds. (For example, one need not attend church to acquire the Protestant work ethic.) Cultural influence begins at the beginning; it is not limited to the evaluation of pre-existing reality (i.e., influencing judgment of the object), but extends to the construction of reality itself (i.e., defining the object of judgment). The individual does not exist apart from cultural influence, but is born into—and can only develop within—particular worlds that come culturally configured.

## THE PSYCHOLOGICAL FOUNDATIONS OF CULTURE

We turn attention now to the topic of psychological foundations. To the extent that one defines culture as a high-entitativity group or reified system, the discussion of psychological foundations is likely to emphasize group dynamics, intergroup relations, or the emergence of stable, macrolevel "cultures." In contrast, a less reifying conception of culture as flowing patterns or dynamic process suggests a different set of psychological foundations related to the microlevel construction of meaning or the production of "common ground" (Clark, 1996).

A list of potential candidates for "psychological foundations of culture" appears in Table 14.1. It includes foundations proposed by contributors to this volume, as well as several that we have seen fit to add ourselves. This list is almost certainly incomplete, and if other writers were to propose a list it would no doubt look different from this one. However, our purpose is not to compile a definitive list, but instead to provide a foundation that stimulates further theory and research. In the following discussion, we elaborate on this list. First though, it is necessary to briefly consider the concept of *psychological.*

### What Is Psychological?

Besides more explicit consideration of the concept of *culture*, the project of articulating the psychological foundations of culture also occasions more explicit consideration of the concept of *psychological.* Here, too, it seems that *psychological* means different things to different scholars.

For scholars who study culture in other social sciences, psychology is sometimes associated with *psychologize*, a phrase typically used as a form of criticism. In some cases, this criticism appears to equate "psychological" with individual-level analysis, and then holds that any such analysis is mis-

TABLE 14.1
Examples of Psychological Foundations of Culture

Evolutionary foundations
- Biologically based dispositions to follow moral norms (Krebs & Janicki)
- Capacity for self-awareness (Solomon et al.)
- Capacity for understanding conspecifics as intentional agents like oneself (Tomasello, 1999)

Neurological systems
- Neural plasticity (Worthman, 1992)
- Sensitive period (Heine & Lehman)

Motivational systems
- Existential anxieties (Norenzayan & Atran)
- Need for closure (Richter & Kruglanski)
- Terror aroused by awareness of death (Solomon et al.)
- Rejection of deviants (Prentice & Carranza; Schachter, 1951)
- Self-interest (Arrow & Burns; Crandall & Schaller)

Affective/emotional systems
- Empathy (Arrow & Burns)
- Mere exposure (Zajonc, 1968)
- Openness of preference and affective experience to social influence (Harton & Bourgeois) and environmental regulation, in general

Cognitive/communication systems
- Interpersonal communication (Harton & Bourgeois; Lau et al.)
- Memorability (Crandall & Schaller; Norenzayan & Atran)
- Perceptual confirmation of belief (e.g., by assimilation to stereotypes; Prentice & Carranza)
- Pluralistic ignorance (Vandello & Cohen)
- Production of common ground (McIntyre et al.)

General psychological principles
- Automaticity of everyday life (Bargh, 1997)
- Dynamic construction of experience (e.g., self-experience; Heine & Lehman)

guided. In other cases, the criticism is not so much about individual-level study but instead concerns the character of that study. In these cases, *psychologize* refers to something like a caricature of psychoanalysis: an attempt to explain phenomena by reducing them to universal psychodynamics (think Oedipus complex), resolution of intrapsychic conflict, or the quest for inner fulfillment. No doubt most readers would object to this characterization of *psychological*. Even so, it is useful to be aware of this characterization, especially when venturing into interdisciplinary territory like the study of culture.

Among psychologists, there is a common tendency to distinguish psychology from other social sciences by identifying *psychological* with *individual*. However, this simple equation of *psychological* with individual-level analysis seems inadequate. On one hand, scholars in disciplines associated with a "collective" level of analysis increasingly consider individual-level functioning. As we noted in a previous section, anthropologists and sociologists who use ethnographic methods have increasingly devoted attention to individual agency in the culture process (e.g., see Comaroff & Comaroff, 1993; Holland et al., 1998).

On the other hand, this simple equation is inadequate because *psychological* extends beyond individual-level processes. It is not limited to intrapsychic, mental worlds, but extends to mental patterns that are made material in institutions, practices, and artifacts. Among contributions to this volume, this perspective is evident in the concept of *common ground* as interpersonal meaning space (McIntyre et al., chap. 10, this volume; see Clark, 1996), the idea of language as a cultural–psychological artifact (Lau et al., chap. 4, this volume; see Vygotsky, 1978), and the call for an epidemiology of representations (Norenzayan & Atran, chap. 7, this volume; see Sperber, 1984). More generally, this perspective is evident in Moscovici's (1984) concept of social representations and in the present conception of culture as dialectically linked, mental and material patterns (Adams & Markus, 2001).

One implication of this extension of *psychological* is to extend the range of appropriate methods to include the study of psychological stuff made manifest in discourse, texts, and other material artifacts (Bar-Tal, 2000; Kim & Markus, 1999). More generally, it suggests that the move to take culture as a phenomenon of study may require social psychologists to venture beyond methodological tradition (i.e., an almost exclusive reliance on experimental and quasi-experimental methods) and consider alternative methods of inquiry. The methodological diversity of contributions to this volume—including computer simulation (Harton & Bourgeois, chap. 3, this volume), analysis of language and discourse (Lau et al., chap. 4, this volume; McIntyre et al., chap. 10, this volume), and the study of demonstration cases (Arrow & Burns, chap. 8, this volume)—adds weight to this suggestion.

## Psychological Systems

### Biological Foundations

For Krebs and Janicki (chap. 6, this volume) the psychological foundations of culture lie in "the biological foundations of the mental mechanisms that give rise to moral norms and other aspects of culture" (p. 125). One framing of "biological foundations" would be to emphasize neural or physiological bases of culture; instead, Krebs and Janicki frame "biological foundations" in terms of evolutionary bases. In the section that follows, we consider both framings.

***Evolutionary Foundations.*** Given an emphasis on evolutionary bases, one might frame the "biological" foundations of culture as the evolved mental mechanisms that enable the process of culture, or the evolved mental mechanisms through which culture and psyche make each other up. This is not the route that Krebs and Janicki take. Rather than evolutionary foundations of *culture* per se, they emphasize that a psychological tendency that is usually thought to be a product of "culture"—specifically, the propensity to follow moral norms—is actually part of human "nature": a genetically encoded, evolved mental mechanism that is cultural only in its secondary manifestations.

One contribution to this volume that does propose an evolutionary foundation of culture is the chapter by Solomon and his colleagues (chap. 2, this volume). Specifically, they propose a social-psychological adaptation, the capacity for self-awareness, as the evolutionary source of a motivation for culture, the existential terror provoked by awareness of mortality. According to this account, the evolved capacity for self-awareness brought with it the terrifying awareness of mortality. Human communities then devised cultural systems like religion to provide an ideological antidote for this potentially paralyzing terror.

Perhaps because they consider culture in terms of relatively explicit and reified systems (like religion), Solomon and his colleagues emphasize the evolutionary priority of *psychological* over *cultural*: "Because all cultural affectations initially originated in minds of individuals . . . all theoretical perspectives that presume the existence of culture without explaining its psychological underpinnings are epistemologically untenable" (p. 17). A more microlevel perspective—where culture is conceived as dynamic, flowing patterns or emergent, common ground—admits a larger role for the cultural shaping of psychological. To illustrate, consider the capacity for self-awareness. Although this capacity is the result of an evolutionary adaptation, actual self-awareness is patterned by (and requires) engagement with other people. This means that the evolutionary adaptation identified as a psychological foundation of culture (self-awareness) is itself based in cultural processes: not in the sense of static, highly reified, macrolevel systems like religion, but instead in the sense of dynamic, microlevel patterns that emerge from interpersonal interaction.

Tomasello (1999) proposed an evolutionary–psychological foundation of culture that is more compatible with this microlevel perspective. First he noted that individuals do not create "cultural affectations" from raw material. Instead, they necessarily draw upon prefabricated, cultural material and pretested, cultural tools (Cole, 1996; Vygotsky, 1978). "Basically none of the most complex human artifacts or social practices—including tool industries, symbolic communication, and social institutions—were invented once and for all at a single moment by any one individual or group of individuals" (Tomasello, 1999, p. 5). Instead these "affectations" arise through a process of *cumulative cultural evolution*, which "ensures that human cognitive ontogeny takes place in an environment of ever-new artifacts and social practices which, at any one time, represent something resembling the entire collective wisdom of the entire social group throughout its entire collective history" (Tomasello, 1999, p. 7). Although culture originates in minds of individuals, these individuals and their mental processes are not pre-cultural. Instead they are positioned in the downstream flow of cultural patterns from a reservoir of activity by preceding waves of actors.

The evolutionary foundation of culture that Tomasello (1999) proposes is the social-psychological adaptation that enabled cumulative cultural evolution: the ability of the human organism to recognize conspecifics as intentional agents with mental lives like itself. According to Tomasello, this social-psychological adaptation made possible cultural learning, which enabled cumulative cultural evolution, which laid the foundation for the higher forms of cognition characteristic of the human species—including human consciousness itself.

***Neurological Foundations.*** Rather than emphasize the evolutionary priority of psychological over cultural, the majority of contributors to this volume emphasize the coevolution of psychological and cultural. Although agreeing that one cannot fully understand culture without reference to its psychological foundations, this perspective adds that one cannot fully understand psyche without reference to its social and cultural foundations (Markus, Kitayama, & Heiman, 1997).

Another way of stating the idea of coevolution is to say that human beings evolved to be cultural. Although naturally selected, mental mechanisms enabled the phenomenon of culture, the emergence of culture also exerted selection pressure on the evolution of mental mechanisms. From this perspective, human beings are evolutionarily shaped and genetically predisposed to seize and make use of cultural resources available in local environments (Heine & Lehman, chap. 13, this volume; McIntyre et al., chap. 10, this volume).

This perspective suggests another "biological foundation" of culture: plasticity. Although the human organism is as an evolutionarily shaped, genetically encoded package of potentialities, it is neither efficient nor adaptive that development be completely preprogrammed. Instead, human ontogeny entails a built-in (and, presumably, selected-for) reliance on environmental patterns for species-typical development (Worthman, 1992). To the extent that this plasticity or reliance on environmental patterns provides a window for the cultural shaping of psyche, it qualifies as a psychological foundation of culture.

Of course, human psyche is not infinitely plastic. Not only are there limits in the extent to which genetically encoded, neural programming is shaped by environmental input. In addition, there are limits to the malleability of neural pathways once they are developed. This implies a psychological foundation that is the flip side of plasticity: the notion of *sensitive period* (Heine & Lehman, chap. 13, this volume). Not only may the ability to experience certain cultural patterns (e.g., tendencies of phoneme discrimination, visual perception, self-experience, and culture-specific emotions) depend on exposure to those patterns during a sensitive period of development. In addition, the shaping of early experience by certain cultural patterns may make later shaping by other cultural patterns more difficult.

### Motivational Foundations

Contributors to this volume suggest two motivational foundations of cultural engagement that we will group together under a general "need to make sense" (Norenzayan & Atran, chap. 7, this volume). One motivational foundation is an *existential need* to make sense of big questions like the meaning of life. For example, Solomon and his colleagues (chap. 2, this volume) propose that people are motivated to construct and engage relatively formalized, cultural patterns like religion as an institutional means of dealing with the potentially paralyzing, existential terror provoked by the awareness of mortality. Another motivational foundation is an *epistemic need* to make sense of day-to-day reality (Richter & Kruglanski, chap. 5, this volume). Reality is often multiple and ambiguous, and people require culture—social influence with a historical and material dimension—to help define reality, sufficient for present purposes. A specific case of this need occurs in interpersonal communication, where people are motivated to engage in a microlevel form of cultural process, the production of common ground (see also Clark, 1996; McIntyre et al., chap. 10, this volume; Richter & Kruglanski, 1999).

### Affective/Emotional Foundations

An aspect of *psychological* that is underrepresented in contributions to this volume is the affective/emotional domain. One candidate for an affective/emotional foundation of culture is the openness of human feeling to social regulation. Phenomena like emotional contagion and empathy (Arrow & Burns, chap. 8, this volume) represent manifestations of this openness.

More generally, one might identify a psychological foundation of culture in the concept of affective primacy: the notion that "preferences need no inferences" (Zajonc, 1980). For present purposes, the essence of this notion is the direct, automatic shaping of moods, feelings and preferences by everyday worlds (Bargh & Chartrand, 1999). To the extent that everyday worlds are culturally patterned, this psychological process provides a mechanism to explain the cultural patterning of mood, feeling, preference, and desire. Institutions, practices, and artifacts often have an affective charge. This affective charge can arise through relatively deliberate means, as when authorities associate negative consequences with acts that they define as taboo or criminal. Alternatively, this affective charge can happen through less deliberate means, as when practices like foot-binding or artifacts like automobiles get associated with sexuality. In any case, people are likely to acquire the affective charge of practices and artifacts, often unwittingly, in the process of engaging cultural worlds. Immersed in worlds where it is taboo to eat meat, people are likely to feel disgust at the sight, sound, or scent of roasting flesh. Immersed in worlds where automobiles have been associated with sex, people are likely to feel sexual desire (or at least arousal) when exposed to certain automobiles.

On a more specific level, one might identify another psychological foundation of culture in the "mere exposure" effect (Zajonc, 1968). Although the relationship between exposure and preference is complicated, the mere exposure process is an engine that drives the mutually constituting, dialectical relationship between environmental prominence and individual preference. People develop tastes in music, clothing, food, and other consumption domains based in large part on familiarity (Crandall, 1985). They then act on these preferences and choose to play certain forms of music, to wear certain styles of clothing, and to cook certain styles of food more than other possible choices. Through this activity, individual actors reproduce local worlds where selected forms of music, clothing, and food are more frequent and potentially familiar than nonselected forms. In other words, individual acts of preference or choice constitute the everyday worlds that shape the preferences and choices of subsequent waves of actors (Kim & Markus, 1999).

### Cognitive Foundations

An important set of cognitive foundations of culture are processes associated with *cultural lag*: the tendency for collective beliefs to lag behind material change. Prentice and Carranza (chap. 11, this volume) note how a process of perceptual confirmation—specifically, assimilation of ambiguous behavior to gender stereotypes—results in the persistence of beliefs about what women and men are like (i.e., descriptive gender norms) that do not correspond to what women and men actually do. Similarly, Vandello and Cohen (chap. 12, this volume) describe how *pluralistic ignorance*—individuals' mistaken beliefs about others' attitudes and values—can promote the persistence of honor-related violence in the absence of material conditions or private endorsement that would support such violence (Cohen, 1998).

More generally, an important contribution of chapters in this volume is to rethink the link between communication and cognition. Locating psyche in individual minds, psychologists have been inclined to treat communication and social interaction as an outcome of more "basic," cognitive processes. Instead, several chapters in this volume consider the extent to which "basic" cognitive-psychological phenomena like language, memory, and consciousness have their roots in social sources and interpersonal communication (Vygotsky, 1978).

This framing suggests that a fruitful place to look for cognitive foundations of culture is communication processes. Accordingly, some chapters consider the features of human cognition that make some information more communicable or memorable than other information, and therefore more likely to be retained across generations of cultural transmission (Crandall & Schaller, chap. 9, this volume; Norenzayan & Atran, chap. 7, this volume). Other chapters emphasize the role of language and interpersonal communication in the emergence of norms (Arrow & Burns, chap. 8, this volume; Harton & Bourgeois, chap. 3, this volume), the production of common ground (McIntyre et al., chap. 10, this volume), and the reproduction of cultural reality (Lau et al., chap. 4, this volume).

## General Psychological Principles

So far, we have organized discussion of the psychological foundations of culture around different content domains or areas of study. An alternative basis for organization is around general psychological principles. In this section, we discuss the implications of two such principles that have emerged as enduring themes in social psychology over the past century: the automaticity of everyday life, and the dynamic construction of psychological experience.

### *The Automaticity of Everyday Life*

Psychological research on culture has tended to focus on internalization and endorsement of explicitly acknowledged values and other forms of ideology associated with readily recognizable groups. In contrast, the more typical case of cultural shaping may be as an indirect byproduct of engagement with "implicit," cultural patterns that are embedded in institutions, practices, and artifacts (Bourdieu, 1990; Shore, 1996; Shweder, Jensen, & Goldstein, 1995; Vygotsky, 1978). A full account of the relationship between cultural and psychological requires greater appreciation for the automatic shaping of experience by patterns that are implicit in everyday life and do not necessarily coincide with explicit, group boundaries.

This conception of cultural influence as direct shaping by implicit patterns resonates with an enduring theme of social psychology—the power of the environmental influence (Ross & Nisbett, 1991)—and especially with recent work on "the automaticity of everyday life" that emphasizes the unmediated nature of environmental influence (Bargh, 1997). According to this perspective, psychological functioning is less often the product of conscious deliberation than the automatic effect of environmental forces on action, goal pursuit, and subjective experience (cf. Bargh & Chartrand, 1999). Although social psychologists who study the phenomenon of automaticity have typically not considered its implications for the study of culture, we find the mutual concern with "implicit patterns" to be a provocative point of intersection. Accordingly, the first principle that we nominate as a psychological foundation of culture is the automaticity of everyday life.

There is, however, a condition to this statement. In order to realize its potential relevance for the study of culture, it is necessary to supplement an appreciation for the automaticity of everyday life with a corresponding appreciation for the extent to which the worlds of everyday life are cultural products–meaning-saturated repositories of psychological activity by preceding waves of human actors (Bourdieu, 1990; Cole, 1996; Shore, 1996; Vygotsky, 1978)–and not culture neutral. The point of this condition is only partly about cultural variation in everyday worlds; instead, the more important point is to suggest how everyday worlds serve as mediators of cultural influence. Products of psychological tendencies at one moment, these worlds carry meaning and force that trigger psychological outcomes in the next. This perspective suggests that perhaps the place to look for human agency is not the ratio of controlled to automatic processing (Bargh & Chartrand, 1999), but instead the meaningful worlds that get constructed during fleeting moments of mindful activity.

### *The Dynamic Construction of Experience*

The second principle that we propose as a "psychological foundation of culture" is perhaps the single, most important theme to emerge from the study of psychology during the past century: what one might call the *dynamic construction* of human psychological experience. Psychological experience is not a passive replication of an objective reality. Instead, people actively construct an experience–perception (Bruner & Goodman, 1947), memory (Bartlett, 1932), emotion (Schachter & Singer, 1962), self (Markus & Wurf, 1987; Mead, 1934), ethnic identity (Deaux, 1993; Sellers, Smith, Shelton, Rowley, & Chavous, 1998), and so on–from indeterminate or potentially ambiguous inputs.

The dynamic construction of experience serves as a foundation of culture in two ways that correspond to the two sides of the mutual constitution dialectic. On one side of dialectic, the dynamic construction of experience opens the door for the cultural shaping of psyche. If people construct an experience based in part on "personal patterns" like habits or implicit theories, then cultural influence happens because–rather than the inevitable unfolding of inborn models–these personal patterns often have cultural sources. These cultural sources may be relatively explicit and direct, as in the case of knowledge structures given expression in cultural ideology. Alternatively, these cultural sources may be more implicit and automatic, as in the case of habitual ways of being developed as a by-product of repeated engagement with culturally patterned worlds. In either case, the dynamic construction of psychological experience provides an opening for cultural influence that would not exist if experience were completely determined by inherent dispositions or properties of stimuli.

On the other side of the dialectic, the dynamic construction of experience provides an engine for the reproduction, maintenance, and modification of cultural worlds. Psychological experience, like cultural transmission (cf. Strauss, 1992), is not a faxlike replication or formulaic combination of received inputs. Instead, each case of psychological activity entails the remaking of received inputs in light of present circumstances. Although psychologists have focused on its consequences for subjective experience, the relevance of this construction activity for the topic of culture concerns its consequences for objective reality. In the process of constructing personal experience, people reconstruct cultural worlds.

The case of language use provides an illustration. With regard to the first side of the dialectic, each case of language use necessarily entails appropriation of the cultural tools embedded in particular languages (e.g., vocabulary, grammar, pragmatics, etc.; see Lau et al., chap. 4, this volume). However, the resulting communicative act usually does not involve rote recitation of a preexisting statement. Instead, each act of linguistic production involves an emergent creation or novel synthesis. With regard to the second side of the dialectic, each case of language use is the mechanism for the reproduction, perpetuation, and extension of received cultural tools. However, this reproduction process does not result in an exact replication of cultural inputs. Instead, each case of language use returns those tools and inputs, modified by usage, back into the common, linguistic reservoir (McIntyre et al., chap. 10, this volume).

***The Dynamics of Culture.*** The present emphasis on the dynamic construction of experience suggests an elaboration or extension of the "dynamic constructionist" approach to culture advocated in this volume by Lau and her colleagues. First, this perspective extends the notion of *dynamic* beyond the limited sense of "motion" or "change" to its more fundamental sense of "active," "forceful," or "generative" (*Merriam-Webster On-Line*, 2002; Markus & Wurf, 1987). The construction process is dynamic, not because it results in change of cultural patterns, but because it entails active re-creation (rather than passive replication) of cultural patterns. Even when cultural patterns appear to be unchanged across generations of transmission, the relevant process is not necessarily one of static persistence but instead entails dynamic maintenance or active homeostasis. (For additional perspectives on *dynamic*, see chapters in this volume by Arrow & Burns, Harton & Bourgeois, and McIntyre et al.)

Second, the present perspective extends the locus of *construction* beyond subjective experience to include objective reality itself (Berger & Luckmann, 1966). The constructionist approach to psychology—as manifested, for example, in the study of social construal (Griffin & Ross, 1991; Ross & Nisbett, 1991)—typically focuses on subjective experience as the relevant outcome of the construction process. However, the experiences that people construct are not restricted to the intrapsychic realm. Instead, people tend to impose their constructions back on the world of experience, resulting in the production of patterned worlds that reflect the patterned psyche of the people who produced them.

***Bridging the Culture–Structure Divide.*** Accordingly, one of the most important implications of the dynamic construction principle for the study of culture is to blur the distinction between cultural and structural varieties of social-scientific explanation (and associated distinctions like mental versus material, idealist versus materialist, or dispositional versus situational; cf. Kashima, 2000; Morawska & Spohn, 1994; Ross & Nisbett, 1991; Veroff & Goldberger, 1995). On one hand, dynamic construction of psychological experience is the means by which structural becomes cultural. It is through dynamic, psychological activity that structural patterns acquire collective meaning and cultural force. This half of the story corresponds to the transition between *behavioral* and *meaning* stages of the Vandello and Cohen model of cultural evolution (chap. 12, this volume). Psychological activity turns structural patterns, like a herding economy or the absence of law enforcement, into the set of cultural patterns referred to as the *culture of honor*.

On the other hand, the dynamic construction of psychological experience is the means by which cultural becomes structural. It is through dynamic, psychological activity that the cultural stuff of this moment gets projected into the objective reality of the next. This half of the story is not explicitly stated in the Vandello and Cohen model, but it is implicit in their program of research. As people act on culturally grounded, psychological tendencies—for example, by treating defense of honor as an exonerating circumstance or regarding defense of person and property to be an individual responsibility (Cohen, 1998; Cohen & Nisbett, 1997)—they re-create worlds in which defense of property is, in fact, an individual responsibility, and violence so committed is, in fact, not blameworthy (e.g., not a barrier to employment). In other words, cultural-psychological tendencies are not merely epiphenomenal byproducts of structural forces; instead, they are the conceptual blueprint by which people reproduce material reality (Crane, 1994; Morawska & Spohn, 1994).

## CONCLUSION

Although increasingly recognized as a topic, exactly how and why *culture* fits into social psychology has not been well articulated. The prevailing model seems to be that culture fits into social psychology as some sort of group process, with an implication that culture is a special case of group membership. This perspective is associated with an overlay model of culture: Basic experience happens first, and then culture–in the form of group membership–modifies or qualifies this basic experience (for a discussion of this point, see Markus et al., 1997). In contrast, the present perspective emphasizes that culture is not a distal force that gets applied on top of basic experience. Instead, culture is also a proximal process of grounding or sense-making that is "basic" in its own right. Just as research during the past 20 years has focused on the importance of culture for the study of social psychology, the contributors to this volume pave the way for the social-psychological study of the basic process called culture.

## REFERENCES

Adams, G., & Markus, H. R. (2001). Culture as patterns: An alternative approach to the problem of reification. *Culture & Psychology, 7,* 283–296.

Appadurai, A. (1996). *Modernity at large: Cultural dimensions of globalization*. Minneapolis: University of Minnesota Press.

Appiah, K. A. (1992). *In my father's house: Africa in the philosophy of culture*. New York: Oxford University Press.

Bargh, J. A. (1997). The automaticity of everyday life. In R. S. Wyer, Jr. (Ed.), *The automaticity of everyday life: Advances in social cognition* (Vol. 10, pp. 1–61). Mahwah, NJ: Lawrence Erlbaum Associates.

Bargh, J. A., & Chartrand, T. L. (1999). The unbearable automaticity of being. *American Psychologist, 54*, 462–479.

Bar-Tal, D. (2000). *Shared beliefs in a society: social psychological analysis*. Thousand Oaks, CA: Sage.

Bartlett, F. C. (1932). *Remembering: A study in experimental and social psychology*. Cambridge, England: Cambridge University Press.

Berger, P. L., & Luckmann, T. (1966). *The social construction of reality: A treatise in the sociology of knowledge*. Garden City, NY: Doubleday.

Betancourt, H., & Lopez, S. R. (1993). The study of culture, ethnicity, and race in American psychology. *American Psychologist, 48*, 629–637.

Bourdieu, P. (1990). *The logic of practice*. Stanford, CA: Stanford University Press.

Bruner, J. (1990). *Acts of meaning*. Cambridge, MA: Harvard University Press.

Bruner, J. S., & Goodman, C. C. (1947). Value and need as organizing factors in perception. *Journal of Abnormal and Social Psychology, 42*, 33–44.

Clark, H. H. (1996). *Using language*. New York: Cambridge University Press.

Cohen, D. (1998). Culture, social organization, and patterns of violence. *Journal of Personality and Social Psychology, 75*, 408–419.

Cohen, D., & Nisbett, R. E. (1997). Field experiments examining the culture of honor: The role of institutions in perpetuating norms about violence. *Personality and Social Psychology Bulletin, 23*, 1188–1199.

Cole, M. (1996). *Cultural psychology: A once and future discipline*. Cambridge, MA: Harvard University Press.

Comaroff, J., & Comaroff, J. (Eds.). (1993). *Modernity and its malcontents: Ritual and power in postcolonial Africa*. Chicago: University of Chicago Press.

Crandall, C. S. (1985). The liking of foods as a result of exposure: Eating doughnuts in Alaska. *Journal of Social Psychology, 125*, 187–194.

Crandall, C. S. (1994). Prejudice against fat people: Ideology and self-interest. *Journal of Personality and Social Psychology, 66*, 882–894.

Crane, D. (1994). Introduction: The challenge of the sociology of culture to sociology as a discipline. In D. Crane (Ed.), *The sociology of culture: Emerging theoretical perspectives* (pp. 1–20). Cambridge, MA: Blackwell.

Deaux, K. (1993). Reconstructing social identity. *Personality and Social Psychology Bulletin, 19*, 4–12.

Greenfield, P. M. (1997). Culture as process: Empirical methods for cultural psychology. In J. W. Berry & Y. H. Poortinga (Eds.), *Handbook of cross-cultural psychology, Vol. 1: Theory and method* (2nd ed., pp. 301–346). Boston: Allyn & Bacon.

Griffin, D., & Ross, L. D. (1991). Subjective construal, social inference, and human misunderstanding. In M. P. Zanna (Ed.), *Advances in experimental social psychology* (Vol. 24, pp. 319–358). New York: Academic Press.

Hannerz, U. (1992). *Cultural complexity: Studies in the social organization of meaning*. New York: Columbia University Press.

Hermans, H. J. M., & Kempen, H. J. G. (1998). Moving cultures: The perilous problems of cultural dichotomies in a globalizing society. *American Psychologist, 53*, 1111–1120.

Herskovits, M. J. (1948). *Man and his works: The science of cultural anthropology*. New York: Knopf.

Hobsbawm, E. J., & Ranger, T. O. (Eds.). (1983). *The invention of tradition*. New York: Cambridge University Press.

Holland, D., Lachicotte, W., Skinner, D., & Cain, C. (1998). *Identity and agency in cultural worlds*. Cambridge, MA: Harvard University Press.

Hong, Y.-Y., Morris, M. W., Chiu, C.-Y., & Benet-Martinez, V. (2000). Multicultural minds: A dynamic constructivist approach to culture and cognition. *American Psychologist, 55*, 709–720.

Jahoda, G. (1984). Do we need a concept of culture? *Journal of Cross-Cultural Psychology, 15*, 139–152.

Ji, L. J., Peng, K., & Nisbett, R. E. (2000). Culture, control, and perception of relationships in the environment. *Journal of Personality and Social Psychology, 78*, 943–955.

Kashima, Y. (2000). Conceptions of culture and person for psychology. *Journal of Cross-Cultural Psychology, 31*, 14–32.

Kim, H., & Markus, H. R. (1999). Deviance or uniqueness, harmony or conformity? A cultural analysis. *Journal of Personality and Social Psychology, 77*, 785–800.

Kluegel, J. R., & Smith, E. R. (1986). *Beliefs about inequality: Americans' views of what is and what ought to be*. Hawthorne, NY: Aldine de Gruyter.

Kroeber, A. L., & Kluckhohn, C. K. (1952). *Culture: A critical review of concepts and definitions*. New York: Random House.

Lachman, M. E., & Weaver, S. L. (1998). The sense of control as a moderator of social class differences in health and well-being. *Journal of Personality and Social Psychology, 74*, 763–773.

Lau, I. Y.-M., Chiu, C.-Y., & Lee, S.-L. (2001). Communication and shared reality: Implications for the psychological foundations of culture. *Social Cognition, 19*, 350–371.

Levy, S. R., Plaks, J. E., Hong, Y.-Y., Chiu, C.-Y., & Dweck, C. S. (2001). Static versus dynamic theories and the perception of groups: Different routes to different destinations. *Personality and Social Psychology Review, 5*, 156–168.

Markus, H. R., & Kitayama, S. (1991). Culture and self: Implications for cognition, motivation, and emotion. *Psychological Review, 98*, 224–253.

Markus, H. R., Kitayama, S., & Heiman, R. L. (1997). Culture and "basic" psychological principles. In E. T. Higgins & A. W. Kruglanski (Eds.), *Social psychology: Handbook of basic principles* (pp. 857–913). New York: Guilford Press.

Markus, H. R., & Wurf, E. (1987). The dynamic self-concept: A social psychological perspective. *Annual review of psychology, 38*, 299–337.

Matsumoto, D. (1999). Culture and self: An empirical assessment of Markus and Kitayama's theory of independent and interdependent self-construals. *Asian Journal of Social Psychology, 2*, 289–310.

Mead, G. H. (1934). *Mind, self, and society*. Chicago: University of Chicago Press.

*Merriam-Webster OnLine*. (2002). Available online: http://www.m-w.com/dictionary.htm (retrieved February 13).

Meyer, B., & Geschiere, P. (1999). Introduction. In B. Meyer & P. Geschiere (Eds.), *Globalization and identity: Dialectics of flow and closure* (pp. 1–16). Oxford, England: Blackwell.

Morawska, E., & Spohn, W. (1994). "Cultural pluralism" in historical sociology: Recent theoretical directions. In D. Crane (Ed.), *The sociology of culture: Emerging theoretical perspectives* (pp. 45–90). Cambridge, MA: Blackwell.

Morris, M. W., Menon, T., & Ames, D. (2001). Culturally conferred conceptions of agency: A key to social perception of persons, groups, and other actors. *Personality and Social Psychology Review, 5*, 169–182.

Moscovici, S. (1984). The phenomena of social representations. In R. M. Farr & S. Moscovici (Eds.), *Social representations* (pp. 3–69). Cambridge, UK: Cambridge University Press.

Phinney, J. S. (1996). When we talk about American ethnic groups, what do we mean? *American Psychologist, 51*, 918–927.

Ratner, C. (1996). Activity as a key concept for cultural psychology. *Culture & Psychology, 2*, 407–434.

Richter, L., & Kruglanski, A. W. (1999). Motivated search for common ground: Need for closure effects on audience design in interpersonal communication. *Personality and Social Psychology Bulletin, 25*, 1101–1114.

Rogoff, B. (1992). *Apprenticeship in thinking: Cognitive development in social context*. Oxford, UK: Oxford University Press.

Rohner, R. P. (1984). Toward a conception of culture for cross-cultural psychology. *Journal of Cross-Cultural Psychology, 15*, 111–138.

Ross, L. D., & Nisbett, R. E. (1991). *The person and the situation: Perspectives of social psychology*. New York: McGraw-Hill.

Said, E. (1978). *Orientalism*. New York: Pantheon.

Schachter, S. (1951). Deviation, rejection, and communication. *Journal of Abormal and Social Psychoogy, 46*, 190–207.

Schachter, S., & Singer, J. E. (1962). Cognitive, social, and psychological determinants of emotional state. *Psychological Review, 69*, 379–399.

Segall, M. H. (1984). More than we need to know about culture but are afraid not to ask. *Journal of Cross-Cultural Psychology, 15*, 153–162.

Segall, M. H., Lonner, W. J., & Berry, J. W. (1998). Cross-cultural psychology as a scholarly discipline: On the flowering of culture in behavioral research. *American Psychologist, 53*, 1101–1110.

Sellers, R. M., Smith, M. A., Shelton, J. N., Rowley, S. A. J., & Chavous, T. M. (1998). Multidimensional model of racial identity: A reconceptualization of African American Racial Identity. *Personality and Social Psychology Review, 2*, 18–39.

Shore, B. (1996). *Culture in mind: Cognition, culture, and the problem of meaning*. New York: Oxford University Press.

Shweder, R. A. (1990). Cultural psychology: What is it? In J. Stigler, R. Shweder, & G. Herdt (Eds.), *Cultural psychology: Essays on comparative human development* (pp. 1–43). Cambridge, UK: Cambridge University Press.

Shweder, R. A. (2001). Culture: Contemporary views. In N. J. Smelser & P. B. Baltes (Eds.), *The international encyclopedia of the social and behavioral sciences* (Vol. 5, pp. 3151–3157). New York: Elsevier.

Shweder, R. A., Jensen, L. A., & Goldstein, W. M. (1995). Who sleeps by whom revisited: A method for extracting the moral goods implicit in practice. In J. J. Goodnow & P. J. Miller (Eds.), *Cultural practices as contexts for development* (pp. 21–39). San Francisco: Jossey-Bass.

Sperber, D. (1984). Anthropology and psychology: Toward an epidemiology of representations. *Man, 20*, 73–89.

Strauss, C. (1992). Models and motives. In R. G. D'Andrade & C. Strauss (Eds.), *Human motives and cultural models* (pp. 1–20). Cambridge, UK: Cambridge University Press.

Takano, Y., & Osaka, E. (1999). An unsupported common view: Comparing Japan and the U. S. on individualism/collectivism. *Asian Journal of Social Psychology, 2*, 311–341.

Tomasello, M. (1999). *The cultural origins of human cognition*. Cambridge, MA: Harvard University Press.

Triandis, H. C. (1972). *The analysis of subjective culture*. New York: Wiley.

Veroff, J. B., & Goldberger, N. R. (1995). What's in a name? The case for "intercultural". In N. R. Goldberger & J. B. Veroff (Eds.), *The culture and psychology reader* (pp. 3–24). New York: New York University Press.

Vygotsky, L. S. (1978). *Mind in society*. Cambridge, MA: Harvard University Press.

Worthman, C. M. (1992). Cupid and Psyche: Investigative syncretism in biological and psychosocial anthropology. In T. Schwartz & G. M. White (Eds.), *New directions in psychological anthropology* (pp. 150–178). Cambridge, UK: Cambridge University Press.

Wrong, D. H. (1961). The oversocialized conception of man in modern sociology. *American Sociological Review, 26*, 183–193.

Yzerbyt, V., Corneille, O., & Estrada, C. (2001). The interplay of subjective essentialism and entitativity in the formation of stereotypes. *Personality and Social Psychology Review, 5*, 141–156.

Zajonc, R. B. (1968). Attitudinal effects of mere exposure. *Journal of Personality and Social Psychology, 9*, 1–27.

Zajonc, R. B. (1980). Feeling and thinking: Preferences need no inferences. *American Psychologist, 35*, 151–175.

# Author Index

C

## Q-R

T

# Subject Index

S